Regulating Finance

Regulating Finance

The Political Economy of
Spanish Financial Policy
from Franco to Democracy

Arvid John Lukauskas

Ann Arbor

THE UNIVERSITY OF MICHIGAN PRESS

2000   1999   1998   1997   4   3   2   1

A CIP catalog record for this book is available from the British Library.

Library of Congress Cataloging-in-Publication Data

Lukauskas, Arvid John.
    Regulating finance : the political economy of Spanish financial
policy from Franco to democracy / Arvid John Lukauskas.
        p.   cm.
    Includes bibliographical references and index.
    ISBN 0-472-10836-0 (alk. paper)
    1. Finance—Spain.   2. Financial institutions—Deregulation—
Spain.   3. Financial service industry—Deregulation—Spain.
I. Title.
HG186.A3S715   1997
336.46—dc21   97-4888
                                                                CIP

To Michael, Robert, and Victoria

Contents

Figures

Tables

Acknowledgments

A great many individuals helped me in the course of writing this book. I owe my largest intellectual debt to the members of my dissertation committee, Joanne Gowa, Howard Pack, and Peter Swenson. This book would not have been possible without their analytical insights, knowledge, and support. José Miguel Andreu, David Baldwin, Eileen Crumm, Fred Frey, Robert Kaufman, Edward Mansfield, José María Maravall, Helen Milner, Richard Nelson, Dani Rodrik, John Ruggie, Jack Snyder, Hendrik Spruyt, and Gabriel Tortella Casares read all or portions of the manuscript and provided exceptional criticisms and suggestions. I will always be grateful for their time and attention. Two anonymous readers for the University of Michigan Press offered extremely helpful comments on content and presentation.

Several people assisted me in carrying out research in Spain. Juan Linz helped me establish contacts with a number of scholars and practitioners that proved to be extraordinarily useful. More important, he raised several major analytical issues at an early stage of this project that led me to improve the design of this study. In Spain, Javier Irastorza Revuelta, Cristóbal Montoro Romero, Luis Angel Lerena, and Fernando Fernández Rodríguez not only shared their experiences with me in interviews, but also supplied advice on conducting research in Spain and arranged several interviews. The staff at the Biblioteca del Banco de España provided expert assistance and cheerfully put up with my never ending requests for photocopies. I am especially grateful to Paloma Gómez Pastor for tracking down elusive data and documents. But most of all, I express my deep thanks to the many individuals who generously took time out of their busy schedules for interviews.

The Council for European Studies at Columbia University and the Columbia University Council on Research in the Humanities and Social Sciences provided financial support for this project. I am also indebted to *Comparative Politics* for permission to reprint parts of the article, "The Political Economy of Financial Restriction: The Case of Spain," volume 27, number 1 (October 1994).

Finally, I reserve my deepest thanks for my family. My wife, Victoria, and son, Robert, endured my long hours at the office with infinite patience and support. The impending birth of my son, Michael, prompted me to finally finish this project. I dedicate this book to them.

Interviews Conducted for This Study

The following Spanish financiers and public officials were interviewed for this study. All interviews were conducted in Madrid, Spain.

Fernando Abril Martorell
    Vice President of Economic Affairs, 1978–80
    Banker, Banco Central
José Miguel Andreu
    Banker, Banco de Bilbao
    Economist, Ministry of Finance
Alberto Cerrolaza
    President of Official Credit Institute, 1970s
Guillermo de la Dehesa
    Various positions in the Ministry of Commerce
    Subsecretary of Economics, 1985–88
Fernando Fernández Rodríguez
    Planning Commission official, 1960s and 1970s
    Banker, Banco de Bilbao
Enrique Fuentes Quintana
    Minister of Economics and Vice President of Economics, 1977–78
    Chief economic advisor to the UCD government, 1978–82
    Various posts in the Confederation of Spanish Savings Banks
Manuel Jesús González
    Planning Commission official, 1960s and 1970s
Fernando Gutierrez Junquera
    Bank of Spain official, 1980s and 1990s
Javier Irastorza Revuelta
    Planning Commission official, 1960s and 1970s
Aristóbulo de Juan
    President of the Corporación Bancaria
    Chief of Banking Inspection at the Bank of Spain
José Luis Leal
    Minister of Economics, 1979–80

Banker, BBV
President of the Spanish Private Banking Association
Luis Angel Lerena
Banker, BBV
Constantino Lluch
Bank of Spain official, 1980s
Angel Luis López Roa
Banker, Banco Atlántico
Mariano Navarro Rubio
Minister of Finance, 1957–65
Governor of the Bank of Spain, 1965–69
Raimundo Ortega Fernández
Bank of Spain official, 1960s and 1970s
General Director of the Treasury and Financial Policy, 1982–85
Director General of Bank of Spain
Banker, BBV
Fransisco Javier Ramos Gascón
Director General of Financial Policy, 1966–74
President of the Madrid Stock Exchange, 1970s and 1980s
Juan José Toribio Dávila
General Director of Financial Policy, 1977–79
Banker, Banco Urquijo and La Caixa
Antonio Torrero Mañas
President of the Spanish Mortgage Bank, 1980s
Victorio Valle Sánchez
General Director of Financial Policy, 1979–81

Abbreviations

AEB	Asociación Española de la Banca Privada (Spanish Private Banking Association)
AP	Alianza Popular (Popular Alliance)
ARs	Asset restrictions
BOS	Banco de España (Bank of Spain)
CD	Coalición Democrática (Democratic Coalition)
CDS	Centro Democrático y Social (Social and Democratic Center)
CECA	Confederación Española de Cajas de Ahorro (Spanish Confederation of Savings Banks)
CEOE	Confederación Española de Organizaciones Empresariales (Spanish Confederation of Employers' Organizations)
CEPYME	Confederación Española de la Pequeña y Mediana Empresa (Confederation of Small- and Medium-sized Businesses)
CP	Coalición Popular (Popular Coalition)
CSB	Consejo Superior Bancario (Superior Banking Council)
EC	European Community
ICs	Investment coefficients
ICO	Instituto de Crédito Oficial (Official Credit Institute)
IMF	International Monetary Fund
INI	Instituto Nacional de Industria (National Industry Institute)
MOC	Ministry of Commerce
MOE	Ministry of Economics
MOEC	Ministry of Economics and Commerce
MOEF	Ministry of Economics and Finance
MOF	Ministry of Finance
NBFIs	Nonbank financial intermediaries
OECD	Organization for Economic Cooperation and Development
PC	Planning Commission
PCE	Partido Comunista de España (Spanish Communist Party)
PDC	Public debt coefficient

PR   Proportional representation
PSOE   Partido Socialista Obrero Español (Spanish Workers'
                Socialist Party)
RRs   Reserve requirements
SMCs   Small- and medium-sized companies
SRLs   Special rediscount lines
UCD   Unión de Centro Democrático (Union of the Democratic
                Center)

CHAPTER 1

Introduction

Many countries have attempted ambitious structural reforms to revitalize their economies in recent years. Financial reform has been a central element of these efforts, for policymakers recognize the critical role that financial markets play in a country's economic and political life. Financial markets are responsible for mobilizing capital and allocating it among competing users, as well as for administering a country's payment services; their ability to perform these tasks greatly affects national economic performance.[1] Moreover, the type of financial system that a country has influences the distribution of wealth and power among private and public actors; it also affects the type of role the state can play in the economy.[2]

Several countries undergoing financial reform began the process with a "restricted" or "repressed" financial system. Restricted systems have been the most common type of financial system worldwide since World War II, especially in the developing world.[3] In a restricted system, the government implements credit, entry, and interest rate controls and impedes the development of direct financial (i.e., bond and equity) markets in order to influence the allocation and cost of credit; it taxes the banking system to obtain government revenue; and it strictly regulates the linkages between domestic and international capital markets.[4] For years, many economists have argued that these policies undermine social welfare. They claim that restriction creates large rents for a few select groups, namely, banks and the firms that obtain preferential credit, at the expense of more general interests, because it lowers levels of investment and reduces financial efficiency.

In some countries with restricted systems, governments have liberalized financial markets by lifting entry, interest rate, and credit controls, privatizing state-owned banks, promoting bond and equity markets and nonbank financial intermediaries (NBFIs, e.g., mortgage societies), reducing taxation of the banking system, and developing stronger linkages between domestic and international capital markets.[5] In others, governments have implemented only minor reforms that have not altered the basic shape of financial policy. Economists have wondered why governments in countries with tightly regulated financial markets have not liberalized more aggressively to reap the advantages of a market-based system. Political scientists, on the other hand, have sought to explain why deregulation, which disturbs the status quo and threatens the interests of established private and public financial actors, has occurred at all.

Spain is one country that has undergone significant financial deregulation. After the Spanish Civil War, the Franco regime pursued a strategy of financial restriction. The government began liberalizing financial markets around 1970, with the most intense reform occurring in the late 1970s and the early to mid-1980s. The Spanish experience is intriguing because it presents several challenges to prevailing explanations of financial deregulation and structural adjustment more broadly. First, Spanish liberalization occurred before the international factors (e.g., increasing capital mobility) that some scholars claim explain recent deregulation efforts became significant.[6] Second, against the predictions of sectoral models of economic policy-making, deregulation took place despite strong opposition from powerful, well-organized private interests, like large national banks.[7] Finally, most financial reforms occurred while Spain was democratizing, a time when many authors suggest governments either avoid or find it difficult to carry out structural adjustment.[8]

This book explores, both generally and in the case of Spain, why governments restrict financial markets as well as why they sometimes liberalize them. Using a rational choice approach, I argue that public officials provide the dynamic behind the evolution of financial policy.[9] They design financial regulation to help themselves attain two goals: retaining power and generating government revenue. I find that restricted and market-based financial systems have distinct political merits whose value to politicians seeking to advance these goals varies across different institutional settings.[10] Restriction enables the government to influence directly the cost and allocation of credit and thus is very useful to leaders whose country's political institutions reward them for delivering benefits to influential private groups. In addition, it enables government officials to raise substantial revenue through taxation of the banking system, though this may severely hurt economic performance. A market-based system, on the other hand, is politically valuable to leaders whose country's institutions provide them with an incentive to supply collective economic goods, such as efficient financial markets, in the pursuit of power. Allowing market forces to determine the allocation and price of credit may also be preferred when leaders wish to avoid having to favor some constituents over others or need to extricate themselves from costly existing commitments. Finally, a market-based system improves the stream of government revenues by promoting long-term growth.

An implication of this analysis is that environmental or institutional changes that increase the relative utility of a market-based system vis-à-vis a restricted one will generate interest among public officials to deregulate the financial system. This may happen when the value of supplying collective economic goods increases relative to that of providing private benefits to select constituents in the pursuit of power. It may also occur when more efficient means of taxation become available and politically feasible. Likewise, leaders will liberalize markets when the costs of maintaining a restricted system outweigh its benefits, turning restriction into a political liability. This takes place when restriction so lowers financial efficiency that it hurts economic performance severely, giving rivals an issue they can use to challenge current leaders.

To undertake liberalization, policymakers must be convinced beforehand that market-based financial systems provide superior economic performance. If they believed, for instance, that a government-controlled system were optimal, they might simply try to intervene more effectively rather than proceed with deregulation. In the contemporary period, dissatisfaction with state financial controls in most countries and strong support for liberalization among economists and international economic agencies (like the World Bank) have elevated to the status of conventional wisdom the view that financial deregulation improves economic performance.

Applying my conceptual framework to Spain, I show that officials in the Franco regime used financial restriction to advance their political goals. The regime imposed elaborate interest rate and credit controls that enabled government officials to allocate preferential credit to private groups in a discretionary manner. Directed credit policies became the primary means of implementing the regime's strategy of supplying material benefits to key constituents in order to secure their support. In addition, they created several mechanisms for taxing the banking system to raise substantial amounts of government revenue. This interpretation contrasts with that of some writers, who have viewed state financial controls during the Franco period as the tools of a technocratic, developmentalist elite seeking to modernize the Spanish economy.[11]

The most striking finding concerning Spanish financial reform is that the country's transition to democracy gave political leaders a powerful incentive to deregulate financial markets. Democratization changed the reward structure confronting leaders, making the supply of public goods, like strong economic performance, more attractive and a narrow defense of special interests less tenable as a political strategy because leaders had to compete against opposition parties for the support of a heterogeneous array of voters to stay in power. The specific features of Spain's new democratic institutions served to support this new reward structure. In particular, electoral rules encouraged the creation of large, broad-based national parties, not small, sectarian parties. In the realm of financial policy, Spanish democratization led leaders to place less emphasis on using financial controls to provide private goods (e.g., preferential credit) than on supplying the collective good of more efficient financial markets in their pursuit of office. In this interpretation, financial liberalization in Spain is a consequence of the decision to adopt a particular form of democratic rule; indeed, I contend that the choice of a different set of electoral institutions in particular might not have provided policymakers with an incentive to remove many financial controls.

This explanation of Spanish financial deregulation bestows less importance on Spain's entrance into the European Community (EC) than other accounts, which see its accession and corresponding need to meet EC standards as the primary cause behind structural reforms, including financial deregulation.[12] This external constraint intensified and deepened financial liberalization in the 1980s, but it cannot account for most of Spain's deregulation efforts, which occurred well before Spain agreed to abide by EC rules. Moreover, reform cannot be attributed to policymakers anticipating EC requirements to facilitate acceptance into the Community. EC rules on financial policy became comprehensive and restrictive only after 1989; until that time, they were ambiguous and limited in scope, granting countries considerable leeway in formulating financial policy. Thus, early Spanish reformers did not have to concern themselves with meeting a set of strict EC demands.

More fundamentally, the argument that Spain's entry into the EC explains why it carried out deregulation incorrectly treats its integration into the Community as exogenously given. The decisions to apply for membership and enter the EC were in fact endogenous policy choices, and in making them, Spanish leaders elected to accept the obligation to undertake certain economic reforms. Therefore, what ultimately needs to be explained is why they accepted this obligation. I contend that the decision to enter the EC was prompted in large part by a fundamental political motive, one that I identify as critical in explaining the course of Spanish economic policy: the drive to improve economic performance in order to generate broad-based political support.[13]

I believe that my findings concerning the impact of the Spanish democratic transition on financial policy are generalizable, and I show in broader analytical terms that democratization often provides political leaders with an incentive to liberalize financial markets.[14] Democratization pushes elected officials to provide for the collective economic good because they must competitively bid for the support of a broad-based, heterogeneous majority in periodic elections; those that appeal only to select social groups or design policies for their benefit may alienate median voters, making it difficult to secure sufficient electoral support. With regards to financial policy, democratization encourages leaders to create efficient markets through deregulation and dismantle inefficient financial controls used to favor particular constituents. In addition, as democratization usually increases the number of groups making claims on policymakers, politicians may dismantle interest rate and credit controls out of fear that they cannot satisfy all the demands for preferential credit and will alienate some constituents. Finally, democratization is often associated with a dramatic surge in demands for government spending. This provides a powerful incentive to eliminate inefficient taxation of the banking system and implement more effective means of raising revenue (e.g., a greater reliance on direct taxes).

I also show that the form of democracy matters. Several institutional features greatly influence the reward structure facing politicians as they formulate financial policy. I focus especially on how variations in electoral institutions affect the incentive to supply collective economic goods, as this incentive has the greatest influence on whether politicians will pursue deregulation and on the profile of their reform efforts. I illustrate these points in the concluding chapter when I show how the specific democratic institutions adopted by Brazil, South Korea, Spain, and Turkey have shaped the course of their financial policy.

The impact of democratization on financial policy merits careful analysis for several reasons. On a practical level, many countries that have recently undergone transitions to democracy confront economic problems that call for financial liberalization. It is thus a matter of immediate relevance to ascertain how democratization will affect their ability to complete badly needed reforms. On a theoretical level, this analysis allows us to examine one important facet of the long-standing hypothesis that democratization spurs the emergence of decentralized markets.[15] More generally, this inquiry contributes to the growing literature on how domestic political institutions shape the incentives facing public officials as they design economic regulatory policy.[16]

It must be noted at the outset that an examination of political institutions, like electoral rules, cannot provide the determinants of political behavior but only indicate an important set of incentives and constraints facing politicians and the likely costs they will incur if they fail to heed them. As the Spanish case study shows, political elite behavior is also influenced by other variables, among them views of how to best attract voters; beliefs about where the majority of voters are located on the left-right spectrum; ideological preferences; and personal ambition. This observation leads me to conclude that this study's rational choice hypotheses capture the effects of political regime change on the reward structures facing political leaders, but that inter- and intragovernmental differences in their actions must be explained by a different set of factors.

Competing Explanations of Financial Regulation

My analytical framework contrasts in important ways with the most prominent explanations found in the existing literature on the political economy of financial policy. I examine these competing explanations in greater depth in the next chapter, but here I will highlight some key differences with my approach. This discussion serves to identify several major issues in the field of political economy that this study addresses and indicates how my findings contribute to the literature on these topics.

Studies of the political economy of restriction have been few. One salient view in the existing literature is that governments in many countries had to opt for a bank-based financial system under tight state control because building effective market-based institutions was too difficult.[17] Alice Amsden, Chalmers Johnson, Robert Wade, and John Zysman claim further that such financial systems have sometimes contributed to excellent economic performance, most notably in "late industrializers" like Japan, South Korea, and Taiwan.[18] In their view, policymakers seeking to promote aggregate social welfare were able to use financial controls to target effectively sectors whose growth was deemed important for the economy's development.

This study contests the view that financial restriction was the only or optimal policy available to policymakers. Governments had an alternative long-term strategy, which was to create a competitive market-based financial system. Even where policymakers faced severe economic constraints in building a market-based system, they could have made progress in some areas while avoiding restriction's worst pitfalls. Moreover, theory and evidence (reviewed later) suggest that restriction was not the optimal policy, although the evidence does not permit us to assert that it was never useful (since a few countries grew rapidly when they had restricted financial systems). Of course, government officials might have chosen restriction in part because they believed it was in the public interest to do so, whether or not this was actually true. I suggest, however, that whatever their initial motives, officials quickly latched onto restriction's political advantages and that their desire to obtain these advantages explains the evolution of financial policy better.

Several scholars have argued, as I do, that public officials regulate financial markets to advance their own private goals. There have been, however, few in-depth studies of how government intervention in financial markets serves the private goals of public officials, and these studies have concentrated mainly on how and why politicians use selective credit programs as a policy instrument.[19] This focus neglects the political logic underlying other features of restriction, most notably its ability to generate substantial government revenue in ways that are largely hidden from public view. One of this study's contributions is that it examines all the features of restriction and demonstrates how they interrelate in the political calculus of public officials.

The literature on the political economy of financial deregulation has concentrated on advanced industrial countries, largely ignoring countries with restricted financial systems until very recently. Much of the work on liberalization of restricted systems has centered on purely economic issues, treating changes in a country's financial system as the product of economic modernization or changing financial conditions, not of political forces.[20] This study seeks to identify the political dynamics underlying financial deregulation as well as understand how they interact with economic factors. It provides a systematic analysis of the stances of the main private and public actors with regard to major financial policy issues and how their stances may change with shifts in key economic and political variables.

Many studies of financial deregulation have relied upon the "economic" theory of regulatory policy.[21] This theory posits that public officials design regulation to favor groups that offer them the greatest political support. Deregulation occurs when a regulatory regime becomes suboptimal for its original beneficiaries or the net balance of interest group demands on public officials shifts because of changes in the bargaining power of its winners and losers.[22] Using this approach, scholars have argued that regulated intermediaries (namely, banks) have provided the impetus for deregulation in advanced industrial countries when changes in their economic environment (e.g., high inflation) made the existing regulatory regime unprofitable for them. Specifically, established banks have sought the removal of financial controls when they limited their ability to compete for deposits with new, unregulated intermediaries or when they faced the threat of disintermediation from direct financial markets.[23]

I contend that the economic events that lead regulated intermediaries to push for deregulation in advanced industrial countries usually do not encourage those operating in restricted systems to seek liberalization. The lack of financial depth in these systems makes it unlikely that such events will alter the costs and benefits of regulation sufficiently for banks to push for deregulation;[24] specifically, few intermediaries exist to challenge banks, and the threat of disintermediation from direct markets is weak. This means that public officials, not private actors, provide the impetus for deregulation in countries with restricted systems; therefore, the society-centered focus used by the economic theory to explain deregulation cannot account for it in restricted systems. More generally, I contend that market structure influences whether public or private actors drive financial deregulation and, therefore, whether state or society should be the center of analysis.[25] This finding highlights the necessity of examining the variables that affect the supply of regulation by public officials as well as the demand for it by private actors. It is also consistent with the emerging consensus that a variety of institutional factors helps to determine the relative importance of state and social actors in influencing economic policy.[26]

Another prominent explanation of deregulation asserts that the recent wave of financial reform has stemmed from policymakers' efforts to improve economic performance in response to common economic difficulties, such as monetary control problems or declining flows of foreign capital.[27] This perspective, called the "public interest" theory, holds that policymakers deregulate financial markets when it becomes clear that government controls are suboptimal from a social welfare perspective. For some, the diffusion of policy-relevant knowledge advocating market-based financial systems through organizations like the International Monetary Fund (IMF) has contributed to deregulation efforts.[28]

The view that widespread economic problems have sparked financial deregulation is intuitively appealing. Mounting economic difficulties, however, have not been a sufficient motive for government officials to undertake deregulation, although they have clearly entered into their calculations. Countries do not necessarily choose to liberalize when faced with tough economic circumstances. The response to major events that have created an apparent common interest in deregulation across countries has not been uniform: some countries have liberalized extensively while others have not.[29] Similarly, the diffusion of policy-relevant knowledge by international agencies has met with a differential response. These observations suggest that factors indigenous to each country, such as its economic and political institutions, leadership's goals, and the balance of interest group demands, greatly influence how financial policy will be affected by changes in economic conditions or the diffusion of new ideas.

A final class of explanations of financial deregulation center on international factors. One contention is that governments have found it increasingly difficult to regulate financial activity, particularly transborder capital flows, as banks and firms have become truly global in their activities.[30] Moreover, international capital flows now respond to a country's economic policies with lightning quickness, putting serious constraints on governments that need to attract capital or prevent its flight. This is forcing international convergence across countries toward similar macroeconomic policies and more open financial systems with less government intervention.[31] Other scholars note that governments often encounter direct pressure from international actors to carry out structural reforms, including financial liberalization.[32]

This study suggests that while some international factors push leaders toward reform, domestic politics still largely determine when, and in what fashion, financial deregulation will occur.[33] Even when international pressures to reform are direct, political leaders evaluate how liberalizing financial markets will affect their ability to achieve their own goals. In the case of financial opening, for instance, they weigh the political advantages of closure (e.g., control over credit allocation) against the benefits of greater openness (e.g., increased capital inflows). Furthermore, countries that integrate their financial system into international markets often retain interest rate and credit controls to dictate how foreign inflows are allocated or to manage the money supply. Nevertheless, once opening is underway, it may lead major actors to modify their stances on key financial policy issues or alter the balance of power among competing interest groups in ways that contribute to greater pressure for further financial deregulation.[34]

Although public interest and international accounts do not tell the whole story, the economic and political trends they identify are increasingly important influences on financial policy. These trends have augmented the *political* costs of maintaining financial restriction, giving leaders a strong incentive to design better financial policy in order to prevent competitors from taking advantage of poor performance to capture support. Even where events have led to similar problems across countries, however, they have not affected the bottom line of the political calculus of leaders equally, indicating again that economic or international factors alone cannot explain financial policy change.

The rest of this chapter analyzes some of the major economic topics pertaining to financial restriction and deregulation. Even if political concerns primarily motivate policymakers, as I contend, economic forces help establish the constraints and opportunities they confront as they design financial policy. First, I consider the economics of financial restriction. I review the theoretical debate over the general strategy of restriction and its attendant controls as well as the empirical evidence on the performance of restricted systems. This discussion is necessary, as it might be the case that policymakers originally chose restriction simply because it was the best or only policy available. I conclude that economic theory and the empirical evidence do not support these contentions. Second, I examine the economics of financial deregulation. I analyze the micro- and macroeconomic issues associated with liberalization and outline the prescriptions of economists who advocate it. In addition, I briefly survey the mixed experience of the countries that have attempted to deregulate their financial systems.

Financial Restriction: Stylized Facts, Rationales, and Performance

Stylized Facts and the Question of Alternatives

In the post–World War II period, policymakers in many countries have pursued a strategy of financial restriction. Several stylized facts character-ize this strategy. First, the government imposes ceilings on both deposit and loan rates of interest, keeping them below "equilibrium" interest rates; in many cases, real interest rates are negative. Second, it designs selective credit policies to channel available funds to sectors it wishes to favor; this results in interest rates that vary arbitrarily across and even within classes of borrowers. These selective credit policies may take the form of the cre-ation of quasi-private development banks or direct intervention in private bank lending (e.g., by imposing credit floors). Third, the government taxes the banking system to obtain revenue. Taxation takes the form of heavy reserve requirements (RRs), asset restrictions (ARs), and forced provision of subsidized credit to favored sectors.[35] Fourth, the government discour-ages the growth of bond and equity markets; consequently, firms rely on credit provided by the banking system or on self-finance. The government often fosters an oligopoly within the banking system by imposing strict controls on entry, so firms and savers deal almost exclusively with a small number of large banks for their financial needs. Not all bank-based finan-cial systems are repressed or should be considered the direct product of government policy; Germany's bank-based system, for example, devel-oped without overt government guidance and is not restricted.[36] Finally, the government limits the linkages between the domestic financial system and international capital markets. There are strict controls on capital flows into and out of the country, and foreign intermediaries are not allowed to enter domestic markets. Controls on inflows are essential because low (or even negative) real yields on domestic assets will push indi-viduals into trying to move their money into foreign assets with higher returns.

It is sometimes suggested that policymakers in many countries had to implement restriction because existing financial markets could not ade-quately support a process of industrialization and agricultural moderniza-tion without government intervention.[37] These countries lacked private financial institutions capable of mobilizing sufficient amounts of invest-ment capital on their own. Moreover, state controls were necessary to allocate available credit efficiently and to prevent financial crises that could devastate the real economy. In short, it is claimed that the structure of a restricted system closely suited the needs of a developing country's stage of economic development.

Restriction was not the only financial strategy available to policymakers, however. An alternative strategy was to create a competitive market-based financial system.[38] This approach required the government to modernize the legal system, clarify financial property rights, remove unnecessary financial controls and barriers to entry in financial markets, promote bond and equity markets, and improve prudential regulation.[39] This promised to be a complex and lengthy process, especially in newly independent countries, because the financial markets that leaders had inherited were often in their infancy and loanable funds were scarce. Nevertheless, it was a long-term, economically viable option. Certainly, policymakers did not have to purposefully hinder the growth of the financial sector by sharply limiting competition among intermediaries, impeding the development of bond and equity markets, establishing a myriad of arbitrary credit and interest rate controls, and heavily taxing the banking system. Leaders determined to industrialize or modernize the economy quickly could have regulated financial markets more discriminately—for example, by sponsoring credit institutions specializing in long-term development finance—while avoiding unnecessary and harmful financial controls. I contend that they chose not to intervene more selectively along these lines because they often had political incentives to regulate financial markets pervasively; I discuss these incentives in the next chapter.

An instructive case of how government policy may thwart the development of viable, preexisting financial institutions needed in a market-based system occurred in India. In the 1950s, Indian capital markets, despite their underdeveloped state, effectively helped to mobilize financial resources for the corporate sector. Their role in industrial finance diminished greatly in later years, however, due largely to government policies that repressed the financial sector.[40]

Theoretical Rationales

Restriction might not have been the only financial strategy open to policymakers, but it might have been the best one for some countries. In this section, I consider the theoretical rationales for pursuing restriction as a general strategy, as well as those for implementing the most important of the financial controls associated with restricted systems, interest rate and credit controls. In addition, I examine the case for developing a bank-based financial system instead of a securities market-based system.[41]

General Strategy

The principle debate surrounding restriction as a general strategy has centered on whether repression of the financial sector bolsters growth of the real economy (i.e., industry and agriculture). Tobin has provided the most compelling theoretical case for adopting financial restriction.[42] He argued that real money balances and productive capital assets are substitutes in the portfolios of economic agents. This implies that to promote productive investment (and thus economic growth) the government must increase the return on capital relative to that on money holdings. It can accomplish this directly, by imposing a ceiling on deposit rates of interest, or indirectly, by permitting an optimal level of inflation. Both policies serve as a tax on money holdings and encourage portfolio shifts away from money toward claims on capital. Policies that limit the development of the financial sector, such as taxation of the banking system, are encouraged as well since they promote the growth of nonfinancial sectors. In a related argument, some scholars advocate loan rate ceilings because they stimulate greater productive investment (and, hence, accelerate economic growth) by lowering real interest rates below the true opportunity cost of capital.[43]

Tobin's views have been widely challenged, but restriction continues to have a few proponents.[44] McKinnon is one of the most persuasive critics of restriction.[45] In his view, growth in real money stock is a necessary condition for capital accumulation because money and capital are complements, not substitutes; accordingly, development of the financial sector is a precondition for real sector growth. Policies that serve as a tax on financial assets, namely, interest rate controls and taxation of the banking system, are perilous because they limit the growth of loanable funds by discouraging savings, thereby restricting the funds available for productive investment. Moreover, interest rate controls distort relative factor prices, while taxation of the banking system increases the costs of financial intermediation and contributes to the inefficient allocation of capital.

Credit Controls

Some scholars suggest that capital market failures caused by imperfect information, externalities, or imperfect competition are widespread and severe in numerous countries, particularly in the developing world.[46] They claim that government allocation of credit is necessary to overcome these failures. In their view, government officials are generally better equipped than the private sector to make allocative decisions because they have superior information and base their choices on social, not private, cost/benefit criteria. Government credit programs socialize some of the risk of private losses from investing in ventures where uncertainty about returns is high or whose payoff occurs late in the life of the project. In this regard, financial policy can be an invaluable tool for entrepreneurial states seeking to develop competitiveness in industrial activities with high returns that are currently not profitable for their firms, but might be in the future with government assistance.[47]

Mainstream economists, as represented by Maxwell Fry and Edward Kane, challenge these assertions, although they acknowledge that capital market failures exist.[48] They dispute that capital market failures are so severe and argue that government control over credit allocation is not the way to correct them in any case; indeed, they claim that state intervention usually distorts the financial system significantly, creating problems far worse than the market failures it seeks to address. They contend that public officials normally do not have superior information about which projects have the highest returns because these officials are removed from the marketplace. In addition, since they do not stand to lose their own funds if they choose projects with inferior returns, unlike private investors, officials may easily introduce noneconomic criteria, notably political expediency, into their allocative decisions.

Bank-Based Financial Systems

A diverse group of scholars, including Alice Amsden, Hugh Patrick, Joseph Stiglitz, and Robert Wade, has argued that governments, especially in late-industrializing countries, should concentrate on constructing a strong banking system consisting of large, entrepreneurial banks instead of attempting to develop broad bond and equity markets.[49] In their view, bank-based systems offer several advantages over securities market-based systems (although they acknowledge that they entail certain risks, such as those identified later in this section).[50] First, they claim that firms in a bank-based system tend to make better investment decisions. A frequent criticism of securities-based systems is that firms adopt an overly short-term investment focus because they fear investors will abandon their bonds or stock if they do not post good results every quarter.[51] This focus discourages managers from investing in potentially high-yielding projects that produce returns primarily late in their lives. In contrast, firms that enjoy close ties to a bank may take advantage of such investment opportunities because the bank is committed to its long-term success and will not cut off credit if returns are not immediately forthcoming. Chung Lee and Robert Wade contend that the government can further improve the performance of bank-based systems by disseminating information on changing investment opportunities and using interest rate and credit controls to socialize some of the risks involved in undertaking new investments.[52]

Second, these authors contend that a bank-based system has superior monitoring capabilities, especially when the information infrastructure of accounting, auditing, and disclosure are underdeveloped, as they usually are in developing countries.[53] Close bank-firm ties lower a lender's cost of acquiring information about a firm's projects, thereby reducing loan risk premia. They may also improve oversight of management performance and facilitate the restructuring of firms in distress.[54]

Finally, as a practical matter, they point out that developing countries usually find it difficult to create efficient bond and equity markets. Demand for bonds and equities is often low because there are few institutional investors, and individuals tend to prefer liquid, short-term assets, not long-term securities. On the supply side, the number of firms capable of issuing securities is often quite small, and information about them tends to be scarce.

Bank-based financial systems, however, are not free of serious weaknesses. First, they seem to be especially prone to moral hazard problems.[55] In bank-based systems, banks frequently give preference to firms in which they have a stake when they make lending decisions, neglecting firms with projects that promise higher returns; this is particularly true when industrialists set up and own banks. Perhaps more importantly, firms associated with banks may engage in risky policies or become less competitive because they anticipate that banks (or the state) will bail them out if they perform inadequately.[56]

Second, bank-based systems have often experienced insolvency problems created by close bank-firm ties. Banks may become insolvent when the economy experiences a downturn and firms with which they have a close relationship default on loans, turning them into nonperforming assets. A difficult economic environment can also depress the value of banks' equity holdings in corporations. The resulting deterioration of bank portfolios can seriously jeopardize the stability of the financial system. Several countries, including Spain, have experienced severe banking crises in which insolvency problems caused by close ties between banks and industry were major contributing factors.[57]

Heavy reliance on debt financing also makes firms vulnerable to reductions in the overall level of liquidity in the banking system, restricting the range of options available to monetary authorities. In particular, authorities may find it difficult to pursue a tight money policy since a decrease in bank credit to the private sector (usually an essential element in strategies aimed at reducing growth in monetary aggregates) may create liquidity problems for many firms.

Finally, the failure to develop direct markets as a source of capital may carry high opportunity costs. Recent studies have suggested that countries with underdeveloped direct markets have experienced higher intermediation costs and lower levels of savings on average.[58] In addition, the lack of effective direct markets may mean that potentially high-yielding but risky projects, which are typically funded through bond and equity markets, do not obtain sufficient financing.[59]

No comprehensive empirical tests of the major issues in the controversy over bank-based financial systems exist. Most work in this area has consisted of in-depth case studies of individual countries or comparisons of several countries.[60] The most sensible conclusion to be drawn from this literature is that the efficacy of bank-based systems depends greatly on several economic and political factors, including the degree of competition among banks, the quality of bank supervision, and the extent of political interference in credit allocation. In chapter 3, I examine the economic and political consequences of Spain's bank-based financial system.

The Empirical Evidence

General Strategy and Interest Rate Controls

Many empirical studies of financial restriction have examined its impact on economic growth. Research in this area has often been conducted using the level of real interest rates as an indicator of the degree of repression, so reviewing it also serves to survey some of the evidence on the effects of interest rate controls. Overall, one cannot draw definitive conclusions on how financial restriction affects aggregate economic performance, but it is clear that it usually does not promote growth. Empirical research has yielded ambiguous results in part due to the difficulties involved in operationalizing and measuring the various dimensions of restriction and controlling for other variables that affect economic performance.

A study by Lanyi and Saracoğlu of the relationship between real interest rates, used as a proxy for degree of restriction, and growth in GDP offers tentative support for the hypothesis that restriction impedes growth.[61] Its findings indicate that countries that have maintained negative real interest rates have experienced slower GDP growth; this relationship is particularly striking in the case of countries with severely negative real rates. This led the authors to conclude that "in the longer run, positive real interest rates contribute to growth in output."[62] Their results are at best suggestive, however, as the study did not control adequately for variables that typically account for GDP growth, such as increases in capital, labor, or total factor productivity, or for the quality of macroeconomic policy.

The World Bank contends that the relationship between real interest rates and growth "appears to operate primarily through the effect of greater financial depth on the productivity of investment."[63] Lowering real rates leads savers to substitute inflation hedges (e.g., real estate) for financial assets in their portfolios; this hurts the efficiency of investment because it takes investment decisions out of the hands of intermediaries, which generally select projects with superior social returns. In support of this hypothesis, the World Bank cites evidence of a positive relationship between real interest rates and the ratio of loanable funds (M2) to GDP, a common measure of financial depth, as well as between real interest rates and growth in real financial assets.[64] Further, the Bank's direct tests of the hypothesized relationship between real interest rates and the productivity of investment show that an increase in real deposit rates was associated with an improvement in productivity, as measured by the ratio of change in GDP to investment.[65] These results, however, do not rule out the possibility that differences in other economic policies account for a significant portion of the observed variations in investment efficiency.

Another explanation for the relationship between low real interest rates and slow growth is that deposit rate ceilings discourage aggregate savings, thereby reducing the quantity of funds available for productive investment.[66] Some studies suggest that real deposit interest rates are positively related to national savings rates in some developing countries but that the relationship can be exploited for policy purposes only when a country has severely negative rates. The World Bank, in a study of eighty-one less developed countries, found that real deposit rates affected national savings rates.[67] Fry reported that real deposit rates significantly influenced savings rates in fourteen Asian countries and that increases in real rates augmented the savings rate.[68] But Giovannini replicated this study with a reestimated savings function and discovered no relationship.[69] Finally, Gupta found that real interest rates affected savings rates in Asian developing countries but not in Latin American countries.[70]

Credit Controls

The empirical record on the merits of credit controls is also inconclusive. To begin with, it is difficult to obtain accurate measures of the impact of selective credit policies on growth. To evaluate their success, one must determine whether additional funds actually reached targeted sectors and whether firms used them to make additional investments or simply substituted cheap credit for credit obtained from the market without increasing investment levels.[71] Second, evaluations of selective credit policies pose difficult counterfactuals: How would the targeted sectors have fared in the absence of directed credit policies? How would the economy as a whole have performed if credit had been allocated differently? Finally, studies suggest that the efficacy of selective credit policies has varied considerably across countries.

The empirical case against credit controls contends that they have resulted in patterns of credit allocation in many countries that are difficult to justify on economic grounds.[72] In addition, policymakers implementing selective credit policies have usually imposed interest rate controls concomitantly, which some scholars claim have limited the pool of investment capital.[73] Furthermore, credit controls have impeded the development of direct markets by encouraging recipient firms to borrow from the banking system.[74] This evidence has led one scholar to conclude that selective credit policies "seem to be an ideal recipe for reducing both the quantity and quality of productive investment."[75]

Other studies cite additional problems with credit controls. There is some evidence that selective credit policies worsen income distribution and increase industrial concentration because they discriminate against small borrowers.[76] Credit controls are also associated with insolvency problems in the banking system, largely due to a sharp rise in the percentage of non-performing loans in intermediaries' portfolios.[77] Firms targeted by selective credit policies often undertake risky investments they might otherwise not attempt because they have access to cheap credit and then find themselves unable to repay their loans. Or they may simply decide to default on their loans because they believe their status as "priority borrowers" will protect them from legal action. Finally, directed credit programs have been linked to a deterioration of monetary control in some countries.[78]

As already noted, scholars of Japan, South Korea, and Taiwan offer a more positive assessment of credit controls. They contend that credit programs in these countries were an integral part of an overall industrial policy that facilitated growth and competitiveness. Amsden contends, for example, that the South Korean government intervened heavily in financial markets, effectively channeling subsidized credit to priority sectors. Its credit policies were important in creating comparative advantage in industrial sectors where a priori Korean firms were not competitive. It succeeded where other states have failed because it exacted performance objectives from firms in exchange for credit subsidies.[79]

Skeptics, however, doubt that industrial policies in Japan, South Korea, and Taiwan have been responsible for their success. They contend that other factors (e.g., well-designed macroeconomic policies) account for their impressive growth better; in fact, some suggest that their industrial policies might have actually hurt economic performance.[80] The part played by financial policy in their overall development strategy is also controversial. Calder and Horiuchi, for example, contend that the Japanese government was far less successful than commonly believed in influencing the allocation of domestic capital; moreover, they claim that state-directed credit was mostly allocated to declining or politically important industries.[81]

Conclusions

The available research indicates that restriction is not the optimal financial strategy for most countries, but it does not allow us to make definitive judgments. The effectiveness of the financial controls associated with restriction has varied across settings. In most countries, a strategy of restriction has apparently hurt economic performance. But Japan, South Korea, and Taiwan grew rapidly while their financial systems were restricted. Although many economists claim that their financial policy had little to do with this success, their performance rules out condemning restriction universally. The East Asian experience suggests that a market-based financial system does not seem to be a necessary condition (nor sufficient condition, as we shall see later) for strong economic performance. As Cole and Wellons assert, "a liberal financial system may not be essential for economic development if other important factors, like fiscal and trade policy, are not seriously distorted."[82]

A likely culprit for variations in the performance of restriction is the nature of political institutions in different countries, especially as it affects politicians' incentives to provide private versus public goods through the financial system, state capacity, and the autonomy of policymakers. The biggest challenge is to explain why the results of East Asian financial policy differed from those of most countries, if indeed they did.[83] Scholars have long argued that East Asian governments implemented superior economic policy in general because unique conditions led political leaders to give "public-spirited" technocrats greater autonomy and there was a broad political consensus that rapid, sustained economic growth was a top national goal.[84] The seemingly singular ability of East Asian policymakers to intervene without causing government failure does suggest that it would be difficult to implement their financial policy model successfully elsewhere.

The Economics of Financial Liberalization

Economists critical of restriction once believed that the optimal policy for countries with a restricted financial system was to establish a market-based system as quickly as possible. They urged policymakers to permit greater entry into the financial sector, deregulate interest rates completely, dismantle most selective credit policies, eliminate taxation of the banking system, deepen bond and equity markets, and integrate the domestic financial system into international markets. Deregulating interest rates would augment the supply of loanable funds and improve the quality of investment.

Allowing private markets to allocate available funds among competing users would distribute capital to its most efficient uses. Eliminating taxation of the banking system would reduce distortion of financial markets by removing the bias in favor of the public sector. Deepening direct markets would expand the range of projects funded and lower the amount of default risk borne by banks. Finally, opening the domestic financial system would permit the injection of badly needed foreign capital. All these steps would increase overall financial efficiency and thus, economic growth.

Unfortunately, some early attempts to liberalize financial markets did not fare well. In the Southern Cone countries, governments carried out a program of wide-ranging financial deregulation in the 1970s as part of broader economic stabilization and structural adjustment plans.[85] Within a few years, these countries saw real interest rates soar to very elevated levels (as high as 60 percent), foreign indebtedness increase unduly, and numerous banks and industrial firms fail. These problems arose largely because policymakers deregulated before controlling high inflation, completing financial deepening, and achieving fiscal restraint (except in the case of Chile). In the end, Southern Cone governments replaced some financial controls and intervened to prop up failing banks and corporations. In Turkey, the government removed all interest rate controls and allowed banks to offer new types of liabilities in 1980. Two years later, however, financial instability (i.e., massive defaults in both the financial and real sectors) led policymakers to replace interest rate controls.[86] It should be noted that most of these countries later liberalized their financial systems again, this time with greater success.

In contrast, several countries have attained greater success with liberalization by adopting a more incremental approach. The South Korean government, for example, removed capital, credit, entry, and interest rate controls gradually and slowly, paying careful attention to the impact of financial deregulation on macroeconomic stability.[87] Greece, Morocco, Portugal, and Spain have also fared relatively well by using an incremental approach to financial reform.[88]

A large body of literature on the micro- and macroeconomics of financial reform has appeared in the past ten years that seeks to explain the differential success of deregulation efforts and determine the optimal course for liberalizing markets. Most economists still agree that liberalization is the best policy, but they now believe that it must be implemented more gradually and discriminately, after first attaining macroeconomic stability. In addition, they emphasize the need for an increase in prudential regulation as deregulation progresses.

Macroeconomic Issues

Many countries with restricted systems confront serious macroeconomic instability; that is, they experience high and variable inflation, wide fluctuations in real interest rates, and large government and balance-of-payment deficits.[89] The consensus among economists is that a stabilization program focused on reducing government deficits, controlling inflation, and fixing the exchange rate at or near its equilibrium level is a precondition for successful liberalization. Failure to carry out such a program is likely to lead to financial and further macroeconomic instability that can derail reform efforts. Let us examine why.

Inflation creates several problems for financial reform. First, high inflation alters the portfolios of savers in ways that constrict the supply of loanable funds. It spurs savers to switch from financial to real assets that serve as inflation hedges, thereby reducing deposits within the banking system.[90] It also impedes the growth of equity and bond markets by making securities less attractive. Second, liberalization under conditions of high inflation has been associated with high real loan rates of interest.[91] In some countries (e.g., in the Southern Cone), the lack of prudential regulation in conjunction with deposit insurance encouraged banks to undertake risky lending at exorbitant real rates. In others (e.g., the Philippines), increased government borrowing caused by large budget deficits drove up real rates. In either case, the combination of inflation and high real interest rates led to serious financial instability and sharply lower productive investment, grinding liberalization efforts to a halt.

Lack of fiscal restraint may frustrate the financial reform process as well. If governments finance deficits by borrowing from the central bank (which augments the stock of high-powered money), as they often do in countries with restricted systems, inflation is bound to increase with all its attendant problems for reform efforts.[92] If the government finances the deficit through the domestic banking system, the supply of credit available to private borrowers is constricted, creating hardship among firms. ARs are particularly onerous since they not only divert resources from the private sector to the government but also force banks to purchase debt at below-market rates; wherever possible, banks will cross-subsidize their low-interest loans to the government by charging private borrowers higher rates. This occurred in Spain with harmful results, as chapter 7 shows. More orthodox means of financing deficits may also pose problems. If the government borrows heavily on the open market at market interest rates, it stunts the growth of private issues in bond and equity markets, inhibiting financial deepening. If it borrows abroad to meet deficits, external debt increases, putting pressure on the balance of payments.

Finally, financial opening under unstable macroeconomic conditions may also lead to damaging capital flows and undesirable changes in exchange rates. In Chile, South Korea, Spain, and Uruguay, financial opening produced sharp capital inflows because it stimulated investment more than savings, and because high real interest rates attracted foreign deposits.[93] Excessive capital inflows had two negative effects. First, they led to an overvalued exchange rate that hurt export competitiveness and encouraged imports. This suggests that countries must actively seek to maintain exchange rates near their equilibrium levels when they open up their markets to avoid a deterioration of their balance of payments. Second, these capital inflows increased the domestic money supply in unpredictable ways, thereby jeopardizing monetary control. The experience of these and other countries has led economists to recommend that countries maintain capital controls until macroeconomic stability is assured and financial deepening has occurred.

Microeconomic Issues

Microeconomic issues concerning the deregulation of restricted financial systems primarily focus on the difficulties of liberalizing under conditions of imperfect information and competition.[94] The Stiglitz and Weiss model of equilibrium credit rationing is the basis of a great deal of theoretical work that concentrates on the problems associated with imperfect information.[95] The model assumes that banks cannot assess the creditworthiness of potential borrowers perfectly because the information costs of determining their risk characteristics are prohibitively high. Under these conditions, a bank's return from lending to a specific group of borrowers may not increase monotonically as the interest rate it charges increases. This is because, as rates rise, the composition of loans that the bank grants become more risky (i.e., they have a higher probability of default). Two factors account for this result. First, as interest rates increase, "safe" borrowers (i.e., those who only borrow if they are sure they can repay the loan) are discouraged, whereas more risk-taking borrowers step forward; this is called "adverse risk selection." Second, as rates increase, borrowers who can choose among various projects select those with higher potential returns on capital but greater risk of default; this is called the "incentive effect."

When government policies do not induce moral hazard, banks themselves try to minimize the adverse selection and incentive effects by setting interest rates at some level below the rate that would equate supply and demand for credit. Unfortunately, moral hazard problems are common in countries undertaking financial deregulation. To secure the banking sector's cooperation and prevent panic among savers, governments typically guarantee that they will rescue the banking sector if deregulation goes awry.[96] In most countries, however, the government's capacity for assessing and limiting the level of risk in bank portfolios is generally weak because qualified inspectors and supervisors are in short supply and prudential regulation is inadequate.[97] This creates a moral hazard problem. Banks have an incentive to make risky loans at high interest rates since (1) if bank loans are repaid, they will make a large profit, and (2) if banks suffer large losses because of defaults, the state will bear most of the losses.

The Stiglitz and Weiss model suggests that the government must play an active role in minimizing the microeconomic problems identified earlier—adverse selection, the incentive effect, and moral hazard—throughout the liberalization process. Several tentative policy proposals can be stated. First, authorities should retain some sort of ceiling on loan and deposit interest rates in the short term to prevent unduly risky lending; however, real interest rates should always be positive. In the words of Cole and Wellons, "the initial goal for financial reform may be an optimal middle ground between a liberal system and controlled interest rates."[98] Second, policymakers must make prudential regulation a top priority. They should increase inspection of bank portfolios, establish adequate own capital requirements, prohibit dangerous banking practices, and strengthen loan-loss provisions to limit excess risk-taking by banks. Interest rate controls should be phased out as soon as effective prudential regulation is established. The government ought to provide deposit insurance to maintain confidence in the banking system's solvency, but premiums should be set so as to discourage moral hazard.[99]

Finally, policymakers ought to promote effective bond and equity markets. Well-functioning direct markets are required to alleviate the credit rationing that occurs even in the absence of interest rate and credit controls.[100] If effective bond and equity markets exist, some risky, high-yield projects that are rationed out of credit markets will find financing; if they do not, many of these projects will not obtain funds. Governments can also promote the efficient allocation of capital by dismantling selective credit policies; however, policymakers must proceed slowly so as to limit financial distress on the part of their beneficiaries. The government should narrow the differential between preferential and market interest rates and provide any subsidies to favored sectors through central bank discounts or direct budgetary subsidies.

Imperfectly competitive financial markets also pose major problems for liberalization efforts.[101] Most restricted systems are characterized by a cartelized or oligopolistic banking sector. Unless policymakers promote competition in the financial sector, deregulation is unlikely to eliminate the inefficiencies that characterize restriction. Removing interest rate controls, for example, seldom provides banks with strong incentives to decrease operating costs or adopt more appropriate interest rates if they face little competition. Experience shows that banks often agree not to engage in serious competition for deposits or loans after deregulation. In several countries with a cartelized banking sector, bank associations took over the role of setting interest rates for their members when government controls were lifted; in others, like Spain, informal networks among bankers helped to restrain price competition.[102]

How should governments encourage competition? An essential step is to create a level playing field among existing intermediaries. Several countries have attempted to do so by moving toward a universal banking model, but other means are available.[103] Policymakers also ought to permit NBFIs, such as finance companies, to enter the market. NBFIs not only increase competition within the sector but also broaden the range of financial instruments available and make the financial system more robust in the face of external and internal shocks. Finally, once domestic intermediaries become more competitive, authorities should allow the entry of foreign banks. Foreign banks usually introduce new financial instruments and operating procedures that lower transaction costs substantially. Throughout this process, policymakers must be careful to balance the need to increase competition with that of safeguarding the solvency of the banking sector.

Finally, liberalization must be accompanied by the elimination of protectionism and other economic controls that inhibit competition. When prices are distorted by price controls and trade barriers, financial reform will probably not improve the allocation of credit. In fact, "deregulation may make matters worse by causing the financial sector to respond more flexibly to bad signals."[104]

Organization of the Book

The rest of this book is organized as follows. Chapter 2 presents my conceptual framework for explaining the evolution of financial regulation. Chapter 3 analyzes the political economy of Spain's restricted financial system during the Franco years in light of the framework I have developed. It also introduces the actors and institutions that play a central role in financial policy-making in Spain. Chapters 4 through 7 examine the process of financial deregulation in Spain. Chapter 4 looks at the origins of liberalization in the late 1960s under the Franco regime. Chapter 5 analyzes Spain's transition to democracy and the impetus that it provided to financial reform; it contains an in-depth discussion of the critical 1977 reforms. Chapter 6 considers financial policy in the years 1978–82, a period marked by a difficult economic and political environment that provoked a pronounced stop-and-go pattern in the reform process. Chapter 7 examines financial policy under the Socialist governments of the 1980s. It demonstrates that a change in governing parties from a centrist to a socialist party did not, as was widely expected, derail the drive for financial liberalization.

Chapter 8 briefly summarizes the study's principal results and considers their wider applicability. It evaluates the implications of the findings for rational choice approaches that explain economic policy-making by analyzing political institutions and the reward structures they impart on political leaders. It also examines how democratization has affected the course of financial policy in several countries other than Spain, namely, Brazil, South Korea, and Turkey. This discussion, in conjunction with the findings obtained from the study of Spain, is intended to help us understand under what conditions democratization is most likely to encourage financial liberalization.

CHAPTER 2

The Political Economy of
Financial Regulation

This chapter develops an analytical framework for explaining why government officials restrict financial markets and why they sometimes choose to deregulate them. It argues that political leaders attempt to shape the financial system to advance their own interests, altering regulatory policy in response to changes in the constraints and opportunities generated by their political environment. I explore the merits of restricted and market-based systems from the perspective of self-interested political leaders and examine which institutional arrangements encourage them to adopt one regulatory framework over the other. I also address several other issues that have traditionally occupied political economists, notably, who benefits and loses from different types of financial systems?

The motives for implementing restriction or liberalizing financial markets surely have varied across settings, so I make no claim that the specific variables discussed here apply to all countries or epochs. I do suggest that my framework identifies strong private political rationales for seeking a restricted or market-based system that may be important in a variety of countries.

The Analytical Approach

Public officials are always involved in the design of financial regulation, whether they take the initiative in the process or react to international or social pressures. As Hugh Patrick states,

> The government designs the architecture of the financial system; the market gives it substance, fills its halls, and even alters the design itself. . . . At the micro level, [government authorities] oversee banks and other financial institutions with prudential regulation and supervision. But they do more than that. They build and modify the institutional structure and hence the industrial organization of finance; they set and enforce the rules of the game.[1]

Public officials may intervene in markets to advance the public interest or their own private interests or, most likely, some combination of both. In this study, I hypothesize that government officials design financial regulation to further their own interests. In this view, to understand financial regulatory policy one must consider the political problems that politicians attempt to solve when they intervene in markets.[2] This belief is central to what are commonly called "rational choice" approaches to political economy. Such approaches explain changes in economic regulation or the structure of markets in terms of the choice processes of the individual participants, taking into account the collective action problems they often face in effecting change.[3]

The most prominent rational choice theory of regulation is the so-called economic theory (or "Chicago School") developed by George Stigler and others. Stigler argued that public officials design regulation to favor groups that offer them the greatest political support. In most cases, regulatory policy ends up benefiting well-organized special interests—producers—at the expense of diffuse social groups—consumers—by redistributing income away from the latter to the former. In sum, "regulation is acquired by the [regulated] industry and is designed and operated primarily for its benefit."[4] Noting that regulatory policy does not always exhibit "capture," other scholars have extended the economic theory to explain why regulation sometimes does not favor producers over consumers and to allow for strategic behavior on the part of politicians. Peltzman argued that politicians attend to the demands of several constituencies when regulating markets.[5] They may, for example, design regulation in ways that limit an industry's profits in order to favor specific consumer groups whose support is deemed critical. Becker demonstrated that public officials must consider overall economic efficiency when establishing regulatory policy in addition to its distributive consequences.[6] They may deregulate markets, for instance, if the existing regulatory regime begins to generate large deadweight economic losses since consumer and producer surpluses are also sources of political support. To my knowledge, this latter argument has not been made with respect to financial policy; instead, scholars drawing on the economic theory have viewed policymakers as largely designing policy in response to social pressures involving distributive issues.

I take as a basic premise that public officials do not simply design financial policy in response to the demands of social groups for regulation; they possess distinctive interests and may attempt to use the instruments of the state to shape markets to further their goals. Thus, I contend that one must look at the factors that influence the supply of regulation as well as the demand for it; analysis that views regulatory policy as simply reflecting the preferences of dominant social groups or emerging from the struggle among interest groups for influence will be incomplete. While I consider private actor demands for financial regulation in this study, my analytical framework stresses the necessity of considering additionally how the preferences of public officials influence financial policy. Indeed, I assert that public officials are the driving force behind financial policy in countries that start out with restricted systems.

As already noted, I initially argue at a high level of abstraction, concentrating on the goals of political leaders who are presumed to have homogeneous preferences. I also assume that principal-agent problems are limited; that is, bureaucrats design financial policy in accordance with their political superiors' preferences. This premise contrasts with that of studies that claim that financial regulation is primarily the product of ongoing, closely guarded negotiations between bureaucratic decision makers ("technocrats") and regulated intermediaries.[7] In this view, politicians typically delegate policy-making to technocrats, partly to avoid taking sides between constituents with competing interests and partly because they rely on their expertise.

In reality, principal-agent problems exist, and politicians may experience difficulty controlling financial policy completely once authority is delegated to bureaucratic officials. Moreover, the goals of bureaucrats may be at odds with those of their political superiors. Nevertheless, I suggest that explanations of financial policy can be strengthened by looking beyond the relationship between technocrats and banks and examining the role of governing politicians in regulatory policy.[8] Political leaders establish the general policy framework in which the bureaucracy must operate, in response to the incentives generated by their political environment. Although politicians often delegate rule-making authority to technocrats, who may then design regulations in consultation with banks within the guidelines set by their political superiors, they ultimately retain control over the regulatory regime. Technocrats, for example, will not eliminate credit controls if their political superiors favor state control over credit allocation. Even in Japan, where the autonomy of bureaucrats in financial policy is considered especially great, Rosenbluth notes, "what deceptively appears to be bureaucratic-led policy making . . . is high politics in disguise, little different in substance from instances of direct political involvement."[9]

In this study, I assume that leaders attempt to solve two fundamental, interrelated political problems. The first is to ensure their own political survival.[10] Positing that politicians are primarily political office seekers does not deny that they may also wish to attain other political or social goals. Rather, as Bates states, "[this assumption] highlights the competitive nature of the political arena and the way in which those who prevail in the competition for office must respond to the pressures and incentives which originate within it, for example by endorsing certain economic policies in a search for political support."[11] The second is the need to raise government revenue.[12] As Levi contends, government revenue facilitates the attainment of a public official's goals, whether they be personal or social.[13] Moreover, leaders will not remain in power if they cannot raise sufficient revenue to provide the services that constituents demand.

Politicians design financial policy in order to advance these two goals, adapting it to the particular reward structure generated by a country's political environment and institutions. For instance, when institutions encourage leaders to court narrow constituencies instead of the general populace in the pursuit of power, they formulate policy that enables them to deliver private benefits to specific groups. When they provide an incentive to appeal to encompassing interests, leaders fashion financial policy that supplies collective goods, like efficient markets.

Seen in this light, restricted and market-based systems have different political merits whose usefulness for politicians varies across institutional settings. Restriction enables politicians to deliver financial benefits to key constituents and raise government revenue, but it often leads to inefficiency. When a country's political setting motivates leaders to target narrow groups in their pursuit of power or raise revenue indirectly, politicians will favor restriction despite its deficiencies. Market-based financial systems promise greater efficiency but do not permit public officials to affect directly the fortunes of specific groups. A more market-based system, however, is valuable when a country's institutions encourage politicians to supply collective goods, such as a strong economy, instead of private goods in the pursuit of power.

This conceptual framework deemphasizes the role of partisanship in shaping financial policy. Other scholars give government partisanship a central place in explanations of economic policy. They claim that governing parties of the left and right prefer different degrees of state intervention in markets.[14] In the case of financial policy, leftist governments are said to favor greater control over markets, especially over the allocation of credit and its cost, than rightist governments. They suggest that transfers of power from rightist to leftist governments (or vice versa) may profoundly alter the evolution of financial regulation.

The view that partisanship matters is not inconsistent with my framework since it holds (as I do) that politicians design policy with an eye to how it will affect their own interests. Few would deny that partisanship can be important in specifying what those interests are. Nonetheless, I suggest that the basic institutional incentives that all politicians must respond to may often predominate and override partisanship concerns. In the case of Spain, I show that a change from a rightist to a leftist government did not alter the basic shape of financial policy despite widespread expectations that it would (although the changeover did affect other features of economic strategy).

The remainder of this chapter considers the political advantages and disadvantages of restricted and market-based systems in detail. It also explores the circumstances under which politicians are most likely to alter the financial regulatory framework, in particular, when they will liberalize restricted financial markets. I begin this analysis in the next section by examining why politicians choose to implement financial restriction.

The Political Economy of Financial Restriction

In the previous chapter, I contested the view that restriction was the only or optimal financial policy available to policymakers in most countries. Economic constraints can explain the existence of only a portion of the financial controls found in restricted systems, and evidence suggests that restriction has often harmed economic performance. This observation provides a strong rationale for considering the political bases of restriction. Even in cases where governments confront great economic constraints in designing financial policy, examining the political benefits that public officials (and other actors) obtain from restriction yields important insights into the formulation and the subsequent evolution of financial regulation.

I argue that the structure of restricted systems may be explained as the product of choices made by officials seeking to achieve the goals of retaining power and generating revenue. Public officials use interest rate and credit controls to direct investable funds through a non-price-rationing system in order to build support among important constituents. They impose ARs, heavy RRs, and other forms of taxation of the banking system to expropriate seigniorage from intermediaries.[15] To maximize seigniorage opportunities, authorities adopt policies that encourage the development of the banking system at the expense of bond and equity markets, as these are markets from which seigniorage is not easily extracted. They resort to taxation of the banking system despite its high efficiency costs because a more effective means of public finance (e.g., a greater reliance on direct taxes) is often not administratively or politically feasible. I examine each of these elements of restriction in detail later.

Although some private actors may seek the imposition of specific regulations associated with restriction, public officials often take the initiative in pursuing a restricted system. Political leaders will favor restriction when a country's institutions primarily motivate them to deliver private benefits to key social groups in their quest to retain power. This is the case for many (but not all) authoritarian regimes, as well as for some democratic regimes, notably those that reward politicians who attend to parochial over collective interests. Leaders also value restriction for its revenue-generating ability when they find it administratively or politically difficult to implement effective means of taxation.

Government officials typically have little trouble implementing restriction when they seek it because powerful private actors—banks and big, politically connected firms—also benefit from it. The relative bargaining power of public officials vis-à-vis private financial actors does influence how the benefits and costs of regulation are distributed. For example, the relative bargaining power of public officials and banks will determine who bears the costs of providing selective credit. Very powerful banks or firms may be able to "capture" the financial policy-making apparatus constructed by the state and become the guiding force behind financial policy.

Banks support restriction even though some of its features impose opportunity costs on them (e.g., credit controls and taxation policies) because they prosper in a restricted system. Governments implementing restriction typically compensate banks to win their cooperation with general financial policy. They do so in two ways. First, they restrict entry into the financial sector to encourage the creation of a banking oligopoly and block the development of direct markets to impede disintermediation. Second, they impose interest rate controls; this facilitates (whether by design or not) a collusive outcome in the banking cartel that they have promoted, enabling established intermediaries to earn supranormal profits. The overall impact of restriction on banks, therefore, is highly favorable; in fact, banks typically become the principal opponents of liberalization efforts. Nonetheless, the finding that several features of restriction go against the preferences of banks suggests that simple capture theory cannot account for financial restriction. I illustrate this with specific examples in the Spanish case.

A competing explanation for why many governments chose restriction in the postwar era is that policymakers believed it was in the public interest to do so, whether or not this was actually the case. In this view, officials sought a bank-based system under close government supervision because they calculated it was best suited to promoting their country's modernization. Certainly, a body of work in development economics at the time promoted this view as did some international economic agencies (although other international actors championed market-based systems).[16] Moreover, the lack of financial depth and difficulty of building effective market-based institutions in many countries made this the least painful choice as well.

Empirical tests of self-interest versus public interest accounts may not yield definitive results as the available evidence on financial policy will often support hypotheses that we can infer from both views.[17] Moreover, most public officials are probably driven by a mixture of motives—some private, some public—when they design regulation, and these may change over time. For instance, officials might initially choose restriction in part because they think it is the best economic policy but maintain it for purely self-interested political reasons as they (or subsequent officials) discover the political benefits that restriction can deliver.

While recognizing these points, this study suggests that the most convincing explanations of economic policy-making regard public officials as self-interest, not social welfare, maximizers. I hold motives constant and contend that a variety of political factors determines whether officials pursue policies that seem only self-serving or that coincide with the general interest. The most important of these are a country's political institutions. In this view, different institutional reward structures account for the variance that leaders show for the public interest across countries or over time.[18] The utility of this approach is evident in the Spanish case. Political leaders altered economic policy away from rewarding narrow, entrenched elites toward advancing the general public interest when the country underwent a transition from an authoritarian to a democratic regime. I contend that this approach can be useful in other comparative or longitudinal analyses of regulation.

Delivering Financial Benefits through Interest Rate and Credit Controls

Whether to institute interest rate and credit controls usually takes center stage in financial policy debates since their introduction can significantly alter the distribution of wealth among financial market participants. These controls prevent market forces from determining the price and distribution of credit and allow the state to make many pricing and allocative decisions authoritatively, creating what economists call "credit rents."[19] Market participants will try to influence credit and interest rate policy in order to obtain these credit rents.

The Politics of Interest Rate Controls
Interest rate controls, in the form of ceilings on loan and/or deposit rates, are among the most common sorts of government intervention in financial

markets. Why do public officials implement them? One answer, offered by capture theory, is that they do so simply to appease the social groups that push for them. The private actors most affected by interest rate policy are financial intermediaries, and they are typically active lobbyists on this issue. Deposit rate ceilings limit the interest paid to bank depositors and, thus, benefit existing intermediaries by lowering the cost of their liabilities. Furthermore, they eliminate the most important form of competition for deposits because banks can no longer bid for deposits by offering higher rates; this facilitates the emergence of a cartel that enables them to earn supranormal profits. But intermediaries do not favor loan rate ceilings because they limit the profits they could potentially earn from charging higher rates. They accept loan rate ceilings, however, if authorities concomitantly impose deposit rate ceilings and entry controls since this set of policies guarantees them a profitable "spread" on all loans they make (assuming no defaults).[20] Bank pressure probably accounts for the observation that countries with nonrestricted financial systems have also had interest rate controls at some points in time. In the United States, for example, banks secured the imposition of deposit rate ceilings in the 1930s through bargaining with financial authorities.[21]

Interest rate policy affects the cost of credit directly, so firms often lobby on this issue as well. The stance of individual firms on interest rate controls should vary across firms. Loan rate ceilings, if binding, create a market in which credit must be rationed since the demand for loans will exceed supply.[22] Some firms will benefit since they will obtain credit at artificially low rates; others, however, will be rationed out of credit markets (either entirely or partially).[23] In theory, however, the business sector as a whole should oppose interest rate controls. Loan rate ceilings require concomitant deposit rate ceilings, which discourage savings in the form of deposits at intermediaries, thereby reducing the long-term supply of loanable funds.[24] This may result in credit shortages that restrict overall levels of investment. In practice, organized business groups have actually favored interest rate controls in many countries. The best explanation for this stance is that large, politically well-connected corporations dominate them, and they are (or expect to be) the recipients of cheap credit.

Public officials have incentives for implementing loan and deposit rate ceilings that are independent of social demands. As noted, when the government imposes loan rate ceilings, non–price rationing of loanable funds must occur since intermediaries no longer allocate credit according to the expected productivity of investment projects.[25] This gives public officials the opportunity to politicize the credit allocation process and create a tremendous source of discretionary power.[26] Indeed, if they can implement effective credit controls, they establish the means to channel credit to social groups they wish to favor and possibly even withhold it from those they wish to penalize. Selective credit policies have a greater political (and economic) impact if policymakers first create a rationed credit market via loan rate ceilings. When rationing exists, they use directed credit policies to grant or withhold access to credit. When it does not exist, they may use these policies only to vary the cost of credit across classes of borrowers.

A key aspect of selective credit policies is that regulators divert part of the profits banks earn due to interest rate and entry controls to help politically important firms. This feature of restriction illustrates Peltzman's contention that regulators often channel some of the profits that the direct beneficiaries of regulation receive—in this case, banks—to favor other important social groups—in this case, firms—in a process known as "cross-subsidization."[27] The costs of credit programs are borne by the diffuse groups of ordinary depositors and firms rationed out of credit markets.

The Politics of Selective Credit Policies

Political leaders often attempt to use selective credit policies to organize political followings and nullify the opposition.[28] If this strategy is successful, preferential credit recipients will provide political support in appreciation for the benefits they derive from selective credit policies.[29] Leaders may attempt to consolidate their power by making continued access to credit contingent upon political loyalty. Government officials, however, cannot allocate credit with total disregard for economic efficiency.[30] Distributing a large percentage of available credit to relatively nonproductive firms may cause a significant decline in economic performance that contributes to a loss of political support for current leadership and a drop in long-term state revenues. Therefore, government officials have a collective interest in considering efficiency criteria when implementing selective credit policies. They may face collective action problems in doing so, however, as individual politicians may not have a sufficient incentive to forgo the political benefits of providing private goods to their key constituents in order to promote aggregate efficiency.

The political utility of directed credit programs varies across countries. First, there may be differences in private demand for preferential credit; where private demand is relatively low (e.g., because firms have other sources of cheap finance), supplying preferential credit has less political value.[31] Second, political leaders might confront different costs in implementing selective credit policies. Haggard and Maxfield find that where macroeconomic instability has proved to be a political liability, leaders may refrain from implementing credit programs that can cause fiscal deficits and monetary control problems.[32]

Some private actors will oppose selective credit policies. Intermediaries resist credit controls for several reasons. First, these controls impose opportunity costs because they require intermediaries to provide credit on preferential terms.[33] Second, they make it difficult for intermediaries to maintain safe loan portfolios by compelling them to grant credit to firms that might not ordinarily receive it because they are poor credit risks; in effect, they force banks to make high-risk loans.[34] In addition, such controls force intermediaries to concentrate their lending in privileged sectors, making their solvency dependent on the health of those sectors. Third, intermediaries become vulnerable to interest rate risk in periods of high and variable inflation since most preferential credit is long term.

Firms rationed out of credit markets and savers also have reason to oppose selective credit policies and their attendant interest rate controls. Firms may be excluded from credit markets totally, in which case they may not be able to survive, or partially, in which case they will have to restrict their investments. Those that have access to credit, but outside preferential credit circles, usually have to pay more for it, as banks will attempt to recover the opportunity cost of providing preferential credit by charging more for other loans (to the extent permitted). Savers are hurt by binding deposit rate ceilings because they lower the yield they receive on their deposits. In periods of high inflation, it is common for savers to receive a negative real return on their deposits since authorities rarely alter interest rate ceilings quickly enough to compensate for rising prices.[35]

Despite the potential for opposition, politicians usually have little trouble sustaining selective credit programs. Savers and firms rationed out of credit markets are unlikely to organize for effective opposition. Savers face severe collective action problems in influencing financial policy. The potential benefits of liberalization for most individual savers are very small; therefore, no saver has sufficient interest to bear the full cost of lobbying the government. Further, the benefits that ensue from the removal of deposit rate ceilings are a public good since all savers will enjoy them whether or not they have contributed to the efforts to achieve reform; this provides individual savers with an incentive to "free ride." Firms partially rationed out of credit markets face similar collective action problems: the costs of lobbying to press for the removal of controls are high for any one firm, but the benefits from deregulation are uncertain. Firms totally rationed out of credit markets have a strong incentive to lobby policymakers since they will find it difficult to survive without access to funds. The resources an individual firm can mobilize in its influence attempts are probably limited, however, and its lobbying efforts are unlikely to be coordinated with those of others since the information costs of identifying other firms with similar fates are high. Moreover, the optimal lobbying strategy for the firm may not be to press for a removal of the controls that cause credit rationing but rather for its own access to preferential credit.

Private intermediaries often refrain from opposing credit controls vigorously out of respect for the implicit bargain by which they benefit from other features of the regulatory regime (e.g., entry and deposit rate controls). Instead, they lobby authorities to choose selective credit policies that minimize their opportunity costs (e.g., differential rediscount rates). In addition, they push for an increase in the remuneration of loans made to priority borrowers and some discretion in determining which firms are eligible to receive preferential credit (so that they can continue to supply credit to companies in which they have a stake). Finally, banks (and other actors) often develop ways to circumvent these controls, a topic I turn to now.

The Limits on Using Interest Rate and Credit Controls to
Deliver Benefits

Although politicians find that interest rate and credit controls are an attractive source of discretionary authority, there are limits on using them to deliver private benefits. These controls often impose opportunity costs on financial actors and have the unintended consequence of encouraging behavior that ultimately undermines their effectiveness and political usefulness.

Policymakers usually find that enforcing interest rate and credit controls fully is difficult. Intermediaries may often circumvent interest rate controls without violating the letter of the law. Banks can raise the effective remuneration on liabilities above deposit rate ceilings by offering depositors free services or gifts. They can bypass loan rate ceilings by mandating "compensating balances." These require borrowers to maintain a percentage of credit they obtain in a non-interest-bearing account for the loan's duration. As the borrower pays interest on the total amount borrowed, this increases the effective interest rate of the loan.[36]

Interest rate controls sometimes spur financial innovation that not only defeats their purpose but also complicates monetary control. In the 1980s, for example, Spanish banks faced a disintermediation threat from newly created short-term public debt that offered higher yields than they were permitted to pay on deposits. Banks circumvented deposit rate ceilings by creating a market for repurchase agreements using this short-term public debt. In this market, banks sold a portion of their public debt holdings to clients with an agreement to repurchase it at a designated future date and price.[37] Through these operations, banks obtained the use of funds that were not legally considered deposits; therefore, they were free to offer savers effective yields that exceeded deposit rate ceilings. Repurchase agreements complicated the efforts of the Spanish central bank to implement a tight money policy since the funds banks obtained in this manner were not included in the monetary aggregates that it used to track money supply growth. Governments can attempt to extend regulation to cope with this sort of financial innovation, but there is usually a significant lag before they are able to implement effective new controls. In the just cited example, Spanish authorities took five years to prohibit repurchase agreements using government debt.

Controlling credit allocation through selective credit policies encounters many problems as well. Funds that are earmarked for priority sectors may not reach their destination. Lenders often attempt to misclassify loans or create channels for redirecting credit from priority borrowers to firms they themselves wish to favor (such as companies in their industrial group).[38] Firms themselves may simply reloan the preferential credit they obtain to others, at a profit. Credit that does reach priority sectors may encourage detrimental behavior by recipients. Preferential loan rates discourage prompt repayment since it is often more profitable to let interest accrue than to pay off the principle; this type of delinquency increases the fragility of the financial system.[39] More importantly, directed credit policies can create moral hazard problems among favored borrowers. Identifying a sector as a priority sector gives the state a vested interest in its success. Privileged borrowers may anticipate a government bailout if their results deteriorate; consequently, they may engage in risky policies or lose their competitive drive. Finally, government officials may find it difficult to stop the flow of preferential credit to sectors once they no longer wish to target them because withdrawing existing benefits can create a severe political backlash. In several countries, this difficulty has led to the steady expansion or "layering" of credit programs over time, as new programs are added without deleting any already in existence.[40]

Taxation of the Banking System

Policymakers following restriction typically tax the banking system to generate revenue and finance government expenditures at low-interest cost. They impose RRs in excess of the optimum minimum requirement that ensures intermediaries can meet their redemption obligations to tap savings mobilized by the banking system at zero- or low-interest cost.[41] The central bank may use the funds intermediaries set aside to meet RRs to invest in assets that generate returns (e.g., foreign bonds); the profits obtained from these investments go to the Treasury and are a source of revenue. Alternatively, the Treasury may borrow these funds to finance the public debt at low cost. Governments establish ARs for similar reasons. ARs require intermediaries to purchase government debt yielding returns below prevailing market rates. Therefore, they enable the Treasury to reduce the cost of financing public sector activities and ensure the placement of government debt issues.

Intermediaries strongly oppose RRs and ARs because they impose opportunity costs in the form of foregone interest that they could otherwise earn on the funds tied up in these obligations. Savers and firms not targeted by directed credit programs are also hurt by heavy RRs and ARs. Intermediaries typically attempt to recover part of their opportunity costs by lowering the rate they pay savers for deposits or increasing loan interest rates (to the extent this is allowed).[42]

There is prima facie evidence that revenue generation has been an important motive for seeking financial restriction in many countries. Giovannini and Melo found that the quantitative importance of revenues generated through restriction is very high worldwide. In a study of twenty-four countries following restriction, the authors determined that forced holdings of government debt alone generated interest cost savings equivalent to an average of 1.8 percent of GDP and 8.8 percent of central government revenue.[43] I show in later chapters that restriction also generated substantial revenue in Spain.

Taxation of the banking system is a highly inefficient means of generating government revenue since it hinders the long-term economic development that ultimately increases the tax base and sustains revenue growth.[44] RRs and ARs substantially increase financial margins and introduce rigidity in the operations of intermediaries and, thereby, lead to a loss of financial efficiency.[45] Moreover, they discourage savings (and, hence, funds available for investment) by contributing to lower deposit interest rates. Consequently, in the absence of political constraints, a policymaker seeking to maximize the present discounted value of the future stream of revenues would not choose to raise revenue through restriction.

Why then do governments tax the banking system to raise public sector revenues? First, some leaders are not able or willing to adopt a strategy that maximizes revenues in the long run because they are not sure they will remain in office for long. These officials have an incentive to maximize current revenue even if this impedes long-term economic performance. Second, revenue production through restriction may be the only viable means of public finance in some countries. More efficient means of revenue generation, namely, greater reliance on direct taxation (e.g., income taxes), may not be feasible for administrative or political reasons. Direct taxation is politically unpopular because it is highly transparent and, if progressive, tends to place a sizable burden on the politically influential middle and upper classes. It is administratively difficult because it requires excellent information gathering and processing services staffed by highly trained personnel. Taxation of the banking system, on the other hand, is attractive because it generates substantial revenues in a way that is largely hidden from public view. Finally, forcing intermediaries to purchase public debt is sometimes the only viable means of financing budget deficits short of printing money. Developing a market for public debt is difficult in some countries because the pool of potential buyers is small.[46] Moreover, government officials are often reluctant to pay market interest rates on debt when deficits can be financed at lower cost.

There are limits on the government's ability to use taxation of the banking system as a source of revenue, however. The imposition of ARs and excessive RRs encourages intermediaries to devise ways of avoiding their opportunity costs. In Spain, banks also created the repurchase agreements involving government debt discussed earlier to develop a source of funds not subject to RRs or ARs (since money raised in this way was not included in the deposit base used by the government to calculate their obligations). As taxation of the banking system increased, intermediaries sought more ways to capture funds that were not subject to RRs or ARs. The result was that the government was able to obtain increasingly smaller amounts of additional revenue despite considerably higher taxation. Furthermore, financial innovation created serious monetary control problems, as already noted.

More importantly, predatory taxation entails a loss of financial efficiency that impedes the country's long-term economic development; this drag on performance may ultimately undermine the government's ability to sustain revenue growth. The state may come to face a fiscal crisis that challenges its legitimacy unless it implements a more effective means of raising revenue. In addition, if political leaders derive much of their support and legitimacy from maintaining a strong economy, a sharp decline in economic performance may allow rivals to challenge the political status quo.

The Suppression of Bond and Equity Markets

Authorities suppress bond and equity markets to promote intermediation through the banking system. They do so for three principal reasons. First, governments can generate more revenue, more easily, by appropriating seigniorage from the banking system than from direct markets.[47] Second, they can control the allocation of available loanable funds more tightly when they flow through the banking sector. For effective bond and equity markets to develop, the government has to allow the final users of funds to deal directly with savers. This makes it more difficult for public officials to influence the distribution of financial resources.[48] Finally, public officials may suppress direct markets to appease banks, which view their expansion as a serious disintermediation threat.

Policymakers have several means at their disposal for discouraging bond and equity markets relative to the banking system. Governments can block measures aimed at modernizing official exchanges or prohibit the introduction of new financial products. They may, for example, disallow the creation of secondary markets for securities sold on the exchanges in order to maintain their relative illiquidity vis-à-vis bank deposits. Second, they can tax assets obtained from the banking system and direct markets at differential rates so that investment in the latter is discouraged. A common tactic is to impose a special capital gains tax on securities traded in the bond and equity markets. Third, they can regulate bond yields and stock dividends to prevent them from competing with bank deposits. Finally, they can impose transaction taxes and stamp duties on the purchase and sale of securities at exchanges.

Suppressing direct markets may involve substantial economic costs, as noted in chapter 1. It also entails political risks. The lack of efficient direct markets means that firms must rely on bank credit and self-finance for investment funds, as they cannot issue securities to obtain them. When firms rely heavily on bank financing, banks gain leverage over the firms to which they lend. The banking sector's hold over industry can become an obstacle to state efforts to shape industrial development or even enable banks to extract concessions from the government through threats to subvert the economic programs that require their cooperation. A reliance on debt financing also limits the ability of authorities to implement a restrictive monetary policy (e.g., to fight inflation) since highly leveraged firms are vulnerable to reductions in the level of liquidity in the banking system.

Closing National Financial Markets

Scholars have identified various reasons why governments may close national financial markets, including the wish to minimize their country's "dependence" on foreign capital, the desire to maintain autonomy over macroeconomic policy, and the fear that such linkages might expose domestic banks and firms to influences that might undermine the political status quo. I specify some additional reasons that stem directly from the political calculus that I claim motivates public officials when they design financial policy.

Governments tend to control capital outflows strictly out of concern that the freedom to move money abroad might lead to massive capital flight, leaving the country devoid of funds for investment. Many governments also regulate capital inflows tightly.[49] One important reason for this policy is to retain control over credit allocation and foreign exchange.[50] Direct foreign investment or borrowing abroad by domestic firms may subvert efforts to promote priority sectors relative to others. Government officials may also be concerned about the impact of flows on monetary policy. This is especially true in countries with restricted systems since authorities find it particularly difficult to sterilize capital inflows they deem excessive.[51] As in the case of suppression of direct markets, limiting capital inflows may carry a high opportunity cost since foreign funds are often needed to bolster economic development. Foreign direct investment in particular may carry additional benefits, such as the transfer of organizational skills or technology.[52]

Nevertheless, some countries have opted to use capital inflows as an important element of their development strategies. Jeffry Frieden, for instance, has identified several countries that relied upon a strategy of "indebted industrialization."[53] These countries, however, still sought to maintain control over the allocation of incoming capital by funneling funds through state-run development banks (e.g., Mexico) or by using a variety of central government agencies to allocate funds (e.g., South Korea). In recent years, more countries have chosen to invite foreign investors, a trend I address later in this chapter.

In restricted systems, governments typically do not authorize foreign banks because they fear that they may come to dominate the banking system (due to their superior competitiveness) and be more difficult to control than domestic intermediaries. In addition, they worry that foreign banks will take advantage of their global network to move capital in and out of the country in ways that disrupt the economy. Finally, government officials may restrict foreign banking to appease domestic banks, which oppose their presence because of the competitive threat they pose.

The Creation of a Financial Oligopoly

Governments pursuing a strategy of restriction usually encourage the emergence of an oligopolistic market in the banking sector.[54] They do so in two primary ways. First, they restrict entry into the banking sector and forbid the formation of new NBFIs. Second, they impose interest rate controls; this facilitates (whether by design or not) a collusive outcome in the banking cartel they have promoted. This combination of policies may entail substantial social costs since the lack of competition increases the cost of financial intermediation (by permitting banks to enjoy wide margins) and decreases the pool of national savings (by allowing banks to pay low deposit rates).[55]

Public officials promote an oligopolistic financial sector despite the welfare losses this policy involves for two primary reasons. They may offer to restrict competition to compensate banks for the aspects of restriction that impose opportunity costs (e.g., credit controls) and, thus, gain their cooperation with their general financial policy. I show evidence of this in Spain. Second, they find it easier to control financial transactions (especially the flow of credit to final users) when the banking sector is oligopolistic since they oversee the activities of fewer financial institutions.[56] For example, moral suasion, a key instrument of financial policy, is more effective when targeted at fewer intermediaries.[57]

Liberalizing Restricted Systems

Restriction creates vested interests that oppose attempts to alter the financial regulatory regime. Private interests that flourish under restriction—preferential credit recipients and established intermediaries—have a big stake in maintaining the status quo. Public officials seemingly have an interest in preserving the financial controls that create a source of revenue and means of delivering benefits to key constituents. On the other hand, the losers in a restricted system—savers and firms rationed out of credit markets—are usually too poorly organized to have an impact on financial policy.

The strength of vested interests and inertia of potential opposition seem to make a movement for financial liberalization unlikely in countries with restricted systems. Nonetheless, a number of these countries have witnessed deregulation of their financial markets. The remainder of this chapter attempts to explain how financial liberalization occurs under such apparently unpropitious circumstances.

The Argument in Brief

Financial restriction can be a valuable tool for politicians seeking to stay in power and raise state revenue. It enables politicians to deliver financial benefits to win the support of constituents they believe are important for maintaining their power and for generating revenue without imposing politically unattractive direct taxes. When a country's political institutions primarily motivate leaders to target narrow constituencies in their quest to retain power, politicians will especially value restriction. Market-based financial systems promise greater efficiency but are seemingly more difficult to manipulate for political purposes because they do not give public officials the means to affect directly the fortunes of particular groups. A more market-based system, however, is valuable when institutions encourage politicians to supply collective economic goods, like a strong economy, instead of private goods, like preferential credit, in the pursuit of public office. For instance, politicians will endeavor to create efficient markets if they must put together a broad-based national coalition to win office, and voters place a high premium on economic performance. A system where market forces determine the allocation and price of credit is also useful when leaders wish to avoid having to favor some constituents over others or need to extricate themselves from costly existing commitments to certain groups. Finally, a market-based system is also desirable because it augments the stream of government revenues by promoting long-term growth.

This analysis implies that changes in the reward structures provided by a country's political institutions or environment may give leaders an incentive to alter the financial regulatory regime. This hypothesis is consistent with the oft-observed correlation between economic policy reform and discontinuous changes in a country's form of government. Specifically, I contend that politicians will liberalize financial markets when institutional changes increase the relative utility of a market-based system vis-à-vis a restricted one. The utility of a market-based financial system for politicians may increase in two ways. First, it may occur when the value of supplying more efficient market arrangements increases relative to that of providing private benefits to select constituents in the pursuit of power. Second, it may happen when more efficient means of taxation become available and politically feasible. Likewise, leaders will deregulate when the costs of maintaining restriction come to exceed its benefits, turning a restricted system into a political liability. This happens when restriction so lowers financial efficiency that it impedes growth, providing rivals with an issue they can use to challenge current leaders. I argue later that the tough economic conditions of the 1970s and 1980s highlighted and accentuated the problems caused by restriction, thereby increasing the political costs of maintaining it (especially as the level of political competition increased in many countries). In addition, increasing capital mobility has made it more difficult and costly for states to control financial activity. To avoid tautological reasoning about when it is in the interest of politicians to liberalize, analysis based on this approach must identify policy options available to leaders and indicate why choosing deregulation rather than other options was in their self-interest.

Events that create an incentive to deregulate may not actually produce liberalization. Government officials must have sufficient autonomy to implement reforms in the face of probable opposition from a variety of private and public actors that benefit from the status quo. In addition, politicians must be able to overcome the collective action problems that they themselves face when seeking to set up more efficient market structures and have a sufficiently long time horizon since the benefits from deregulation are usually not immediate.

Applying this framework to Spain in chapters 4 through 7, I identify two factors that were critical in producing financial deregulation. First, an increase in political dissent fueled by dissatisfaction with economic policy prompted the Franco regime to liberalize financial markets partially starting in the late 1960s; officials hoped a more market-based system would help sustain rapid growth and that prosperity would defuse hostility toward the regime. Second, Spain's transition to democracy in the late 1970s encouraged government officials to reopen the process of financial liberalization after it had stalled. The country's new democratic institutions provided leaders with a relatively greater incentive to supply collective goods instead of private goods to select groups in the quest for electoral support. In the realm of financial policy, this led them to try to create efficient financial markets via deregulation and to dismantle the controls previously used to deliver preferential credit to key constituents. In addition, greatly increased demands on state expenditures brought on by democratization eventually pushed them to eschew inefficient taxation of the financial sector and seek more effective means of raising government revenues. Overhauling fiscal policy, a long-needed reform that was off limits to policymakers during the Franco era, was made possible by democratization.

I believe that democratization often gives political leaders an incentive to liberalize financial markets, and I examine why this is so in a later section. First, I elaborate upon my theoretical framework by examining how it differs from existing explanations of financial deregulation. I distinguish among four competing views (even though there is substantial overlap among them). This discussion indicates why existing explanations cannot fully account for deregulation in restricted systems and highlights major theoretical issues in the study of regulatory policy and my contribution to them. I do not believe my own and competing views are mutually exclusive, however; in fact, they often complement one another in interesting ways.

Contrasts with Existing Theory

The Economic Theory
Many studies have relied upon the economic theory of regulatory policy to explain financial liberalization.[58] In this view, deregulation occurs when a

regulatory regime becomes suboptimal for its beneficiaries or the net balance of interest group demands on public officials shifts because of changes in the bargaining power of its winners and losers.[59] As it is generally agreed that the losers in restricted systems, savers and firms rationed out of credit markets, are unlikely to initiate the fight for deregulation due to collective action problems, studies have focused on understanding when the preferences of the beneficiaries of highly regulated systems are likely to change.

Using the economic theory, several authors have explained deregulation by arguing that regulated financial intermediaries (namely, banks) have provided the impetus for deregulation when economic changes, such as inflation, have made the existing regulatory regime unprofitable for them. Specifically, the literature suggests that deregulation has often originated in the efforts of regulated banks to eliminate deposit rate ceilings. In general, intermediaries favor deposit rate ceilings because they limit competition for deposits and raise profits. But regulated intermediaries will seek the removal of ceilings when they limit their ability to compete for deposits with new, unregulated intermediaries or when they face the threat of disintermediation from direct financial markets. The U.S. experience with deregulation illustrates this point well. In the 1970s, U.S. banks could not compete with NBFIs offering liabilities, such as money market mutual funds, that were not subject to deposit rate ceilings as inflation increased. Consequently, they lobbied authorities and obtained the removal of interest rate controls in 1980.

Interest rate deregulation is especially significant because it typically sparks more extensive financial deregulation. In the U.S. case, it exposed unequal playing fields in areas of non–price competition. Intermediaries left at a competitive disadvantage lobbied to reform regulations in these areas. As policymakers altered regulatory policy in response, other rules became controversial, and they came under fire to modify them as well. In conclusion, partial deregulation created a "deregulatory snowball" that eventually led to calls for a thorough deregulation of the financial sector.[60]

Several studies have sought to specify the factors that alter the distribution of costs and benefits of financial regulation sufficiently to generate pressure for reform. Among those that they have identified are (1) the onset of high and variable rates of inflation; (2) greater integration of domestic and international financial markets; (3) major advances in communications and data processing technology with direct application to financial markets; and (4) a rapid accumulation of financial assets by nonfinancial sectors.[61]

I contend that these economic events will usually not encourage regulated intermediaries operating in restricted systems to seek deregulation.

The lack of financial depth in these systems makes it unlikely that such events will alter the costs and benefits of regulation sufficiently for banks to push for deregulation. This means that public officials, not private actors, will initiate deregulation in countries with restricted systems; thus, the society-centered focus used by the economic theory to explain deregulation in well-developed systems is unlikely to account for it in restricted systems.

Two differences in financial depth between restricted and more market-based financial systems limit the utility of the economic theory for explaining deregulation in restricted systems.[62] First, NBFIs are few in restricted systems, and authorities control their growth and range of activities more closely than in market-based systems. Thus, investors and borrowers must often deal with banks almost exclusively when investing or raising funds. Second, in nonrestricted systems, mature bond and equity markets exist, so disintermediation takes the form of substitution from indirect to direct financial claims (such as equities). In restricted systems, on the other hand, the lack of efficient bond and equity markets means that disintermediation takes the form of capital flight or substitution from deposits with banks to "curb markets" or tangible assets that are used as inflation hedges (e.g., real estate).[63]

These differences in financial depth imply that banks in restricted systems often do not have an incentive to seek deregulation in situations where their counterparts in more advanced systems do. Without the threat of strong domestic or foreign competitors, or disintermediation from direct markets, banks oppose the removal of interest rate controls since these controls do not hinder their ability to attract deposits or maintain their share of credit to the private sector.[64] The other major beneficiaries of restriction, firms targeted by selective credit policies, rarely have an incentive to press for the removal of financial controls either.[65]

These findings may not hold strictly in all contexts. First, the most and least competitive banks may take different stances on deregulation, as the most competitive banks may want less regulated markets to try to expand their market share.[66] However, even competitive banks may not wish to give up guaranteed, risk-free profits for potential but uncertain higher profits in a less regulated environment. Empirical evidence, in fact, suggests that banks tend to act as a bloc on most financial policy issues, often replacing informal agreements for official regulations when deregulation occurs.[67] Second, the existence of conglomerates containing banks and industrial firms, a common feature in countries with restricted systems, sometimes leads banks and firms to define their interests somewhat differently.[68]

Banks may press for other financial reforms. For instance, banks and

internationally oriented firms have been important in pushing for the elimination of controls on foreign financial transactions so that they can take
advantage of opportunities in international capital markets.[69] If capital
controls are removed, however, other forms of deregulation will not necessarily follow. Studies suggest that countries with restricted systems that
liberalize their capital account often retain other financial controls (e.g.,
interest rate and credit controls) to dictate how foreign flows are allocated
and manage the money supply.[70]

In sum, private actors are unlikely to provide the impetus for deregulation in restricted systems. Those that benefit from restriction rarely have
an incentive to pursue deregulation; those with an interest in liberalization
find it difficult to organize themselves to effect change. This suggests that
public officials most likely will be the force behind deregulation, if they
have sufficient autonomy and can overcome the collective action problems
that they often face in supplying efficient markets. In other words, I contend that a state-centered focus is required to explain financial deregulation in restricted systems.

More generally, it seems that market structure influences whether
public or private actors drive financial deregulation in any given case and,
therefore, whether state or society should be the center of analysis. This is
consistent with the growing consensus that a variety of contextual factors
help determine the relative importance of state and social actors in
influencing economic policy. It highlights the importance of examining the
variables that affect the supply of regulation by public officials as well as
the demand for it by private actors.

Attention to the factors that influence government supply of regulation might strengthen the predominant explanation of deregulation in
countries with more advanced financial systems. The economic theory
treats the existence of unregulated competitors that challenge banks as an
exogenous rather than endogenous variable. In reality, politicians chose to
allow other intermediaries to enter the financial sector at some point in
time; moreover, they opted to exclude these intermediaries from the regulatory controls imposed upon existing banks. This decision to permit entry
without imposing regulatory controls was ultimately responsible for creating the dynamic that drives the deregulatory process. This suggests that
understanding why politicians chose to eschew a more tightly regulated
financial sector and seek the greater efficiency associated with financial
deepening has the potential to improve studies of deregulation in countries
with nonrestricted systems.

This claim must be qualified, however. In deciding to authorize other
intermediaries and exclude them from the regulatory regime, policymakers
might not have set out to create the challenge that these entities come to

represent for regulated intermediaries. This is particularly true in the United States where regulatory authority is shared by a myriad of agencies at the state and federal level that may have contradictory goals.[71] At the time they permit entry, policymakers may not be aware of the economic developments that will enable new intermediaries to threaten the dominance of existing ones. They may simply be responding to demands to authorize new financial institutions in order to increase the flow of credit to specific sectors, such as housing, or to aid small savers or investors.

The Public Interest View
Some authors have contended that financial liberalization has stemmed from efforts by public officials to promote social welfare.[72] This "public interest" view holds that policymakers deregulated financial markets to improve economic performance when they became aware of the costs associated with government financial controls. Specifically, governments in countries with restricted systems liberalized when they confronted low financial efficiency, a lack of monetary control, balance-of-payments problems, or declining flows of foreign capital and decided that they could best overcome these problems by abandoning a strategy of restriction. In this perspective, the serious economic difficulties that many countries have faced in the past two decades have sparked the recent wave of financial reform. Some scholars have extended this argument by suggesting that the World Bank and IMF greatly aided deregulatory efforts by diffusing a set of ideas showing that countries can improve their economic performance through financial liberalization; I examine this line of argumentation separately later.[73]

The view that widespread economic problems have sparked a wave of financial deregulation is intuitively appealing, but it is incomplete. In reality, mounting economic difficulties have not been a sufficient motive for initiating deregulation. To begin with, countries do not necessarily choose to liberalize when faced with economic problems. The response to major events that have apparently created a common interest in deregulation across countries has not been uniform. For example, faced with monetary control problems generated by the breakdown of Bretton Woods, France deregulated its financial markets while Finland chose to refine its existing financial controls.[74] This suggests that factors indigenous to each country influence how governments will respond to global economic trends.

Second, the economic problems caused by restriction are usually a perennial difficulty for public officials. As a result, most countries suffer several bouts of poor performance attributable in part to deficiencies in the financial sector before a movement for liberalization takes hold; arguing that previous crises were not "severe enough" to cause reform merely begs the question: how severe must a crisis be?[75] Economic difficulties alone, therefore, cannot explain the timing of deregulation.

The critical point here is that even very poor economic results may not damage the prospects of current rulers sufficiently to entice them to seek more efficient financial markets; economic performance most often becomes a motivating factor when rulers confront rivals who are able to channel social dissatisfaction over problems into a viable source of political opposition. If leaders do not have serious competitors, they may have no reason to forsake a financial regulatory regime that provides several important benefits (e.g., the ability to raise government revenue). When they do face political competition, a sharp increase in financial inefficiency can provide self-interested politicians with an incentive to design better financial policy in order to prevent rivals from taking advantage of declining economic performance to win support. Slowing growth may also jeopardize the position of current leaders vis-à-vis internal and external rivals if it cuts into state revenues and limits their ability to deliver basic services or provide for the national defense.[76]

While economic problems alone cannot account for financial reform, economic crises have often been associated with reform for good reason.[77] In the absence of an economic crisis, leaders often avoid major reform because demand for it is probably low and altering the status quo is politically costly.[78] The ill economic effects of restriction, for example, were not difficult to withstand politically in the high-growth era of the 1950s and 1960s, but they became less tolerable (and more noticeable) with the onset of economic problems in the 1970s.

A sharp rise in financial inefficiency due to global economic trends partly explains the apparent but uneven general trend toward financial reform in the 1980s. The significance of these trends is that they have increased the political costs of maintaining restriction, thereby altering the bottom line of the cost/benefit calculations of political leaders. In many countries, economic problems have come at a time when there has been an increase in political competition or, in some instances, outright political liberalization. This is not mere coincidence: evidence indicates that economic crises have helped to spark demands for political reform in authoritarian regimes.[79] Nevertheless, even where trends have led to similar economic problems across countries, they have not affected the political calculus of leaders in the same way, suggesting again that economic factors alone cannot explain policy change.

Internationalization of Finance and External Pressures
A third class of explanations of financial deregulation centers on international factors. Some scholars note that governments often encounter direct

pressure from international actors to carry out structural reforms, including financial liberalization.[80] Governments that turn to international agencies for funds to overcome temporary balance-of-payments problems or initiate structural reforms usually must meet conditionality requirements that include financial reforms, notably the dismantling of credit and interest rate controls.[81] They may also face demands by foreign banks, firms, and their governments to open markets to foreign intermediaries or capital flows.[82] In addition, if a government wishes national banks to expand abroad to take advantage of international capital markets, the norm of reciprocity dictates that it open domestic markets to intermediaries from countries that grant its country's banks access.[83]

Another contention is that governments, especially in advanced industrial nations, now find it difficult to control financial activity, particularly transborder capital flows.[84] It is argued that banks and firms have become truly global in their activities, making it possible for them to evade government financial controls.[85] This trend has made government efforts to control capital movements more costly and ineffective. It has also increased the influence of holders of nonfixed capital, enabling them to obtain their preferred policy of openness.[86] More generally, because of a variety of factors, including technological innovation, international capital flows now respond to a country's economic policies with lightning quickness, placing serious constraints on governments who wish or need to attract capital or prevent its flight. This increasing capital mobility is forcing international convergence across countries toward similar macroeconomic policies and more open financial systems with less government intervention.[87]

These factors impose serious constraints on policymakers in restricted systems, but they are not so great that financial policy simply responds to international trends.[88] First, some of the factors that scholars have identified as important in prodding governments in advanced industrial nations to open their markets are usually not as constraining in countries with restricted systems, and, in general, barriers to international financial intermediation remain significant in them.[89] For instance, most industrializing country firms and banks do not have comparable global reach, putting less pressure on authorities to open up their financial systems. On the other hand, these countries do tend to have a greater need to attract capital to finance balance-of-payments or government deficits. Second, as already noted, if foreign banks are permitted greater access to national markets or controls on transborder capital flows are removed, other forms of financial deregulation will not necessarily follow; indeed, the financial policy mix in countries that have begun to liberalize vis-à-vis external markets remains very diverse. Moreover, countries can attenuate their reliance on foreign funds by choosing to foster their domestic savings. Chile, Singapore, and South Korea, for example, have attempted to augment their domestic investment pools by providing tax incentives to save long term or encouraging the growth of pension plans.

More importantly, political leaders evaluate how liberalizing financial markets will affect their ability to achieve their own goals even when international constraints are direct and pressing, as when countries negotiate to obtain official aid. In deciding whether to open financial markets, for example, they assess the merits of forgoing the political advantages of closure—enhanced control over credit allocation, appeasement of domestic banking interests, and possibly greater macroeconomic policy autonomy—to obtain the benefits of liberalization. The evidence in fact suggests that states carry out structural reforms prescribed by international agencies only when a country's leadership is already committed to policy change.[90] Even in advanced industrial countries where pressures to open financial markets are greatest, governments liberalize only after careful cost/benefit calculations. In his study of financial opening in four advanced industrial countries, Louis Pauly concluded, "no state was required to admit or legitimate the direct presence of foreign banks. . . . Idiosyncratic domestic structures mediated between common [international] pressures and changing national policies."[91]

In conclusion, it seems that international factors play an important but not determining role in financial reform in restricted systems. The timing and nature of reforms are still determined by domestic factors, notably the calculations of political leaders, the degree of political competition, and the balance of interest group demands. Nevertheless, international constraints are growing in importance as barriers to international financial intermediation diminish (e.g., due to technological innovation), raising the costs of maintaining closed, highly regulated financial systems. Furthermore, once opening is underway, it may lead major actors to change their stances on key financial policy issues or alter the distribution of power among competing interest groups in ways that contribute to pressure for further financial deregulation, for the reasons suggested by Frieden and Kurzer.

The Role of Ideas

As already noted, it is sometimes argued that the World Bank and IMF have greatly contributed to deregulatory efforts by diffusing a new set of ideas indicating that countries can improve their economic performance through financial liberalization. For some authors, these organizations advanced these ideas out of a genuine belief that they would best serve countries in their development efforts;[92] for others, they promoted them primarily because adoption of their prescriptions would serve the interests of the advanced industrial democracies that dominate these agencies.[93]

The spread of policy-relevant knowledge by economists and international agencies has played a significant role in liberalization efforts. Public officials in many countries were disillusioned about the effectiveness of their financial policies by the 1960s, and the spread of ideas promoting deregulation provided a focal point for deciding what had to be done to improve economic performance. The diffusion of this policy-relevant knowledge, however, has not been sufficient to produce deregulation, as new ideas have been met with different responses: some countries have sought to deregulate, but others have not. This again suggests that factors indigenous to each country, such as the structure of its economic and political institutions or leadership's goals, mediate the impact of the spread of new ideas on financial policy.[94]

Still, beliefs about what type of financial system will improve economic performance are important to my analytical framework. Leaders and policymakers must believe that liberalization, not refinement of an interventionist apparatus, is the way to promote economic growth and modernization. In the Spanish case, by the mid-1960s there was a consensus among mainstream economists and policymakers, based on their training and critical assessment of financial restriction, that a market-based system was superior; contacts with the Organization for Economic Cooperation and Development (OECD) and IMF only reinforced their views. When Spanish political leaders decided that improving economic performance was politically important, economic policymakers had no trouble agreeing that the development of a more market-based financial system was a top priority. In other countries, however, the diffusion of policy-relevant knowledge, particularly in the 1970s, was critical in fostering the belief that liberalization was the correct financial policy choice to improve economic performance.

The difficulties that some countries have experienced with financial liberalization and studies that view government intervention in financial markets in Japan, South Korea, and Taiwan in a positive light have raised doubts about the desirability of deregulation. Indeed, differences in belief about what type of financial system will improve economic performance remain; several scholars, for example, think that a bank-based system under government supervision is often best for developing countries. Nevertheless, while some question the standard prescription of liberalization, mainstream economists still argue that it is the best policy if done prudently. With a few exceptions, even authors who praise East Asian financial policy believe that a strategy of restriction must eventually give way to the creation of a more market-based system; Japan and South Korea in fact have undergone significant deregulation in recent years.[95] Moreover, international agencies, which play a key role in influencing ideas about economic policy in many developing states, continue to promote a market-based financial system as the optimal choice.

Democratization and Financial Policy

Traditional sectoral approaches cannot explain financial liberalization in restricted systems because public officials, not private actors, are the driving force behind it. Public interest and ideational accounts of deregulation are incomplete because political leaders view economic conditions and new policy-relevant knowledge through the filter of their own self-interest. Similarly, identifying external pressures to liberalize markets does not fully explain financial reform since leaders decide whether to acquiesce based on their calculations of how compliance will affect their ability to achieve their own goals. But it must be recognized that global economic and political trends probably play an increasingly significant role because they augment the political costs of maintaining restriction.

I contend that politicians liberalize financial markets when changes in a country's political environment or institutions augment the political utility of a more market-based system relative to that of a restricted system. Identifying all the events that may increase the utility of a market-based system is not feasible; the exact nature of the factor that sparks interest in liberalization will vary across countries or over time since the specific features of a country's economic, political, and social context matter. What I do instead is examine in depth a fundamental institutional change that may give an impetus to deregulation in a wide variety of settings: democratization. The following discussion examines how democratization affects the ways politicians design financial policy both to stay in power and raise government revenue.

I do not suggest that all transitions to democracy will lead politicians to deregulate financial markets. Transitions and the democracies that emerge from them are so different that one conclusion cannot possibly cover all cases. In Spain, democratization encouraged financial deregulation, but in other countries it has had little impact (at least as of yet). The reason why is that the form of democracy that emerges from the transition matters. This raises a basic issue that this study addresses: under what circumstances is democratization likely or unlikely to lead to financial liberalization? In considering this topic, I concentrate more on how different types of democratic regimes vary in the incentives they provide to initiate financial deregulation than on the ability of their leaders to implement it (even though these two topics are related). Until recently, the most salient view in the literature was that "strong" authoritarian states alone were able to carry out structural economic reforms. But now a burgeoning body of work contends that there is a "democratic equivalent" of a strong state.[96] This literature suggests that structural reform is most likely to occur in democratic settings in which the government has a clear majority in the legislature and a strong executive that empowers a competent, cohesive technocracy and shields it from political pressure.[97] In the case study of Spain, I find similar results.

Furthermore, I do not suggest that only democratic regimes engage in financial deregulation. Authoritarian regimes that rely on strong economic growth for their legitimacy or to promote national security may also undertake deregulation. Salient cases of liberalization by authoritarian regimes include Chile in the 1970s, Indonesia at several points in the last twenty-five years, Spain in the early 1970s, and Thailand in the 1980s. I examine one reason why authoritarian regimes might pursue financial deregulation in the following section and discuss the Spanish case in detail in chapter 4.

Democratization, Political Survival, and Financial Policy

The Impact of Greater Political Competition
Democratization may reduce the utility of financial restriction in helping politicians to achieve both of their two basic goals: holding power and generating government revenue. Many countries begin the process of democratization with noncompetitive political systems in which institutions give national leaders a relatively greater incentive to supply private instead of collective goods in their quest to maintain power. In these systems, the ability of rulers to deliver private benefits (like preferential credit) to key social groups is most critical for retaining power, insofar as their hold on office often rests on the support of narrow groups of powerful constituents. Providing collective economic goods for the general populace is less important—unless economic performance deteriorates so much that internal or external rivals are able to challenge the regime—since rulers often need only the acquiescence of a national majority, not its active support. This suggests that creating restricted financial markets to devise a means of delivering private benefits has the highest payoff in political systems in which there is an absence of political competition.[98] It deserves noting that most authoritarian regimes have followed a policy of restriction and that many regimes that still exhibit a lack of meaningful party competition (e.g., several sub-Saharan countries) continue to have restricted systems.

In democratic regimes with a competitive party system, on the other hand, institutions give public officials a relatively greater incentive to supply collective goods like efficient markets, even though delivering private goods to important constituents may retain considerable value.[99] In general, national parties in a competitive democracy must appeal to voters by advocating policies that provide for the collective economic good since they are bidding for the support of a broad-based, heterogeneous majority in periodic elections. A party that appeals only to select narrow groups or designs policies for their benefit once in power may be seen as hostage to their interests and, thereby, alienate median voters, making it difficult for it to secure adequate electoral backing. In addition, policies designed to benefit only select groups are less likely to proliferate in democracies than in autocracies because constituents have the ability to oust rulers who mismanage the economy.[100] Therefore, movement toward a competitive democratic regime may result in a larger supply of collective economic goods; in the realm of financial policy, this may spark efforts to increase the efficiency of financial markets through liberalization. It may not be coincidence that the "third wave" of democracy and the movement toward more free-market policies have occurred almost simultaneously.

The claim that politicians or parties must make aggregate economic performance a top priority—and, hence, that they must concern themselves with the efficiency of financial markets—implies that electors "vote their pocketbook." Kiewiet finds strong evidence that voters' perceptions of general macroeconomic performance have a significant impact on their voting decisions.[101] Voting on the basis of general macroeconomic conditions need not be altruistic. Self-interested voters "may construe the performance or policies of the party in power as a public good, and thus use information about the condition of the nation's economy as an indicator of the present administration's ability to promote their own economic well-being—and incidentally that of their fellow citizens as well."[102]

My argument should not be construed to contend that democracies as a group will enjoy higher growth, as many variables affect economic performance (e.g., factor endowments).[103] Instead, I suggest that within a particular country, democratization will contribute to superior performance because politicians must aggregate the interests of a broader range of social groups. Democracies, once established, will not necessarily pursue economic policies that are optimal from a social welfare point of view. As Olson has argued, keeping well-organized narrow interests from dominating economic policy in mature democracies can be difficult. Olson himself contends, however, that democracies have inherent economic advantages over nondemocratic regimes.[104]

An increase in political competition in semicompetitive democratic systems (e.g., one-party democracies) or mounting political opposition in authoritarian regimes, especially if coupled with discontentment over economic policy, may also generate interest among leaders in improving economic performance. Failure to adjust a deteriorating economy may weaken the bargain between leaders and key support groups and increase the probability that opposition will be directed at the basic character of the regime itself.[105] Faced with growing competition or dissent, leaders frequently give technocrats a mandate to rectify economic problems and a freer hand in designing strategy. In many countries, policymakers confront a variety of economic problems that call for financial liberalization (e.g., monetary control problems), so they often identify it as an essential step in economic adjustment. What I describe here occurred in Spain, as I show in chapter 4. Rising political dissent fueled by dissatisfaction with economic policy led the Franco regime to permit policymakers to partially liberalize financial markets starting in the late 1960s.

Differences across Democracies
The incentive of parties and the politicians within them to appeal to encompassing interests and supply collective goods once in office varies greatly across democracies. Indeed, some democracies reward parties or politicians who develop close ties to select constituencies. In these systems, one would expect politicians to have a greater interest in financial restriction. Japan, for example, had a financial system that exhibited many elements of restriction until very recently. Calder argued that Japanese financial policy reflected the distributive, clientilistic nature of Japanese democratic politics.[106] Japan's electoral system and political culture were biased toward securing power through the cultivation of small, intense support groups with material benefits.[107] Japanese politicians aggressively used financial controls to distribute preferential credit to key constituents, such as small businesses in the provinces.

The extensive literature on democracy offers no firm maxims about which types of systems encourage leaders to supply collective as opposed to private goods or which tend to be more stable over time, thereby allowing politicians to carry out reformist agendas.[108] Although scholars have identified certain broad traits with particular types of democratic systems, countries with similar formal institutions often exhibit considerable differences in how they function. This is due to variations in microlevel institutional variables as well as basic differences in political culture and history, population, and social institutions. Here I offer some observations on which sorts of democratic systems are more or less likely to give national leaders an incentive and capacity to supply collective goods concentrating on electoral and party systems and constitutional frameworks. This is meant to be an intuitive, not exhaustive, exercise. In the concluding chapter, I show how institutional variations in several newly democratic countries have influenced the formulation of their financial policy.

An analysis of political institutions cannot provide the determinants of political behavior. Identical electoral institutions, for example, may yield different political results depending upon the characteristics of political elites and the populace. Moreover, institutions, like electoral rules, themselves must ultimately be treated as endogenous variables. Fundamental political variables, such as the distribution of power among social groups or historical experience, greatly influence the choice of a country's institutions. A systematic analysis of this issue is beyond the scope of this study, but I do examine the sources of Spain's institutional framework, particularly its electoral laws, in chapter 5.

The features of a country's electoral and party systems critically affect the incentive to appeal to encompassing interests and the ability to supply collective goods. Electoral systems vary greatly in the reward structure that they present to politicians and in their capacity to create legislative majorities capable of introducing credible policy initiatives. Scholars identify three variables as most important in shaping the political effects of electoral systems: electoral formula, such as plurality or the different types of proportional representation (PR); district magnitude (i.e., the number of representatives elected per district); and electoral threshold (i.e., the minimum support a party needs to gain representation).[109] These factors have a direct impact on the degree of multipartism and fragmentation as well as on the proportionality of electoral outcomes, including the tendency to generate majority victories.

Whether parties function on the basis of "open" or "closed" list systems is also significant, as this influences how much control party leaders exercise over individual party members.[110] In open list systems, party leaders do not determine who appears on the ballot or the order in which candidates are listed. Thus, they lack an important means of controlling candidates who wish to follow a private agenda. In closed list systems, party leaders make up electoral lists and, hence, can control individual party members. Therefore, party systems that use closed and blocked lists should generally lead to greater party unity and less parochialism.

Another institutional feature that seems to have a bearing on the incentive and ability to supply collective goods is a country's constitutional framework, that is, whether a democracy has a presidential or parliamentary system. Much recent literature claims that parliamentarianism is more favorable for building stable democracies capable of promoting the public good than presidentialism.[111] In principle, a presidential system might encourage the provision of collective goods because presidents must appeal to a heterogeneous, national constituency. The appeal of a strong, energetic executive focused on the public interest is in fact why some countries opt for a presidential system. Many scholars, however, suggest that presidentialism suffers serious deficiencies compared to parliamentarianism in practice. Stepan and Skach, for example, argue that presidential systems possess a lower propensity for governments to have majorities to implement their programs; a lesser ability to rule in a multiparty setting; a greater proclivity for executives to rule at the edge of the constitution; and a lesser tendency to provide long party/government careers, which add loyalty and experience to political society.[112] Mainwaring claims that the combination of presidentialism and multipartism, common in new presidential democracies, is especially inimical to the creation of a stable political system.[113]

The significance of electoral institutions and constitutional frameworks can be illustrated by creating ideal types of democratic systems that seem the least and most conducive to the supply of collective goods. Democracies with highly fragmented party systems, especially presidential regimes, where parties operate with open lists are probably the least conducive to the supply of collective economic goods. Politicians in such systems are able to pursue private agendas and have an incentive to appeal to local or other parochial interests in their pursuit of office. This is especially true if the bases of electoral support are geographically concentrated (as is the case in countries divided along cultural or ethnic lines) or if national politics are highly polarized ideologically. In these circumstances, a politician's prospects hinge upon her ability to deliver benefits to her home region or maintain a clear ideological stance. In addition, legislative majorities are more difficult to achieve in highly fragmented systems. If a transition results in this type of democracy, politicians will value financial restriction for its ability to target specific groups and liberalization will be unlikely in the short run. In chapter 8, I show that Brazil is an example of a democratic system with a presidential regime that has provided few collective action incentives for reform because it encourages politicians (with some exceptions) to court narrow local or regional interests.

Democratic systems exhibiting a low degree of party fragmentation or polarization, where parties operate with closed lists, are probably most amenable to the supply of collective economic goods. Generally, one would expect that the closer a democratic regime gets to a two-party system based on heterogeneous "catch-all" parties, the more likely it is to produce an optimal level of public goods for the reasons already identified.[114] Contemporary Spain, as I discuss in chapter 5, is an example of a country with such a system. Its electoral laws penalize small, sectarian parties with geographically dispersed support and encourage the emergence of large,

national, broad-based parties. Spanish parties must appeal to encompassing interests to gain adequate electoral support and have an incentive to
supply collective goods once in office to retain power.

Of course, in any democratic system, including one like Spain's,
politicians could attempt to construct a minimum winning coalition by
making deals with a number of narrow groups. This strategy is often too
costly and impractical, however, because it involves tremendous information and transaction costs; in addition, the demands on politicians are
often conflicting, especially when groups base their electoral support on
more than one issue. For these reasons, minimum winning coalitions tend
to be highly unstable and difficult to manage over time.[115] Finally, this
strategy distorts markets and actor incentives, thereby reducing society's
economic output, a serious problem if leaders are judged by their economic record.[116]

Democratization and Interest Group Demands

Democratization leads to a reshaping of the political landscape, as individuals previously excluded from political activity gain a voice in public
life through the ballot box and, sometimes, identify common interests and
organize for political action. In theory, this may give politicians greater
freedom to move away from courting entrenched groups and develop new
constituencies. In practice, politicians concerned with their immediate survival may have to turn to established groups for support in the short term
since new political actors may not be organized (or may be difficult to
organize) into constituencies capable of providing effective support. In the
longer run, however, politicians will have to consider the interests of newly
empowered groups if they want to succeed electorally.

In the case of financial policy, new groups will probably make
demands that require gradual changes in the regulatory regime that can
initiate the deregulatory snowball effect identified by Hammond and
Knott. Take middle-income workers as an example. They will want deeper
and more efficient mortgage markets to finance the purchase of homes.
They will also desire new financial instruments and deeper bond and
equity markets to facilitate long-term saving for other goals, such as education and retirement saving, and to diversify their assets away from only
short-term, highly liquid instruments. Such groups, however, are unlikely
to organize for lobbying on financial policy issues because of collective
action problems. The most likely way that their demands will find a voice
in the political system is through political entrepreneurs. Entrepreneurs
may target these issues in an attempt to mobilize the relevant groups and
win their votes; this will compel others to address and act upon these issues
as well. Of course, if groups favoring deregulation are among the key sup-

porters of the party that comes to power, the odds of liberalization are increased.

Changes in interest group demands are important in another way as well. In a nondemocratic society, the use of credit and interest rate controls to generate support is cost effective because providing benefits to a few key social groups is often sufficient. After democratization, it is usually no longer an efficient means of mobilizing support since political leaders will have to respond to pressure for credit rents from a much larger set of interest groups and confront the issue of what is a "fair" distribution of preferential credit. If they do not provide credit rents to all those who demand them, excluded groups may turn hostile to the democratic process; if they do, they will place impossible demands on state resources and further distort the functioning of financial markets. Under these circumstances, political leaders have an interest in eliminating selective credit policies, thereby closing a channel of disruptive and insatiable social demands. Abolishing credit programs has the additional advantage of reducing the revenue needs of the government.

Although they share a common motive in eliminating selective credit policies to suppress demands for financial handouts, incumbents and opposition parties may also have different reasons for supporting this policy. Opposition groups may view liberalization as a means of impeding incumbents from using their control over financial markets to consolidate their hold on power. Incumbents, on the other hand, may wish to decrease the risk that financial controls be used against them when they find themselves out of power. In addition, incumbents, especially if they are linked to the previous authoritarian regime, may face charges of enjoying overly close ties to groups previously favored by authoritarian leaders. Dismantling interest rate and credit controls is a way of defusing these accusations.

The Temporal Pattern of Financial Reform

The prospects for financial reform are likely to change over time. Przeworski shows that, because many structural reforms entail high short-term costs and produce benefits only in the long term, they are difficult to sustain once started since leaders must cope with rising discontent among the populace and political competitors who try to capitalize on it.[117] Transitional governments may face special problems in implementing structural adjustment because their leaders feel pressure to provide immediate material benefits to an impatient population, and they have insecure tenure in office; this can lead them to adopt a short time horizon. Moreover, the institutional structure needed for formulating and implementing reforms may be lacking. Therefore, with regards to financial policy, one might expect the transition to lead to some financial reform immediately (especially if economic conditions are deteriorating) and then a period of retrenchment as the short-term costs of reform are felt fully. Later, there may be a renewal of the liberalization process as the benefits from earlier measures become clear or the costs of not deepening the reform process rise and governments develop the autonomy and institutional structures needed to implement structural adjustment successfully.

Nelson finds empirical support for this pattern. She notes that first or second posttransition governments have found it difficult to sustain tough structural reforms. Mounting economic difficulties coupled with broadened recognition that partial measures were not effective, however, later led to further reform in some countries.[118]

Democratization, the Need for Revenue, and Financial Policy

Democratization also affects restriction's utility in helping public officials achieve their second goal: obtaining adequate government revenue. Democratization is often associated with a dramatic surge in demands on the state that translate into a need for more revenue. As Adam Przeworski writes, "the advent of democracy is accompanied by an explosion of expectations: for most people democratization promises not only political rights but also social transformations."[119]

The pent-up demands for social welfare services, income redistribution, and the like are unlikely to be met by expanding indirect taxes, such as taxation of the banking system. Governments may initially try to deepen restriction to extract more revenue, but at a certain point this becomes self-defeating. Intermediaries will undertake innovation to circumvent financial controls that act as a tax, thereby limiting the amount of additional revenue that the state can raise by this means. More fundamentally, excessive taxation of the banking system generates inefficiencies that slow the economy's development and, hence, limit the expansion of the overall tax base; this will ultimately restrict the growth of government revenues. Unless a more effective means of raising revenue is implemented, the state may face a fiscal crisis that ultimately weakens its legitimacy. Thus, democratization provides a powerful long-term incentive to dismantle restriction and implement more effective means of taxation (e.g., a greater reliance on direct or value-added taxes).

Abrupt increases in the need for government spending have in fact often led to fundamental changes in the nature of revenue generation. Notably, a number of countries have implemented income taxes to finance rapidly growing government expenditures. A good example is Britain, which instituted an income tax in 1799 to meet the costs of foreign conflicts and service a rising government debt.[120] The United States and Germany have also experienced similar changes in tax policy due to sharply higher government expenditures.

The advent of democracy may also facilitate the implementation of a system of direct taxation because it is often accompanied by a change in notions of legitimacy and demands for greater social justice. In many countries undergoing transitions, fiscal policies emphasize highly regressive indirect taxation because politicians have tried to avoid direct taxes, especially income taxes, since they are opposed by their key constituents. A transition to democracy will create pressure for a more equitable distribution of the tax burden, especially the adoption of progressive direct taxes (including taxation of corporate profits), by those disadvantaged by indirect taxes. Government officials who wish to overhaul fiscal policy can take advantage of this pressure to secure support for tax reform.

Conclusion

In contrast to sectoral explanations of regulatory policy, like the "economic theory," the analytical framework developed in this chapter suggests that financial policy is best explained by examining the preferences and choice processes of political leaders. Politicians follow a strategy of restriction when they have institutional incentives to provide private benefits to key social groups and generate revenue without relying on more efficient but politically difficult taxation. To understand liberalization in restricted systems, one must explain why politicians conclude that establishing more efficient markets is essential for staying in power and why they are able and willing to forgo the government revenue that restriction can generate. Accounts that focus on economic problems, new policy-relevant knowledge, or international economic or political pressures only partially explain financial reform because political leaders view these variables through the filter of their self-interest. Starting with the next chapter, I apply the theoretical framework developed here to the evolution of financial policy in Spain.

CHAPTER 3

Financial Restriction in Spain

This chapter examines the political economy of Spanish financial policy during the years 1939–75 in light of the analytical framework developed in the previous chapter. In this period, Spain was governed by the authoritarian Franco regime, which adopted a strategy of financial restriction upon taking power. The height of restriction occurred in the 1960s, but some of its features were present much earlier.

Several stylized facts about financial restriction in Spain are noteworthy. First, the government imposed controls on both deposit and loan interest rates. Table 3.1 indicates that rates were held at very low levels, as evidenced by the prevalence of negative real interest rates throughout much of the 1960s and 1970s. The degree of financial repression, therefore, was high. Second, the overwhelming majority of credit to the private sector flowed through the banking system and not direct financial markets. Direct markets were responsible for only about 6 percent of total credit to the private sector throughout the 1960s and 1970s.[1] Moreover, the degree of self-financing among Spanish firms was the lowest of any industrialized country.[2] Third, the percentage of government-allocated credit was high, ranging from 30 to 40 percent in the 1960s and 1970s.[3] Policymakers used a variety of mechanisms to channel credit into specified sectors; they are discussed later. Fourth, the government taxed the banking system to obtain revenue. Intermediaries had to invest in low-yield government securities and provide credit at preferential rates to specific sectors; after 1977, they were also subject to high RRs. Fifth, the Spanish financial market was almost completely isolated from international capital markets. The government established strict controls on capital flows, prohibited entry of foreign financial intermediaries, and restricted international transactions by domestic firms and financial institutions.

The structure of Spain's financial system was not the product of purely economic factors, like the country's level of development. The Franco regime inherited an underdeveloped financial system, one that it could not transform dramatically in the short run. Nevertheless, it actively sought to deepen financial repression rather than work toward a more market-based system. I argue that political calculations primarily motivated Franquist officials when they designed financial policy. This is not to say that they were totally unconcerned with advancing the public interest. Rather, officials believed that a tightly controlled financial system would allow them to pursue their political goals without sacrificing too much in the way of economic growth or modernization.[4] Finally, I contend that the nature of financial policy was not dictated by broader economic strategy, for example, the drive to industrialize.[5] As I show later, the Franco regime lacked a coherent overall economic strategy; it shaped its economic policies largely in response to its political concerns.

Until about 1960, Spanish financial regulation primarily reflected the interests of the large national banks, which had great bargaining power due to their central economic role and position as important backers of the regime. Starting in the late 1950s, however, the Franco regime decided to alter its economic strategy to gain the support of new and emerging business interests and increasingly militant workers. Consequently, the regime appointed several new top-level economic policymakers—dubbed the Opus Dei technocrats[6]—and permitted them to design a new economic strategy. The technocrats gradually transformed financial regulation as part of their reform efforts. By the mid-1960s, they had established controls that created a means of using financial markets to obtain government revenue and distribute financial benefits to influential social groups. Sev-

TABLE 3.1.   Real Loan and Deposit Interest Rates in the 1960s and 1970s

	Real Deposit Rate[a]	Real Loan Rate[b]
1965	−10.5	−8.5
1966	−5.5	−3.5
1967	−3.6	−1.1
1968	−0.6	0.6
1969	2.3	4.4
1970	−0.4	1.9
1971	−3.4	−1.6
1972	−4.3	−2.3
1973	−7.0	−4.4
1974	−10.3	−7.7
1975	−10.9	−8.9
1976	−9.0	−7.0
1977	−18.1	−15.4
1978	−11.7	−10.8
1979	−7.3	−6.7

Source: Banco de España, "Boletín Económico," April 1980, and Molinas et al. 1987, Cuadro V.6.

[a]Real Rate = Nominal Short-term Rate − Inflation
[b]Real Rate = Rate on Commercial Discount − Inflation

eral features of the new regulatory regime went against banking interests, suggesting that simple capture theory cannot account for the evolution of Spanish financial policy.[7] Regime leaders supported the new financial policy because they believed it would provide an attractive source of revenue and co-opt key social groups.

This chapter begins with a brief analysis of the Franco regime and its general economic strategies to provide the political and economic context for the discussion of its financial policy. It then describes the primary private and public financial actors in Spain in the post–Civil War period. Finally, it examines the political economy of finance during the Franco period in depth.

The Institutions and Political Economy of the Franco Era

Political Institutions

The "Nationalists" gained control over Spain after the defeat of Republican forces in the Spanish Civil War (1936–39). General Francisco Franco emerged as the prominent figure within the nationalist camp.[8] After the war, Franco became chief of state and president of the government, and he succeeded in concentrating a great deal of power directly in his hands. As chief of state, Franco appointed (directly or indirectly) all important state officials, and they were ultimately responsible only to him. The regime's "inner circle," consisting of Franco and his closest personal advisors (such as Carrero Blanco), reserved all major political decisions for itself and was able to exercise veto power over all others.

In the 1940s, the regime created a single political party, the Movimiento, but it never played a central role in Spanish politics. In fact, over time, the Franquist regime evolved into what observers have described as an authoritarian, personalistic, no-party system, characterized by limited pluralistic competition within its political structures.[9] Although Franco established himself as the clear head of the new regime, many political "families" constituted its supporting coalition, among them the Catholics, Falangists, military, monarchists, and technocrats.[10] Competition for power among these groups was intense, occasionally even leading to acts of violence. Franco manipulated the existing rivalries astutely, using a divide-and-conquer strategy to maintain personal control. He awarded high-level posts in the government to reward loyalty or win support, and the composition of the cabinet usually reflected the relative power of the various families. Over time, political competition within the regime became even more pronounced; in the early 1970s, Franco's failing health set off a vicious scramble for power.[11]

The political institutions of the Franquist state were created haphazardly over a period of years. Authority was concentrated in the executive branch, with administrative functions centralized in Madrid. The Council of Ministers, presided over by Franco, was the nation's highest policy-making body and also had responsibility for the administration of all public policy. In general, Franco delegated a great deal of authority to his ministers, who formulated and implemented policy subject to the constraint of not undermining the regime's basic principles and strategies. Franco actively participated in policy-making only when it involved issue areas he felt were critical to the maintenance of the regime.[12] He also exercised strong control over the nominally independent Cortes (the Spanish legislature). He appointed the president of the Cortes who in turn chose the members of legislative committees. In practice, therefore, the Cortes usually acted as a rubber stamp, approving the Council of Ministers's proposals with only slight modifications.

The regime relied on support obtained by providing material goods to important social groups to stay in power; it did not govern by intimidation alone. The coalition backing the Franco regime changed substantially during its rule. Initially, *latifundistas,* established capitalists, the large national banks, the army, the Church, and the politico-military government bureaucracy were the regime's main supporters. As modernization created new interests, such as a middle class, the regime tried, with varying degrees of success, to co-opt them into the prevailing political structures without alienating traditional constituencies. Toward the end, the regime had few active backers apart from the military and the financial oligarchy; most social groups merely tolerated the regime, waiting for Franco's death to bring about change.

The Political Economy of the Franco Period

The Franco regime intervened extensively in the economy, including financial markets, throughout its period of rule. The regime usually did not have a coherent economic doctrine or strategy. Instead, its economic policies were largely formulated with an eye to maintaining its power. It designed policies that benefited key constituents to obtain or retain their backing, subsequently modifying them when new constituents emerged or existing policies threatened to increase social and political disorder. Strong clientilistic ties between policymakers and disaggregated private interests came to characterize many areas of economic policy.[13] This section provides an overview of economic policy under Franco, divided into three broad periods.

The Period of Autarky: 1939–51

After the Civil War, the Franco regime had two primary objectives: to install a socioeconomic system—corporatism—that had its roots in Italian fascism; and to achieve autarky.[14] The corporatist system the Franco regime sought rejected "horizontal" organizations, such as labor unions, and posited that society should be ordered along "vertical" or "functional" lines. Its basic organizing principle was that all owners of capital, managers, and workers engaged in the production of a good (broadly defined to include entire industrial sectors, e.g., "energy") should be arranged in a single hierarchically structured corporation supervised by the state. The regime operationalized this principle by creating twenty-seven sectoral "syndicates," which encompassed the whole gamut of economic activity in Spain. The law required all employers and workers to join the syndicate corresponding to their sector.

Corporatism was designed to achieve two basic goals: control labor and regulate production. Regime leaders wanted to prevent labor from organizing since they believed that unions fomented class conflict. They also wanted to keep wages low to benefit capitalists and promote a form of forced savings that would encourage productive investment. The regime succeeded on this score; real wages in 1945, 1953, and 1956 were only 25, 50, and 75 percent of prewar wages, respectively.[15] In compensation to labor, the regime guaranteed workers full employment. This combination—low wages but full employment—would be a mainstay of Franquist political economy.

The regime pursued autarky by cutting Spain off from international markets and attempting to guide agricultural and industrial development.[16] This decision was not entirely voluntary, since Spain was isolated internationally (due to displeasure over the Nationalist uprising); only Germany and Italy traded freely with Spain in the aftermath of the Civil War. The goal of autarky was consistent with the Falangists' traditional infatuation with national economic self-sufficiency. As explained later, however, autarkic economic policies were guided as much by a desire to ensure the loyalty of key economic interests, namely, banks, *latifundistas,* and established industrialists, as by a grand economic strategy.

Immediately following the war, the regime's top priority was to achieve self-sufficiency in agriculture because of the impending threat of widespread starvation. The regime tried to encourage greater agricultural production by implementing a series of price supports for key foodstuffs, especially wheat. In addition, policymakers used their control over both agricultural and industrial prices to shift the terms of trade in favor of agriculture.[17] These policies helped secure the support of the powerful *latifundistas* but were not very effective in bolstering agricultural production.

The government also sought to direct industrial growth. In 1939, legislation permitted policymakers to identify sectors of "national interest" and promote their growth. Measures to assist favored sectors included privileged access to scarce foreign exchange and import licenses, tax reductions, and other government help. Scholars agree that economic policymakers wielded their discretionary authority in this area in an entirely arbitrary and self-interested manner.[18] In 1941, the government founded the Instituto Nacional de Industria (INI), purportedly to lead industrial development.[19] The INI served as a holding company for the numerous public enterprises created to increase production in priority sectors.

A key aspect of autarkic industrial policy was the promotion of oligopolies in all major industrial sectors (and the financial sector) through the use of entry and price controls as well as other measures to limit competition. Policymakers also favored large firms when allocating scarce inputs (e.g., foreign exchange), licenses, and permits. In principle, these policies might have been a rational response to the reconstruction tasks facing Spanish policymakers. Concentration of capital with investment guided by the government was potentially one way to allocate scarce resources efficiently. As already noted, however, scholars concur that the regime's industrial policy was implemented in a decidedly arbitrary fashion. The results were in fact disastrous: Spanish national output grew at an annual average of only 1.6 percent in the 1940s and, in absolute terms, remained below prewar levels until the early 1950s.[20]

The political rationale behind the regime's industrial policy is easy to discern. It locked in market share and profits for established industrialists, thereby securing their support in spite of other government policies that hurt their terms of trade relative to agriculture. The broad lines of Spanish industrial policy also reflected Franco's conviction that economic liberalism was inherently connected to social and political liberalism and, hence, instability. This belief was central to the economic policies of Primo de Rivera, the Spanish dictator who ruled the country in the 1920s and was an important influence on Franco.[21] At the same time, Franco was deeply distrustful of big business and banking and intent upon preventing the concentration of too much economic power in a few hands, since this could become a challenge to his authority.

Liberalization and the Stabilization Plan: 1951–63
Poor economic performance in the 1940s and early 1950s—namely, high inflation, slow growth, and severe balance-of-payments problems—exposed the utter failure of autarkic policies. Until the early 1950s, the

regime believed that slow economic growth was a reasonable price to pay for policies that secured the backing of its primary constituents and maintained social peace. In 1951, however, political and social stability started to erode. Workers in some parts of the country protested low real wages and the chronic scarcity of basic consumer goods.[22] Newly emerging industrialists pressed the government to liberalize the economy and remove the bias in favor of agriculture.[23] In response, the regime announced it would begin to liberalize trade, remove controls that restricted competition, and foster economic growth based on rapid industrialization. To promote industrialization, the government used price controls to shift the terms of trade in favor of industry, lifted some import restrictions on capital goods, and created additional enterprises (under the auspices of INI) to expand production in key sectors. The start of U.S. aid to Spain in this period made this new approach possible by alleviating Spain's balance-of-payments problems and permitting the import of needed capital goods. Perhaps more importantly, it also marked the beginning of the end of Spain's international isolation.

The government, however, did not implement the liberalizing elements of its new economic strategy fully. "The conservative oligarchy . . . [with] its traditional terror of changes in the economic system, including those necessary for its own objective economic benefit, could not support policies that would break with the past and introduce a modern capitalist economy."[24] Consequently, the regime backed off, and most trade restrictions and price, entry, and production controls remained in place.

In 1956–57, economic conditions deteriorated dramatically, contributing to an increase in dissent toward the regime, especially among workers and students.[25] The inner circle calculated that it could no longer rely on an economic strategy favoring only traditional regime supporters to attain sufficient political backing. It decided reluctantly that the regime needed to gain the support, or at least acquiescence, of rising industrial interests (e.g., exporters) and increasingly militant workers. As a result, Franco appointed several new top-level economic policymakers—the Opus Dei technocrats—who entered government in 1957, and allowed them to chart a different economic policy course.

The technocrats had an immediate impact on economic policy in the form of the "Stabilization Plan" of 1959.[26] Mariano Navarro Rubio and Alberto Ullastres, the ministers of finance and commerce, respectively, were the Plan's principal architects and proponents. The IMF provided temporary balance-of-payment funding and played important roles in designing the program and selling it to Spanish leadership.[27] The Plan called for classic stabilization measures and structural reforms to liberalize the economy. The former included reduced government expenditures, slower monetary growth, and a realistic exchange rate; the latter, the removal of some trade barriers, and import and export restrictions, the easing of the most onerous price, entry, and production controls, and liberalization of foreign direct investment.

Policymakers implemented the stabilization measures quickly and successfully. In the short run, they provoked a recession, but inflation fell and the balance of payments improved dramatically. The recession subsided by 1961, and the economy started to grow without significant internal and external imbalances. Measures to liberalize the economy met a different fate. Although the government liberalized foreign investment and established lower tariffs, little was accomplished in other areas.

Franco was not enthusiastic about the Stabilization Plan but deferred to the counsel of his economic experts and those in the inner circle, especially Luis Carrero Blanco,[28] who argued that economic modernization was essential for the regime's long-term stability. They believed that the regime could gain legitimacy amongst most of the populace through its economic achievements, notably a sustained increase in standards of living, and crush any remaining dissent through repression. This was to be done without a major redistribution of income, something Franco virulently opposed; instead, the goal was to increase the size of the pie to be divided. This strategy was not without risks; the regime was to create a populace whose political loyalty would depend on continuing prosperity.[29]

In general, Franco would permit the technocrats great autonomy in economic policy-making in the years to come. Most economic policy questions fell within Franco's "zone of indifference," and the Council of Ministers typically shied away from formulating or administering specific economic policies. Nevertheless, the inner circle made it clear that the technocrats had to respect the regime's basic social and political foundations. For example, tax reform, desired by many economic policymakers, remained strictly off-limits because it would anger traditional regime supporters.

Development Planning: 1963–75

The regime's flirtation with "liberal" economic policies proved to be short lived. The early 1960s saw a return to government efforts to guide the economy, albeit with a far less heavy hand than in previous decades. In addition, it abandoned the tighter monetary stance implemented during the Stabilization Plan. Nevertheless, the regime's emphasis on designing economic policies that would create sufficient affluence to deflect opposition remained central to its political strategy.[30]

In 1963, the regime adopted the French indicative planning model. In the following years, it prepared three four-year plans. The plans established production objectives for "priority" sectors; these objectives were binding for public enterprises but merely "indicative" for private firms. Those favored were primarily "high-linkage" industries such as steel, chemicals, shipbuilding, metals, and automobiles. The plans also introduced measures to rationalize key sectors by reducing the number of firms through mergers (to obtain scale economies) and encouraging firms to adopt modern technology and export. Finally, some programs developed under the aegis of the plans sought to promote the development of "backward" regions and reduce income inequalities. To obtain the cooperation of private actors, the government offered incentives for new entrepreneurs to enter priority sectors or set up operations in backward regions and for existing firms to meet production and productivity targets. These incentives included fiscal advantages, favorable labor policies, and most importantly, access to preferential credit through an elaborate system of selective credit policies.

For some, Spain's plans were the product of a development elite that sought to rationalize the economy, promote growth through rapid industrial development, and make the country competitive in international markets.[31] Others argue that planning was politically motivated and, further, that it hurt economic performance.[32] Spain's chief planner himself asserted that planning was meant to "provide continuity to the regime," adding that "a development plan could only be considered to have any real significance in relation to politics."[33] This study also contends that the regime engaged in development planning for political reasons. I argue that one political motive was particularly important. Establishing a planning apparatus created an important source of discretionary power for regime officials, one they could use to target and secure the support of important sets of constituents.

Spain did enjoy high growth in this period. The average annual growth rate of Spain's real GNP—9.8 percent—was second only to Japan's in the period 1961–73. Nevertheless, major imbalances in regional wealth and national income distribution actually worsened.[34] Moreover, economists agree that Spain's development plans had little to do with the country's phenomenal growth; indeed, the consensus is that the economy performed well in spite of government intervention.[35] Growth was, in fact, fastest in the years 1961–64, before the Development Plans were put into place. Several other factors explain Spain's rapid economic progress much better. Large tourist receipts, emigrant workers' remittances, and heavy foreign direct investment sharply augmented the funds available for capital formation, sparking a surge in investment.[36] A worldwide economic boom provided ample markets for Spanish goods.

Ironically, the economic takeoff that the regime hoped would legitimize and stabilize its power ultimately contributed a great deal to its undoing. Economic development created new interests and unleashed modernizing forces that the regime's antiquated political structure could ultimately not co-opt or destroy. By the early 1970s, many within the regime had abandoned the idea of preserving an authoritarian regime based on the Franco model and began to join moderate opposition groups in pressing for reform.

Spanish Financial Actors and Institutions in the Franco Era

The Banking System

This section introduces the primary private and public actors involved in Spanish financial markets. The discussion of private financial actors in Spain must by default concentrate on those operating in the banking system. Direct financial markets in Spain were largely inconsequential during the Franco era, a result of both economic factors and government policy. The features of bond and equity markets are discussed later when we examine government policies aimed at suppressing them. The Spanish banking system in the Franco era consisted of "universal" or "mixed" banks, savings banks, public banks, and a few insignificant NBFIs. I discuss each of these in turn in the following sections.

Universal Banks

Universal banks, intermediaries that perform the functions of both commercial and investment banks, have dominated the Spanish financial sector in the post–Civil War period. Table 3.2 indicates that universal banks provided the majority of banking system credit to the private sector in the 1950s and 1960s.[37] As I show later, their dominance was assured by government policies. In particular, the so-called status quo regulations, issued in the period 1939–42, closed the financial sector to new entrants and limited competition among existing banks.[38] These regulations, combined with deposit rate ceilings, encouraged the consolidation of an oligopoly in the banking sector and enabled existing banks to earn large profits.

The Banking Law of 1962 tried to discourage the growth of universal banking by encouraging banks to become either strictly commercial or "industrial" (i.e., development or investment) banks. Industrial banks were to dedicate themselves to providing medium- and long-term credit (which was very scarce) to the private sector and to promoting new firms. Commercial banks were to concentrate on short-term lending and providing services to the public. The Ministry of Finance (MOF) encouraged but did not require existing universal banks to choose between commercial or industrial banking. Few did, as they had little incentive to give up the benefits of being a universal bank.[39]

The Banking Law of 1962 permitted the MOF to authorize new banks. Those it authorized usually chose to be industrial banks to take advantage of less stringent entry requirements. Most of these new banks were established by industrialists seeking to create a guaranteed source of cheap credit. They were very poorly run, largely because their operations were subordinated to the interests of their industrial groups. Almost all of these banks later failed, contributing decisively to a major banking crisis in the late 1970s. In short, the effort to create industrial banks was half-hearted and produced none of the desired results. By 1974, authorities had conceded as much, and they readopted the universal banking model.

Several scholars have claimed that banks wielded tremendous political influence in the Franco regime.[40] They contend that this influence stemmed from their active and early support for the Franco regime and the leverage obtained from the central role that banks played in industrial financing. Moreover, they suggest that the extensive familial ties among bank owners and managers made it possible for them to act collectively in their lobbying efforts. Banks in fact enjoyed ample "representation" in the upper levels of the bureaucracy and all the major government economic advisory bodies; from 1946 to 1975, bankers filled fifty-six administrative posts at the level of minister, undersecretary, and general director.[41] The most important advisory body dealing with financial policy was the Consejo Superior Bancario (CSB, Superior Banking Council). The CSB provided advice on most banking and financial matters, and the government

TABLE 3.2. Share of Credit to the Private Sector by Financial Entity (as a percentage of total credit)

	Universal Banks	Savings Banks	Public Banks	Industrial Banks	Other Entities
1954	76.9	7.2	15.9	n/a	—
1956	77.3	6.7	16.1	n/a	—
1958	75.8	8.8	15.4	n/a	—
1960	73.9	9.0	17.1	n/a	—
1962	75.4	9.7	14.9	n/a	—
1964	67.1	14.9	14.7	2.5	0.8
1966	62.2	16.8	15.9	3.9	1.2
1968	57.3	20.4	15.4	4.9	2.0

Source: Adapted from Gala 1969, cuadro 8.
Note: n/a = not applicable; — = negligible

took its recommendations very seriously. The CSB consisted of representatives from the private banking sector, mainly the large national banks,
and officials from the MOF. More generally, the relations between policymakers and banks were cordial. In exchange for usually favorable regulation, banks provided information, helped draft regulations, and promised
policymakers lucrative jobs in the private sector.

Nevertheless, there is reason to doubt that banks had the sort of
sweeping political power often attributed to them. Early on, banks did
have great influence over financial policy, obtaining very favorable legislation and regulation. As time progressed, however, policymakers asserted
greater independence and pursued policies that ran counter to the interests
of the banking sector. The existence of banking representatives in government certainly did not guarantee policies favoring their sector. In fact,
most important financial reforms were initiated by public officials with
strong connections to the banking world.[42]

In addition, banks found it increasingly difficult to act collectively to
influence financial or general economic policy as their interests grew more
diverse (due to differences in their size, geographic location, and competitive position) over time.[43] Individual banks were able to exert pressure on
specific issues, frequently with considerable success. The most powerful
banks have been called the "Big Seven" because they have long occupied
the top seven positions in the "ranking" of Spanish banks.[44] The ranking
is established on the basis of share of total deposits in the banking system.
Bank managers greatly value their ranking, and holding a top position has
been a key motivation. This scramble for rank within the sector also
detracted from banks' ability to act collectively.

Savings Banks

Savings banks are the second most important Spanish financial intermediary. Until recently, they could only carry out operations of a "socially
munificent" nature, although private ownership was permitted. In the
1920s and 1930s, the government began to intervene extensively in the
affairs of savings banks. Legislation regulated their internal management and limited their range of financial activities. In addition, the state
started intervening directly in their loan portfolios. They were required
to invest a percentage of their resources in "public funds," that is, bonds
issued by local or national government agencies or firms in government-
favored sectors. Control over their portfolios increased dramatically in
the post–Civil War period. By 1970, 80 percent of their total credit was
controlled by the state.

Until the 1960s, most savings banks were poorly run since managers
had little incentive to perform efficiently. In many cases, political not eco-

nomic criteria were the primary basis for operational decisions. The boards of directors of savings banks were traditionally occupied by local dignitaries and loyalists to the regime (often members of the Movimiento hierarchy). They used their authority to channel available funds to their friends or supporters of the regime, not to the most productive projects. In addition, the regime sometimes gave savings banks the power to oversee the granting of factory licenses, and the like, in their region.[45]

Policymakers began treating savings banks as true financial intermediaries (while maintaining their nonprofit character) in the late 1960s. In response, the professionalism and nonpartisanship of managers improved. Until 1977, financial authorities maintained tight restrictions on the range of activities of savings banks. They were not permitted to discount commercial paper, conduct international transactions, or issue many different sorts of liabilities. These restrictions limited their ability to compete with banks or intermediate between savers and the final users of funds efficiently.

Public Banks
The Spanish public bank system, consisting of seven banks founded mostly in the 1920s, has played an important but not pivotal role in the financial system.[46] Its share of total credit to the private sector has averaged about 15 percent in the post–Civil War period. Although most public banks were founded with private capital, the government has always exercised at least some control over their lending and borrowing activities. In 1962, the regime nationalized all public banks, except the Exterior Bank of Spain, and placed them under the direct supervision of the MOF's Instituto de Crédito a Medio y Largo Plazo (ICMLP, Medium- and Long-term Credit Institute). Policymakers greatly increased the volume of public bank lending in the 1960s and 1970s in order to deliver credit to sectors targeted by Spanish plans. In the Franco era, public banks normally offered loans with very long maturities, averaging about fifteen years; in sharp contrast, the maturities on loans granted by private intermediaries averaged less than a year. Interest rates on these loans were extremely low, usually in the 2.5 to 6.5 percent range; thus, real interest rates on public bank credit were usually negative.

Nonbank Financial Intermediaries
Until recently, NBFIs have played an insignificant role in the Spanish financial system. Authorities prohibited the creation of certain types of NBFIs and made sure that existing NBFIs did not challenge the market dominance of banks and savings banks. The most important NBFIs have been the *cajas cooperativas* (credit unions) and *cajas rurales* (rural savings

banks). Until 1987, the "cooperative" nature of these institutions limited their activities to taking deposits from and lending to their members. At their peak in the late 1970s, they held about 2 percent of the total assets and 4 percent of the total deposits of the banking sector; before 1970, their share of the market was negligible.[47] Spain has had only a small and underdeveloped curb market.[48]

Government Agencies

The Ministry of Finance
The MOF had virtually complete control over financial and monetary policy in the Franco era. Most formal authority was vested directly in the person of the minister, who served at the pleasure of the inner circle. Although certain administrative posts traditionally went to members of specific administrative corps, the minister had the authority to make several high-level appointments, greatly facilitating his control over the activities of the ministry. Typically, the minister and his closest advisors personally formulated monetary policy and supervised the central bank and the Treasury. The Dirección General de Política Financiera (Financial Policy Directorate) had responsibility for general financial policy and regulating the activities of all private intermediaries.[49] The ICMLP and, after 1971, the Instituto de Crédito Oficial (ICO, Official Credit Institute) supervised public banks.

The MOF's control over the budgetary process made it the most powerful economic ministry throughout much of the Franco period.[50] The MOF had some influence over the overall distribution of state expenditures among ministries but little over how expenditures were allocated within individual ministries. It could not design a grand economic strategy because it lacked the authority to coordinate the activities of the various economic ministries.

The Bank of Spain
The Banco de España (BOS, Bank of Spain) is the Spanish central bank. In the nineteenth century, the BOS resembled an ordinary private bank, although its activities were primarily geared toward government finance, and it had monopoly of issue after 1874. The BOS attained some functions of a modern central bank, notably the role of lender of last resort, in the early 1900s. In this period, it also began to consider how its operations affected money supply, although it did not formulate an explicit monetary policy or have the instruments necessary for implementing one. The BOS officially became the central bank with its nationalization in 1962. In theory, the 1962 Banking Law granted the BOS operational responsibility for implementing monetary policy and for all matters (supervision, control,

and inspection) concerning private intermediaries. In practice, its independence was severely restricted, as the MOF and political leaders jealously retained their authority over financial and monetary policy and even impeded the development of institutional capacity that would have given the Bank greater autonomy.[51] The BOS's lack of independence from political control was still evident in the 1980s despite reforms meant to grant it greater autonomy in carrying out financial and monetary policy.[52]

The banking sector had several ways of influencing BOS policies. The Big Seven had representatives on the BOS's board of directors, its formal decision-making body. However, the BOS's governor had final authority over all policy decisions, and he answered directly to the minister of finance. The extensive personal contacts between top BOS officials and private bankers were perhaps more critical. The governor had monthly lunches with the presidents of the Big Seven, where policy disputes were often resolved informally. Banks, for example, could expect the BOS to help them overcome temporary liquidity problems (by providing a line of credit) or overlook small rules violations in exchange for agreeing to set interest rates in line with BOS preferences or increase their lending to a particular sector.[53]

The Political Economy of Financial Restriction in Spain

The Franco regime inherited a financial system that was underdeveloped by European standards. Table 3.3 indicates that the ratio of financial institutions' assets to national product—a common indicator of financial development—was lower in Spain than in other industrial countries in 1935. Spanish bond and equity markets were relatively shallow and dominated by public securities. Therefore, the Spanish financial system would have been difficult to transform radically—for example, to a securities market-based system—in the short run. The regime made no such effort, however; instead, it sought to deepen financial repression. Consequently, although the structure of Spain's financial markets during the Franco era was partly influenced by the country's level of development and other economic variables, it was also the conscious product of government policy. The sections that follow examine Franquist financial policy in detail.

Policies to Suppress Direct Financial Markets and Close the
Financial Sector

Direct Financial Markets
Until the 1980s, Spanish financial policy purposefully encouraged the growth of a cartelized banking system at the expense of direct financial markets. Consequently, bond and equity markets played an insignificant

part in financing Spanish economic development. It is unlikely that direct markets would have played a dominant role in the absence of government policies. In the nineteenth and early twentieth centuries, the development of direct markets was hindered by savers' preference for short-term liquid assets, the small size of most Spanish firms, and their monopolization by government bond issues. Moreover, only a small number of individual investors had sufficient funds to delve into direct markets, and there were very few institutional investors (e.g., insurance companies) to compensate for this deficiency. Nonetheless, public policy was clearly designed to suppress the development of direct markets. This policy ran counter to mainstream economic theory that indicates that the growth of direct markets yields considerable benefits.[54]

The MOF implemented several policies designed to impede the development of bond and equity markets. First, it opposed all proposals to modernize official exchanges, create or expand secondary markets, or broaden the range of financial products traded. Second, an MOF agency, the Junta de Inversiones (Investment Board), had to approve bond and stock issues before they could be sold on the exchanges.[55] It also regulated bond yields to prevent them from competing with bank deposits.[56] The effect of these policies was to discourage most companies from attempting to raise funds in direct markets.[57] Third, the MOF required investors to

TABLE 3.3. Ratio of Financial Institutions' Assets to National Product, 1860–1938 (in percentages)

	1860[a]	1880	1900	1913	1929	1938
Spain	13	31	39	33	69	75[b]
Belgium	31	73	114	158	89	99
Britain	57	71	94	109	85	140
Denmark	n/a	95	147	184	186	198
France	19	50	96	104	90	130
Germany	n/a	95	93	103	131	158
Holland	n/a	46	62	83	110	187
Italy	n/a	36	61	97	95	137
Norway	n/a	107	136	166	241	187
Sweden	n/a	89	123	136	138	161
Switzerland	56	153	184	287	261	325
United States	28	49	86	91	129	185
Europe	n/a	77	104	133	136	163

Source: For Spain, Tortella 1973, cuadro IX-8, and Martín Aceña 1987, table 6.5; for other countries, Goldsmith 1969, tables 4.7, 4.12, and 4.23, and Cameron 1967, table IX.1.

[a]Data indicated are for Spain, 1864; Belgium, 1865; Britain, 1860; France, 1860; Switzerland, 1860; United States, 1860.

[b]Figure is for 1935.

n/a = not available

report their purchases of bonds and stocks but not their deposits in the banking system. In addition, the "banking secret" established in 1940 allowed banks to withhold all information concerning customer accounts. These policies provided savers with an incentive and opportunity to conceal their wealth in the banking system. Finally, income earned on securities faced a special capital gains tax of 15 percent.

Data on private sector financing suggest the effectiveness of these policies. The banking system provided only 30 percent of company financing in the period 1920–35 but more than 60 percent in the period 1940–69.[58] As already noted, by the 1960s and 1970s, direct markets provided only about 6 percent of total credit to the private sector. Even the hundred largest Spanish firms, those with the greatest presence in direct markets, obtained only about 40 percent of their funds from bond and equity markets in the mid-1960s.[59]

The regime blocked the development of bond and equity markets partly to placate key constituents, especially banks. Banks opposed a greater role for direct markets for two basic reasons. First, they feared their expansion would lead to disintermediation. Disintermediation threatened to reduce their share of credit to the private sector, thereby limiting their profits and long-term growth potential. Second, more developed direct markets would have allowed firms to diversify their financial structure, thereby weakening the banking sector's influence over industry.

The Junta Sindical de los Agentes de Cambio y Bolsa (Association of Stock Brokers) also opposed the modernization of the official exchanges. Members of the Junta, a very small and select group, completely monopolized trade on Spain's four exchanges. Although the government's policy of suppressing direct markets restricted the volume of activity on the exchanges, the Junta's monopoly position permitted its members to earn handsome, guaranteed profits. Reforms to modernize the exchanges would have necessarily begun by redesigning their antiquated system of brokerage and ending the Junta's monopoly.

The regime also impeded the development of direct markets to help achieve two broader goals, especially after 1960. First, it believed it would be easier to control the overall allocation of credit if direct markets were inconsequential. Second, it realized it would be more difficult to extract seignorage from bond and equity markets than from the banking system. I examine these two goals later in this chapter.

The policy of suppressing direct markets, however, eventually created several problems for policymakers. Perhaps the most serious was that it allowed banks to gain leverage over industry. Firms had to rely almost exclusively on self-finance and bank credit for their funds. Banks used their control over credit to influence the behavior of individual firms. This leverage was augmented by the fact that the vast majority of credit was short term.[60] The banking sector's influence over industry was an obstacle to the government's attempts to shape industrial development in the 1960s. Its subsequent efforts to reduce banks' influence over industry by legislation proved ineffective, as I discuss later.

Heavy reliance on debt financing also made firms vulnerable to reductions in the overall level of liquidity in the banking system. Their vulnerability restricted the range of options available to the MOF when it set monetary policy. In particular, the MOF could not easily implement a tight money policy, since a drop in bank credit to the private sector would leave many firms without adequate funds. Finally, insufficient direct markets increased the risk of financial instability. In countries with well-developed financial markets, bond and equity markets are typically the primary source of financing for risky, high-return projects. In Spain, the banking system financed these projects and assumed excessive default risk. This jeopardized its solvency and contributed to a severe banking crisis in the period from 1978 to 1985.

A Closed Financial Market

The Franco regime tightly regulated foreign transactions in order to isolate the Spanish economy from international financial markets. Strict controls limited flows of capital into and out of Spain. The government allowed very few firms, most of them state-owned companies, to borrow funds in international capital markets, and they had to obtain authorization on a case-by-case basis; no Spanish firms were authorized to engage in direct investment abroad. It prohibited Spanish banks from participating in international lending or acquiring positions in foreign exchange. Finally, it barred foreign intermediaries from entering the Spanish market.

Two major rationales underlay this policy. One was to maintain control over the allocation of credit and foreign exchange. In particular, policymakers feared that external borrowing would weaken their ability to dictate who received credit and at what cost. Second, the regime believed that integration into international capital markets would expose Spanish banks and firms to influences that might undermine the regime's stability.[61]

The regime opened the financial market somewhat as a result of the Stabilization Plan of 1959. It declared convertibility of the peseta, established a single exchange rate, and liberalized some minor foreign financial transactions. In addition, it allowed substantial foreign direct investment in certain industrial sectors after 1960. Spanish borrowing and investment abroad, however, remained strictly controlled. Significant liberalization of these transactions would have to wait until the late 1970s.

Policies to Encourage an Oligopolistic Banking Sector

In the post–Civil War period, the regime fostered an oligopolistic financial sector dominated by a handful of large national banks. It ensured the dominance of these banks with the aforementioned status-quo regulations. These regulations, promoted by the minister of finance, Jose Larás, closed the financial sector to all NBFIs, prohibited the creation of new banks or the entry of foreign banks, and placed strict restrictions on the opening of new offices and the expansion of paid-in capital. In short, they severely limited competition within the financial sector, effectively encouraging and sanctioning the consolidation of a banking cartel. This increased the costs of financial intermediation and impeded the mobilization and efficient allocation of financial resources.[62] Later legislation permitted new banks, but only a handful actually received authorization until the 1960s.[63]

Why did the regime promote a financial oligopoly? The primary reason was to appease the powerful national banks, which wished to limit competition in the financial sector so they could earn supranormal profits. Franco met their demand because he wished to reward banks for their financial backing of the Nationalist faction during the Civil War and ensure their continued support for the regime.[64] This policy was also consistent with Franco's conviction that economic competition created tensions that might lead to social and political instability, although it did run counter to his suspicion of big business. For their part, financial policymakers wanted to win the banking sector's cooperation in reconstructing the Spanish economy along a new autarkic course.[65] Not surprisingly, large national banks earned huge profits. The gross profits of the five largest banks increased by 3,000 percent from 1940 to 1960. In 1950, a typical year, the return on equity capital for the large national banks was 35 percent.[66]

Local and regional banks opposed the new regulations because they feared they would lock them into an inferior competitive position (e.g., because they had fewer branches).[67] Their fears proved to be justified. Until the late 1950s, authorities accentuated the initial inequalities among banks by implementing the limits on expansion unequally. They permitted the large national banks but not local and regional banks to open new offices and increase their capital.[68] They also allowed national banks to take over local and regional banks.[69] This process led to the formation of large banking groups, typically consisting of a big national bank, an industrial bank, and several small local and regional banks. By 1967, the six largest groups contained fifty-four banks and controlled almost 80 percent

of the total deposits in the banking system.[70] These policies also contributed to a drop in the number of banks in the banking sector, from 250
in 1940 to 126 in 1967. Nevertheless, the concentration of total deposits
among banks, as measured by the Herfindhal and Entropia concentration
indices, actually declined from about 1950 on, despite the fall in the total
number of banks, as local and regional banks gained market share.[71]

The regime adopted one regulation in the early 1940s that did not
favor banking interests. The MOF ruled that banks could not pay out cash
dividends whose value was greater than 6 percent of their paid-in capital.[72]
This meant that banks had to increase their capital if they wanted to raise
their dividends. The status-quo regulations were supposed to restrict this
type of capital expansion. In practice, however, the MOF allowed the
large national banks to increase their capital while it restrained small
banks from doing so.[73]

The limit on dividends was a concession to an important political
group within the regime, the Falangists. The Falangists were hostile to big
business and banking, and they had urged Franco to break up the dominance of the large national banks and limit their profits.[74] Since the regime
had actually sanctioned and not destroyed the financial status quo, it limited dividends to appease the Falangists. The dividends rule was also
designed to encourage banks to invest profits that could not be paid out as
dividends into equity in industrial firms, thereby increasing overall levels
of investment.[75] This policy had a large and ultimately unintended impact.
By the mid-1950s, the largest six banks had obtained a controlling interest
in 745 leading firms.[76] Interlocking directorates between banks and firms
also became common; bank representatives were on the boards of directors of 2,321 private firms in 1968.[77] This was significant because in Spain
the board of directors exercises some managerial control over a firm's
operations. The apparent concentration of economic power in banks led
some scholars to speak of the emergence of a "financial oligarchy."[78]

This does not mean that banks had automatic or complete influence
over industry, however. First, bank representatives did not always have
sufficient expertise to influence a firm's operations significantly.[79] Second,
the financial stake banks developed in firms actually gave them some leverage over banks. Banks typically gave firms in which they had an interest
preference in obtaining credits (whether or not they had high default risk
or their projects promised the highest returns), especially when liquidity
was tight.

The dividends policy, along with others that concentrated resources
in the hands of a cartel of powerful national banks, could be interpreted as
consistent with an economic strategy of using banks to lead and shape
development in a late industrializing country in which other actors lack

sufficient expertise and large accumulations of capital are necessary for efficient investment.[80] As noted in chapter 1, some scholars, particularly of Japan, have argued that entry and interest controls can improve efficiency in underdeveloped financial systems because they permit a few strong banks with superior information and monitoring capability to manage available resources. In the 1940s especially, promoting a few strong banks might have been a rational response by policymakers to Spain's economic problems (notably its daunting reconstruction tasks) given the state of its bond and equity markets and its weak entrepreneurial class.

This motive was probably a factor in the design of Spanish financial policy, at least in the 1940s; efforts to shape financial markets to meet tasks like reconstruction are not inconsistent with the motives that I ascribe to policymakers. However, there is reason to doubt that it was the sole or primary rationale, as political factors were clearly relevant in the design of financial and industrial policy. Certainly, this rationale disappeared over time as Spain emerged from the devastation caused by the war, capital grew more abundant, and savers became ready to diversify their assets by purchasing bonds or equities. Moreover, this set of policies was implemented in ways that had little to do with economic logic; Spain's economic performance in the 1940s and 1950s, when banks were rapidly building economic power, was dismal as we have seen.

More importantly, although Spanish banks exercised influence over firms because of their control over financing, they did not guide industrial development in the way that banks have in other European countries, like Belgium and Germany, or in Japan; nor did the government actively encourage them to take on this role.[81] As already noted, the state itself guided (albeit tentatively) the creation of national industry throughout the Franco era, a task most scholars contend it did poorly and with little regard to economic criteria.[82] In the 1960s, foreign investors also became significant in charting out new economic territory through their direct investments.

In fact, the regime soon came to believe that it had permitted the banking sector to acquire excessive economic power, and it actively sought to reduce its dominance of the financial sector and leverage over industry.[83] The Banking Law of 1962 was partly designed to weaken the power of the large national banks. First, it facilitated entry into the financial sector. Fanjul and Maravall note that this increased competition among banks slightly and reduced concentration within the banking sector.[84] The Law also limited the amount of equity banks could hold in firms to a percentage of paid-up capital. However, banks did not decrease subsequently their equity holdings as policymakers had expected. Instead, they circumvented the restriction by increasing dramatically their capital, thereby demonstrating their determination to maintain their leverage over firms.[85] In 1968, policymakers proposed legislation intended to stop the proliferation of interlocking directorates; it sought to prohibit bank presidents, vice presidents, board members or general directors from occupying similar posts in other financial institutions or firms. Banks virulently opposed the legislation and succeeded in weakening its key provisions. The legislation passed in 1969, but was not enforced fully.[86]

Delivering Financial Benefits through Interest Rate and Credit Controls

Interest Rate Controls
The Spanish government first approved a form of interest rate controls in 1921 when it gave the newly created CSB the authority to establish deposit rate ceilings. In 1927, new legislation gave the CSB the power to set minimum loan interest rates. The decision to grant the CSB control over interest rates was tantamount to officially sanctioning price-fixing by the banking industry given its heavy representation on the CSB.

The Franco regime authorized the MOF to establish deposit rate ceilings but required it to consult with the CSB beforehand.[87] The regime kept deposit rate ceilings in place to placate banking interests.[88] Banks were anxious to maintain the ceilings because they lowered the cost of liabilities and eliminated price competition for deposits, thereby facilitating the formation of a cartel. In addition, the regime allowed banks to negotiate several pacts among themselves, called "Agreements to Limit Competition," to fix minimum loan interest rates.[89] The combination of official maximum deposit rates and unofficial minimum loan rates ensured banks a profitable spread on all loans.[90]

After 1960, policymakers asserted more control over interest rate policy and gradually shaped it to advance their own interests. The MOF negotiated loan rate ceilings with private banks even though initially it had no clear legal basis for establishing them.[91] MOF officials could enforce these agreements because they controlled access to lines of credit at the BOS; uncooperative banks might find themselves cut off from informal BOS lending. In addition, banks did not oppose the loan rate ceilings too vigorously because deposit rate controls enabled them to continue to lend profitably.

Officials stated that lowering real interest rates via loan rate ceilings would encourage productive investment and, thereby, promote aggregate growth. This rationale, however, was fallacious, a point brought to the attention of Spanish authorities by the World Bank and OECD.[92] Barring serious market failures, if the expected return on a project does not cover the cost of borrowing in the absence of controls, it is not productive from a social welfare perspective and should not be undertaken. In addition, loan rate ceilings actually created several immediate problems. Perhaps the most serious was that they distorted relative factor prices by artificially lowering the cost of capital, thereby encouraging firms to adopt overly capital-intensive modes of production.[93]

I contend that the regime imposed loan rate ceilings for a political purpose: to help create an important source of discretionary power. Loan rate ceilings, combined with credit controls, made it possible for officials to create non–price rationing in credit markets and influence directly the credit allocation process. Their efforts to do so are discussed in the next section.

Selective Credit Policies

In the 1960s and 1970s, the Franco regime imposed an elaborate system of new controls to influence the allocation of credit.[94] The legal mechanisms used in the period from 1962 to 1975, the apex of what Spaniards called the "privileged credit circuits," are summarized in table 3.4. As already noted, government-controlled credit as a percentage of total credit to the private sector was high, averaging about 35 percent. The percentage was somewhat smaller before 1962, averaging about 25 percent; savings banks supplied most of this credit. In addition, authorities often employed moral suasion to induce private intermediaries to invest in certain sectors.[95] Until about 1980, most preferential credit was long term and interest rates were highly subsidized, averaging well below the rates charged for short-term loans.[96] Interest rates, therefore, varied arbitrarily across classes of borrowers; there were even substantial differences in rates among types of privileged borrowers.

A few of the selective credit policies listed in table 3.4 deserve special comment. The coefficients imposed on banks and savings banks (e.g., the "public funds" coefficient) required them to invest a fixed percentage of their deposits in public debt or securities issued by government agencies and favored industrial sectors. Savings banks had much higher coefficients than banks; in 1969, for example, the coefficients involved 80 and 20 percent of savings bank and bank assets, respectively. Therefore, savings banks carried more of the burden of subsidizing privileged sectors. Intermediaries disliked the coefficients because they imposed opportunity costs in the form of foregone interest they might have obtained on other assets. They did not oppose them strongly, however, because they respected the implicit bargain by which they were amply compensated by other aspects of financial policy.[97] Instead, they focused their lobbying on gaining the inclusion of firms they controlled into the privileged circuits.

TABLE 3.4. Spanish Selective Credit Policies, 1962–74

Banks
  1962–71
    "Public funds" coefficient

    Special rediscount lines

  1971–74
    "Investment" coefficient

"Public funds" coefficient	Banks were required to invest 15 to 20 percent of their deposits in public debt and bonds used to raise funds for public banks.
Special rediscount lines	The Bank of Spain was obliged to rediscount loans made by banks to "priority sectors." The rediscounting operation provided banks with instant liquidity and a small profit.
"Investment" coefficient	The public funds coefficient and special rediscount lines were combined into a single coefficient. Under the new coefficient, loans to priority sectors could not be rediscounted.
Savings Banks	
"Public funds" coefficient	Savings banks had to invest 50 to 60 percent of their deposits in bonds issued by public enterprises and private bond and equity issues approved by the Ministry of Finance.
"Special regulatory credits" coefficient	Savings banks were required to invest 10 to 30 percent of their deposits in specified industrial sectors (e.g., housing).
Public Banks	
Direct Provision of Subsidized Credit	Public banks provided subsidized credit to priority sectors and regions through a variety of programs (e.g., "Development Poles"), drawing on funds supplied through the "public funds" coefficient of private banks.
Bank of Spain	
Direct financing of public enterprises	The Bank of Spain typically covered the deficits of public enterprises operating in priority sectors. It also funded agriculture through credits provided to FORPPA, an agricultural development agency.
Ad hoc policies	The Bank of Spain occasionally purchased securities of firms in priority sectors when private entities had already met their coefficients.

Special rediscount lines (SRLs) encouraged lending to certain priority sectors by allowing banks to rediscount credits granted to them at the BOS. In the 1960s, the primary beneficiaries of these lines were the shipbuilding industry, heavy machinery manufacturers, and exporters.[98] Banks embraced the rediscount lines because they were a means of obtaining liquidity that was outside the control of monetary authorities. Moreover, they put the burden of subsidizing favored sectors on the BOS, not on banks. The MOF eliminated SRLs in 1971; at the same time, it established new coefficients (discussed in chap. 4) that forced banks to lend at subsidized rates to the same sectors. This shifted the cost of providing credit to favored sectors onto banks.

In the 1960s and 1970s, directed credit policies were an integral part of Spain's development plans. The government stated it was establishing credit controls to channel funds to priority sectors whose growth was deemed essential for economic development. Preferential credit was also intended to encourage priority sectors to modernize, adopt more rational industrial organization, and increase productivity and exports.[99]

The plans and their attendant financial policies were apparently very successful, as Spain enjoyed high growth in this period. A closer look, however, reveals a different picture. As noted earlier, most scholars agree that Spain's plans had little to do with its strong growth; a sharp increase in investment capital and a worldwide economic boom explain its performance more satisfactorily. Moreover, the evidence suggests that selective credit policies allocated funds in an economically inefficient manner; with a few exceptions, beneficiaries were not the optimal final users of credit.[100] In fact, many recipients later failed or suffered serious losses. Furthermore, in contrast to South Korea and Taiwan, directed credit policies did not encourage most targeted sectors to improve their performance.[101] Finally, credit controls often were surrounded by corruption, as shown particularly in the "Matesa Affair."[102] International agencies and leading Spanish economists repeatedly told government policymakers that credit controls were hurting economic performance, but this did not produce a change in policy.[103]

I contend that government officials implemented the planning apparatus and credit controls to enhance the regime's ability to create and satisfy particular interests.[104] Plan proponents, notably López Rodó (head of the Planning Commission [PC]) and López Bravo (minister of industry), sought the discretionary power that the planning process gave those in charge of management of the economy.[105] Programs developed under the aegis of the development plans were designed to enable public officials to deliver benefits in the form of tax breaks, subsidized credit, or other scarce inputs (e.g., foreign exchange) to select private groups.

Not all economic policymakers favored planning. Navarro Rubio, the minister of finance, and several other officials in the MOF, BOS, and the Ministry of Commerce (MOC) opposed the plans because they feared they would lead to excessive and ineffective state intervention in the economy and movement away from the greater macroeconomic orthodoxy won at such great cost with the Stabilization Plan. However, López Rodó, who was Carrero Blanco's protégé and derived a great deal of power from this relationship, was able to prevail. In fact, until his star faded in 1973, López Rodó was the single most powerful official involved in economic policy-making. Among his exploits, he was able to move some authority over interdepartmental investment priorities away from the MOF to the PC, push through administrative reforms that facilitated the implementation of the development plans, and even exercise influence over the composition of the new government formed in 1969. Navarro Rubio left his post as minister of finance to become governor of the BOS in 1965, largely because of disagreements over the PC's encroachment upon the MOF's jurisdiction and the government's planning efforts. As related in chapter 4, Navarro Rubio created a team of top economists at the BOS who favored liberal economic policies and distinguished themselves by their opposition to state efforts to manage the economy. This team was to play a decisive role in later financial liberalization efforts.

Directed credit programs quickly became the principal means of distributing private benefits to favored groups. They were especially attractive to policymakers because they did not require direct budgetary expenditures. Their direct costs could be imposed on the financial sector; their indirect costs, mainly a loss of financial efficiency and higher inflation, would be diffused throughout society. Growth in fact remained robust despite low financial efficiency, making it possible for those favoring planning to deflect criticism of the government's financial policy.

Officially, the Council of Ministers, chaired by Franco, designated priority sectors and determined the overall sectoral distribution of privileged credit. In practice, intense bargaining in interdepartmental committees (such as the Official Credit Commission) decided these matters. In these negotiations, a minister's personal political influence and negotiating skills largely determined the amount of credit economic sectors overseen by his ministry would receive.[106] State control over credit allocation also went well beyond targeting broad sectors. First, many categories of recipients were very narrowly defined. For example, a special rediscount line was set up solely for apricot growers. Administrators also had discretion in deciding whether a specific firm was eligible for inclusion in a given category. In one notorious case, a small shipbuilding firm with no export operations obtained funds reserved exclusively for exporters. Finally, several programs, notably "Development Poles" and "Concerted Action," were deliberately designed to allow administrators to allocate credit on a firm-by-firm basis.[107]

Policymakers at the ministerial level selected the specific recipients of privileged credit, being careful to respect the inner circle's ground rules. In general, they attempted to channel credit to firms owned by friends or family or those who promised them financial rewards or might contribute to the success of the programs they ran.[108] The inner circle was satisfied with this arrangement because it was not overly concerned with exercising tight control over the exact allocation of subsidized credit. It believed that its agents' choices were consistent with the overall goal of increasing broad-based support for the regime. Moreover, it believed it was better to increase the amount and scope of privileged credit than to restrict it and exclude groups that might then become hostile to the regime. The steady expansion of selective credit programs, especially SRLs, contributed to rapid and largely unpredictable monetary growth; this severely undermined the efforts to assert control over inflation that began with the Stabilization Plan.[109]

Firms targeted by credit controls were (along with banks) the big "winners" of financial restriction in Spain. Interest rate and credit controls guaranteed them access to scarce long-term credit at artificially low rates. Firms competed intensely for access to privileged credit, engaging in classic rent-seeking behavior. Savers and firms rationed out of credit markets lost the most. Deposit rate ceilings lowered the yield that savers received on their deposits, often leaving them with a negative real return in periods of high inflation. Interest rate and credit controls produced credit rationing that forced some firms to restrict their investments.[110] Small- and medium-sized companies (SMCs) were the most affected. Whenever liquidity fell, banks stopped lending to SMCs first, forcing them to turn to curb markets or restrict their investments.

The scarcity of financing for SMCs was especially severe in the provinces. The absorption of local and regional banks by the large national banks siphoned funds collected in the provinces and channeled them to Spain's industrial centers. In order to survive, many SMCs offered banks a seat on their board of directors or stock to ensure the flow of credit when liquidity was tight. In exchange, banks demanded a voice in the firm's affairs.[111] SMCs in Cataluña were an exception. A traditional fear of bank financing led Catalan firms to rely more on self-finance than firms in other parts of Spain.

The regime generally incurred low political costs in using financial policy to benefit select groups since savers and firms rationed out of credit markets did not organize for effective opposition due to collective action problems. Indeed, the optimal course for a saver was not to press for changes in government policy but to strike an individual deal with a bank to obtain better rates. Moreover, whereas the Franco regime permitted firms to exert pressure on lower-order economic decisions, it strongly discouraged lobbying on issues of broad economic policy.[112]

Regime officials encountered limits in using interest rate and credit controls to deliver benefits, however. These controls imposed opportunity costs on intermediaries and, hence, stimulated efforts to circumvent them. Banks devised several means of evading interest rate controls legally. For example, they bypassed loan rate ceilings by requiring borrowers to maintain "compensating balances" (see chap. 2). Similarly, controlling credit allocation through selective credit policies was problematic. Subsidized credit did not always reach its intended final users. Lenders sometimes misclassified loans or created channels for redirecting credit from priority sectors to those they wished to favor.[113] Funds that did reach priority sectors created moral hazard problems among recipients. Favored borrowers, especially in heavy industry, believed that the government would support them, even if they racked up losses; consequently, they often expanded production recklessly or failed to remain competitive.[114] Finally, forcing intermediaries to supply funds to favored sectors seriously weakened their portfolios since their lending was overly concentrated and preferential credit recipients were poor risks. This eventually compromised the solvency of the banking system. In the 1970s, a deteriorating economy led many privileged borrowers to default on their loans, greatly contributing to Spain's severe banking crisis.[115]

Taxation of the Banking System

The Historical Roots of Taxation of the Spanish Financial Sector

The Spanish state has traditionally sought to use the private banking system as a source of low-cost funds. Spain's banking system took shape in the early 1800s and evolved largely in response to the government's need to finance its activities and deficits. In many cases, financiers created intermediaries with the express purpose of financing government activities. For example, the founding and development of the Bank of San Carlos, the first modern Spanish bank, "was directly related to the growth of public debt."[116] The state encouraged its formation to manage the liquidation of *vales reales,* a form of public debt that served as currency. Similarly, the Bank of St. Ferdinand (later to become the BOS), lent huge sums to the government against its future tax receipts. At one point, 75 percent of the Bank's profits came from its lending to the government.[117] The state's efforts to cast private banks in the role of government financier continued throughout the nineteenth century. In 1874, legislators granted the BOS monopoly of issue in exchange for loans to the government totaling 125 million pesetas.[118] This measure "reduced the financial system's level of competitiveness and placed control of the credit market in the hands of a single institution [the BOS]—an institution that did not always function in a manner conducive to the economy's growth."[119] Public debt, along with securities associated with state-backed projects in the private sector (e.g., railroad construction), also dominated bond markets.[120]

Economic historians concur that the banking sector's close ties to the state held back Spain's financial development and slowed the growth of industry and the overall economy. Tortella argues that rather than taking an active entrepreneurial role, as banks did in other European countries, Spanish banks submissively followed the state's short-sighted and politically driven economic policies.[121] By the mid-nineteenth century, the country's financial development was already well behind that of other European countries as measured by the ratio of financial institutions' assets to national product (see table 3.3). A weak financial sector led to overdependence on foreign capital for investment and a deficient payments mechanism that hindered commerce.

In 1917, the state developed a new legal instrument, ARs, to extract revenue from the financial sector. ARs required intermediaries to purchase low-yielding government debt. The Primo de Rivera regime used ARs intensely in the 1920s to finance a major public works program that was a key element in its state-led industrial development strategy. It opted to increase public debt rather than augment direct taxation because it feared progressive income taxes would cause social unrest. One consequence of the government's heavy reliance on bank lending was that Spanish financial development continued to lag behind that of other European countries.

The Post–Civil War Period

The Franco regime also taxed the banking system to finance government activities at zero- or low-interest cost. It turned to taxation of the financial sector because it was reluctant to implement a more efficient tax system based on direct or value-added taxes.[122] The regime was particularly unwilling to tax the middle and upper classes, both essential constituencies, for fear of losing their political support. The level and composition of state revenues reflects this. Fiscal receipts as a percentage of GDP in Spain were among the lowest of any OECD country.[123] Direct taxes accounted for less than one-fourth of all tax revenue in the 1960s and early 1970s, a very small figure by international standards.[124] Income taxes were especially low, contributing only 1 to 2 percent of all revenue.[125] Overall, the taxation system was highly regressive, placing an unfair burden on the lower classes.[126]

In the 1940s and 1950s, policymakers did not tax banks heavily because of their strong bargaining power. After the Civil War, they reestablished ARs requiring banks to purchase government debt with returns fixed below prevailing market rates. However, they eliminated the opportunity cost this represented for banks by giving them the option of rediscounting up to 90 percent of their debt purchases at the BOS. The rediscount option gave banks a ready source of liquidity and made public debt very popular with banks.[127]

The rediscount option complicated monetary policy as it converted the operation of issuing public debt into one of borrowing from the central bank, albeit with an intermediate step. Banks usually rediscounted a large portion of the debt they purchased, so new government debt issues increased the money supply and created inflationary pressures. It should be noted that authorities did not attempt to control the money supply until the 1970s. Instead, they allowed the money supply to grow passively in response to the demand for money. This passivity was due to two factors. First, Spanish authorities lacked the tools to implement an active policy effectively.[128] Second, until the 1960s, many high-ranking government officials believed that authorities should accommodate the demand for money to support industrialization.

Passive monetary policy contributed to moderate-to-high inflation in several periods, notably in the 1950s and mid-1960s. The regime tolerated inflation, however, as long as the economy grew at an adequate pace. Navarro Rubio, a former minister of finance, noted that "inflation [is] the most useful instrument for satisfying the best organized interests while transferring costs to those who are politically unimportant because they have not been able to organize."[129] The regime accomplished this trick by allowing firms to pass on price increases to customers but restraining wage growth. Consequently, the real income accruing to capitalists increased while real wages held steady.

Eventually, the need to finance expanded government activity led policymakers to intensify their efforts to extract seignorage from the banking system. In particular, starting in the 1960s, they sought to obtain more resources to distribute as preferential credit to favored groups. Forcing banks to shoulder part of the burden for financing public expenditures was critical because the inner circle had made it clear that policymakers could not increase orthodox taxation substantially to generate more revenue.

The first step in shifting the cost of financing public expenditures onto banks was the abolition of the rediscount option on new public debt in

1959.[130] Without the rediscount option, the obligation to purchase debt represented an opportunity cost for banks in the form of foregone interest they might have obtained on other assets. In 1962, the regime created additional means of taxing the financial sector to raise revenues by authorizing the MOF to establish a "public funds" coefficient and RRs. The public funds coefficient set up a new legal framework for requiring banks to purchase public debt. In addition, it obligated banks to purchase "Cedulas de Inversión" (Investment Certificates) from the Treasury at below-market rates. The MOF used the proceeds from their sale to finance lending by public banks. In effect, this measure replaced state funding of public banks, thereby eliminating a large budgetary item, while creating a new pool of funds to meet the growing demands for preferential credit.[131] Savings banks were required to purchase securities issued by state-run enterprises at below-market rates; this also reduced the government's direct budgetary expenditures.

An estimate of government revenue generated by financial restriction in this period reveals that it was lower than the average that Giovannini and Melo found for the twenty-four countries in their study, but still substantial.[132] ARs generated cost savings equal to 1.0 percent of GDP and 7.4 percent of government revenue in 1971.[133] Meanwhile, obligatory bank lending to the public banking system through Investment Certificates represented a cost saving for the government equivalent to 0.9 percent of GDP and 6.9 percent of government revenue in 1970.[134]

The MOF, on the other hand, did not take advantage of RRs immediately. It postponed establishing RRs for banks (except industrial banks) until the early 1970s, mainly because banking interests strongly opposed them. At that time, RRs were not set at excessive levels (5.75 percent) and, thus, did not constitute a blatant attempt to expropriate seignorage. In fact, their implementation was closely tied to their use as an instrument of monetary policy.

The government did not try to maximize seignorage opportunities because it did not feel much urgency to increase revenues. It faced little pressure from its citizenry to expand government spending (until the late 1960s) and no external security threat. Moreover, its leaders believed that keeping government expenditures low was the optimal policy because seeking greater revenues by raising either direct or indirect taxes might be politically costly. Gunther has argued that this led the regime to adopt a strategy of "revenue budgeting."[135] In revenue budgeting, fiscal authorities adjust expenditures to the expected level of revenues to avoid running large budget deficits. In the period from 1952 to 1974, government expenditures were very low by international standards, and the state ran a budget deficit only eight years.[136]

Starting in the late 1970s, Spain's newly elected democratic govern-ments increased efforts to extract revenues from the banking system through both ARs and RRs; this came in response to the need to finance large budget deficits caused by rapidly growing expenditures and the con-tinuing difficulty in raising revenue by more efficient means (such as direct taxation) during the early period of Spain's democratic transition. This change in policy is discussed in chapter 7.

Conclusion

Financial restriction in Spain had its roots in the nineteenth century. State officials shaped the financial sector around the need to fund government activities and state-backed projects in the private sector. The Franco regime further repressed the financial system upon taking power. It adopted policies that encouraged the consolidation of an oligopolistic financial sector dominated by large national banks. The regime sup-pressed bond and equity markets and closed off the Spanish economy from international capital markets. Finally, it established strict interest rate controls. These policies reduced financial efficiency and hurt eco-nomic performance.

This regulatory environment reflected the strong bargaining power of the banking sector. Interest rate and entry controls limited competition and risk, allowing established banks to dominate financial markets and earn high, risk-free profits. The regime also permitted banks to secure great leverage over industry by authorizing them to purchase equity in firms and obtain representation on their boards of directors. In Spain, the promotion of a bank-based financial system under close government supervision did not provide important economic and political advantages. Although such systems have been beneficial in some countries, in Spain it concentrated economic power in the hands of a banking cartel that failed to manage industrial firms wisely, led to financial instability and inefficient allocation of credit, and created moral hazard problems among firms.

A change in the orientation and makeup of the regime in the late 1950s led to a transformation of financial regulation. Regime officials gradually implemented financial controls that were used to advance their private interests. By the mid-1960s, interest rate and credit controls enabled officials to distribute financial benefits to select groups and shift the cost of providing subsidized credit onto the banking system. Policy-makers established mechanisms for extracting seignorage from the finan-cial sector, although they did not take full advantage of them until pres-sures on government spending demanded it. Although these new controls imposed costs on banks, they continued to support the regulatory regime because they still benefited from most of its elements (e.g., entry and interest rate controls).

The odds of a major change in Spanish financial policy seemed remote in the 1960s. Powerful interests stood ready to oppose attempts to alter the regulatory status quo, and few actors appeared interested in deregulating markets. Nevertheless, the government soon launched a set of reforms aimed at liberalizing the financial system. I analyze the forces that sparked deregulation and the political economy of the reform process in the following four chapters.

CHAPTER 4

The Origins of Financial Liberalization in Spain

Financial Deregulation in Spain: An Overview

The Spanish government initiated the process of financial liberalization in 1969. Progress toward liberalization has been episodic. Major financial reforms have been followed by periods in which the deregulation process has stalled. Moreover, at times the government has reduced its control over financial markets in some ways (e.g., by deregulating interest rates) while it has deepened its intervention in others (e.g., by increasing taxation of the banking system).

Public officials, not private actors, provided the impetus for financial deregulation in Spain. Private actors active in financial policy strongly opposed liberalization. In particular, banks, which have led deregulation efforts in advanced industrial countries, aggressively lobbied against most reforms; only in the late 1980s did banks accept (though not embrace) deregulation. Private groups that stood to benefit from deregulation, notably savers and firms rationed out of credit markets, were not organized and did not apply pressure on the government to alter financial policy. In sum, the impetus for deregulation did not result from a change in the preferences of restriction's private sector beneficiaries or the net balance of interest group demands on policymakers, as the economic theory might predict.

The strongest advocates of financial reform were MOF and BOS officials. They had an interest in liberalization because they had to manage the serious economic problems that restriction created, notably financial inefficiency and lack of monetary control. Political leaders retained control over financial policy, however, so these officials could not deregulate financial markets until political leaders were willing to give up the political advantages of restriction for better economic performance. In addition, financial policymakers faced challenges from other public officials who opposed many aspects of deregulation.

I argue that deregulation occurred in Spain when political leaders determined that it was politically advantageous to seek the greater efficiency that a market-based financial system promised. The specific concerns that created interest in better economic performance varied across time, but they all centered on the goal of generating political support. In the Franco era, a swell in political dissent in the late 1960s sparked interest in financial reform among regime leaders. They decided to permit the MOF to pursue limited structural reforms aimed at increasing economic efficiency and growth as well as lowering inflation. They hoped that rising standards of living and stable prices would reduce hostility toward the regime and eliminate a potential basis of support for opposition groups. Later, Spain's transition to democracy ushered in a competitive political environment that pushed national leaders to improve economic performance in order to secure broad-based electoral support; in the realm of financial policy, this encouraged them to liberalize financial markets. Of course, other variables—notably economic conditions and Spain's entry into the EC—have also had a major impact on the evolution of financial regulation; I discuss these factors in detail in the chapters that follow.

Analytically, the differences between my explanation of Spanish financial reform and one based on the "public interest" perspective are obvious. In the public interest view, leaders pursued financial liberalization to improve social welfare, the ultimate goal of policy, when it became evident it was the optimal strategy. I contend, on the other hand, that they deregulated markets when political conditions made providing for the public interest the best means of retaining power and generating revenue. Nevertheless, as both explanations suggest that Spanish politicians sought deregulation to advance collective interests, albeit for different reasons, the task of determining empirically which is superior is challenging.

Although the data are somewhat consistent with both interpretations, a close reading of the evidence suggests that political, not economic, factors determined the timing and pace of reforms. In the 1960s, some (but not all) technocrats wished to reform the financial system, but could not do so—even as Spain experienced worsening economic problems—until their political superiors decided that deregulation was in their interest. In the 1970s and 1980s, the liberalization process stalled several times (most notably, in 1975–76 and 1979–80) despite an increasingly evident need to reform; political events (e.g., Franco's death and subsequent political uncertainty) best explain this pattern. The evolution of the scope of the reforms also suggests that political calculations underlay the liberalization process. Policymakers delayed dismantling selective credit policies and reducing taxation of the banking system, even though these steps were obviously necessary, because politicians initially did not support those measures. In sum, the calculations of political leaders, not economic conditions or beliefs about financial policy, dictated the course of financial policy.

It deserves noting that personnel changes at the top level of government agencies conducting financial policy often coincided with major innovations in Spanish financial regulation. In particular, major policy shifts occurred with the entrance and exit of Barrera (1973, 1974); Fuentes Quintana (1977, 1978); Abril Martorell (1978, 1980); and García Díez (1980, 1982); these episodes are discussed below. One reason for this is that each minister brought a different agenda and set of ideas with him into office. The importance of shifts in personnel in explaining the course of financial policy should not be exaggerated, however. New ministerial appointments were usually made by the Franco inner circle, or later, the leaders of the parties that formed governments after Spain's transition to democracy, in response to changes in their political strategies; new ministers secured their posts because their views were consistent with the plans of their political superiors. This is not to deny that ministers might have influenced the beliefs of political leaders; rather, it indicates that policy output was generally consistent with the preferences of leaders. Clearly, regulatory policy did not simply reflect the product of negotiations between technocratic policymakers and the intermediaries they oversaw, as some scholars have contended.[1]

Overall, Spanish financial reforms have largely followed the course recommended by economists who advocate liberalization as a remedy to restriction. The pace of the reforms has also been largely appropriate given Spain's frequent macroeconomic troubles. The key elements in the liberalization strategy have been as follows:

1. Interest rate liberalization
2. The elimination of selective credit policies
3. The bid to improve the efficiency of financial intermediation by increasing competition in financial markets
4. Efforts to expand and deepen bond and equity markets
5. Attempts to improve prudential regulation of intermediaries
6. Reduction of taxation of the banking system and implementation of more orthodox fiscal policies

As I examine the evolution of Spanish financial policy in detail, I analyze why political leaders sought deregulation, why policymakers concentrated on the policy objectives just cited and not others, the measures they chose to achieve them, the controversies reforms generated, the stances of major private and public actors on the liberalization process, and the factors that determined the success or failure of the various reforms.

The ultimate aims of deregulation were to improve financial efficiency and monetary control. Policymakers were convinced that they could attain these goals only if they succeeded in reducing the dominance of the banking system by large national banks and creating deeper, more diversified financial markets. In their efforts to break up the bank oligopoly, policymakers liberalized interest rates; promoted new intermediaries and bond and equity markets; eliminated differences among intermediaries, moving toward a universal banking model; and improved prudential regulation and supervision of banks. This program closely matched the recommendations of economists who have researched how to best liberalize financial markets under conditions of oligopoly.[2] It took time for these policies to have their intended impact; banks lost market share only slowly, and their financial margins and profits remained high until the 1990s. This outcome is not surprising, since deregulation under conditions of oligopoly is exceedingly difficult and has yielded similar results in other countries.[3] Still, as chapter 7 details, these policies eventually achieved their intended impact in Spain.[4]

Financial policymakers had to temper their liberalizing reforms out of an awareness that they could not run roughshod over banks. The large national banks in particular wielded great economic power, and the state needed their cooperation to carry out economic modernization. As a result, even while determinedly seeking reform, policymakers sometimes made important concessions to banking interests and the reform process clearly took on a negotiated character.

It is possible to identify three major periods in the liberalization process. The first, 1969–76, occurred during the twilight of the Franco regime. Policymakers initiated financial liberalization after regime leaders decided that they needed to sustain rapid economic growth to keep their hold on power. It is significant that Spain began to liberalize its financial markets before the global wave of financial deregulation in the early 1980s. This indicates that Spain's financial reforms were not simply a response to the same international events or diffusion of ideas that some scholars have argued motivated financial reform in a variety of countries but had more to do with indigenous economic and political factors. The second period, 1977–82, took place during Spain's transition from an authoritarian to a democratic regime. Government officials undertook major financial reforms in this period, but progress toward a more market-based system was hampered by the strong opposition of social and state actors and the development of severe crises in both the real and financial sectors. The third, 1982–90, saw the rise to power of the PSOE, the Spanish Socialist Party. The Socialists implemented the most far-reaching reforms in the period of study and have largely completed the move toward a market-based financial system. This chapter examines the first of these three periods.

The Initial Moves toward Financial Liberalization

The late 1960s and early 1970s were an important era in Spanish financial policy. The government took the first steps toward liberalizing interest rates, implemented policies that increased competition among intermediaries, and began to follow an active monetary policy based on the control of monetary aggregates. The reforms implemented in this period were relatively minor (except in the case of monetary policy), but they laid the foundation for future changes in financial policy. This section begins by demonstrating why an analytical focus on private actors cannot account for the changes in Spanish financial policy. Then, it examines why the Franco regime sought limited deregulation and identifies the public officials who advocated and opposed financial reform. The second half of the chapter analyzes the evolution of financial policy in this period in detail.

Private Actors and Financial Policy

Private actors did not provide the impetus for financial deregulation in this period. The social actors most active in financial policy-making—namely, banks and firms targeted by selective credit policies—strongly opposed liberalization. The Big Seven banks were the most vigorous opponents of any changes in the financial status quo; they enjoyed influence over financial policy because they were well organized and had both informal and official channels of access to government officials.[5] They had good reasons to oppose reforms. Existing entry and interest rate controls along with policies that suppressed direct markets continued to make the restricted system very comfortable for them. Although Spain experienced the economic events that have stimulated banks in other countries to press for deregulation (e.g., high inflation), these did not pose a major threat to Spanish banks because they faced few real competitors. As a result, profits remained strong, with return on equity capital averaging about 13 percent in the early 1970s.[6] As table 4.1 indicates, Spanish bank profits (expressed as a percentage of volume of business) were very high by international standards.

Groups possessing a potential interest in deregulation played virtually no part in financial policy-making (with the exception of savings banks[7]) because they were poorly organized.[8] The collective action problems savers and firms rationed out of credit markets typically face in organizing to influence financial policy were accentuated in Spain. The corporatist system that the Franco regime imposed upon Spanish society (discussed in chap. 3) impeded interest aggregation. In theory, social actors seeking to influence economic policy could only express their demands through the corporatist apparatus maintained by the state. At their peak, the corporatist syndicates were fairly effective at direct lobbying of the government on behalf of individual firms, but they "did not play a particularly useful role in aggregating a unified policy position for their clientele, or participating in the design of measures or objectives of the economy as a whole."[9] In practice, the regime tolerated attempts by firms to gain direct, informal access to government decision makers as long as they did it on an ad hoc basis to solve specific problems, not to shape general economic policy. Only the most powerful private actors, such as large industrial firms, consistently enjoyed close ties to state officials and exercised any influence on broad policies.

Spanish corporatism impeded the emergence of coalitions that bridged sectoral lines in particular. In the case of financial policy, this

TABLE 4.1.   Financial Margins in OECD Countries, 1970 (expressed as ratios to volume of business)

	Interest Margin	Gross Earnings Margin[b]	Profit before Tax[c]
Australia	n/a	4.77	1.00
Austria	2.13	3.15	1.10
Belgium	1.44	3.68	0.54
Canada	n/a	3.49	1.14
Denmark	4.65	5.21	1.63
Finland	1.90	2.96	0.59
France	n/a	4.16	0.39
Germany	1.88	2.13	0.49
Greece	2.16	3.76	0.73
Italy	2.72	3.34	0.82
Netherlands	2.42	3.72	0.89
Norway	2.97	4.06	0.96
Spain	2.73	4.44	1.63
Sweden	2.19	2.92	0.52
Switzerland	0.73	2.08	0.70
United States	3.19	3.83	0.89
Yugoslavia	1.94	2.35	1.60

Source: Compiled from Revell 1980, tables 3.1, 3.2, and 3.3.
n/a = not available
[a]Interest Margin = Interest Received – Interest Paid
[b]Gross Earnings Margin = Interest Margin + Other Income
[c]Profit before Tax = Gross Earnings Margin – Operating Costs + Other Credits (net)

made it difficult for firms from different sectors to identify their common interest in deregulation and organize to press for reform. Indeed, since the corporatist system encouraged sectoral identification, it gave firms an incentive to lobby the state to increase the flow of subsidized credit to their sector rather than to dismantle financial controls.

The Origins of Financial Reform within the State

The Franco regime initiated financial deregulation in the late 1960s because it confronted a new set of economic and political constraints that decreased the attractiveness of restriction. First, the economic problems associated with existing financial and monetary policies increased, making it more costly to maintain a restricted financial system. Second, the inner circle began to value greater economic efficiency and growth more highly for political reasons. MOF and BOS officials who were advocates of structural reform took advantage of the inner circle's interest in better performance to pursue a more market-based financial system, which they viewed as essential to improving the economy's long-term prospects.

The economic costs attributable to prevailing financial and monetary policies were becoming increasingly hard to ignore by the late 1960s. There were two primary problems. First, Spain was experiencing persistent inflation primarily due to steady increases in the money supply. Concern over monetary policy was especially great in 1969, and again in 1971–73, when authorities had difficulty containing money supply growth generated by sharp rises in bank lending and capital inflows. MOF and BOS officials wanted to substitute a more "activist" stance based on control of monetary aggregates for the traditional accommodative one. This led them to advocate financial liberalization, since targeting monetary aggregates required the elimination of many financial controls, especially interest rate controls.[10]

Second, inefficiencies in the financial sector threatened to make it difficult for the Spanish economy to continue to enjoy sustained growth, especially in light of changing international economic conditions. Studies by Spanish economists and various international organizations, particularly the OECD, published in the 1960s, and a major financial/political scandal, the Matesa Affair, helped to raise awareness of restriction's inefficiencies.[11] Critics of Spanish financial policy had three basic concerns. First, they claimed that the artificially low cost of capital was encouraging firms to adopt overly capital-intense modes of production.[12] Second, they argued that administrative (as opposed to market) allocation of credit was not distributing available resources efficiently. Government credit programs seemed to be tying up available funds in sectors where the return on capital was low, leaving potentially dynamic sectors with inadequate funding.[13] Third, they pointed out the high costs involved in permitting the lack of competition among financial intermediaries to persist. As table 4.1 indicates, financial margins in Spain in the 1970s were higher than those in other OECD countries.[14] High financial margins reduced the volume of funds received by the real sector and, hence, limited investment.

Although the costs associated with restriction rose in the late 1960s, a desire to reduce inefficiency by itself cannot account for the government's decision to initiate liberalization. Inefficiency had been a perennial problem in the Spanish financial system; therefore, it alone cannot explain why policymakers began the deregulation process at that particular moment in time. Indeed, previous economic slowdowns (e.g., in 1965–66) had not resulted in efforts to implement financial reforms.

Moreover, liberalization was not an inevitable response to mounting inefficiency. The regime could have chosen to work strictly within the interventionist apparatus it had created over the years; in fact, policymakers had dealt with economic problems in the past by tinkering with rather than eliminating financial controls (e.g., in 1962), mainly because the regime's leaders opposed deregulation. Exposure to economic doctrine promoting a market-based financial system helped to shape the content of the reforms, but it was not a decisive factor. Starting as far back as the late 1950s, international agencies and leading Spanish economists had repeatedly told policymakers that Spain's financial system was inefficient and should be reformed along more market-oriented lines, and their commentary had found sympathetic ears within the MOF, BOS, and MOC.[15] Many policymakers in these organizations, especially younger technocrats, believed that some deregulation was necessary and had occasionally advocated liberalizing reforms. They were only able to act on their ideas, however, when their political superiors decided that a change in financial policy was politically valuable. In sum, new ideas played only a permissive role in the reform process.

The timing of financial deregulation is best explained by the Franco regime's heightened interest in achieving greater efficiency in order to sustain rapid growth. This interest was aroused by concern over mounting social unrest, especially among workers, fueled in part by dissatisfaction with the distributional effects of economic policy. Regime leaders believed that sustained strong growth was the key to defusing political opposition to the regime. Prosperity would create a depoliticized populace willing to accept an increased standard of living in lieu of political liberties.[16] They decided to permit financial policymakers to implement some deregulatory reforms when they became convinced that they were necessary to improve economic performance. Signs that growth was slowing and that existing economic institutions, particularly the financial system, were not operating efficiently acted as a catalyst for reform efforts.

The clearest manifestation of political and social unrest was a dramatic increase in strike activity starting in 1967; moreover, the strikes themselves became increasingly politicized in this period.[17] The upturn in labor unrest occurred even though strikes were illegal and workers faced the possibility of dismissal and arrest. One particularly significant incident saw one hundred thousand workers demonstrate against the high cost of living in Madrid.[18] Student protests against the regime, also partly motivated by disillusionment with economic policy, increased sharply in this period as well.[19] Finally, the Catholic Church, a traditional supporter of the regime, began to clamor publicly for economic justice and greater political freedom.[20]

Growing social unrest emboldened clandestine political movements to step up their efforts to organize social groups dissatisfied with the regime, although most of their activities were moderate and restrained.[21] In the most highly publicized action, 131 of the leaders of the semilegal and illegal opposition presented Franco with an open letter demanding democratic reforms in December 1969. The letter greatly embarrassed the regime throughout Europe at a time when Spain was again seeking entry into the EC.

Protestors were largely correct in their assessment of the distributive effects of government policy. Although Spain experienced rapid growth in the 1960s, the distribution of national income remained inequitable. "Between 1960 and 1970 there was practically no change in the distribution of disposable income. If anything, disparities widened and, while the numbers of very poor households diminished, those with high levels of income tended to increase."[22] Wages and salaries as a percentage of GNP rose only slowly, from 41 percent in 1960 to 43 percent in 1970, a figure well below the average in other OECD countries.[23] Moreover, "most Spanish workers still worked ten hours a day and often engaged in overtime work or had a second job."[24] Finally, the level of social services, particularly housing, educational, and medical facilities, remained very poor.

Although it did not threaten the regime's immediate stability, this dissent deeply preoccupied some of its leaders. It led Carrero and the Opus Dei technocrats to reassert their position, one they had maintained since the late 1950s, that the regime's long-term legitimacy was best secured by sustaining rapid economic growth that would have trickle-down effects.[25] The technocrats pushed specifically for further and more rapid economic modernization, achieved through increased (but still cautious) reliance on market forces and greater incorporation into the world economy. In the last regard, they hoped to secure Spain's admission into the EC. These policies would raise standards of living and reduce hostility toward the regime, eliminating a potential basis of support for opposition groups. Finally, they recommended superficial political reforms to reduce the pressure for a fundamental change in political institutions.

It is important to note that the technocrats could not consider policies aimed explicitly at redistributing income or wealth as part of their overall strategy of achieving economic and political stability. Franco and other members of the inner circle had always made it clear that redistribution, whether through tax reform or greatly expanded government services, was politically unacceptable because it would alienate the regime's core constituents. By default, the technocrats had to hope that the trickle-down effects from rapid sustained growth would be sufficient to mollify those beginning to oppose the regime.

Other public officials, particularly those with ties to the military and Falange, contended that the regime should restore the hard-line policies of the immediate post–Civil War period to deal with the problems facing the regime.[26] They opposed political liberalization and urged a return to the strictly controlled economy of the 1940s and early 1950s. They asserted that the regime could best deal with the growing protest movement through the use of strong-arm tactics. Carrero did not entirely disagree with this last stance; he had long advocated a policy of repressing the opposition that economic progress did not quell.

Carrero ultimately prevailed in the internal battle over strategy because of his great personal influence with Franco and astute handling of the infamous Matesa Affair. The Matesa Affair was the greatest financial and political scandal of the Franco years.[27] The affair got its name from the firm implicated in the scandal, the Spanish multinational firm, Maquinaria Textil, S.A. (commonly known as Matesa). In the mid-1960s, Matesa's director, Vilá Reyes, misrepresented the number of foreign orders for his firm's new mechanical loom in order to obtain additional export credits from one of Spain's public banks, the Banco de Crédito Industrial (BCI).[28] The director general of Spanish customs, a Falangist associated with the Movimiento, discovered and denounced the irregularities in the summer of 1969. Although this type of fraud was not new, it quickly turned into a major scandal because of the size of the loans and because Vilá Reyes had close ties to several of the Opus Dei technocrats. The Falangists wasted little time in implying Opus Dei complicity in the incident in an attempt to discredit their archenemies and prompt a reorganization of the Council of Ministers.[29]

This tactic backfired. The incumbent ministers of finance and commerce, both with Opus Dei ties, were forced out of their posts, but the new Council of Ministers announced in October actually represented a swing in favor of the Opus Dei technocrats. In fact, political observers labeled the new government the "monocolor government" because many of the new ministers were associated with either Opus Dei or the Asociación Católica Nacional de Propaganda.[30] The new cabinet was chosen by Carrero and reflected his preferences.[31] Carrero had become vice president of the government in 1967 and taken charge of its day-to-day management. In early 1969, Franco had decided to allow Carrero to make most key appointments within the government because his failing health had sapped his vitality. In selecting the new cabinet, Carrero broke with Franco's traditional practice of seeking a rough balance of power among all the major political families making up the regime. Instead, he used the reorganization as an opportunity to banish his political enemies (the Falangists) and surround himself with his allies (the Opus Dei technocrats).

Although Carrero prevailed and had his economic team in place, the debate on basic political and economic strategy persisted within the regime. Hard-line elements stepped up their demands for strong-arm tactics to control protesting workers and crush the political opposition and regional separatists. The regime, in fact, unleashed a violent wave of repression starting in late 1969 that was widely criticized abroad.[32] It did not, however, return to the extensive state control of the economy that had characterized the 1940s and 1950s, as the hard-liners urged.

MOF and BOS officials took advantage of the regime's greater concern with efficiency and growth to begin financial reform. They viewed a more market-based financial system as critical to improving the performance of the economy.[33] In particular, they viewed the removal of some interest rate controls and the rationalization of others as necessary to permit a more active monetary policy, the top priority of financial and monetary policymakers at the time. Interest rate reform would also promote greater financial efficiency by increasing competition in the banking system and boosting savings. Financial reformers did not touch selective credit policies because they recognized they were simply too valuable to political leaders. In addition, the influential PC and its head, López Rodó, remained firmly in favor of credit controls. In supporting limited financial deregulation, regime leaders calculated that the political benefits of better economic performance were worth the risk of estranging the banking sector.

A decrease in the relative bargaining power of the banking sector gave the MOF sufficient autonomy to implement the controversial financial reforms. By the mid-1960s, banks had fallen somewhat out of favor with the Franquist inner circle. Franco himself had grown suspicious of the large national banks and was concerned that too much economic power had become concentrated in the banking sector.[34] In addition, the banking system came under attack by academics and the popular press in this period. Several widely read books and articles warned that the large national banks had gained control over the economy because of their domination of financial markets and close ties to industry.[35] This literature had a strong impact on leaders and the general public, who became increasingly distrustful of and hostile toward the national banks.

The relative autonomy of financial policymakers was evident in that reformers in other areas encountered serious social opposition and were unable to carry out their initiatives as effectively. Efforts to implement a more liberal commercial policy, for example, met with strident opposition from import-competing groups. Of course, some structural reforms (e.g., the introduction of collective bargaining or major tax reform) were still strictly off-limits to policymakers. Ministers who dared to attempt significant reforms in these areas quickly found themselves out of office.[36]

Divisions on Financial Policy within the Franquist State

Support for financial reform within the Franquist regime was not universal. A debate over financial policy emerged that tied into a broader controversy over the proper role of the state in the economy. Liberalization proponents confronted a long tradition of active government management of the economy. Although state intervention had reached its peak in the immediate post–Civil War period, many public officials, including some among the top political leadership, remained convinced that a greater reliance on market forces was unwise. Moreover, they relished the discretionary power that heavy involvement in the economy provided them. These officials were anxious to retain the political benefits of government regulation of markets and skeptical of the advantages to be obtained from removing financial controls.

The primary proponents of financial deregulation were officials at the BOS, MOF, and MOC. As their political superiors developed an interest in promoting economic efficiency, they gained influence because of their expertise and were able to implement some of their policy preferences. BOS officials were the most consistent advocates of liberalization in the 1960s and 1970s, but they had little formal authority over monetary and financial policy. This authority rested in the hands of MOF officials, and they carefully reserved all important decisions for themselves. Nevertheless, the BOS played an important role in policy-making because of its superior competence in monetary and financial affairs. The BOS's research department was staffed by the leading young economists in Spain, attracted there by Mariano Navarro Rubio (governor during much of the 1960s), who realized that expertise was the BOS's best means of influencing policy; many of these officials became central figures in reform efforts in the 1970s and 1980s.[37] The BOS also possessed the best economic data in Spain, which it jealously guarded from other actors.[38]

High-ranking MOF officials, especially after 1969, also generally supported financial liberalization, but their stance was more ambivalent. These officials had to attend to a number of (often conflicting) objectives at once and, sometimes, mediate between feuding departments. Occasionally, this was reflected in reversals on issues or a delay in reforms. For example, the objective of the General Directorate for Financial Policy of removing interest rate controls provoked strong opposition from the Treasury when this policy threatened to increase the cost of financing budget deficits. This conflict contributed to the MOF's decision to proceed incrementally and slowly with interest rate reform. As already noted, the MOF was also more prone to pressure by private groups opposed to reform, like national banks and big business.

Policymakers from a few other economic ministries, notably the MOC, also supported financial deregulation.[39] In the late 1960s, a coalition favoring a more market-based financial system developed among these officials. The "Committee of Experts," an interdepartmental group consisting of representatives from the BOS, MOF, MOC, and PC, was the most salient manifestation of this coalition.[40] This committee was officially established to carry out econometric studies of the Spanish economy, but it soon became the center of bureaucratic efforts to reform the economy along more market-oriented lines.

Proponents of deregulation faced resistance from other public officials, especially with respect to interest rate deregulation (the most contentious financial policy issue until the mid-1970s). Officials in the ministries of Industry and Agriculture were particularly outspoken critics. They opposed interest rate reform on the grounds that it would raise the cost of credit and, thereby, hurt the growth of industry and agriculture. Their postures differed in one important respect, however. Ministry of Agriculture officials lobbied vigorously against any interest rate liberalization. They contended that removing interest rate controls when the prices of agricultural products were still fixed would place an intolerable burden on already disadvantaged producers. Ministry of Industry officials, on the other hand, viewed liberalization as inevitable, and, to a certain extent, as desirable in the long term, since it would increase the flow of credit to potentially productive firms. They opposed reform in order to appease an important constituency, industrial firms that disliked any measures that might increase the cost of credit.

Officials in the ministries of Industry and Agriculture skillfully exploited the inner circle's fears that an increase in the cost of credit could

provoke an economic slowdown that might unravel the increasingly fragile coalition of social actors supporting the regime.[41] Their arguments did
not stop the financial reform process but did persuade regime leaders to
insist upon a cautious, gradual approach.

The Evolution of Financial Policy, 1969–77

Implementing an Active Monetary Policy

MOF and BOS officials made implementing an active monetary policy
their top priority once they had the green light to undertake limited structural reforms because of their increasing inability to manage money supply
growth. The desire to adopt a new monetary policy was the primary factor
that generated a strong interest in deregulation among financial policymakers in the late 1960s, and initial reforms were designed to accomplish
this goal.

In 1969, the Spanish economy was finally starting to recover from a
recession that had lasted two years. In the summer, monetary authorities
began to fear that the economy was "overheating," as bank credit to the
private sector had risen abruptly. In addition, Spain faced a rising balance-
of-payments deficit. They decided to limit bank credit growth to 18 percent that year to curtail demand and stave off inflationary pressures. To
this end, the MOF instructed the BOS to cut back ordinary rediscount
lines and raise its discount rate from 5 to 6 percent. These measures were
only partially effective. Banks were unwilling to reduce credit to the private sector; they turned to the SRLs, over which the BOS had no control,
to obtain funds.[42] Confronted with continued excess liquidity, the MOF
took more drastic steps to reduce the money supply at the end of the year,
notably imposing quantitative restrictions on bank credit. These measures
succeeded in limiting credit growth, but their effect was overly harsh,
throwing the economy into another recession that lasted well into 1970.

The events of 1969 marked a turning point in the evolution of Spanish monetary and financial policy. Monetary authorities became more
determined than ever to design a better means of controlling the money
supply. They ruled out attempts to refine direct administrative controls,
since it had become painfully obvious that they were inadequate.[43]
Instead, they sought to establish orthodox instruments of monetary control, namely, an effective discount rate policy and RRs, and to eliminate
money creation through the SRLs.

The first steps in monetary and financial reform occurred in 1969 in
the form of four ministerial orders concerning interest rate controls.
Although issued by the MOF, the reforms were formulated by the afore-

mentioned Committee of Experts. The new regulations established a basic discount rate and linked all other interest rates (e.g., short-term deposit and loan rates) to it via differential margins. Previously, there had been no direct connection between the various rates, so that when the BOS had altered its discount rate there had been little effect on loan rates (and, hence, on the volume of bank lending). Policymakers hoped the new interest rate structure would reduce market segmentation and, thus, provide the BOS with the ability to use the discount rate strategically.

The ministerial orders also deregulated some interest rates. First, they removed all interest rate controls on interbank operations to promote the development of an efficient interbank market. Second, they liberalized loan rates for maturities of three years or more to encourage intermediaries to increase their supply of long-term credit to the private sector.[44] This objective also motivated the decision to lift ceilings on deposits of two years or more at industrial banks. Industrial banks, originally envisioned as major suppliers of long-term credit, had found it very difficult to attract deposits; consequently, they had shown limited effectiveness in this role. The new regulation sought to increase their share of total deposits.

MOF officials had initially hoped to remove ceilings on long-term deposits at universal banks as well. They retreated on this issue, however, in the face of opposition from banks, firms, and the ministries of Agriculture and Industry. Banks fought the removal of deposit rate ceilings because they feared it would spark price competition for liabilities. Already upset by the removal of controls on long-term loan rates, firms also resisted the measure. They argued that an increase in the cost of liabilities due to the removal of deposit rate ceilings would raise their cost of credit even further. Officials in the ministries of Industry and Agriculture shared this concern and expressed their opposition to the reform in the Council of Ministers. The combined resistance of these groups was so intense that financial policymakers had to postpone further interest rate liberalization for several years.

The MOF instituted RRs for universal banks in December 1970. Although the authorizing legislation had been available since 1962, only industrial banks, whose default risk was perceived to be substantially greater, had faced RRs up to then. The MOF had not imposed RRs on commercial and universal banks because of their opposition. The decision to extend RRs to these banks in the early 1970s showed policymakers' growing willingness and ability to challenge the banking sector. RRs were extended to savings banks in 1972 and to all other intermediaries in following years.[45]

The MOF succeeded in eliminating the SRLs in 1971. In its place, it created "investment coefficients" (ICs), which required intermediaries to invest a percentage of their total liabilities in "public funds" (e.g., public debt) and specified industrial sectors.[46] The stipulation to invest in public funds was not new, since banks had faced this requirement since 1962; authorities now merely included this obligation in the newly created ICs. The requirement to lend to designated industrial sectors was a major change. The sectors favored by the new policy were precisely those that had benefited from the SRLs. Thus, whereas previously the BOS had borne the cost of subsidizing these privileged sectors, now banks were forced to assume it.

The BOS led the initiative to dismantle the SRLs. The existence of the SRLs had made it almost impossible for the BOS to control money creation by the banking sector. Therefore, their abolition was deemed essential for implementing a more active monetary policy. The BOS also had a purely pecuniary motive for wishing to eliminate the SRLs. The opportunity costs of having to rediscount paper presented by banks (instead of using these resources to acquire other assets) were high and had a negative impact on the BOS's balance sheet. The MOF found both of these reasons compelling and supported the BOS's initiative to shift the burden of funding priority sectors to the banks.

Banks did not like the new ICs but did not mount a major challenge against them. First, they believed they would be able to increase the cost of long-term loans (whose interest rates were no longer state-controlled) sufficiently to recover the losses imposed by the ICs. Second, banks respected the implicit bargain under which they tolerated some unfavorable measures in exchange for generally advantageous financial policy. In fact, the MOF rewarded banks for their acquiescence on this specific matter. In the past, it had been usual practice to compensate banks for policies that imposed costs on them, typically by widening margins between administratively controlled loan and deposit interest rates.[47] It was not coincidence, therefore, that the MOF lowered deposit ceilings (while most loan ceilings remained unchanged) soon after the ICs were put into effect.

Accelerating inflation in the years 1971–73 consolidated the movement toward a more active monetary policy. Inflation reached 14 percent in 1973, almost double the average for the last fifteen years (7.8 percent). As in some other OECD countries, high inflation was partly due to rapid growth in high-powered money caused by sizable capital inflows; an exchange rate that undervalued the domestic currency vis-à-vis the U.S. dollar stimulated these inflows.[48] Monetary authorities attempted to sterilize the rapid increase in foreign reserves, but they quickly realized that existing instruments for influencing the money stock were inadequate.

The definitive change in Spanish monetary policy occurred in late 1973 when the BOS adopted official targets for growth in the principal money aggregate, *disponibilidades líquidas* (the equivalent of the U.S. M3 measure). Authorities decided to manage the money stock by targeting the evolution of bank reserves. In practice, the BOS controlled the level of bank reserves through RRs and its net lending to the banking sector. On a day-to-day basis, the BOS drained liquidity by selling Treasury bonds to banks or injected it by granting credits to banks through an instrument called *préstamos de regulación monetaria* (monetary regulation loans). Once the BOS determined its total daily net intervention in credit markets, it offered each bank a share of the total fixed in proportion to its share of total deposits, a policy that greatly favored the large national banks. The BOS kept interest rates on monetary regulation loans well below interbank market rates, thereby making the loans extremely attractive. "Giving an assured profit margin to banks . . . was the price paid for achieving quantitative control of bank reserves."[49]

A key point here is that "the burden of short-run adjustments imposed by monetary control fell, via changes in the BOS's net lending to banks, upon bank lending to the private sector."[50] Consequently, adopting a restrictive monetary stance was politically costly for leaders because firms encountered an immediate drop in the availability of credit. This feature of Spanish monetary policy was largely responsible for the stiff opposition mounted by firms and banks throughout the 1970s and 1980s toward the use of a tighter monetary policy to slow inflation.

Other Financial Reforms, 1971–74

Reform of the Public Banking System
In addition to its macropolitical effects, the Matesa Affair focused attention on the problems of the public banking system and provided a major impetus to reform it. First, critics noted that current practice required some public banks to supply credit to sectors in which they had little expertise. The BCI, for instance, had no experience in providing export credits and did not have the organizational capabilities to oversee this type of operation. These deficiencies made public banks vulnerable to fraudulent petitions by applicants. Second, critics charged that the public banking system was overly politicized and, thus, did not allocate credit among competing users efficiently. Public banks had little control over the allocation of their lending. If a firm's application met the minimum requirements for obtaining credit established by the relevant ministry, public banks had to grant the loan even if there were factors that made it unadvisable. In practice, some ministries established requirements so that specific firms would get credit or even instructed public banks to provide loans to a firm they wished to favor when it did not meet minimum requirements. In

short, government officials used the public banking system to deliver preferential credit to key constituents.

Recognition of these problems led the regime to overhaul the Spanish public banking system. A major piece of legislation, the Official Credit Act of 1971, was the result of this reform movement. It attempted, with some success, to rationalize the structure of the system and depoliticize its credit allocation process.[51] In addition, authorities slowly brought interest rates on preferential credit more into line with market rates starting in 1971 in order to reduce the credit rents created by selective credit policies.

Interest Rate Reform

Interest rate liberalization took another step forward in 1972. The MOF eliminated maximum commissions for banking services and established minimum commissions in their place. Regulators allowed banks to treat the collection of discounted bills as a service and, thus, to set as high a commission as they wished for this operation. This meant that the interest rate for discounted commercial paper (the most common credit instrument in Spain) was completely liberalized in practice since banks had an easy means of exceeding the administratively stipulated rate for this operation.[52]

The move from maximum to minimum commissions is best understood as a means of carrying out further interest rate liberalization without labeling it as such. MOF officials, aware that business and the ministries of Industry and Agriculture would oppose the removal of additional loan rate ceilings, decided to seek it in a less direct fashion.[53] Firms were undoubtedly aware that the costs of discounting paper had increased; however, several respondents pointed out that banks quoted and calculated commissions in a way that made it difficult for firms to compute the final cost of credit in advance.[54]

The "Barrera Reforms"

The most important financial reforms of the 1969–77 period occurred in the summer of 1974. Their architect was Antonio Barrera de Irimo, the minister of finance who entered office during a minor cabinet reorganization in June 1973. Although he was an ex-banker, and later returned to the private sector, Barrera quickly demonstrated that he was not a point man for banking interests. The political environment of 1974 was very different from that of previous years.[55] The "monocolor government" that had been in place since 1969 was gone, replaced by a government led by Carlos Arias Navarro. It had taken office in January 1974, a few weeks after Carrero's assassination by terrorists in December 1973. Arias had forced the

Opus Dei technocrats out of office and formed a cabinet that "seemed designed to guard the deathwatch of Franco."[56]

Although it rejected political opening, the new government did not oppose limited market-oriented economic reforms. Top regime officials retained their interest in policies aimed at greater efficiency because of continued apprehension over the connection between poor economic performance and social unrest.[57] Franco himself insisted that Barrera, whose interest in economic reform was well known, be retained in his post as minister of finance when Arias formed his cabinet in January 1974.[58] Barrera exacted a price from Arias for his continuance: he chose the ministers of commerce and industry and, thereby, was able to create a coherent economic team.[59]

In early 1974, encouraged by the regime's concern over economic performance and the discredit of development planning, Barrera formulated a comprehensive plan aimed at dismantling the extensive system of state controls over the economy.[60] It called for the implementation of financial reforms in August and a package of "real sector" reforms in October.[61] The MOF, anticipating strong opposition (especially from banks), did not, as was its custom, consult with key private actors before implementing the financial reforms. Instead, it waited until August—when Spain shut down for summer holidays—to submit the reforms to the Council of Ministers, thereby avoiding a major battle over the proposals.[62] In supporting financial reform, regime officials calculated, as they had in 1969, that the political benefits from an improvement in financial performance outweighed the loss of support from the banking sector and firms that might protest an increase in loan interest rates.

The 1974 financial reforms sought to improve financial efficiency and monetary control, which policymakers continued to believe were the keys to achieving better economic performance.[63] The reforms had three basic elements: (1) measures to increase interbank competition; (2) regulations to promote competition among different types of intermediaries; and (3) the liberalization of all long-term interest rates. Policymakers intended the first two elements to prod financial entities to perform their intermediation role more efficiently (i.e., to lower their financial margins). They enacted interest rate liberalization to facilitate monetary control, improve the supply of long-term credit, and further stimulate competition among intermediaries. Unfortunately, policymakers did not implement prudential regulation because they did not realize that increased competition would create insolvency problems in the banking sector; this lack of foresight later proved very costly.[64]

To foster interbank competition, the MOF permitted existing banks to open more offices and made it somewhat easier for new banks to enter the market. This had an immediate and dramatic effect on the number of offices but not on the number of banks. In as little as five years, the number of offices doubled, but few new banks were authorized.[65] Some banks had lobbied for greater freedom to open offices and were initially pleased by the new regulations. As the race to open offices to attract new clients intensified, however, many discovered that their operating costs were increasing sharply.

The belief that any increases in costs from expansion could be passed onto borrowers best explains why some banks initially wished for greater freedom to open new offices. This did turn out to be the case for the sector as a whole, though not necessarily so for individual banks. Table 4.2 indicates that banks recovered the increased operating costs brought on by rapid expansion by widening financial margins.[66] In fact, as column 3 shows, they actually inflated margins over and above the increase in costs. Moreover, bank profits remained stable and very high by international standards.[67] Banks' ability to pass on higher operating costs to clients was a major blow to the government's goal of improving the efficiency of intermediation (as measured by financial margins).

The MOF attempted to foster competition among different intermediaries by reducing differences in the regulatory treatment of universal, industrial, and savings banks, thereby creating "a more level playing field." In fact, the 1974 reforms were a deliberate move back toward universal banking. First, the MOF allowed industrial banks to carry out operations previously reserved for universal banks. Second, it permitted uni-

TABLE 4.2. Banks' Operating Costs, Financial Margins, and Profits as a Percentage of Total Assets, 1970–78

	[1] Operating Costs[a]	[2] Financial Margins[b]	[3] [2] – [1]	[4] Profits before Taxes[c]
1970	2.61	3.79	1.18	1.21
1971	2.57	3.77	1.20	1.18
1972	2.43	3.61	1.18	1.22
1973	2.46	3.70	1.24	1.30
1974	2.55	3.74	1.19	1.29
1975	2.88	4.09	1.21	1.26
1976	3.00	4.29	1.29	1.22
1977	3.33	4.66	1.33	1.03
1978	3.50	4.87	1.37	0.87

Source: Banco de España, "Boletín Estadístico," April 1983.
[a]Operating Costs = Personnel Costs + General Expenses + Taxes + Amortizations
[b]Financial Margin = Average Yield on Loans – Average Costs of Deposits + Commissions
[c]Profits before Taxes = Column 3 + Other Profits – Loan-Loss Provisions

versal and savings banks to issue certificates of deposit, an instrument previously limited to industrial banks. Third, it started to bring the ICs of different intermediaries more into line with each other. The ICs of industrial banks were raised (from 8 to 18 percent), whereas the coefficients of savings banks (which covered 70 percent of their resources as compared to only 22 percent for universal banks) were scheduled for a slow reduction.

MOF officials hoped that these new regulations would enable industrial and savings banks to challenge the dominance of large national banks in obtaining deposits and supplying credit to the private sector. The new playing field, however, did not accomplish this goal, at least in the short run. Figure 4.1 demonstrates that the 1974 reforms had little immediate impact on the respective shares of the most important intermediaries in financing the private sector. Figure 4.2 shows similar results for their respective shares of total deposits. Moreover, as noted earlier, the measures apparently did not prod universal banks to improve their efficiency either.[68]

Several factors help explain the lack of effectiveness of reforms that sought to increase the market share of other intermediaries. First, there was bound to be some delay as intermediaries adjusted to the new opportunities created by the reforms. Second, many firms doubted that other intermediaries could guarantee them adequate lines of credit or provide the same level of service as universal banks. Consequently, they were unwilling to run the risk of severing their relations with a large national bank to obtain slightly more favorable terms from another intermediary.

The 1974 reforms liberalized interest rates for all operations with maturities of two years or more but required intermediaries to use long-term deposits to lend long term. The MOF was under pressure from business to increase the supply of long-term credit, and policymakers hoped that packaging interest rate reform together with this requirement would ease its traditional objection to the removal of interest rate controls. Business reaction to interest rate deregulation was in fact muted. Banks, especially the Big Seven, however, wasted no time in expressing their displeasure but could do little in the wake of the new regulations except try to limit the damage.[69] Their chief strategy was to attempt to curtail price competition for deposits by negotiating "gentlemen's pacts" among themselves. These pacts established informal deposit rate ceilings on long-term liabilities. The results were mixed. In some oligopolistic markets, the threat of a price war is sufficient to enforce a collusive outcome. In this case, however, the emphasis the financial community placed on each bank's "ranking" led a few banks to try to gain market share; the temptation to improve one's ranking by offering higher rates than competitors was simply too great for some bankers to resist.[70]

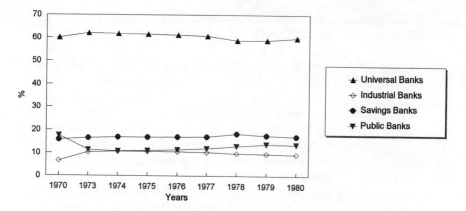

Fig. 4.1.   Share of credit to the private sector by financial intermediary as a percentage of total, 1970–80. (Data from Banco de España, "Boletín Estadístico," April 1983.)

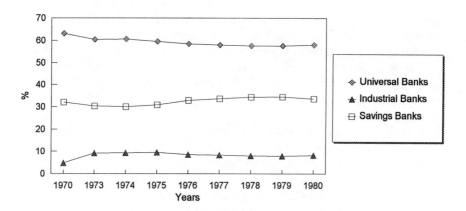

Fig. 4.2.   Share of total deposits by financial intermediary as a percentage of total, 1970–80. (Data from Banco de España, "Boletín Estadístico," April 1983.)

Efforts to reduce state control over credit allocation were conspicuously absent from the reforms. The one regulatory change that decreased state control over credit allocation, the reduction of the coefficients of savings banks, was more than offset by the increase in the ICs of industrial banks and the imposition of the long-term financing requirement. The MOF omitted steps to decrease state control over credit for political reasons. The ministries of Agriculture and Industry would have certainly resisted any measures to dismantle selective credit programs, which would possibly have jeopardized the approval of other financial reforms in the Council of Ministers if such measures had been included in the 1974 package. Of course, the recipients of preferential credit, highly influential political actors, would have also opposed the removal of credit controls. Finally, Spain's political institutions still provided top regime officials with an incentive to maintain the flow of benefits to key supporters, and credit controls were excellent instruments for accomplishing this. As the next chapter shows, this incentive diminished with Spain's transition to democracy.

In summary, the 1974 reforms were not a great success. They did not lead to greater financial efficiency or reduce universal banks' dominance of the financial system. Policymakers did not realize that deregulation under conditions of oligopoly might not lead to greater intermediation efficiency but rather only increase the cost of credit for the nonfinancial sector. Still, it would be wrong to judge the reforms or the officials who instituted them too harshly. Policymakers faced strong opposition from a wide range of actors who sought to maintain the status quo, and they had to overcome traditional suspicion of free-market policies. The reforms were a valiant first effort to overhaul key parts of the financial system, and they served as the foundation for later liberalization efforts.

The Early Transition Years, 1975–77

In contrast to the early 1970s, the period from 1975 to mid-1977 witnessed no major changes in financial policy. The lack of reforms was due to the political crisis brought on by Franco's death.[71] In this period, a fierce struggle, barely contained during Franco's final years, surged within both state and society over whether Spain would remain an authoritarian state or undergo democratization. King Juan Carlos, Franco's handpicked successor, took on the role of head of state upon the dictator's death. The king, despite his ultimate intentions to transform Spain into a democracy, retained the cautious Arias Navarro as president of the government.[72] Not wishing to break with the Franquist status quo, the Arias Navarro government proposed a gradual, meek reformist program intended only to quell escalating political tensions. This strategy, however, was clearly untenable for very long. The opposition, unwilling to accept piecemeal, minor reform, was already trying to force dramatic political change (*ruptura*), while the military and the "Bunker" (ultraconservatives within the regime) stood poised to prevent any real movement toward democracy or perceived breakdown of political and social order. Aware that his policies pleased no one, Arias resigned in July 1976, seemingly leaving Spain on the verge of political and social chaos. Miraculously, the king's new appointment to the presidency, Adolfo Suárez, was able to carry out a series of political reforms that resulted in a successful transition to democracy. The next chapter discusses these reforms.

The uncertainty about the type of political regime that would emerge in Franco's absence led government officials to postpone major initiatives in all policy areas. Political leaders concentrated on managing a complicated political transition, and bureaucrats awaited the outcome of the struggle for control over the state. This cautious, short-term focus was particularly conspicuous in economic policy-making. Politicians were anxious to maintain strong growth and employment, as they feared that an economic slowdown would provoke business and labor at a time when social stability was essential. Consequently, economic policy in this period was expansive, demonstrating the government's unwillingness to address increasingly evident internal and external imbalances in the economy.[73] Indeed, both the Arias Navarro (1974–76) and Suárez (1976–77) governments launched economic programs under the slogan "selective expansion." These programs attempted to boost output in key sectors, such as housing and capital goods, by increasing the flow of preferential credit to them. Political leaders ordered public banks to increase their supply of credit and they raised the ICs of banks (by 1 and 2 percent in 1975 and 1976, respectively).[74] These measures represented a setback for the liberalization process, since they extended state control over available financial resources, and financial policymakers opposed them. Nevertheless, political leaders did not heed persistent calls to reimpose interest rate controls.

The expansionary policies did not include an overly permissive monetary policy. As discussed earlier, the BOS began targeting monetary aggregates in 1973, intending to gradually impose a tighter monetary policy over a period of years. The MOF succeeded in implementing this plan more or less successfully in the transition period despite strong pressure (when credit to the private sector got tight) to increase the money stock.[75] Its ability to do so indicates that by this time the political elite had come to accept the goal of monetary control.

In summary, this period's economic policies reflected the constraints facing political leadership. Leaders did not have an incentive to implement a stabilization program or structural reforms that imposed significant short-term adjustment costs because they were not sure they would reap their long-term benefits. Moreover, with the distinct possibility of *ruptura* ever present, they feared the political and social repercussions of serious economic reforms. Consequently, their policies concentrated on maintaining short-term economic performance.

Conclusion

Public officials provided the impetus for financial liberalization in Spain in the period from 1969 to 1977. Social groups with an interest in liberalization—savers and firms rationed out of credit markets—were too poorly organized to have an impact on financial policy. Those most active in financial policy-making, notably banks, vigorously opposed deregulation. Economic factors that have led banks in other countries to press for deregulation—for example, high inflation and technological change—did not pose a major threat to Spanish banks since there were few other intermediaries to challenge their dominance of the banking system, and the threat of disintermediation from direct markets was insignificant.

The strongest advocates of financial reform were policymakers in the MOF and BOS. Regime leaders allowed them to implement minor financial reforms in the late 1960s and early 1970s because they were concerned with sustaining rapid economic growth and controlling inflationary pressures. They hoped that increased prosperity would defuse mounting political opposition to the regime. By the late 1960s, the costs of maintaining restriction had also increased significantly. The BOS's inability to control the money supply sparked inflation, the lack of competition in financial markets contributed to excessive financial margins, and rigid financial controls led to inefficient allocation of credit.

The major reforms of the period attempted to facilitate monetary control by removing interest rate controls and to improve the efficiency of financial intermediation by increasing competition in the financial sector. Policymakers did not eliminate selective credit policies because politicians still valued their utility in delivering benefits to key constituents. The MOF was able to implement reforms because the bargaining power of the banking sector was on the wane by the late 1960s.

The momentum behind liberalization dissipated during the early phase of the political transition. Government officials put economic policy initiatives on hold as they waited to see what type of political regime would emerge in Franco's absence. Significantly, the government resisted calls to reimpose the interest rate controls that had made financial restriction so comfortable and profitable for certain social groups, especially banks. Consequently, when the first democratic government resurrected deregulation in 1977, it built upon the substantial foundation established in this period.

CHAPTER 5

Spain's Transition to Democracy and Financial Liberalization

Spain's first post–Civil War democratic elections took place in June 1977. The elections followed a period of intense political reform that fashioned a peaceful albeit tense transition to democracy after Franco's death. This and the next two chapters examine how Spain's transition to and consolidation of democracy affected its financial policy, covering the period up to 1992.

I contend that Spain's democratic transition fundamentally altered the calculus of political leaders in economic policy-making. Democratization made the supply of collective economic goods more attractive and a narrow defense of special interests less tenable for political leaders because they had to compete against opposition parties for the electoral support of an ever broader array of voters to stay in power. The particular features of Spain's new democratic institutions served to support this reward structure. Electoral rules encouraged the creation of large, broad-based national parties, not small, sectarian parties. Moreover, newly formed parties were pushed to generate electoral support by appealing to encompassing interests, not narrow constituencies. Once in office, political leaders had an incentive to supply collective goods to maintain political support among a heterogeneous electorate. This analysis does not imply that providing private benefits to select groups lost all its importance or usefulness; rather, it suggests that the relative utility of providing collective benefits increased.

Achieving strong economic performance through the creation of efficient markets was crucial because voters' perceptions of the efficacy of government economic policy were key factors in their voting decisions.[1] This was partly a legacy of the Franco regime's strategy of building support and legitimacy through its economic achievements. Democratic leaders faced a much greater political imperative to supply economic growth than had Franquist officials because they could be held accountable through the ballot box.

In the realm of financial policy, Spain's transition gave politicians an incentive to, first, dismantle the credit, entry, and interest rate controls that had traditionally been used to provide benefits to select groups and instead promote efficiency by giving market forces greater reign; and, second, replace the government's reliance on taxation of the banking system with more orthodox and efficient fiscal policies to generate revenue, like a value-added tax and direct taxes. Overhauling fiscal policy, a long-needed reform that was off-limits to policymakers during the Franco era, was also made possible by democratization. Of course, politicians also confronted countervailing political incentives. Abandoning financial controls entailed eliminating an important source of discretionary power and possibly alienating the current beneficiaries of financial regulation. Replacing taxation of the banking system with more efficient forms of taxation required increasing more visible taxes and possibly estranging key constituents.

The two parties that won elections and formed governments after the transition, the Unión de Centro Democrático (UCD, Union of the Democratic Center) and the Partido Socialista Obrero Español (PSOE, Spanish Socialist Workers Party), responded to the reward structure generated by Spain's democratic institutions, albeit in varying degrees and with differential success. Despite significant differences in their ideology, party structure, natural constituencies, and historical policy preferences, they both took steps to stabilize the economy and introduced badly needed structural reforms designed to promote aggregate social welfare and eliminate special privileges for entrenched economic elites.[2] Of course, other factors influenced the economic reform process as well. The most important were changes in economic conditions, shifts in the composition of the economic policy-making team, and Spain's entry into the EC. They are discussed in depth in the chapters that follow.

A long-term view reveals that Spain's movement toward a liberal market system, particularly in the area of financial policy, has been far-reaching, especially when compared to the experience of other countries that have recently undergone democratization. Moreover, Spain's economic record in the post-Franco era has been excellent, ranking it second among Western European countries in the period 1979–95 in terms of overall performance according to one source.[3] Its success is all the more remarkable because at the time of the transition there seemed to be huge obstacles to completing deep economic reform. The "financial oligarchy," which was staunchly wedded to the economic status quo, was still entrenched at the center of economy and prepared to defend its interests.[4] Labor, which had shown its willingness to cause public disturbances to achieve its objectives, seemed determined to obtain material benefits without delay, not to tolerate austerity measures or possibly high short-term adjustment costs. Moreover, establishing an economy based on impersonal market forces required a basic change in social attitudes, as Spain's economic and political institutions had always functioned on the basis of clientilism.[5]

On the other hand, several factors favored the prospects for a transformation of economic policy in Spain. The Franco regime had already completed some structural reforms, most notably in the areas of financial and monetary policy.[6] Consequently, Spain's new democratic leaders did not have to start the reform process from scratch but rather had the far easier task of extending efforts already underway. In addition, as the transition did not include a purge of the state bureaucracy, they could call upon a well-trained cadre of policymakers, some intimately involved in earlier reform efforts (see chap. 4), to design a coherent economic program. The economy itself had modernized and grown considerably in the previous two decades and was strong enough to withstand some short-term adjustment costs. Furthermore, highly conservative budgeting by the Franco regime meant that outstanding public debt was low.[7] These were advantages that many countries undertaking political and economic liberalization, particularly in the former Eastern Bloc, have not enjoyed. Finally, there was a consensus among major politicians that economic stability was essential for the consolidation of democracy, and they were willing to cooperate to facilitate economic adjustment.

My interpretation of the post-Franco period is at odds with that of some authors who have claimed that the UCD chose not to pursue economic reform aggressively.[8] They suggest that the UCD failed to carry out reforms either out of fear that deep structural adjustment would disrupt the fragile democratic transition or because the party was beholden to vested economic interests or afraid of provoking labor. In their view, Spain witnessed serious economic adjustment only after the PSOE took office in 1982. Thomas Lancaster takes this argument a step further, claiming that the democratic transition has not brought about a transformation of Spanish economic policy because powerful elites have successfully blocked any real change.[9]

I contend that UCD leadership entered office intent upon carrying out structural adjustment and, in fact, proposed and implemented several major reforms, especially in the financial, monetary, and trade policy areas.[10] After 1978, however, they encountered obstacles that made it very difficult to carry out their initial proposals completely. The UCD's party structure made it ill equipped to be a reformist party. Further complicating matters, it lacked a parliamentary majority and did not have autonomy from key social groups that retained inordinate influence over public policy. In addition, the UCD had to contend with urgent political issues (e.g., the drafting of a new constitution) that drained its political capital.

Finally, the UCD governments had to cope with the difficult international economic environment of the late 1970s, which created severe policy problems for all industrial nations. The PSOE did not suffer from the same constraints when seeking to implement a similar economic program. It was not as constrained by private economic interests, enjoyed a huge parliamentary majority, took office when many of the political reforms associated with the transition had already been completed, and had the advantage of learning from the UCD's mistakes.

It must be stressed from the outset that an examination of political institutions, like electoral rules, cannot yield the determinants of political behavior but can only indicate the incentives facing parties or politicians and the likely costs they incur if they fail to heed them. This lack of determinism is evident in two facets of the Spanish experience. First, Spanish parties have not always responded "rationally" to electoral incentives and constraints. Some small nationwide parties have continued to run for office despite their poor prospects for gaining electoral representation. Further, large national parties have not always followed strategies consistent with maximizing their representation. As Richard Gunther has shown, several intervening factors—for example, ideological or programmatic incompatibility with potential coalition partners—have occasionally led party leaders to place other concerns above the short-term maximization of parliamentary representation.[11] Nevertheless, large parties that did not respond appropriately to electoral constraints suffered huge defeats; this indicates that the electoral system compels parties to behave "rationally" if they wish to be major participants in Spanish politics and shape the country's economic policies.

Second, not all politicians within the two parties that have governed interpreted the incentives generated by Spanish electoral institutions in the same way. There was intense disagreement within both the UCD and the PSOE over basic political and economic strategy because of different calculations of how to maximize electoral support as well as diverse ideological stances. At the most basic level, the disputes pitted officials who advocated public policies designed to appeal to encompassing interests against those who wished to favor key constituencies. Ultimately, a strategy consistent with institutional incentives prevailed within both parties. The PSOE, for instance, generally adopted an economic strategy of structural adjustment intended to improve aggregate social welfare, even though it sometimes made concessions to important constituent groups.

In short, my theoretical framework adequately captures the effects of regime change on the reward structure that confronted Spanish political leaders, but it cannot explain all of the variance in elite political behavior. I consider the sources of intra- and intergovernmental differences in the actions of politicians further in this and the following chapters. The concluding chapter considers the implications of these differences for the explanatory scope of my conceptual framework.

This and the following two chapters follow rough chronological order. In addition to recounting the key events of the period, each chapter concentrates on a different set of analytical topics. This chapter presents the argument that Spain's transition to democracy gave political leaders an incentive to pursue financial deregulation. It also examines the financial reforms introduced immediately after the 1977 elections. In many ways, these reforms were the most important of all those that make up the Spanish liberalization process. They represented the first systematic effort to reduce all aspects of state intervention in financial markets, and they greatly expanded efforts to foster greater competition within the sector.

Political Reform and the 1977 Elections

The first post-Franco elections followed a rapid succession of political reforms in late 1976 and early 1977.[12] In July 1976, King Juan Carlos dismissed the first post-Franco government, headed by Arias Navarro, and appointed a former Movimiento official and Franquist minister, Adolfo Suárez, as the new president. Suárez's appointment was initially unpopular. Opposition groups believed that Suárez would try to block movement toward democracy and seek to preserve the basic institutions of the Franco regime as the Arias government had. Conservative elements in the government, especially the Bunker, feared that Suárez, who they thought opposed significant democratization, lacked the skills to maintain an authoritarian regime in the face of mounting political opposition.

Suárez soon surprised everyone (except King Juan Carlos) by firmly committing himself to achieving a peaceful transition to democracy within the existing legal framework. The obstacles to such a transition were tremendous. On the one hand, Suárez confronted a populace that increasingly clamored for major political and social change. Leftist parties had begun to organize the most politically active elements of the population, notably the emerging labor unions, to overthrow existing political institutions. On the other, ultraconservative forces, especially the military, threatened to intercede if political change was too dramatic.

Fortunately, Suárez proved adept at finding a middle ground. In October 1976, he convinced the Franquist legislature to commit what was in effect political suicide by approving the Political Reform Law.[13] This law disbanded the Franquist Cortes and established the procedures by which a democratic legislature would undertake future political reforms. Soon after, the Movimiento was disbanded and political parties were officially authorized. In March 1977, the Suárez government and representatives from various opposition groups negotiated a law that established the rules for electoral competition and the method of determining seat allocation. Finally, the government granted pardons to political prisoners and legalized the Partido Comunista de España (PCE, Spanish Communist Party).

The Electoral Law

The formulation of an electoral law was a critical step in the transition to democracy. The law was the object of intense negotiation among political groups. Different groups favored the adoption of different electoral institutions in accordance with their estimations of the size and geographical distribution of their respective blocs of supporters.[14] Nevertheless, Spain's politicians also collectively hoped to create institutions that would ensure the consolidation of democracy. Their challenge was to strike a "difficult balance . . . between the need to create a party system conducive to stable government and the need to represent the interests of significant political and social groups."[15] In particular, politicians wished to create electoral rules that would prevent excessive fragmentation and a return to the political and social conflict that tore Spain apart in the 1930s and contributed to the Civil War. The desire to avoid repeating the past served as a powerful constraint on simple self-interest maximization by future party leaders.

The electoral law of March 1977 represented a compromise among the conflicting demands of the various parties. To promote the legitimacy of the new democracy, the law embodied broad PR principles so that all major groups would have a voice in the democratic process. Voters would cast ballots for closed and blocked party lists in each district, and each party's share of the vote would determine the number of seats it returned from that district in the new Congress of Deputies or Cortes.[16] However, several "correctives" were introduced to reduce party fragmentation that might impede energetic, purposeful state action. First, the law established a minimum threshold of votes for obtaining parliamentary representation (3 percent of votes in the given district). Second, many small electoral districts were created (mostly corresponding to the provinces), each with a minimum of three representatives. Third, the D'Hondt "highest average" method of seat allocation was chosen.[17]

The correctives introduced into the electoral law penalized small, sectarian parties with geographically dispersed support and encouraged the emergence of large, national, all-encompassing parties.[18] The bias is obvious in the results of the 1977 elections, which are listed in table 5.1. The PSP-US and Alianza Popular (AP, Popular Alliance) polled 4.4 and 8.0

percent of the vote, respectively, but obtained only 1.7 and 4.6 percent of the seats in the Congress of Deputies. Small parties grouped under the heading "Others" fared even worse: they received 9.9 percent of the vote but only 1.1 percent of the seats. On the other hand, the UCD and PSOE won 34.0 and 28.9 percent of the vote, respectively, but secured 47.1 and 33.7 percent of the seats in the Congress. Spain has in fact displayed the highest degree of disproportionality of any country with an electoral system based on PR.[19]

The two parties receiving the most votes continued to win the lion's share of seats in later elections, as table 5.2 shows, and the effective number of parties steadily declined.[20] This is because over time the electoral law's "mechanical" effects (the law's translation of votes into seats) were reinforced by "distal" or "psychological" effects.[21] Spanish voters and contributors exhibited "strategic behavior," favoring larger parties because of the expectation that the system would discriminate against smaller parties.[22] The Spanish party system, therefore, is best characterized as a two-party dominant system,[23] approximating the type of democracy that Downs and others have claimed results in the greatest provision

TABLE 5.1. The Results of the 1977 Elections for the Congress of Deputies

Party	Votes	% of Votes	Seats	% of Seats
UCD	6,309,991	34.0	165	47.1
PSOE	5,371,466	28.9	118	33.7
PCE-PSUC	1,709,870	9.2	20	5.7
AP	1,488,001	8.0	16	4.6
PSP-US	816,582	4.4	6	1.7
PDC	514,647	2.8	11	3.1
PNV	314,272	1.7	8	2.3
EC	143,954	0.8	1	0.3
EE	64,039	0.3	1	0.3
Others	1,853,448	9.9	4	1.1
Total	18,586,270	100.0	350	100.0

Source: Ministerio de la Gobernación, Dirección General de la Política Interior 1977.
Note:
UCD: Unión de Centro Democrático
PSOE: Partido Socialista Obrero Español and Socialistes de Catalunya
PCE-PSUC: Partido Comunista de España and Partit Unificat de Catalunya
AP: Alianza Popular
PSP-US: Partido Socialista Popular-Unidad Socialista
PDC: Pacte Democratic per Catalunya
PNV: Partido Nacionalista Vasco
EC: Esquerra de Catalunya
EE: Euskadiko Ezkerra

of collective goods. The only small, nonnational parties that have fared well in Spain have been Catalan and Basque nationalist parties (e.g., the PDC and PNV), which have succeeded by concentrating on regional issues (e.g., regional government autonomy). This result was intended by the framers of the electoral law, who designed it to give Basque and Catalan parties the opportunity to gain sufficient representation to reduce tensions between these regions and the central government.[24]

In sum, the features of the electoral system meant that parties aspiring to play a major role in Spanish politics had an incentive to seek broad-based national majorities. Electoral rules favored doing this by appealing to encompassing interests, in that it would be hard to generate sufficient electoral support by logrolling a coalition of narrow constituencies. Once in office, governing parties had an incentive to maintain support among a heterogeneous electorate by supplying collective goods. Closed and blocked party lists gave party leaders the means to exercise some control over individual legislators and prevent them from concentrating on local interests at the expense of the party's national agenda.

Electoral laws alone, however, cannot entirely explain why Spanish politicians created parties that sought to build a broad-based, national constituency through the provision of collective goods. Variables associated with Spain's general political environment must also be considered. As already noted, Spanish politicians placed a premium on economic and political stability and energetic state action because they feared a return to the divisiveness and policy incoherence characteristic of the 1930s. These concerns, of course, had contributed to the choice of Spain's electoral institutions in the first place. For their part, Spanish voters, who were normally distributed across the political spectrum, had a pragmatic orientation toward public policy that stressed good results, not particular con-

TABLE 5.2.   Seats Won by Various Types of Parties in the Congress of Deputies, 1977–96

	Two Largest Parties	Small Nationwide Parties	Regional Parties
1977	283	41	26
1979	289	33	28
1982	308	18	24
1986	289	26	35
1989	282	31	37
1993	300	18	32
1996	297	21	32

Source: "Anuario El País 1996," 70, and Ministerio de Justicia e Interior 1996.

tent.[25] They viewed parties that favored public policies seeming to benefit only select groups as illegitimate because such an orientation reminded them of the arbitrariness and favoritism of much government policy during the Franco years.

The 1977 Elections

The rapid pace of events gave Spain's nascent parties little time to develop into functioning political organizations before the June polls. In most cases, the parties were brand new and had no party apparatus or membership. Only the PCE, which had maintained a sizable clandestine organization throughout the Franco years, had an organization already capable of carrying out the functions normally associated with a political party. Other parties confronted the daunting task of simultaneously establishing an organizational structure and membership, preparing a strategy for the elections, and raising funds to finance the campaign.

The major parties, faced with the reward structure provided by electoral institutions and the character of the Spanish electorate, all adopted strategies aimed at obtaining broad-based electoral support in the first (and subsequent) democratic elections.[26] The UCD, a coalition of centrist and conservative groups headed by Suárez, was conceived as a catch-all party that sought the votes of all but the most extreme right and left. The AP, a coalition of conservative groups (many of them headed by ex-Franco ministers), was also originally envisioned as a catch-all party, but tactical errors by its leaders eventually turned it into a reactionary, "clientilistic" party in the eyes of the public. The two major leftist parties, the PSOE and PCE, also adopted strategies designed to maximize broad-based electoral support. They took moderate positions on the major issues in an effort to be perceived as socially responsible and in the political mainstream.

Economic issues had a prominent place in the 1977 campaign since the Spanish economy was struggling. Although the main focus was on topics such as inflation and unemployment, financial policy was an issue in the campaign. Some parties declared that the state should continue to intervene in financial markets to promote social goals. The AP, for example, argued that financial policy should be an integral part of a comprehensive economic planning process; to this end, selective credit policies were to be used to channel funds to priority sectors. The major leftist parties initially advocated nationalization of the banking system, a stance that unnerved the banks and mainstream voters. They greatly moderated their stance, however, as the elections grew near. Only the Partido Popular, the precursor to the UCD, explicitly came out in favor of financial liberalization.[27]

Several parties acted as political entrepreneurs in the financial policy area by championing the cause of savers and firms rationed out of credit markets. The PSOE, for example, criticized existing selective credit policies on the grounds that they favored large firms at the expense of SMCs. It proposed the creation of a public bank that would lend exclusively to SMCs as a remedy.[28] The Partido Popular, which generally favored financial liberalization, promised to institute a new credit floor requiring banks to lend to SMCs. It also argued that interest rate controls should be lifted to permit savers to earn a reasonable return on their deposits.[29]

Banks played an important role in financing the 1977 campaign. They provided loans to several parties (even the PCE), but the majority of credit went to AP.[30] Their decision to back AP was based primarily on two factors. First, the AP was opposed to both nationalization of the banking sector and financial deregulation. The UCD, on the other hand, based on statements made by the Partido Popular, had come out in favor of deregulation (including the much feared removal of interest rate controls). Second, early opinion polls showed AP to be ahead in the race. The decision to back AP ultimately proved a grave tactical error since it fared badly in the elections. UCD leadership resented the major banks' decision to back the AP and showed little concern for their interests once in office. Indeed, relations between the UCD and banks remained very poor throughout the party's stay in office.

The results of the 1977 elections are indicated in table 5.1. The two parties most closely associated with the "center," the UCD and the PSOE, gathered the vast majority of the votes. The AP, which had initially been expected to win the elections, finished a distant fourth. The electorate was frightened away from the AP by the inclusion of several reactionary figures from the Franco period on its party lists and the authoritarian rhetoric used by leading party officials throughout the campaign. The UCD did not win enough votes to hold an absolute majority but did not have to create a formal coalition with other parties to form a government. The Council of Ministers announced in June did not include politicians from other parties. The UCD's status as a minority government, however, meant that it sometimes had to make deals with other parties prior to major votes in the Cortes.

The UCD and Its Economic Strategy

The UCD as a Political Party

The nature of the UCD as a political party influenced its economic policy throughout its tenure in office. The UCD formed as a coalition of disparate "centrist" groups, such as the Christian Democrats, Social Democrats, Liberals, ex-Movimiento officials, and the "Blues." That is, original UCD membership included elements of the moderate opposition to Franco as well as former Franquist officials who had not been tarnished by their association with the regime. The coalition originally came together because the component groups realized they could not exist as viable electoral entities on their own. In addition, constructing a party around Suárez was attractive because of his access to state funds, control over government patronage, and influence over the state-run radio and television networks.[31] Many of the groups making up the UCD initially did not want to institutionalize the coalition as a permanent party for fear of losing their identity. Nevertheless, Suárez secured the dissolution of the elements of the coalition into a party united around his leadership in 1978. The component parts of UCD accepted unification "not out of ideological affinity but only to guarantee their proximity to the fount of power."[32] Indeed, Suárez had to reward group leaders with ministerial and other high-ranking government posts in return for their acquiescence.

Although Suárez was the indisputable leader of the UCD, the heads of some component groups, called the "barons," had power resources not connected to the party. The barons were politicians who held a prominent place in Spanish politics before joining the UCD because of their position within the Franquist state or proximity to powerful social interests. The leaders of the Christian Democrats, for example, had close ties to industry and the banking world (in addition to their claim on the allegiance of Catholics). The barons were not always willing to submit to party discipline or give up their own political initiatives. Suárez sometimes had to work out deals with the barons before major votes to ensure the passage of legislation.

In comparative perspective, the UCD displayed several of the characteristics of what Shefter has termed an "internally mobilized" party.[33] Internally mobilized parties are those "founded by elites who occupy positions of power within the prevailing regime and who undertake to mobilize a popular following behind themselves in an effort to gain control over the government or to secure their hold over it."[34] They are linked to their popular base through politicians whose loyalty is purchased by patronage and are dependent on these politicians to maintain themselves in power. Internally mobilized parties are in a position to use the resources of the state to acquire a political following and have every incentive to make use of that advantage. "Externally mobilized" parties, on the other hand, are "established by outsiders who did not hold positions within the prevailing regime and who organize a mass following either in an effort to gain entry into the political system for themselves and their supporters or in an effort to overthrow that system."[35] They do not have access to state patronage when founded and must turn to other means to acquire a following; specifically, they rely on appeals to the general interest or the supply of collective goods, regardless of the composition of their social base. In Spain, the PSOE (discussed in chap. 7) is an example of an externally mobilized party.

One would expect an internally mobilized party, like the UCD, to develop a political strategy based on supplying material benefits to well-established interest groups and not to attempt to attract a large, hetero-geneous constituency through appeals to collective interests. Spain's new democratic institutions, however, generated a reward structure that pushed the UCD to do the latter, not the former. An intense controversy among top officials over what sort of party the UCD should aspire to be evidenced the contradictory incentives facing party officials.[36] Suárez and his immediate circle, whom I will refer to as "party leadership,"[37] envisioned the UCD as a progressive, catch-all party located in the cen-ter-left of the political spectrum, where they believed most voters were clustered. They argued that electoral institutions dictated that the UCD appeal to a broad-based, nationwide constituency if it was to succeed. A key element of this strategy was to develop a reformist economic pro-gram designed to promote aggregate social welfare. Several barons con-tested this strategy. In their view, the UCD needed to court influential interest groups, such as professional, business, and community organi-zations, by devising policies that advanced their interests and create institutional links to them to secure their long-term support. They feared that efforts to attract a broader constituency might alienate the UCD's core constituency.

Suárez had several tools at his disposal in the battle over strategy even though his control of the party was incomplete. He influenced the compo-sition of the party's electoral lists and, in principle, could ask for the resig-nation of a deputy at any time.[38] He also had great control over the UCD's financial (and other) resources. Consequently, he was able, at least ini-tially, to impose his view of the type of party the UCD should be and to largely shape its overall political strategy. The UCD followed a catch-all strategy in both the 1977 and 1979 elections and, despite tremendous pres-sures from powerful interest groups, avoided designing policies targeted at narrow constituencies.[39]

The UCD's Economic Strategy

The overall direction of the UCD's initial economic strategy became clear when Suárez appointed Enrique Fuentes Quintana to be the vice president for economics. Fuentes was a well-known economist with little political experience; in fact, he did not belong to any political party. This highlights the fact that Suárez chose him for his economic expertise. In the early 1970s, Fuentes helped design the fiscal reform plan that was vetoed by the Franco inner circle. Later on, he aggressively advocated more market-oriented economic policies from his prominent posts as the director of the Fiscal Studies Institute and, subsequently, the Foundation for Economic and Social Studies. Several months before his appointment as vice president, Fuentes harshly criticized the government's economic policies and outlined an ambitious program of stabilization and structural reforms in a widely publicized interview.[40] It is important to note that although politicians disagreed as to which economic strategy was best for Spain, professional economists (including technocratic policymakers) were virtually unanimous that the country needed to undertake a comprehensive economic reform program of the sort advocated by Fuentes.

Fuentes demanded complete discretion in formulating economic policy as a condition for accepting the post.[41] Although Suárez granted this request, he also appointed other economic ministers, like Alberto Oliart as minister of industry, whose views differed from those of Fuentes. This occurred because various UCD factions demanded representation in the economic ministries, and the party's coalitional structure made it hard for Suárez to refuse. The result was a lack of consensus on basic economic strategy among top-level policymakers. Fuentes soon discovered that he could formulate stabilization and structural reforms but would be unable to ensure their complete implementation.

Fuentes proposed an ambitious set of policies designed to correct internal and external imbalances as well as structural defects in the Spanish economy.[42] He contended that a stabilization plan alone was insufficient to solve Spain's economic problems. They were the consequence of long-standing, ill-advised economic policies that had created serious structural deficiencies, not merely of a temporary disequilibrium. The first elements of a more social democratic state were evident in the proposed economic program as well. It included plans to raise expenditures on social welfare, particularly in areas like health, education, and worker compensation programs. Increased state spending in this area was certainly a concession to labor but was also intended to remedy the severe deficiencies caused by the Franco regime's practice of strictly limiting government expenditures.

The measures contemplated to rectify internal and external imbalances constituted an orthodox stabilization plan. They included the devaluation of the peseta, a tighter monetary policy, a strict incomes policy, and an overall decrease in government current spending. To correct structural deficiencies, Fuentes envisioned major financial reforms, an overhaul of the tax system, further liberalization of trade, and the dismantling of the still extensive system of price controls and state subsidies. This set of policies was intended to promote aggregate social welfare while eliminating the rents and other privileges bestowed upon entrenched economic elites by prevailing government policy. The UCD was careful not to promise dramatic short-term economic improvement. In a television appearance after the 1977 elections, which was well received by the populace, Fuentes told Spaniards that they would have to withstand a tough period of adjustment before the economy could resume steady growth.

Spain's economic situation at the time—moderately high inflation, a balance-of-payments deficit, stagnating growth, and growing unemployment—in fact required forceful measures, although the country's problems were not atypical of those facing many European nations.[43] The existence of economic problems alone cannot account for the decision to pursue reforms, however. Spain had recently experienced several periods of poor performance without seeing reform.[44] Some of the measures implemented in 1977 had been talked about for several years but had languished because policymakers were paralyzed by the political uncertainty surrounding Franco's death. Nevertheless, deteriorating economic conditions certainly provided an additional impetus to initiate the reform process.

I argue that the UCD sought reforms in response to the reward structure provided by Spain's new democratic institutions to eschew the provision of benefits to narrow social groups and instead improve general economic performance in order to capture broad-based electoral support. Electoral concerns were already present since national elections would be convened as soon as a new constitution was approved. The UCD also opted for a strategy of appealing to collective interests because it did not want to become too closely identified with entrenched interest groups.[45] It was already on the defensive because some party officials with ties to the Franco regime were closely associated with the financial oligarchy and big business. Party leaders feared that further appeals to these groups would alienate large segments of the electorate.

To facilitate implementation of his program, Fuentes secured the creation of a new ministry, the Ministry of Economics (MOE).[46] The MOE was given the authority to formulate general economic policy and coordinate the activities of other economic ministries, although its real influence over other ministries was limited in practice. The MOE also took over most of the responsibility for financial and monetary policy, an area previously handled almost exclusively by the MOF. The MOE now supervised the BOS, the Official Credit Institute, and the General Directorate for Financial Policy. The MOF retained control over the Treasury and the General Directorate for Insurance. Fuentes himself filled the post of minister of economics.

Fuentes viewed the creation of the MOE as a way of circumventing any potential bureaucratic opposition to financial reforms and insulating policymakers from societal pressures. Several departments within the MOF, in fact, opposed certain financial reforms. The Treasury argued against the removal of deposit rate ceilings because it would increase the cost of issuing new public debt. Officials supervising the Junta de Inversiones (Investment Board) opposed its elimination because they did not want to give up their discretionary power. Although top MOF officials generally supported financial reform, such internal dissent would have made it more difficult to implement the proposed policy changes successfully. Moreover, the MOF had always been vulnerable to interest group pressure, especially from the large national banks. Fuentes believed all of these problems could be avoided by creating a new ministry, staffed by handpicked personnel, to handle financial and monetary affairs. It could also engender a more cohesive financial policy team.[47]

Finally, Fuentes also wished to give the BOS, then under the MOF's supervision, a more autonomous role in monetary policy. He believed that unless the BOS was allowed to act independently, in a fashion similar to central banks in other OECD countries, an effective monetary policy was impossible.[48] The MOF had shown itself reluctant to grant the BOS more autonomy in the past and probably would have relinquished its control over monetary policy only grudgingly.

The Moncloa Pacts

The UCD was well aware that it might not have sufficient political strength to implement its economic program successfully. In the realm of financial policy, MOE officials generally had the legal authority to introduce new regulations whenever they wished, except in a few select areas where legislative reform was required. But they realized that an attempt to impose basic reforms without the cooperation of other political parties and key interest groups would jeopardize their long-term success and severely strain the political environment. UCD leaders were especially concerned about the attitude of labor, since workers had electoral clout and had shown through their strike activities that they had the capacity to cause public disturbances that might disrupt the transition.[49]

To overcome its political limitations, the UCD sought the input and cooperation of other political parties and labor in formulating and carrying out its economic reforms. This consensus-building process resulted in the signing of the "Moncloa Pacts" in October 1977, an agreement in which Spain's major political actors expressed their support for the process of economic and political reform.[50] The Moncloa process was intended to make key political actors feel that they had a stake in the consolidation of democracy. The pacts themselves would permit the UCD to deflect some of the responsibility for unpopular measures (e.g., wage caps and tight monetary policy) by presenting these policies as the product of a broad consensus.

Business was mostly excluded from the Moncloa process, lacking even the indirect representation in the negotiations that labor enjoyed via the participation of the PCE and PSOE.[51] The UCD did not court business actively because some party leaders, notably Suárez, did not want the party to be seen as catering to entrenched economic interests. Consequently, business was openly hostile to the Moncloa process and criticized the agreement when it was announced.[52] The sour relations between the UCD and business continued throughout the party's time in office, if anything, getting worse and more public over time.[53]

In obtaining the Moncloa agreement, the UCD capitalized on the widespread apprehension among opposition politicians that a prolonged economic crisis could disrupt Spain's fragile new democracy and invite military intervention. In this regard, the pacts demonstrated that the leaders of the major political parties were willing, at least initially, to forgo the potential benefits of attacking the UCD's policies in order to cooperate on reforms that seemed important to assure a stable democratic transition. Fear of recreating the divisive political climate that had ripped apart Spain's first democracy or of replicating the postrevolution experience of neighboring Portugal also lay heavily on the minds of the political elite. Moreover, none of the parties wanted to be excluded from the economic policy-making process. In particular, the PCE and PSOE believed their participation would project a moderate and responsible image to the electorate and ensure that the interests of unionized labor were represented.

Maravall and Przeworski have argued that Spain's "consensual" approach to basic economic reforms has advantages over technocratic, "neoliberal" strategies that emphasize insulation of decision makers from social demands and the imposition of reforms from above.[54] They claim that consultation with all relevant actors increases cooperation with reform efforts, improves their design, and increases their overall legitimacy. In Spain at least, their argument rings true; if the UCD had attempted to impose reforms from above, it would have alienated wide sectors of society and weakened the legitimacy of the new democratic regime. Of course, the consultation process that Maravall and Przeworski favor may also lead to capture if state officials cannot resist strong private actors or to policy paralysis if participant viewpoints are widely divergent.

The primary economic goals of the Moncloa Pacts were to control inflation and generate momentum for fiscal reform. Government officials recognized that a tight monetary policy alone could not tame inflation; wage growth had to be brought under control. Wage increases in the period leading up to the pacts were substantial, often exceeding the inflation rate, as many firms offered higher real wages in an effort to pacify their workforce. A negotiated incomes policy seemed to offer the only credible way of moderating wage growth and, thereby, breaking the inflationary spiral.

The pacts sought to limit wage increases to 22 percent in 1978, a figure well below the prevailing rate of inflation, 29 percent. The wage cap was binding for public enterprises and "indicative" for private companies. The PSOE and PCE pledged to seek the consent of the two major unions associated with their parties, the UGT and CCOO, respectively, for moderate wage growth. In fact, the major unions generally abided by the wage agreement, despite some reservations, because the pacts implicitly recognized their central role in the economic policy-making process. In exchange for wage restraint, the UCD promised to intensify its efforts to implement structural reforms (especially fiscal reform) aimed at achieving a more just distribution of national income and wealth. In addition, it promised increased government spending on job creation and maintenance, unemployment insurance, and pension payments.

In most respects, the pacts supported the goal of financial liberalization. The participants backed the expansion of bond and equity markets, the creation of a secondary mortgage market, and the promotion of institutional investors. They believed that these measures would be popular with the middle class since they would provide financial instruments to facilitate saving for housing, education, and retirement. There was also support for granting the BOS greater autonomy in monetary policy and reducing state financing of public banks. The one exception (albeit a minor one) to the general liberalizing tone was a proposal to require savings banks to channel more credit to SMCs since this measure threatened to introduce an additional element of rigidity in the process of credit allocation.

The Moncloa Pacts brought mixed results. On the positive side, they helped to slow inflation considerably by 1978.[55] The money growth targets established in the pacts were met (with a slight delay), and wage growth during 1978 was under the 22 percent objective. This initial success encouraged future attempts to reach social pacts on wage increases.[56]

Other reforms, however, met with less fortune, at least in the short run. The most conspicuous failure was the government's inability to carry out fiscal reform fully because of the concerted opposition of the wealthy and business; this is discussed later in this chapter. Major financial policy reforms were also delayed. Legislation governing the BOS was not passed until 1980; measures to expand bond and equity markets and create a secondary mortgage market were not adopted until the early 1980s; and public banks continued to rely on Treasury financing, although they began to raise some capital in private markets. I explore the reasons behind the delay in implementing these financial reforms in chapters 6 and 7.

The Organization of Business and Banking Interests

Exclusion from the consultation process culminating in the Moncloa Pacts prodded banks and business to intensify their efforts to organize. Many business leaders feared that unless they formed effective peak organizations, they would be unable to negotiate with the government on equal terms with labor or play a more direct role in economic policy-making.[57] In addition, they suspected that their traditional informal access to top government officials might wane and lose effectiveness with changing political conditions; concerted political action was envisioned as the means of promoting their interests in its place. In general, the business and financial organizations that emerged were weak and divided, however.[58] Nonetheless, they managed to augment and alter the nature of private sector participation in financial policy-making. Here, I briefly identify the relevant associations and discuss the most important issues concerning their formation and evolution.

The Banking Sector

The Asociación Española de la Banca Privada (AEB, Spanish Private Banking Association) was formed in the winter of 1977. Previously, private banking representatives on the CSB had acted as the lobby group for the banking sector. Local and regional banks had been unhappy with this arrangement since they lacked a voice within the CSB. Consequently, they pushed for a banking association that would represent all banks. The Big Seven banks also favored the creation of such an association because they wanted the sector to show solidarity on specific issues, especially wage negotiations with labor. They also believed that they would be able to dominate the affairs of the new association.

Sharp internal divisions have often prevented the AEB from presenting a cohesive front in dealings with the government and business. In particular, many issues have pitted local and regional banks against the large national banks. The variety of stances on deposit rate ceilings in the 1970s and early 1980s illustrates the diversity within the AEB. The Big Seven banks, which held the largest share of deposits, benefited the most from these ceilings since they tended to lock in each bank's current share of total deposits. They also fared better in the non–price competition that took the place of price competition for deposits since they had superior resources and visibility. Consequently, they supported deposit rate ceilings. Several banks with smaller shares of the market opposed the ceilings because they believed they would be able to gain market share in an unregulated market. Other local and regional banks, however, preferred the guaranteed profit margins that ceilings provided to a potential, but uncertain, greater share of an unregulated market.

In the final analysis, the AEB normally took positions that reflected the preferences of the large national banks since they still dominated the banking sector. Moreover, the Big Seven banks did not hesitate to lobby the government separately on key issues (e.g., the 1981 reforms). Nevertheless, the cohesiveness of the Big Seven was slowly beginning to deteriorate, though they managed to engage in cartel-like behavior on certain issues, notably deposit rates, well into the 1980s (see chap. 6).[59]

The Confederación Española de Cajas de Ahorro (CECA, Spanish Confederation of Savings Banks) is the primary trade association of savings banks. All savings banks have a voice in the CECA, but the largest institutions enjoy greater influence because they have more representatives. The CECA first became active in lobbying the government in the mid-1970s when policymakers considered various financial reforms. The CECA's influence on financial policy improved markedly after Fuentes became minister of economics. Its lobbying efforts peaked when the UCD and PSOE governments considered legislation concerning the governing institutions of savings banks.

Business

The Confederación Española de Organizaciones Empresariales (CEOE, Spanish Confederation of Employers' Organizations) is the major business association in Spain. The CEOE was formed in June 1977 when four different national business organizations joined together to form one representative body. Originally, the CEOE had few members and had to compete with several other business groups. By the early 1980s, however, it had the affiliation of businesses representing 80 percent of industrial employment.[60] Currently, although most firms belong to the CEOE, they are also members of a variety of other organizations, such as those representing the interests of their sector or region.[61] In many cases, their loyalty to these narrow organizations is stronger.

A critical issue business faced when it started to organize was whether large and small and medium-sized companies (SMCs) should coexist in the same organization or establish separate associations since their interests were likely to diverge on many issues. Initially, SMCs created their own organizations, the principal one being the Confederación Española de la Pequeña y Mediana Empresa (CEPYME, Confederation of Small-and Medium-sized Businesses), and refused to join forces with the CEOE because they feared their interests would be sacrificed in favor of those of large firms. The CEPYME eventually decided, however, that it lacked the political weight to influence economic policy on its own, and it incorporated itself into the CEOE in 1980.[62]

The AEB joined the CEOE in late 1977.[63] Some (but not all) corporate leaders wanted the AEB to be part of the CEOE because they believed it would give the confederation more clout in its dealings with the government. Banks sought CEOE membership because their multiple links to industry (equity holdings, etc.) gave them a strong stake in the policy stances adopted by the organization. Conflicts of interest between banks and firms on policy issues arose frequently, contributing to the emergence of deep divisions within the CEOE.[64] The AEB has played a less central role in the CEOE with the passage of time.

The Structural Reforms of the Summer of 1977

Fiscal Reform

Fuentes and the minister of finance, Francisco Fernández Ordoñez, announced the government's intention to overhaul Spain's antiquated fiscal policy upon taking office. Previous fiscal reform had been blocked by the Franco inner circle who feared that the implementation of more efficient taxation policies would alienate the middle and upper classes. The transition to democracy greatly increased interest in fiscal reform. First, political leaders realized they would have to generate more revenue to cover anticipated higher government expenditures. Higher government spending would be necessary to satisfy the pent-up demands for government services unleashed by the transition and to overcome huge deficiencies in physical and social infrastructure, a legacy of restrictive Franquist budgeting practices. Second, the transition raised issues of social justice, especially those concerning how to distribute the tax burden equitably. Leftist groups in particular were clamoring for a reduction of regressive indirect taxes and greater reliance on a progressive income tax and corporate taxes.

Opposition to fiscal reform arose immediately, with business and the wealthy launching an intense lobbying campaign against it. This pressure and administrative constraints soon made it apparent that a truly comprehensive reform was impossible, despite the political support offered through the Moncloa Pacts. The MOF, therefore, decided to proceed in an incremental manner. It implemented the so-called Urgent Measures in November 1977 to obtain an immediate expansion of revenue and proposed a series of reforms for coming years. The Urgent Measures increased the tax burden on the upper classes by raising taxes on wealth and attempted to reduce tax evasion.[65] Steps to curtail tax evasion included the repeal of the "banking secret" that had been in force since 1940. Banks bitterly opposed its removal since it eliminated one of the primary attractions of bank deposits vis-à-vis bonds or stocks. In practice, the abolition of the banking secret did not have a dramatic impact in the short run, in that authorities permitted banks to continue to keep information about certain types of accounts confidential. The Cortes passed legislation governing other aspects of fiscal policy in 1978 and 1979. The legislation introduced new income and corporate tax codes and modified existing taxes on wealth. Nevertheless, these laws did not constitute a major overhaul of the fiscal system but only a series of stopgap measures. A systematic reform of the fiscal system would have to wait until the 1980s when the Socialists were able to overcome social opposition to more efficient tax policies.[66]

The UCD's moves succeeded in increasing state revenues significantly. Between 1975 and 1982, tax revenues increased from 20 to 26 percent of GDP.[67] However, they also angered business considerably and aggravated its already tense relations with the government.[68] Business's sense of betrayal by the UCD's policies contributed to a prolonged slump in private investment that held back economic growth.[69]

Monetary Reform

In early July, the MOE began taking steps to establish a tighter monetary policy. First, it announced that it was revising M3 growth targets downward from 21 to 17 percent, to be achieved by the end of the year. Second, the BOS notified intermediaries that, starting in September, it would reduce its discretionary lending to the banking sector and increase its cost. These measures led to an immediate drop in credit to the private sector; the decrease was short lived, however, as the supply of credit soon began to grow again, although at a slightly lower rate.[70] Finally, the BOS devalued the peseta by almost 20 percent against the dollar to bring the exchange rate more in line with its equilibrium value.

Business and labor protested the tighter monetary policy because they feared it would reduce significantly the amount of credit available to the private sector and raise its cost and, hence, provoke a recession. Business argued that it was a particularly bad time for a decrease in liquidity because a great number of firms were struggling to remain solvent. Organized labor was concerned that the reduction in credit would lead to increased unemployment.[71] Banks also opposed the tighter monetary stance, particularly the reduction in central bank lending, because it would limit the volume of their lending activity. They also feared a reduction in liquidity would increase the number of defaults and bankruptcies by firms, severely compromising the integrity of their loan portfolios. As chapter 6 shows, this in fact did happen, and it contributed to a major banking crisis.

Groups opposed to a more restrictive monetary policy achieved one victory, albeit a minor one. The government announced in September that it would not reduce M3 growth to 17 percent until April 1978. This small concession, however, did little to appease business and labor, although it calmed financial intermediaries. In fact, tension over monetary policy became a constant feature of the relations between the government and business well into the 1980s.

The Financial Reforms

The MOE introduced its financial reforms immediately after the elections to take advantage of the favorable political climate and to make it hard for opposition to the reforms to organize. They were the most important steps yet toward liberalization since they reduced most forms of state intervention in financial markets, including some areas untouched by past reform efforts, and further increased competition within the financial sector. The immediate objectives of the reforms were to (1) reduce state control over credit allocation, replacing funds channeled through selective credit policies by direct state subsidies where warranted; (2) further deregulate interest rates; (3) increase competition among financial intermediaries; and (4) establish guidelines to "democratize" savings banks.[72] I focus primarily on the first three here. As already noted, opposition parties generally expressed their support for these measures in the Moncloa Pacts.

Overall, the 1977 reforms sought to create more efficient financial markets and improve monetary control, while actually reducing the ability of public officials to exercise discretionary authority over financial markets, particularly over the allocation of credit. Their design, then, was consistent with the incentives provided by Spanish political institutions to capture political support by supplying collective not private economic goods. In addition, UCD leaders hoped that the reduction of government credit programs would help defuse charges (stemming from the presence of several former Franquist officials in the party) that it was beholden to big business and other powerful social groups. Opposition parties, on the other hand, saw financial deregulation as a means of preventing the UCD government from attempting to use its interventionist capacity in financial markets to consolidate its hold on power.

More generally, all Spanish elected officials also shared a basic rationale for dismantling selective credit programs. Democratization had begun to introduce new groups into the political process, and it was likely that the state would confront pressure for preferential credit from a much larger set of social groups. If political leaders did not provide such credit to all those who demanded it, excluded groups might turn hostile to the democratic process; if they did provide it, they would place impossible demands on state resources and severely distort the functioning of financial markets.

If the transition had resulted in a different set of electoral institutions, or if Spain's overall political context were different (e.g., leading politicians to place less emphasis on stability), then significant financial reform in some areas, particularly the removal of interest rate and credit controls, might not have occurred. For instance, if the transition had created an electoral system that rewarded parties with close ties to narrow constituencies, politicians would have had an incentive to maintain existing selective credit policies, or even expand them, so that they could direct preferential finance to important constituents. In Brazil, a country with such an electoral system, selective credit policies actually expanded after its redemocratization.[73]

There were certainly pressures to expand selective credit policies in Spain. As discussed more fully in chapter 6, several groups, notably the construction industry and SMCs, repeatedly requested credit controls to aid their sectors. The government did not bow to these pressures. It did take other steps to help some sectors, but many of these measures were justified from an economic point of view and did not involve the use of financial controls.

Reduction of State Control over Credit Allocation
As table 5.3 shows, the percentage of government-controlled credit in the 1970s was high, totaling about 40 percent of total credit. Policymakers believed it was essential to reduce government control over credit in order

to improve allocative efficiency. They also hoped that curtailing credit programs would facilitate industrial restructuring, as the flow of preferential credit to recipients in declining sectors would drop, forcing them to rationalize their production.

The ICs of banks and savings banks were the primary targets of efforts to decrease the amount of administratively controlled credit.[74] In July 1977, the MOE lowered the ICs of savings banks significantly; it also announced a timetable for gradually reducing the ICs of banks and for further cutting those of savings banks starting in January 1978.[75] In addition, the MOE raised interest rates on funds lent through ICs and asserted that it would gradually bring them into line with market interest rates.[76] Nevertheless, it did not give intermediaries greater freedom in allocating funds among the various categories of recipients of preferential credit, something they had long demanded.

The government also reduced state intervention in credit allocation by eliminating the Junta de Inversiones. The primary function of the Junta had been to rate private bond issues (granting or withholding inclusion in the list of assets whose purchase fulfilled the "public funds" coefficient of savings banks) and fix yields on the bonds issued. The decree that abolished the Junta granted automatic "public funds" eligibility to bonds issued by local governments, INI companies, and utilities but stipulated that all other bond issues were ineligible. This meant that most firms would henceforth have to compete for funds on equal terms in the bond market. The elimination of the Junta, therefore, opened the way for the develop-

TABLE 5.3.   Preferential Credit in the 1970s

	As a % of Total Credit[a]	Annual Growth
1971	41.7	n/a
1972	39.0	18.0
1973	36.4	16.1
1974	36.8	19.6
1975	37.4	18.6
1976	38.0	24.2
1977	37.2	16.0
1978	36.7	12.8
1979	36.5	14.8
1980	38.0	12.2

Source: Adapted from Poveda Anadón 1986, cuadro XLI.

[a]Includes preferential credit granted by the Bank of Spain, banks, savings banks, credit cooperatives, and public banks.

n/a = not available

ment of an efficient bond market by allowing market forces, not public officials, to drive activity.

Intermediaries had lobbied for the elimination of credit controls for several years, and they responded favorably to the measures.[77] They opposed selective credit policies, especially ICs, because they were required to supply long-term credit at interest rates fixed below what they could charge for ordinary loans.[78] Credit controls also made it difficult for intermediaries to create safe loan portfolios. By the mid-1970s, some sectors targeted by credit controls, especially capital goods producers (e.g., heavy machinery) were in serious trouble. The requirement to lend to these firms, therefore, forced intermediaries to take on a great deal of default risk. Finally, selective credit policies exposed intermediaries to interest rate risk as they had to provide long-term loans at preferential rates.

Firms without access to preferential credit did not lobby to reduce government control over credit; moreover, a subsequent slowdown in the reduction in ICs (discussed later) elicited only a timid protest from them.[79] This behavior seems anomalous given the potential benefits that the elimination of credit controls would bring these firms, especially at a time when credit was tight and firms were struggling to obtain financing. It is best explained by the collective action problems these firms usually face in organizing to take action on this issue (see chap. 2). Government officials apparently did not attempt to mobilize firms that might benefit from financial deregulation to support the reform process. The late 1970s, however, were a difficult time for creating such a coalition since economic conditions were deteriorating and the government could not point to many immediate positive results from its reforms.

The termination of the Junta de Inversiones met with strong disapproval from firms that had benefited from "qualified" bond and equity issues since it meant they would no longer enjoy a guaranteed market for their bonds and would be forced to pay competitive yields to attract investors. The reductions in ICs also encountered intense opposition from their beneficiaries, principally capital goods producers, exporters, and shipbuilders. The reductions threatened capital goods producers in particular since the funds they obtained through the ICs accounted for about one-quarter of their total financing.[80] Through their trade association, SERCOBE, they pressured top government officials to reinstate the ICs at previous levels, or at least to suspend their reduction.[81] Several shipbuilding firms were also very active, drawing on the help of their unionized workforce in their lobbying efforts.[82] This pressure was especially effective since the government was attempting to establish good relations with labor. Firms were aided by officials in the ministries of Agriculture, Public Works, and especially Industry, in their attempt to maintain credit controls. The Ministry of Industry, for example, argued that firms in the capital goods and shipbuilding sectors would face bankruptcy if they lost their access to preferential finance. This would create large unemployment and dampen industrial output in the short run and cause irreparable long-term damage to the Spanish industrial sector.

All these lobbying efforts paid immediate dividends. In October 1977, the scheduled reduction in banks' ICs was slowed; however, the timetable for cuts in savings banks' ICs was left unchanged, reflecting both the MOE's determination to place banks and savings banks on more equal footing and effective counterpressure by savings banks. This modification did not entirely placate those in favor of credit controls, and they intensified their lobbying. In March 1979, the MOE, confronted with this pressure and deteriorating economic conditions, froze further reductions in banks' ICs until March 1980.

Measures to Increase Competition
As in 1974, the government's principal goal in increasing competition among intermediaries was to improve the efficiency of financial intermediation. The MOE hoped to achieve this goal by creating a level playing field for all intermediaries; this mainly entailed reducing the privileged status of universal banks in the financial sector. The MOE's most important measures involved equalizing the ICs and RRs of intermediaries. First, it lowered the ICs of savings banks more aggressively than that of banks, as already noted. Second, it increased the RRs of savings banks to the same level as those of universal and industrial banks.[83] Finally, it authorized savings banks to engage in commercial operations previously the exclusive domain of industrial and universal banks. Specifically, it allowed them to discount commercial paper and bills, finance import and export operations, and engage in certain international transactions (e.g., the buying and selling of foreign exchange).

Savings banks had been pressuring state officials since the mid-1970s to improve their competitive position vis-à-vis banks, and they greeted these measures enthusiastically.[84] Their efforts had strained their relations with banks. Banks viewed savings banks as potentially strong rivals and, therefore, had responded by lobbying authorities aggressively to maintain the status quo. Banks were especially intent on stopping savings banks from obtaining authorization to engage in commercial operations and gaining access to discretionary BOS credit. They argued that savings banks enjoyed fiscal advantages that would give them an edge if they were allowed to compete in areas previously reserved for banks alone.[85] They also contended that the specialization that had developed among different intermediaries was highly beneficial and should not be jeopardized.

One explanation for why policymakers implemented reforms that leveled the playing field over the objections of banks is that savings banks were more effective in their lobbying of the MOE. In this regard, the appointment of Fuentes, the former director of studies of the Spanish Federation of Savings Banks, certainly did provide savings banks with a sympathetic ear within top-level policy-making circles. A more accurate view, however, is that policymakers implemented the reforms because they were determined to increase competition, and a principal means of doing so was to establish greater equality between banks and savings banks. They had already demonstrated their commitment to improve the competitive position of savings banks, and it is reasonable to suppose they would have proceeded with the reforms in the absence of lobbying by savings banks.

At least initially, banks' fears that savings banks would penetrate their traditional markets were not borne out. Savings banks found it difficult to gain clientele among the biggest users of discounted bills and import/export finance operations—large corporations. Moreover, as shown in figures 4.1 and 4.2, they did not capture significantly greater shares of total deposits or credit to the private sector as a direct result of the reforms.

Finally, policymakers also tried out a new means of increasing competition within the financial sector: encouraging the entry of new intermediaries. The most significant new intermediary authorized in this period was the leasing company.[86] The immediate impact of this move, however, was minimal; leasing companies only started playing a noticeable role in the financial system in the mid-1980s.

Interest Rate Liberalization

In July 1977, the MOE announced that it was liberalizing all deposit and loan interest rates for maturities of one year or longer. It also indicated that it would remove controls on all interest rates by the summer of 1978. Interest rate deregulation had been planned for several months, but the political climate had led to its postponement. Although the measure was widely expected, interest rate deregulation quickly became the most controversial element in the package of financial reforms.[87] In fact, the outcry was so intense that in September the MOE gave up hope of deregulating all interest rates by the summer of 1978 and announced instead that it would occur by June 30, 1979.

The banking sector publicly resisted interest rate reform en bloc as it had in the past. Its stance on this issue was quietly diversifying, however. Most banks continued to oppose liberalization because it would increase competition, but a few viewed it as an opportunity to gain market share at the expense of less efficient institutions.[88] They hoped that the removal of controls would allow them to increase their deposit base by enticing savers with higher rates.

Savings banks, as intermediaries with a smaller market share of both total deposits and assets, had a potential interest in promoting interest rate deregulation. Interest rate reform, however, could only benefit savings banks if it occurred under conditions of relative competitive strength between banks and themselves. If interest rate controls were removed without first equalizing the burden imposed by ICs, savings banks would be at a competitive disadvantage vis-à-vis banks. They would find it difficult to compete for deposits, for instance, when a larger portion of their assets were tied up by the various coefficients at low returns.[89] Consequently, savings banks made their support for the removal of interest rate controls conditional on movement toward greater equality, particularly in the matter of ICs.

Business once again opposed interest rate deregulation because it believed it would increase the cost of credit. Its concern on this issue was heightened by the simultaneous tightening of monetary policy that threatened to decrease the availability of credit. Banks attempted to take advantage of business's anxiety over the cost of credit by urging firms to pressure the government to stop interest rate reform. Many firms heeded this advice and lobbied state officials, particularly those in the Ministry of Industry, on this issue. The minister of industry (as well as the ministers of public works and agriculture) took up their cause and resisted interest rate reform in the Council of Ministers and the Economic Commission. As already noted, all this pressure was effective. Although interest rate controls were not reimposed, their further deregulation was frozen until 1981.

The Foreign Banking Controversy

In the Franco era, the Spanish financial market was closed to foreign intermediaries. Only four foreign banks, all authorized before the Civil War, were operating in Spain in the 1970s. In the early 1970s, policymakers periodically raised the possibility of authorizing foreign banks, but the banking sector's strident opposition led them to shelve the idea. Moreover, policymakers viewed other financial reforms (e.g., interest rate deregulation) as more fundamental, and they opted to implement them before beginning what promised to be a difficult battle to open the financial system.

Villar Mir, minister of finance under Arias Navarro, made the first formal proposal to authorize foreign banks in the spring of 1976. His initiative did not fare well. Banks fought the proposal at a meeting of the CSB in the spring of 1976, and the government quietly let the matter drop. In early 1977, financial policymakers again expressed interest in a new foreign banking law; Suárez, however, decided to put the matter on hold when it was determined that elections would be held in June.[90]

The UCD reopened the foreign banking issue after the 1977 elections. Fuentes believed that opening financial markets was an essential element of liberalization, and he promised a new foreign banking law by the end of the year. José Toribio Dávila, the MOE's director of financial policy, personally worked with BOS officials to draft the legislation. Policymakers had three basic rationales for opening up Spain's financial markets. The first was to increase competition within the banking sector. Spanish banks were woefully inefficient compared to their foreign counterparts. Policymakers believed that the entry of foreign banks would increase competitive pressures on Spanish banks, spurring them to greater efficiency. The second rationale was to encourage financial innovation and improve the managerial competence of domestic banks. Foreign banks were expected to introduce new management techniques and financial instruments that would diffuse throughout the banking sector. Finally, policymakers anticipated that financial opening would give Spanish banks the opportunity to increase their presence in international markets through the principle of reciprocity. In particular, they hoped that Spanish banks would be able to establish branches in foreign countries (particularly the United States), thereby facilitating import/export operations.[91]

Foreign governments applied some pressure on the Spanish government to open its financial markets. In the mid-1970s, Spain was the only OECD country that did not permit foreign banking, and several member countries urged Spain to give foreign intermediaries greater access to its markets. In addition, a number of foreign banks lobbied the Spanish government directly. Pressure by U.S. and German banks was particularly intense in 1977 and early 1978. Nevertheless, the overall drive to achieve greater efficiency is what chiefly explains the decision to open markets since interest in financial opening on the part of Spanish policymakers clearly preceded foreign lobbying. International pressure was most important in helping would-be reformers in their struggle with those that opposed financial opening.

A draft of the foreign banking legislation was ready by November 1977, and it quickly found its way into the hands of the banking sector. Banks immediately launched a fierce lobbying campaign against it, claiming it was too "liberal."[92] Nevertheless, they realized that international pressure as well as the MOE's determination made authorization of foreign banks inevitable. Consequently, they concentrated their efforts on limiting the damage that foreign institutions might inflict. Specifically, banks sought to limit the range of activities open to foreign banks; restrict their ability to compete for deposits; establish stiff entrance requirements to discourage all but the most determined applicants; and sharply restrict the ability of foreign banks to purchase domestic institutions.

The government established new regulations governing foreign banking in June 1978.[93] The regulations demonstrated that Spanish banks had succeeded in restricting the operations of foreign banks. Government officials backed off from their initial proposals to avoid angering banks even further at a time when the MOE had just implemented several unpopular measures (and was contemplating additional liberalizing reforms). The banking sector still played a dominant role in the economy, and its cooperation was needed to restore growth. In addition, the UCD knew that it would have to rely on bank loans to finance the upcoming electoral campaigns.[94] The imposition of heavy restrictions on foreign banks despite external pressure showed that domestic politics still carried more weight in determining financial policy.

The regulations permitted two types of foreign banks: branches and affiliated banks.[95] To gain entry, foreign banks had to fulfill all the entry requirements (e.g., paid-in capital) that domestic banks had to meet. In addition, they faced the following restrictions: (1) they were limited to three offices in Spain; (2) they could not hold equity in Spanish firms; (3) a maximum of 40 percent of their working capital could be raised in the Spanish market, although funds obtained from the interbank market were excluded from this restriction; and (4) the BOS would inspect them annually. The government authorized twenty-three foreign banks within thirteen months of the new regulations, but allowed only ten to start operations immediately; most of the other banks began operations in early 1980.[96] U.S., German, French, and British banks dominated the early entrants.

Despite the severe restrictions, foreign banks had an immediate impact. Foreign banks' share of total banking system assets rose dramatically, from 0.7 percent in 1979 to about 6.5 percent in the mid-1980s, where it stagnated.[97] Foreign banks also demonstrated their superior competitiveness. Table 5.4 indicates that they earned very large profits compared to national banks (which were themselves highly profitable by international standards).

As policymakers had anticipated, foreign banks quickly made a qualitative impact as well. Interest rate margins fell with the entry of foreign banks, the result of greater competition in the banking sector, but this was mostly a one-time effect.[98] Foreign banks were also responsible for deepening several specific markets and introducing new financial instruments. The most significant development of this kind was the expansion of the interbank market.[99] The Spanish interbank market formed in the early 1970s to help banks cover their reserve and liquidity requirements. The

BOS promoted the interbank market because it believed it would facilitate its strategy of targeting monetary aggregates and provide a reference interest rate for other financial markets.[100] The market stagnated, however, because bank managers believed that borrowing from other banks was a sign of poor management. After foreign banks began operating in 1980, the interbank market finally took off.[101] Policymakers had purposefully not restricted the amount of funds foreign banks could obtain from the interbank market in order to encourage its growth.

In a related development, the government began to integrate the Spanish financial system into international markets. The government lifted some capital controls in 1977. In 1978, it introduced a draft bill that established a new legal foundation for international financial transactions; the Cortes approved it in December 1979. This legislation liberalized international transactions in two important ways. First, it permitted intermediaries to engage in a wider variety of transactions without prior government approval. Second, it allowed all Spanish firms to raise capital in international capital markets and with fewer conditions; the government, however, retained the right to limit external borrowing whenever it wished.[102] Banks and large firms, which had pressed for reform in these areas for several years, embraced these measures.

Conclusion

The 1977 financial reforms were a watershed in Spanish financial policy. They represented the first systematic attempt to reduce most dimensions of state intervention in financial markets, increase competition within the financial sector, and develop stronger linkages between Spanish financial markets and the international financial system.

Public officials once again provided the impetus behind this stage of financial deregulation. Spain's transition to democracy ushered in political

TABLE 5.4.   Comparison of Banking Ratios between Spanish and Foreign Banks Operating in Spain, 1986

	Return on Equity Capital[a]	Profits/Total Resources[a]	Profits/ Employee[b]
Spanish banks[c]	16.49	1.26	1.35
Foreign banks	26.11	5.86	5.20

Source: Consejo Superior Bancario 1986.
[a]Expressed as a percentage
[b]In millions of pesetas
[c]Large national banks

institutions that gave politicians a relatively greater incentive to supply collective economic goods, such as efficient financial markets, rather than private benefits, such as credit rents, to select groups in the pursuit of power. The first UCD government responded to these incentives. Suárez brought in a team of economic policymakers, led by Fuentes Quintana, who implemented a classic stabilization plan and initiated a series of structural reforms aimed at promoting overall social welfare while abolishing the rents conferred upon entrenched economic elites by prevailing government policy. In seeking reform, the UCD astutely took advantage of an early consensus among major political actors that deep economic adjustment was necessary to promote economic and political stability. This consensus resulted in the signing of the Moncloa Pacts in October 1977, an agreement in which Spain's major political parties expressed their support for many structural reforms, including financial liberalization.

Nevertheless, government officials did not succeed in mobilizing groups that might benefit from financial deregulation in order to provide support for sustaining the reform process. As general economic conditions deteriorated after the 1977 reforms and political tensions within the UCD deepened, the drive behind the liberalization process dissipated. The next chapter examines these events.

CHAPTER 6

Sustaining Financial Reform in Hard Times: 1978–82

Starting in mid-1978, the UCD government turned its attention to the political issues surrounding the democratic transition and temporarily put aside active economic adjustment. Financial deregulation was one casualty of the slowdown in structural reforms. In addition, Spain's economic situation deteriorated further. Deregulation opponents were able to associate financial reforms with Spain's economic distress, and this put pressure on the government to postpone additional liberalization. Some technocratic policymakers also decided that certain reforms should proceed at a slower pace until greater financial and macroeconomic stability was achieved. The government, however, did not repeal reforms already implemented or extend its control over financial markets in new ways; in fact, liberalization continued in several areas.

The slowdown in structural reforms suggests that the argument that Spain's transition led to economic adjustment must be qualified somewhat. First, although Spain's new democratic institutions encouraged political leaders to promote aggregate economic performance by creating efficient markets, the UCD was unable to complete the process of structural adjustment required to achieve this goal, despite its initial efforts. As discussed in chapter 5, the UCD was poorly constituted to be a reformist party, and it lacked a parliamentary majority. This suggests that the character of the governing party and its parliamentary strength are critical variables in determining economic policy outcomes during a transition.

Second, the UCD lacked sufficient autonomy from banking and business interests opposed to many of the proposed structural reforms. In addition, labor's potential to disrupt the transition meant the government had to seek its cooperation with the economic adjustment program. The UCD government did not yield to most of the demands made by these groups, but the need to consult with and occasionally appease them constrained its ability to sustain structural adjustment. The importance of autonomy is highlighted by the observation that in policy areas where the government was more autonomous, like finance, it was more successful at achieving reform; even the Socialists, who were far less dependent on entrenched economic groups, found it very difficult to achieve reform in certain policy areas (e.g., energy).

From a comparative perspective, the Spanish experience confirms Przeworski's hypothesis that transitional governments face special problems in implementing structural reforms (even when they have good reasons for attempting them) and that a period of retrenchment typically ensues as the immediate costs of reforms are felt fully. Nonetheless, it indicates that such changes are still possible. In Spain, the leaders of a weak and divided party, faced with daunting political issues and a struggling economy, still managed to initiate and even successfully implement several important structural adjustment measures.

Significantly, financial deregulation began again in 1981. Policymakers implemented a major reform package in January and several other liberalizing measures during the year. Liberalization resumed in part because UCD leaders realized that the electorate had become disenchanted with the government's policies and apparent inability to deal decisively with the struggling economy. Party leaders decided that further delay could lead to a severe economic crisis and would destroy the UCD's chances to succeed in the upcoming 1982 elections. In addition, the Social Democrats, the political group most in favor of economic reform within the UCD, took over key economic posts in a 1980 cabinet reorganization; their greater power was due in part to the perception that they would breathe new life into the government's economic policy.

The first part of this chapter examines the political and economic events that led the UCD to slow financial liberalization after mid-1978. In particular, it explores the complex interactions between the state of the economy and the prospects for financial reform. The second part analyzes why the UCD reopened the financial deregulation process in 1981 and the measures it undertook. I examine the politics surrounding these reforms in depth because they reveal the calculations of major private and public sector actors concerning key policy issues.

Financial Reform in a Period of Political and Economic Crisis, 1978–79

The Political Crisis

Tension among government officials over economic policy grew throughout the fall of 1977. Fuentes became increasingly bitter and disillusioned because the ministries of Industry, Agriculture, Public Works, and Transportation did not always cooperate with the government's stated policy objectives. Although he was vice president of economic affairs, Fuentes did not have the authority to compel other ministries to follow his overall strategy because of their autonomy in their respective policy domains. Officials in these ministries had agendas of their own, which did not always coincide with Fuentes's plans. A few top-ranking officials contested Fuentes's policies in the Council of Ministers, the Economic Affairs Committee, and the Undersecretaries Commission.[1] On most issues, Fuentes had allies in the ministers of finance and commerce, Francisco Fernández Ordoñez and Juan Antonio García Díez, respectively, both Social Democrats. Suárez himself publicly and privately supported Fuentes's economic strategy.[2]

Fuentes's disputes with Alberto Oliart, the minister of industry, over how to deal with struggling industrial sectors, especially steel and shipbuilding, illustrate the clash in perspectives.[3] Oliart favored propping up these sectors with subsidized loans and other state aid until the economy improved sufficiently to allow them to regain solvency. Fuentes, on the other hand, wanted to pare them down (primarily by streamlining INI firms) to reflect market realities.

In early December, Fuentes threatened to resign his posts unless Suárez granted him greater control over economic policy (through an administrative reorganization) and replaced the ministers of agriculture, transportation, and industry.[4] Suárez was sympathetic, but he could not and would not meet all of Fuentes's demands. The Christian Democrats and others who opposed rapid economic reform warned Suárez that they would withdraw their support from the UCD if he granted Fuentes greater authority. Their threats were potent at the time, since Suárez was completing negotiations on turning the UCD electoral coalition into a permanent party.

Aware that he would never obtain greater authority over the government's overall economic policy, Fuentes resigned on February 11, 1978.[5] Suárez appointed Fernando Abril Martorell, a trusted friend and political advisor, to replace him as vice president of economic affairs and minister of economics.[6] He convinced Fuentes to remain as his chief economic advisor. Abril had little training in financial or monetary economics but had served as minister of agriculture in the first Suárez government. Highly regarded for his negotiating skills and extensive political contacts, the Spanish press quickly dubbed Abril the "fireman" summoned to put out the flames of dissent within the party and government.[7] A major cabinet reorganization also ensued. The two Social Democrats, Fernández Ordoñez and García Díez, retained their portfolios, but all other economic ministers were replaced. In an apparent effort to smooth ruffled feathers in the business community, the new minister of industry, Augustín

Rodríguez Sahagún, was drawn directly from the CEOE, where he had been vice president.[8] The government stated that the cabinet reorganization would not affect its economic policies, stressing particularly that the Moncloa Pacts would be implemented fully.

The UCD's declarations notwithstanding, Fuentes's resignation did mark a shift in the government's economic strategy away from active, comprehensive structural reform. Abril believed that resolving the political issues associated with the consolidation of democracy should take precedence over deepening economic reforms, however necessary the latter might be. In fact, the government confronted an imposing set of political issues. First, it had to contend with demands for regional autonomy. In the Basque country, political violence, especially ETA terrorism, threatened to unravel an already shaky social and political environment.[9] Second, it faced the threat of armed forces subversion, partly as a result of dissatisfaction over the government's "soft" handling of terrorism. Finally, it had to draft and gain support for a new constitution. Abril personally led this effort, undertaking secret negotiations with Alfonso Guerra, the vice president of the PSOE, the main opposition party, on the basic outlines of a new constitution immediately after taking on his new post.

With Suárez's acquiescence, Abril adopted a more passive adjustment strategy featuring a more gradual, less controversial reform of fiscal and financial policy. The decision to slow financial deregulation displeased MOE technocrats who wished to proceed with more aggressive reform. The government also decided to continue to increase social welfare spending and postpone industrial restructuring to prevent further layoffs. In effect, UCD leadership calculated that the short-term benefits of not exacerbating social and political tensions temporarily outweighed the advantages of seeking greater efficiency through structural reforms. The success of the transition depended on maintaining social peace, and social peace depended in large part on not alienating labor.

In addition, UCD leaders realized that the transition had not completely destroyed the privileged status of national banks and big business. The government would have to proceed slowly in the face of their stiff resistance to reforms, since they had the potential to disrupt the economy (e.g., by withholding capital or investment). Nevertheless, at Suárez's insistence, the UCD continued to avoid formulating its policies to benefit powerful economic interest groups. This contributed to tense relations between top UCD leaders, especially Suárez, and the business community, which, because of its close ties to some UCD politicians, expected policies designed to advance their interests.[10]

Finally, the collaboration among political parties that had created a climate propitious for undertaking stabilization and economic restructuring, as seen in the signing of the Moncloa Pacts, had largely crumbled. Opposition parties viewed Fuentes's resignation as an indication that the UCD was backing off from its commitment to implement fundamental reforms and decided that they had little incentive to support the government's economic program.[11] Thereafter, opposition parties, especially the PSOE, took every opportunity to malign UCD's handling of the economy and gain the support of those dissatisfied with prevailing policies.[12]

The Deepening Economic Crisis

In 1978, Spain's already bad economic situation deteriorated further, increasing the public's distress over the state of the economy. As table 6.1 indicates, all major economic indicators, except inflation and the balance of payments, worsened.[13] In comparative perspective, Spain's economic situation was only somewhat worse than that of other European countries in this period.

Opponents of financial liberalization, namely, banks, business organizations, and the beneficiaries of selective credit policies, attempted to associate economic problems, especially climbing interest rates and stagnation in the industrial sector, with financial reform in order to put pressure on the government to stop the deregulation process. This lobbying campaign helped convince Abril that financial reform should proceed very slowly. In addition, some policymakers decided that economic circumstances counseled a more gradual approach to certain aspects of financial reform, notably interest rate deregulation. Increasing insolvency among

TABLE 6.1.   Some Indicators of the Economic Crisis, 1974–82 (in percentages)

	Annual Real GNP Growth	Unemployment	Annual Inflation Rate	Balance of Payments/ GNP	Annual Capital Investment Growth	Annual Industrial Production Growth
1974	5.7	3.2	17.9	−3.7	6.6	6.2
1975	1.1	4.0	14.1	−3.3	−3.9	−0.6
1976	3.0	4.9	19.8	−4.0	−2.0	3.4
1977	3.3	5.7	26.4	−1.8	−0.2	4.7
1978	1.8	7.4	16.5	1.1	−2.4	2.0
1979	0.2	9.1	15.5	0.6	−4.5	−0.1
1980	1.5	11.8	15.5	−2.5	3.0	0.4
1981	0.1	14.6	14.5	−2.7	1.0	0.0
1982	1.1	16.5	14.4	−2.4	−0.9	−0.3

Source: Banco de España, "Boletín Estadístico," various issues, and Ministerio de Comercio, "Balanza de Pagos," various issues.

firms and banks, combined with high inflation, produced an economic climate that was in fact ill suited for rapid deregulation. As discussed in chapter 1, removing interest rate controls quickly under inflationary conditions may provoke high real interest rates and excessive risk taking by intermediaries. Moreover, the sudden halt of selective credit policies may lead their beneficiaries to collapse, with all the attendant problems for the stability of the financial system.

Three interrelated issues became the focus of the financial policy debate: the scarcity of credit and high interest rates; stagnant investment, growing unemployment, and bankruptcies in industry; and the emergence of a severe banking crisis. I examine these issues and their impact on financial policy in the following sections.

Tight Money and High Interest Rates
"High" interest rates and scarce credit became the object of major controversies in the period between 1978 and 1980, largely because business put these issues at the top of their political agenda. Business stepped up its traditional opposition to tight monetary policy, claiming that it was directly responsible for a drop in the availability of credit. It supported the fight against inflation that motivated the tight money policy but argued that the government should put more effort into controlling its spending, as well as designing and winning support for an incomes policy that could hold down wage growth.[14]

In reality, the money supply was growing at a pace faster than that desired by monetary authorities, helping to keep inflation up around 16 percent in 1978. Table 6.2 shows the evolution of money supply (as measured by M2) and several of its components. Higher government expenditures, a greater volume of exports, and sharp capital inflows (due to increased foreign borrowing) raised money supply growth to an annual rate of 18.3 percent in 1978, above the 17.0 percent targeted by the MOF. The BOS tried to offset the liquidity injected by the external and public sectors by limiting credit to the private sector (primarily by reducing bank access to BOS lines of credit). Consequently, many firms did suffer liquidity problems because real levels of credit to the private sector actually dropped.[15]

Business also complained bitterly about the rise in interest rates, contending that it was a principal cause of low levels of investment and its declining profitability. (Table 6.3 shows the evolution of key interest rates in this period.) Increases in the cost of bank credit were especially troubling for Spanish firms because they were dependent on debt finance and had few alternative sources of funds; that is, their demand for bank credit was highly inelastic. Table 6.4 shows that firm financing costs in fact rose sharply in the period. Cuervo has argued that this increase was a principal reason why firm profitability decreased in the late 1970s.[16] In contrast, Argandoña Ramiz has contended that higher interest rates had only a marginal impact on firm profitability.[17]

Business leaders attributed high interest rates to two basic causes. First, they argued that the government's tight money policy had reduced the supply of credit sharply, thereby pushing up its price. They chose not to direct their hostility at the government alone, however. They also complained bitterly that banks were taking advantage of their dominant posi-

TABLE 6.2. **Monetary Growth and Credit to the Public and Private Sectors, Annual Growth Rates, 1974–82**

	M2	Credit to the Public Sector	Credit to the Private Sector
1974	19.0	18.8	25.5
1975	19.0	20.5	22.7
1976	19.2	5.1	23.5
1977	18.9	1.1	22.0
1978	18.3	40.1	13.7
1979	19.3	15.7	20.5
1980	17.1	38.2	18.4
1981	15.3	41.0	17.6
1982	16.6	35.2	18.2

Source: Banco de España, "Boletín Estadístico," various issues.

TABLE 6.3. **The Evolution of Various Interest Rates, 1974–84**

	Banks[a]		Savings Banks[b]		Interbank Market[c]	
	Nominal	Real	Nominal	Real	Nominal	Real
1974	9.3	−7.8	n/a	n/a	10.7	−4.8
1975	10.5	−7.0	8.8	−7.9	8.8	−6.5
1976	10.8	−6.6	9.1	−7.6	10.5	−4.0
1977	12.0	−11.7	9.7	−13.1	14.4	−7.4
1978	13.9	−6.9	12.2	−9.1	20.2	1.6
1979	15.4	−2.4	12.6	−5.0	15.1	−0.5
1980	16.0	1.2	13.3	−1.6	15.2	1.8
1981	16.7	1.9	14.3	−0.4	15.5	2.0
1982	16.3	1.8	14.9	−0.1	15.8	2.2
1983	15.9	4.1	14.7	2.4	18.8	8.1
1984	16.0	5.0	14.7	2.7	14.8	2.4

Source: Banco de España 1985.

[a]Nominal rates were on loans not controlled by authorities; real rates were on discounted bills.
[b]Nominal rates were on loans not controlled by authorities; real rates were on all lending activity.
[c]Nominal rates were on day-to-day operations; real rates were on one-month loans.
n/a = not available

tion in industrial finance to raise interest rates and commissions excessively. They claimed that bank profit margins were actually widening and that net profits remained outrageously high although most economic sectors were suffering losses.[18] Second, business leaders argued that recent financial deregulation, especially the removal of deposit rate ceilings, had sparked a deleterious race for deposits that had bid up the cost of bank liabilities; the primary consequence of this was higher loan rates. Consequently, high interest rates became business's rallying cry against financial deregulation.[19]

Banks blamed high interest rates mainly on the government's recent financial reforms. Specifically, banks argued that the removal of deposit rate ceilings and their continuing obligation to provide preferential credit had left them with no choice but to increase loan rates.[20] They claimed that they faced higher operating costs that cut into their financial margins and vehemently denied the charge that their profits were excessive. They were unhappy that the MOE's tight monetary policy had reduced liquidity in the banking system but generally approved of its efforts to keep inflation low.

MOE and BOS officials disputed the charges leveled against the government's monetary and financial policies. They argued that a restrictive monetary policy was a necessity in the fight against inflation and that current policy was not overly tight. Nominal interest rates, they claimed, were not excessively high, since real rates remained negative or extremely low.

TABLE 6.4.   Measures of Firm Profitability, 1974–85 (expressed as percentages)

	Return on Investment[a]	Return on Equity Capital[b]	Profits/ Sales	Cost of Finance/ Sales
1974	11.57	19.11	7.33	3.98
1975	9.54	12.12	6.08	4.61
1976	9.80	12.50	5.88	4.76
1977	11.17	13.10	4.77	4.48
1978	11.10	8.90	2.94	5.51
1979	11.00	8.60	3.52	5.69
1980	8.60	2.70	1.00	5.77
1981	5.80	−0.50	−0.23	6.46
1982	6.70	−0.20	−0.09	6.95
1983	6.42	0.02	0.06	7.13
1984	6.57	1.00	0.06	7.04
1985	7.00	3.21	1.69	6.20

Source: Adapted from Cuervo 1988, cuadro 3.4.
[a]Return on Investment = Profit before Taxes/Total Assets
[b]Return on Equity Capital = Profits before Taxes/Equity Capital

In any case, they contended that the increase in nominal rates was due to inflation and the lack of competition in the financial sector, not to deregulation. They argued that increasing competition in the financial sector through deregulation would reduce the cost of credit in the long run since it would reduce intermediaries' financial margins.

The available evidence suggests that banks were able to pass the burden of higher operating costs and more expensive liabilities onto firms through higher loan rates. Table 6.5 demonstrates that banks maintained or even increased their financial margins despite the economic downturn and the competition-augmenting reforms implemented in 1977, undoubtedly because they still faced little competition. As table 6.6 indicates, savings banks, anxious to capture a greater market share, were less effective in passing along higher operating costs. Bank profits, nevertheless, were not higher as business charged, despite augmented margins. The drop in profits was primarily due to higher loan-loss provisions.[21]

Academic studies also indicate that deregulation was not the primary cause of higher interest rates. The consensus among Spanish economists was that interest rates rose due to inflation, increased operating costs in the banking sector, and a tighter monetary policy.[22] The removal of deposit rate ceilings had only a marginal impact compared to these other factors. Moreover, higher interest rates apparently had little effect on overall

TABLE 6.5. Banks' Operating Costs, Financial Margins, Loan-Loss Provisions, and Profits as a Percentage of Total Assets, 1974–85

	[1] Operating Costs[a]	[2] Financial Margin[b]	[3] [2] - [1]	[4] Loan-Loss Provisions	[5] Profits before Taxes[c]
1974	2.55	3.74	1.19	0.10	1.29
1975	2.88	4.09	1.21	0.09	1.26
1976	3.00	4.29	1.29	0.18	1.22
1977	3.33	4.66	1.33	0.36	1.03
1978	3.50	4.87	1.37	0.62	0.87
1979	3.53	5.02	1.49	0.72	0.83
1980	3.52	5.11	1.59	0.83	0.76
1981	3.36	5.01	1.65	0.79	0.76
1982	3.11	4.65	1.54	0.82	0.60
1983	3.01	4.88	1.87	1.05	0.64
1984	2.75	4.54	1.79	0.94	0.59
1985	2.65	4.32	1.67	0.68	0.73

Source: Banco de España, "Boletín Económico," various issues.
[a]Operating Costs = Personnel Costs + General Expenses + Taxes + Amortizations
[b]Financial Margin = Average Yield on Loans – Average Cost of Deposits + Commissions
[c]Profits before Taxes = Column 3 + Other Profits – Column 4

investment levels, although they might have hurt firm profitability, as Cuervo contends.

Nevertheless, some UCD leaders, especially Abril, feared that high interest rates might become a political liability. Consequently, he made finding ways to increase the supply of credit to the private sector and lower its cost a top priority. In mid-1978, at the behest of business leaders, he sought the voluntary cooperation of the banking sector in controlling the cost of credit. He asked the AEB to prepare a proposal outlining the conditions under which banks would be willing to increase medium- and long-term lending and decrease interest rates. The AEB presented the MOE with its proposal in November.[23] Banks offered to supply more medium- and long-term credit in exchange for a reduction in the amount of preferential credit they had to supply or an increase in its cost. The government ultimately rejected these and similar AEB proposals, as is discussed later.[24]

One reason policymakers were able to turn aside the banking sector's demands as well as press on with reforms it opposed was the hostility exhibited toward banks by much of the political class (notably Suárez) and the populace. Banks met with disapproval because of their continued high profits at a time of sharp economic downturn. In addition, banks were exposed to fierce ideological attack because they were perceived to have been among the primary supporters and beneficiaries of the Franquist regime. Rumors circulated widely that banks were withholding credit to

TABLE 6.6.   Savings Banks' Operating Costs, Financial Margins, Loan-Loss Provisions, and Profits as a Percentage of Total Assets, 1976–85

	[1] Operating Costs[a]	[2] Financial Margin[b]	[3] [2] - [1]	[4] Loan-Loss Provisions	[5] Profits before Taxes[c]
1976	2.45	3.60	1.15	n/a	1.20
1977	2.79	3.84	1.05	n/a	1.06
1978	3.00	3.80	0.80	0.34	0.88
1979	3.06	3.99	0.93	0.32	0.96
1980	3.24	4.16	0.92	0.36	0.99
1981	3.38	4.33	0.95	0.53	1.00
1982	3.46	4.63	1.17	0.57	1.00
1983	3.42	4.76	1.34	0.89	1.07
1984	3.23	4.66	1.43	0.64	1.04
1985	3.05	4.51	1.46	0.52	1.06

Source: Banco de España, "Boletín Económico," various issues.
[a]Operating Costs = Personnel Costs + General Expenses + Taxes + Amortizations
[b]Financial Margin = Average Yield on Loans – Average Cost of Deposits + Commissions
[c]Profits before Taxes = Column 3 + Other Profits – Column 4
n/a = not available

damage the economy and discredit the new democracy or that some were secretly financing rebellious military officials. Banks vehemently denied these allegations but to little avail. Nevertheless, as the foreign banking controversy shows, the UCD believed it was best to choose its battles with banks carefully to avoid antagonizing them unduly because of their important position in the economy.

The Industrial Crisis

In 1978, economic policymakers increasingly turned their attention toward what they considered to be a growing "industrial crisis." The data reveal that the downturn in the industrial sector was significant. Table 6.1 shows that fixed capital investment and industrial production declined precipitously. In addition, the number of firms declaring suspension of payments and bankruptcy increased sharply in 1978 and 1979.[25] Finally, table 6.4 shows that the profitability of industrial firms, measured in various ways, generally declined. The impact on workers of these trends was large, resulting in big increases in jobs eliminated, layoffs, and workday reductions.[26] The second OPEC oil shock of 1979 and a slowdown in the world economy helped to further erode the strength of the industrial sector in the early 1980s.

As already discussed, business contended that the government's financial and monetary policies were responsible for many of industry's problems, and the UCD found itself on the defensive. The government did not yield to the demand for a more permissive monetary policy. However, confronted with growing hostility from firms and workers, it did adopt several "soft budgeting" measures to support distressed firms, especially to prevent additional unemployment. It decided to bail out several large distressed private firms by nationalizing them, adding to the already huge burden state-owned enterprises imposed on government finances. Altogether, it nationalized thirty firms between 1976 and 1980, many of them in steel and shipbuilding, purchasing virtually worthless stock from shareholders at very favorable prices.[27] In addition, the blanket nationalizations created potential moral hazard problems among other firms since the government's actions indicated that it would not allow large private firms to fail.

Second, the government opted to maintain the flow of subsidized credit to firms in distress. As discussed in chapter 5, the government slowed the reduction of banks' ICs in late 1977 (and froze them entirely in 1979) in response to pressure from their beneficiaries. In 1979, it imposed ICs on credit unions and rural savings banks in a move that increased slightly the quantity of funds flowing through privileged circuits.[28] This policy had one important liberalizing dimension, however: it eliminated the competitive advantage credit unions and rural savings banks had enjoyed over banks and savings banks because of their exclusion from ICs. Thus, this measure helped to level the playing field among existing intermediaries, a feature MOE officials highlighted in their statements.

The government's policy of postponing industry's adjustment to a changing domestic and world economy proved to be costly. At a time when some European countries were going through a period of active adjustment, Spain was delaying the inevitable. This made industrial restructuring in the 1980s all the more difficult and expensive. In particular, it contributed to larger government deficits, which acted as a brake on financial liberalization (see chap. 7). It should be noted that UCD officials were aware of the necessity of carrying out industrial restructuring. They announced their intention to begin this process several times and later passed broad enabling legislation.[29] They failed to carry through on their plans, however, when they confronted high short-term economic and political costs.

Finally, the government decided to provide direct help to SMCs. In July 1978, the government authorized the formation of Sociedades de Garantía Recíproca (SGRs, Mutual Guarantee Companies).[30] SGRs were intended to help SMCs that could not obtain adequate financing due to insufficient collateral. SMCs could join a SGR by contributing a specified amount of capital. They were then eligible to list the pooled resources of the SGR as collateral when applying for credit. Twenty-two SGRs were created between 1978 and 1981 with total capital resources of 2.3 billion pesetas.[31] The government also created the Instituto de la Pequeña y Mediana Empresa (Institute of the Small- and Medium-sized Company) in the Ministry of Industry to promote the growth of SMCs, but it never played a major role in economic policy-making. The steps to help SMCs were probably warranted from an economic perspective. In most countries, SMCs find it difficult to obtain financing but are often responsible for a large proportion of growth in output and employment. Thus, many economists have suggested that governments should actively seek to improve their financing.[32]

The government's decision to create SGRs was the direct result of intense pressure by SMCs through their associations, CEPYME and COPYME.[33] In addition, CEPYME lobbied hard for the creation of a subcoefficient within the ICs that would have required banks to lend to SMCs. Significantly, these groups did not seek the elimination of the financial controls that were at the root of credit rationing. They believed that their optimal strategy was to obtain their own piece of the preferential credit pie rather than seek general reform.

MOE officials opposed the creation of a subcoefficient for SMCs, and top-level government officials backed them on this point.[34] They felt that an additional subcoefficient, even if it was offset by a reduction in other subcoefficients, would open the door for further requests for credit controls. Indeed, they were already under intense pressure from construction firms to establish a subcoefficient for their sector. Policymakers finally agreed to the creation of SGRs because they believed they would not greatly distort the functioning of financial markets but would reduce pressure for more harmful credit floors. In fact, they were able to avoid implementing any new credit controls favoring specific sectors until the mid-1980s. The government's handling of acute pressure for new credit controls showed that it was committed to not broadening state control over credit allocation and is further evidence that the UCD carefully avoided reliance on a political strategy based on nurturing ties to narrow constituencies.

The Banking Crisis

Largely unbeknownst to financial authorities, by late 1977 the Spanish banking system was on the brink of mass insolvency. The Spanish banking crisis, which lasted from 1978 to 1985, affected 56 out of 110 Spanish banks and 27 percent of the total capital of the banking system according to official sources.[35] The crisis severely undermined confidence in the banking system and was only resolved at a tremendous cost to taxpayers.

Many factors contributed to the Spanish banking crisis.[36] One set of factors involved the close ties between banks and firms. Bank ownership of firms encouraged banks to provide ample credit to firms in which they had a stake, whether or not this lending was justified on purely economic grounds. In addition, selective credit policies forced banks to lend excessively to certain sectors, many of them in decline. Overconcentrated lending exposed the banking system to severe default risk, especially as macroeconomic conditions deteriorated. In Spain, these problems were exacerbated because banks often rolled over bad loans rather than writing them off when defaults occurred.[37] Finally, banks incurred heavy losses on their equity holdings as firms struggled. In short, close bank-firm ties led to risky loan portfolios that collapsed under the weight of the economic slowdown; accounting procedures and poor banking practices hid the extent of the banking system's insolvency problems. This aspect of Spain's banking crisis illustrates one of the potential dangers of a bank-based financial system: it can cause serious insolvency problems when the real economy struggles and firms default on loans.[38]

A grievous lack of prudential regulation also contributed mightily to the crisis. Control over entry into the banking profession was overly lax. In the 1960s and 1970s, the MOF authorized the creation of new banks or the purchase of existing banks by investors who did not have the qualifications or experience to be bankers. The purchase of eighteen banks by the Rumasa industrial group is perhaps the most glaring example of this negligence. Incredibly, almost every bank created or purchased in the 1960s and 1970s failed during the course of the crisis.[39] More importantly, until the crisis broke, many policymakers believed that the banking system was not at risk and, thus, did not require close supervision. High, steady bank profits (some of them fictitious, as noted earlier) convinced officials that the banking system was essentially sound. Consequently, until 1977, supervision was directed mostly toward gauging compliance with interest rate and credit controls, not on examining the overall level of risk of a bank's loan portfolio or its capital adequacy.

Finally, earlier deregulation had increased competition among banks without concomitantly increasing prudential regulation. The 1974 reforms had a particularly deleterious effect on bank solvency. The rapid increase in the number of bank branches and offices produced by the reforms sharply augmented operating costs.[40] The lack of competition within the financial sector and inelastic demand for bank credit allowed banks to increase financial margins to cover their increased costs. This increased the overall riskiness of their loan portfolios because it raised the probability of default by borrowers. The government compounded the mistake of not overseeing bank lending by creating deposit insurance in 1977. The Fondo de Garantía de Depósitos (FGD, Guaranteed Deposits Fund) was meant to increase depositors' confidence in the banking system during the uncertain political and economic climate of the transition. Deposit insurance, however, created a moral hazard problem. It gave intermediaries an incentive to gamble with deposits by making high-return but risky loans, since their liability was limited to paid-in capital. Anecdotal evidence suggests that some banks did increase risky lending practices after the creation of the FGD.[41]

The banking crisis broke in February 1978 when the BOS announced that the Banco de Navarra and Banco Cantábrico, two small regional banks, were insolvent. As more banks failed, the government scrambled, on a case-by-case basis, to limit losses and preserve the integrity of the banking system, primarily by injecting capital into failing banks.[42] Private banks also provided capital reluctantly, agreeing to do so only after the government threatened to withhold funds if banks did not shoulder some of the rescue costs. The crisis culminated when the first PSOE government expropriated the eighteen Rumasa banks in 1983.[43] The official tally of the cost of the crisis was staggering: the government contributed 1.4 trillion pesetas ($14 billion) and the banking sector 365 billion pesetas ($4 billion) to bail out insolvent banks.[44] Most observers believe that the cost was actually much higher.

Liberalization opponents, particularly banks, wasted little time in blaming financial deregulation for the banking system's instability. They argued that past reforms that had increased the cost of liabilities and the level of competition within the sector had provoked financial instability by encouraging intermediaries to take excessive risks. Moreover, they contended that the financial system could not withstand further deregulation. Significantly, this argument found sympathetic ears within policy-making circles. As the extent of the crisis became evident, even some deregulation advocates, notably the subgovernor of the BOS, stated that certain aspects of liberalization, especially interest rate deregulation, should proceed more gradually to avoid putting more intermediaries at risk.[45]

Summary
Financial liberalization was not responsible for Spain's economic problems in the late 1970s. Interest rate deregulation contributed only slightly to an increase in the cost of credit. Higher interest rates themselves had little effect on the level of investment; in fact, the level of savings might have been lower without the removal of deposit rate controls, provoking an even greater scarcity of funds available for investment.[46] In short, "the problems facing the Spanish economy would have arisen without liberalization, and it would have encountered additional problems."[47] The consensus among economists is that several other factors, notably a sharp increase in the cost of energy, inflexible labor markets, and antiquated technology explain the industrial crisis more convincingly.

Spain's economic difficulties, however, inhibited the process of financial reform. Macroeconomic and financial instability counseled prudence in proceeding with certain aspects of deregulation. More significantly, deregulation opponents succeeded in creating the impression that financial liberalization was mostly to blame for the industrial and banking crises; this placed pressure on the government to halt the liberalization process. The slowdown was most obvious in 1979 and 1980. The next section examines financial policy in this period.

The Halt in Financial Deregulation: The 1979 Measures

The UCD won the 1979 elections, again coming up just short of an absolute majority in the Congress of Deputies. The results are shown in table 6.7. As in 1977, the UCD did not have to seek a coalition with other parties to form a government. It announced a new cabinet immediately after the elections. Abril maintained his post as vice president of economic affairs but relinquished the post of minister of economics to José Luis Leal. Fernández Ordoñez, with whom Abril had had serious disagreements, left his post as minister of finance; another Social Democrat, Jaime García Añoveros, replaced him. The principal motive for the cabinet reorganization was Suárez's desire to create a loyal, cohesive Council of Ministers. After his triumph in the elections, Suárez believed that he was sufficiently strong politically to exclude the troublesome barons from his cabinet.[48]

The year 1979 marked the height of the UCD's "passive adjustment" strategy. Shortly after the elections, the government presented an economic program the purported goals of which were to increase investment and employment while continuing the fight against inflation through a

TABLE 6.7.   Results of the 1977 and 1979 Elections for the Congress of Deputies

Party	1977 % of Votes	1977 Seats	1979 % of Votes	1979 Seats
UCD	34.0	165	35.1	168
PSOE	28.9	118	30.5	121
PSP-US	4.4	6	n/a	n/a
PSA	n/a	n/a	1.8	5
PCE-PSUC	9.2	20	10.8	23
AP-CD	8.0	16	6.1	9
PDC-CIU	2.8	11	2.7	8
ERC	0.8	1	0.7	1
PNV	1.7	8	1.7	7
EE	0.3	1	0.4	1
HB	n/a	n/a	1.0	3
Others	9.9	4	9.2	4
Total	100.0	350	100.0	350

Source: Ministerio de la Gobernación, Dirección General de la Política Interior 1977, and Ministerio del Interior, Dirección General de la Política Interior 1979.

Note:

UCD: Unión de Centro Democrático and Centristes de Catalunya
PSOE: Partido Socialista Obrero Español and Socialistes de Catalunya
PSP-US: Partido Socialista Popular-Unidad Socialista
PSA: Partido Socialista Andaluz
PCE-PSUC: Partido Comunista de España and Partit Socialista Unificat de Catalunya
AP-CD: Alianza Popular and Coalición Democrática
PDC-CIU: Pacte Democràtic per Catalunya and Convergència i Unió
ERC: Esquerra de Catalunya and Esquerra Republicana de Catalunya amb Front Nacional de Catalunya
   i Partit Social Democrata
PNV: Partido Nacionalista Vasco
EE: Euskadiko Ezkerra
HB: Herri Batasuna
n/a = not applicable

tight monetary policy. In reality, the plan offered few concrete proposals for meeting its investment and employment objectives and generally postponed major structural reforms. The UCD designed this strategy without any input from other political parties; thus, it did not reflect a broad consensus as its 1977 program had.

The financial policy measures included in the program signified a clear slowdown in the liberalization process.[49] First, the MOE directed banks to deposit 1 percent of their liabilities in special accounts at the BOS called *depósitos remunerados* (remunerated deposits). The MOE stated that the sole objective of the new requirement was to help slow growth in the money supply. The measure, however, also conveniently created a source of government revenue at a time when budget expenditures were increasing rapidly. To reduce bank opposition, the BOS paid interest on these deposits; however, the rate was well below what intermediaries could earn by lending these funds to the private sector.

Second, the MOE required banks to invest 1.8 percent of their deposits in the form of long-term loans (maturities of three years or more), or be obliged to deposit these funds with the BOS at zero interest. From an efficiency standpoint, this policy was far less harmful than other credit controls since it permitted banks to choose credit recipients and set interest rates. Authorities imposed the new credit floor without reducing banks' ICs, as the AEB had requested in 1978, but they did raise interest rates on all preferential credit by 1 percent.

Finally, the MOE required firms to deposit 25 percent of the credit they obtained abroad in a non-interest-bearing account at the BOS. The MOE sought to reduce foreign borrowing in order to help stem the large capital inflows that were appreciating the peseta and contributing to disruptive money supply increases.[50] Inflows began after authorities removed some capital controls in 1977; they picked up in volume when differentials between peseta- and Eurocurrency-denominated loan rates grew large. As seen in chapter 1, this experience is typical of countries that liberalize capital flows before achieving macroeconomic stability and financial deepening. The government's policy, although a step back from liberalization, was not inappropriate given the circumstances.

The UCD's economic program was not well received in the Cortes. Opposition parties claimed that the proposals for increasing investment and employment were vague and attacked the government's reliance on a tight monetary policy to combat inflation. The CEOE also criticized the economic program but less harshly.[51] It contended that the measures to increase long-term credit were appropriate but insufficient. It opposed the imposition of import deposit requirements and the *depósitos remunerados,* asserting that they would increase the cost of credit. It supported the decision to maintain banks' ICs; in fact, it requested that the reduction of savings banks' ICs also be frozen for six months.

Although the financial reform process slowed in this period, policymakers managed to implement some liberalizing measures. The most important concerned the promotion of new NBFIs and markets. The MOE gave finance companies, credit unions, and rural savings banks greater operational freedom and permitted savings banks to open additional branches within their home region. In addition, it sent legislation to the Cortes to modernize mortgage markets and expand the role of institutional investors; this legislation was approved in 1981. Policymakers took these steps because they believed that the best way to lower the cost of credit was to increase competition in the financial sector and, thereby, force banks to reduce financial margins. Moreover, these reforms were attractive from a political perspective because they provoked only mild protests from banks.[52]

On the monetary front, the government granted the BOS somewhat greater independence. After the signing of the Moncloa Pacts, MOE and BOS officials started drafting a bill to create a new legal framework for the central bank; the bill was ready by early 1979. It contained two major parts. The first proposed a reorganization of the BOS. This portion of the bill later became law with only minor revisions. The second concerned the functions of the central bank. It would have given the BOS full authority in monetary policy and the right to refuse the financing of government budget deficits.[53] This part of the bill encountered stiff resistance from several public and private actors. Officials in the so-called spending departments (e.g., the Ministry of Transportation) opposed limits on the government's ability to borrow from the BOS to finance deficit spending. Many politicians, in both the UCD and opposition parties, did not wish to relinquish elected officials' control over monetary policy to an autonomous technocratic agency. Private actors, like business, feared that the BOS would pursue a tight monetary policy even more aggressively if made independent. Consequently, key provisions of the proposal's second part were excluded from the law passed by the Cortes, and political control over the BOS was maintained.

In its final form, the 1980 law gave the BOS more responsibility for formulating and implementing financial and monetary policy, and succeeding governments in fact accorded the central bank somewhat greater independence. It also established longer (four-year) terms for the governor and subgovernor to reduce their vulnerability to direct political interference. Nonetheless, in the final analysis, the MOE retained the authority to establish general policy objectives and force the BOS to lend to the Treasury; therefore, the central bank ultimately remained subservient to political control. Its subordination was evident throughout the 1980s as the Ministry of Economics and Finance (MOEF) continued to dictate monetary targets to the central bank, which BOS officials found unacceptable much of the time.[54] Moreover, Treasury borrowing from the BOS also persisted, causing numerous economic problems and making it difficult for the Bank to meet its monetary objectives. The BOS finally obtained full independence, along the lines of Germany's Bundesbank, in 1994.

The Resumption of Financial Liberalization, 1980–81

Financial deregulation recommenced in 1981. The MOE implemented a major reform package in January and several important liberalizing measures throughout the year. I discuss these measures and their genesis later, after first examining the factors that motivated the UCD to renew the reform process.

A loss of political support for the UCD due to the struggling economy provided the impetus for financial reform. By 1980, the economy had still not begun its long-anticipated recovery, hindered partly by factors outside the UCD's control, like the global recession. Inflation had stabilized, but unemployment and the budget and balance-of-payments deficits were growing. The electorate was disenchanted with the UCD's constant internal struggles and lack of action and felt it no longer had the creativity and skill to design solutions to Spain's economic and political problems. The UCD had fared badly in three regional elections in early 1980, and opinion polls indicated that voters who had cast ballots for the party in 1979 were defecting in large numbers.[55] Some UCD officials, notably the Social Democrats, argued that the government's current economic strategy was incapable of generating adequate electoral support. The party needed to demonstrate that it was confronting Spain's economic problems head on; further delay in carrying out basic reforms, they reasoned, would cost the party the slim chance it still had to succeed in the upcoming 1982 elections.

The turn in economic policy became evident in September 1980. Speaking before the Cortes, Suárez stated that overcoming the economic crisis was the primary objective of the government, and he outlined an ambitious set of structural reforms in the areas of energy, financial, fiscal, industrial, labor, and trade policy.[56] In effect, Suárez was announcing a return to the original economic strategy of the first UCD government in 1977.

The change in strategy did not come without a struggle. The tensions among economic policymakers had persisted despite the reorganization of the Council of Ministers in 1979. The proponents of gradual economic adjustment, Abril and Leal, and the ministers of commerce, García Díez, and of industry, Carlos Bustelo Leal, both reform-minded Social Democrats, had frequent angry confrontations over the appropriate pace of structural reforms.[57] Until Abril left the government in July 1980, after particularly harsh criticism of the government's economic policies by the PSOE and CEOE, an active adjustment strategy was out of the question. In addition, some political groups within the party strongly opposed redirecting the government's economic policies. The Christian Democrats in particular protested economic reforms that might go against business and financial interests.

The UCD's political unity, already precarious, was also under increasing strain. Suárez's hold over the party was rapidly diminishing, leaving the party without strong leadership. In the past, Suárez had wielded great power largely because of his popularity with the electorate. As his and the party's public standing declined throughout 1980, Suárez began to face stiff internal opposition. Several barons, desirous of more power, publicly attacked Suárez, creating deep rifts within the UCD. Eventually, these internal conflicts led to Suárez's resignation as prime minister in January 1981, the defection of key groups within the party, a humiliating defeat in the 1982 elections, and the UCD's dissolution in 1983.

In an attempt to quell internal dissent, Suárez agreed to two cabinet reorganizations in 1980. The first, in May 1980, gave the Christian Democrats a more prominent role. This new cabinet did little to improve the UCD's public image or unify the party, however. In fact, the government barely turned back a vote of no-confidence launched by the PSOE later that month.[58] The second, in September 1980, revealed that Suárez had been compelled to give several of the barons a greater role in the government. The Social Democrats fared particularly well in the new cabinet. García Díez became the head of the Ministry of Economics and Commerce (MOEC),[59] García Añoveros remained the minister of finance, and Fernández Ordoñez returned to the government as minister of justice. Two factors explained the rise of the Social Democrats. First, Suárez had to give them a more significant role because the Socialists had been urging the Social Democrats to split with the UCD and enter into a coalition with the PSOE.[60] Second, Suárez believed that the Social Democrats would infuse new life into economic policy and, with it, improved electoral prospects.[61]

In the reorganization, Leopoldo Calvo Sotelo took over the post of vice president of economic affairs from Abril. Calvo Sotelo was a political conservative with liberal economic views, a well-known advocate of structural adjustment. Calvo Sotelo and García Díez wasted little time launching major reforms. In October 1980, they eliminated most price controls, and in November they proposed or began to carry out a series of concrete structural adjustment measures, building on the broad policies outlined by Suárez in September.[62] They put special emphasis on intensifying the processes of financial liberalization and industrial restructuring and working with business and labor to reach a new accord on wages. In the following year, they succeeded in implementing a number of major financial reforms, which I discuss in the following sections.

The 1981 Financial Reform Package

The Negotiations behind the Reforms

When Calvo Sotelo and García Díez began preparing the new round of financial reforms in late 1980, they decided to confer with all major private and public actors in the hopes of obtaining their cooperation with the reform process. Consequently, the MOEC asked the BOS, AEB, CECA, and CEOE for position papers on several proposed reforms and informally consulted with a wider range of private and public actors. Financial policymakers expressed a willingness to negotiate with all affected parties.

In its position paper, the BOS argued for the complete but gradual removal of interest rate and credit controls. The BOS noted that high real interest rates abroad—the U.S. prime rate reached 19 percent in 1980—combined with deposit rate ceilings in Spain were provoking extensive capital outflows.[63] To stop capital flight, authorities needed either to liberalize deposit rates or reimpose capital controls, and the BOS deemed the latter course infeasible. The BOS argued that loan interest rates should also be liberalized and that intermediaries be required to publish their prime loan rates on a regular basis to increase the transparency of credit markets. In addition, it recommended that the MOEC establish maximum commissions for banking services. This would stop the banking sector's practice of camouflaging the real cost of credit by charging relatively low interest rates but high commissions (see chap. 4).

Not all other state actors were as supportive of financial liberalization. In particular, officials in the ministries of Industry, Agriculture, and Public Works again expressed their opposition to further deregulation. As in the past, they protested the removal of interest rate controls because they believed it would increase the cost of credit. They resisted a reduction in preferential credit because they feared it might cause firms in key industrial sectors to fail.

Negotiations with the banking sector largely took place with the Big Seven banks, even though the government asked the AEB to prepare a policy statement.[64] The AEB report stated that while banks favored deregulation, they could only support it under certain conditions.[65] Two stood out. First, the government should liberalize the rest of the economy (e.g., free the labor market) before deregulating the financial sector. Second, it should cut spending to achieve greater fiscal discipline; banks feared that otherwise they ultimately would be required to purchase additional public debt on unfavorable terms.

The AEB's stance on specific reforms offered few surprises. As in the past, banks were most concerned with changes in interest rate policy. The AEB report argued that loan interest rates and commissions should be completely liberalized. On the other hand, it vigorously opposed the removal of deposit rate ceilings, stating that it would be dangerous given the prevailing economic situation.[66] It contended that deregulation of deposit rates would lead to sharp increases in the cost of credit in the short term, thereby lowering levels of investment and causing some firms to default. But it intimated that banks might not resist the removal of controls on large (i.e., over one million pesetas) six-month deposits. The AEB also asserted that other measures to increase competition in the banking system should be avoided because they might encourage some intermediaries to follow risky policies, thereby jeopardizing the solvency of the financial sector. Banks strongly backed a reduction of RRs and ICs. The AEB's report asked the government to replace preferential credit with direct budget subsidies over a period of several years, and allow intermediaries to charge market interest rates on preferential credit and choose which firms in favored sectors obtained loans immediately.

Savings banks viewed the proposed reforms with mixed feelings. They argued that the removal of deposit rate ceilings would be unfair and harmful unless further measures were taken to create a level playing field.[67] Specifically, they requested the MOEC to reduce their ICs to the level of banks and increase interest rates on preferential credit. Savings banks mostly favored the remaining proposals.

The CEOE made major pronouncements on financial policy in June 1980 and January 1981.[68] Many of its statements concerned the issue of how to lower the cost of credit. For instance, the CEOE called for deposit rates ceilings to be retained. It also requested the government to decrease RRs to allow intermediaries to lower loan interest rates but require them to channel funds freed from RRs into long-term lending to the private sector. In addition, the CEOE suggested a strategy for reactivating the economy: targeting industrial sectors with high backward linkages, such as the rail, communications, and energy sectors. It asked the government either to include these sectors in the ICs or subsidize credit to them directly. The CEOE also appealed to the government to stop reductions in ICs favoring shipbuilding and capital goods producers. It suggested that banks be compensated for the opportunity costs ICs imposed by a concomitant increase in interest rates on preferential credit.

The CEOE's stance revealed that it still represented the interests of a few firms at the expense of the business sector as a whole. Keeping deposit rate ceilings would benefit firms with access to credit but continue to discourage savings in the form of deposits at intermediaries, thereby decreasing the overall supply of loanable funds. Maintaining or creating additional ICs would help preferential credit recipients but continue to limit the credit available for other industries or increase its cost.

The Reform Package
The MOEC announced its financial reform package in January 1981. The final version of the reforms showed that the government genuinely had attempted to balance the competing demands of the groups it had consulted. The goals of the package were similar to those of previous reform efforts: improve financial efficiency and monetary control; increase the transparency of financial markets; and augment long-term financing to the private sector. Overall, the package was a huge step toward a market-based system; its scope and depth were probably as ambitious as possible given the state of the economy.

The centerpiece of the reform package was interest rate deregulation. The MOEC eliminated all loan rate ceilings except those on preferential credit but maintained all short-term deposit rate ceilings, with one exception: interest rates on six-month deposits of quantities exceeding one million pesetas. In a concession to banks and the CEOE, the MOEC dropped its original plan to remove controls on three-month deposits by 1982 and on all deposits by 1983. In another effort to increase competition, the MOEC removed the restriction on the amount of dividends that banks could distribute (although banks needed the BOS's prior approval to exceed the existing 6 percent cap until 1983).

The MOEC took two steps to increase the transparency of credit markets, notwithstanding the banking sector's opposition. It established maximum commissions for bank services, fixing commissions of 0.4 percent for most operations (banks had been charging between 1.5 and 2.0 percent), and required intermediaries to publicize their prime rates. Finally, the MOEC also increased the pace of reduction of ICs but rejected the use of direct subsidies to favor priority sectors because of concerns over mounting budget deficits.[69] However, it increased the long-term lending coefficient it had created in 1979, requiring banks and savings banks to lend 7 and 10 percent, respectively, of their liabilities (up from the initial

1.8 percent) long term. The MOEC also announced it would seek the "voluntary" cooperation of intermediaries in financing the housing sector by promoting "pacts" between itself, banks, and construction firms.[70]

Reaction to the 1981 reforms was critical despite their negotiated nature, suggesting that private actors wished to distance themselves from any negative impacts they might produce. The AEB asserted that the reforms were technically flawed and would force banks to raise interest rates.[71] The CEOE expressed disappointment that deregulation had not been extended to other areas of the economy, such as labor markets.[72] It stated financial deregulation by itself would only deepen the economic crisis by increasing interest rates, and it reiterated its proposals to lower the cost of credit. Finally, the largest opposition party, the PSOE, argued that the reforms would hurt the real sector and perpetuate the privileged status of the banks.

Other Major Financial Reforms in 1981

Suárez resigned as prime minister and president of the UCD in January 1981, motivated by a complex set of political calculations.[73] Calvo Sotelo took on the post of prime minister and immediately made it clear that his government would give economic affairs high priority. In February, Calvo Sotelo announced an economic program that built upon the broad strategy outlined by Suárez in September 1980.[74] The program emphasized the need to intensify financial deregulation, industrial restructuring, labor market reform, and trade liberalization. Progress on some of these issues turned out to be disappointing.[75] In the area of financial policy, however, the new UCD government accomplished many of its objectives.

Promoting Direct Financial Markets

Starting in 1977, financial policymakers stated that the promotion of direct markets was a top priority. They hoped that their expansion and modernization would improve the financial structure of corporations (i.e., lower dependence on bank financing), mobilize savings by giving savers the opportunity to diversify their assets, and generate venture capital to fund risky but high-return projects. The Moncloa Pacts established a commission to study the reform of bond and equity markets, and its findings were ready by 1978. The commission's principal recommendations were to improve the information available on firms issuing securities, modernize the system of contracting and brokerage, encourage institutional investors, and integrate Spain's four official exchanges. The MOE was ready to act upon these recommendations by 1979, but fierce private sector opposition forced it to postpone reforms until 1981.

The strongest opposition came from banks and the Association of Stock Brokers (ASB).[76] Banks opposed the expansion of bond and equity markets primarily because they feared disintermediation. They also fought the promotion of institutional investors since they posed a threat to their traditional dominance of the sale and purchase of securities on the exchanges. The stance of Spanish banks toward the expansion of bond markets differed significantly from that of similarly positioned Japanese banks in the same period.[77] Japanese banks supported measures to expand bond markets because Japanese firms had gained access to Eurocurrency markets where they could borrow at a much lower cost than from domestic banks. Banks hoped that the expansion of domestic bond markets would encourage firms to raise funds in Japan, where at least they could underwrite bond issues. In Spain, few firms had access to Eurocurrency markets, so the disintermediation threat posed by international capital markets was small; therefore, banks had no reason to support the expansion of domestic bond markets.

For its part, the ASB favored the expansion of direct markets but opposed any measures that challenged its monopoly of brokerage activities on the exchanges. Since such measures were an essential element of any plan to overhaul the exchanges, the ASB resisted comprehensive reform efforts. Although it was a small organization, the ASB's directors had considerable political influence, in part because they enjoyed close ties to important government officials, especially García Díez.[78]

Business was ambivalent about the modernization of bond and equity markets. On the one hand, corporations viewed it as an opportunity to develop new sources of capital and diversify their financial structure. On the other, most firms opposed reforms requiring them to provide investors with better financial information and submit to periodic audits. Some firms feared that greater disclosure would reveal weak balance sheets that would drive away investors; others feared that it would reveal earnings that would make them liable for higher taxes.

The MOEC implemented (or permitted the exchanges to carry out) several important reforms in 1980 and 1981 but carefully avoided several controversial reforms.[79] Among the principal measures were (1) new disclosure requirements for firms; (2) new rules on takeovers; (3) a new system for quoting securities; and (4) the authorization of leveraged stock purchases. The official exchanges also launched several new financial instruments, notably a market in discounted bills. Nevertheless, the MOEC did not attempt to change the system of brokerage or introduce market-makers, nor did it do much to encourage institutional investors. A more systematic reform of the stock exchanges including these and other essential measures would have to wait until 1988. Due in part to these omissions, bond and equity markets remained weak throughout the early 1980s.[80]

The Creation of New Markets and Intermediaries

In 1981, the MOEC took several steps to increase competition within the Spanish money market. The most important was the authorization of the Sociedades Mediadoras en el Mercado de Dinero (SMMD, Money Market Intermediaries).[81] The SMMD were to serve as market-makers in the interbank market by taking and placing deposits from and with banks. In addition, they were to challenge bank dominance of money markets by competing in the buying and selling of short-term financial instruments (e.g., Treasury bills) directly from and to the public. To ensure competition with banks, the MOEC prohibited banks from owning or operating a SMMD. The MOEC hoped to achieve two basic objectives by fostering competition in money markets: (1) buttress their other efforts to force banks to become more efficient; and (2) help the BOS to improve monetary control by preparing the stage for open market operations.

At the behest of government leaders, the MOEC also attempted to deepen mortgage markets by creating a market in mortgage-backed securities. Politicians promoted this policy because it met a growing demand among the middle class to increase the availability and lower the cost of mortgages. A 1981 law permitted all intermediaries to issue mortgage-backed securities to obtain long-term funds;[82] previously, this had been the exclusive privilege of a public bank, the Banco Hipotecario de España (Mortgage Bank of Spain). It also permitted the creation of Sociedades de Crédito Hipotecario (SCH, Mortgage Credit Companies). Policymakers hoped the SCH would compete with banks and savings banks in granting mortgages and in obtaining long-term funds.

Banks opposed the creation of both the SMMD and SCH because of the competitive threat they posed. They did not make this a top priority, however, since their authorization seemed inevitable and their immediate impact promised to be slight. Instead, banks concentrated their lobbying on other disintermediation threats that loomed larger: the expansion of the public debt market (discussed in chap. 7) and private bond and equity markets.

Prudential Regulation

In the early 1980s, financial authorities began to address the lack of prudential regulation that had contributed to the banking crisis. First, the MOEC strengthened the BOS's authority in the supervision and inspection of intermediaries. The BOS's formal sanctioning power, however, remained limited. Consequently, it had to rely on its discretionary authority (e.g., granting or withholding short-term credits) to control intermediaries. Second, the BOS issued regulations aimed at obtaining better information on the net worth of intermediaries, reducing risky lending, establishing adequate levels of loan-loss provisions, and eradicating unacceptable banking practices. It implemented standardized accounting procedures and required banks to submit to periodic outside audits. It imposed limits on lending to any one firm (or conglomerate) or type of activity; in addition, certain banking practices, like "cross loans," were strictly prohibited.[83] Finally, authorities established strict capital adequacy requirements or "solvency" coefficients.

Two stances emerged within the banking sector on efforts to augment prudential regulation. Banks experiencing solvency problems resisted greater prudential regulation. They feared that improved supervision, especially increased inspection of assets, would place their management under greater scrutiny. Stricter rules concerning the riskiness of loan portfolios would restrict their flexibility in making investments. Tougher loan-loss provisions would impose opportunity costs because funds used to meet them could not be invested in performing assets. Solvent banks supported increased prudential regulation despite the fact that some rules would also impose opportunity costs on them. Prudential regulation offered a means of bringing problem banks into line, thereby stabilizing the banking system and reducing the cost of bailing out failed intermediaries (to which they had to contribute). In addition, it gave financially strong banks a competitive advantage since meeting the new requirements would place a larger burden on less solvent competitors.

While the primary goal of prudential regulation was to safeguard the solvency of the banking system, authorities also hoped that the regulations would lead to mergers since small banks would find it difficult to meet some of the requirements (especially paid-in capital requirements). They believed that mergers would "rationalize" the sector and create banks that would be better equipped to compete in foreign markets, especially in EC countries. The United States, among other countries, has also sought to encourage mergers using similar policy changes in recent years.

The Economic Impact of the 1977 and 1981 Financial Reforms

Policymakers hoped the 1977 and 1981 reforms would improve the efficiency of the financial system. Measures to level the playing field among intermediaries (and other competition-augmenting reforms) would diminish banks' dominance of the sector (as seen in market share) and lower financial margins, thereby increasing the efficiency of intermediation. A decrease in state control over credit allocation would improve allocative efficiency, thereby improving the social return on available financial resources. Over time, the improvement in financial efficiency would contribute to significantly better economic performance.

The evidence on the impact of the reforms on financial efficiency reveals that they achieved only partial success. The 1977 reforms had little effect on intermediaries' relative market shares of both total deposits and total credit to the private sector, as figures 6.1 and 6.2 indicate. Other intermediaries did not gain ground on banks as policymakers had hoped. The 1981 reforms, on the other hand, did have an impact. Banks lost market share in the competition for deposits to savings banks and, to a lesser extent, to public banks, credit cooperatives, and rural savings banks, leading the OECD to herald a clear increase in competition in the banking system.[84] Similarly, banks lost market share in the supply of credit to the private sector, primarily to savings banks.[85]

Tables 6.5 and 6.6 indicate that the 1977 reforms did not improve the efficiency of intermediation as measured by financial margins. The margins of both banks and savings banks increased rather than decreased following the reforms. Moreover, column 3 indicates both types of intermediaries were able to pass increased operating costs onto borrowers (albeit with differing degrees of success). After the 1981 reforms, bank margins did decrease, although column 3 indicates banks did not lower their margins in pace with the decline in operating costs. Bank profits did fall significantly over this period. This might indicate that, the analysis of financial margins notwithstanding, competition was forcing out surplus rents. It is more likely, however, that the fall in profits was due to sharp increases in loan-loss provisions, a consequence of the industrial crisis. The margins of savings banks increased but remained lower than those of banks, and their profits remained stable. This is consistent with an expansion of market share based on the removal of barriers to competition.[86] Chapter 7 examines the evolution of margins in the late 1980s and early 1990s.

Why didn't competition-augmenting reforms force out banks' surplus rents more effectively? One must note, first of all, that this phenomenon is not unique to Spain. Many countries seeking to deregulate a financial system dominated by a banking cartel have encountered similar problems. In Turkey, for example, authorities liberalized only to find that large national banks actually increased their dominance of the banking sector.[87] The economics literature offers several explanations for why deregulation does not weaken cartels more quickly, among them the inability of new intermediaries to offer the wide range of services large corporate clients need in the short run.[88]

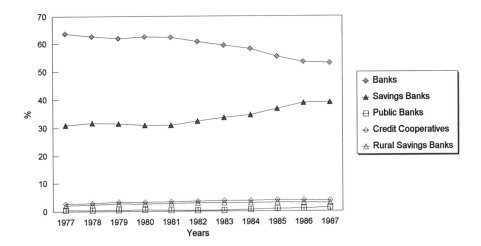

Fig. 6.1. Share of total deposits by financial intermediary as a percentage of total, 1977–87. (Data from Banco de España, "Boletín Estadístico," various issues.)

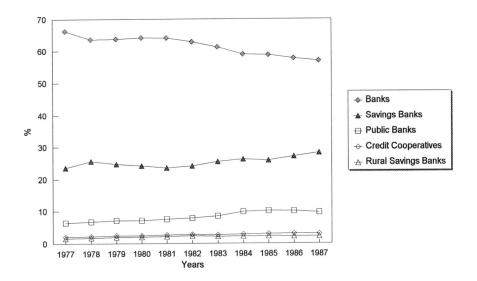

Fig. 6.2. Share of credit to the private sector by financial intermediary as a percentage of total, 1977–87. (Data from Banco de España, "Boletín Estadístico," various issues.)

In Spain, banks, especially the Big Seven, retained surplus rents partly because they were often able to collude to maintain favorable interest rates. As other intermediaries (such as savings banks) were capturing market share only slowly, this was economically feasible. Collusion amongst banks was aided by sociological factors.[89] Extensive familial ties among the owners and managers of Spain's largest banks persisted in the 1980s.[90] In addition, the presidents of the Big Seven met monthly to discuss current issues, apparently facilitating coordination on several matters. The banking cartel eventually unraveled in the early 1990s because of increased competition sparked by further deregulation. As a result, the efficiency of the banking system finally improved significantly. These developments are discussed in the next chapter.

It is notoriously difficult to measure the allocative efficiency of financial markets. The Spanish case is no exception. One readily available measure of allocative efficiency, the crude incremental output/capital ratio, indicates that it did improve as a consequence of the reforms.[91] As table 6.8 shows, the ratio dropped immediately after the 1977 reforms but increased substantially in the mid-1980s. In addition, anecdotal evidence offered by financial market participants unanimously supports the view that allocative efficiency improved substantially.[92] These results, however, are at best suggestive.

Conclusion

Upon taking office in 1977, UCD leadership decided that the party's long-term electoral prospects demanded the adoption of a reform-oriented economic strategy. Indeed, the entire Spanish political class believed that consolidating the new democracy required improving economic performance through stabilization and major structural reforms. The result was a commitment to economic adjustment symbolized by the Moncloa Pacts. By the end of 1978, however, the UCD had shifted to a "passive adjustment" strategy. A deteriorating economy, internal party divisions, and fear of alienating key constituents convinced UCD leadership that it could not maintain its existing level of commitment to structural reform.

TABLE 6.8.   Incremental Output/Capital Ratio, 1975–91

Average 1975–77	Average 1978–80	Average 1981–83	Average 1984–86	Average 1987–89	Average 1990–91
0.14	0.06	0.11	0.38	0.26	0.30

Source: Calculations based on data from World Bank 1994.

Opponents of financial deregulation, notably banks and the beneficiaries of selective credit policies, astutely associated Spain's economic problems with liberalizing reforms. Abril became concerned about the high cost of credit and the political dangers of reducing subsidized finance to key industrial sectors. In addition, a severe banking crisis raised serious doubts about the stability of the Spanish banking system, leading even the BOS to urge caution on some reforms, like the removal of interest rate controls. All these factors contributed to a marked slowdown in the process of financial liberalization.

In 1980, the UCD reopened the process of structural reform when party leaders realized that the government's lack of progress in dealing with major economic problems was costing it political support. The return to a more reform-oriented economic strategy was aided by a realignment of forces within the UCD, namely, the rise of the Social Democrats. Financial deregulation was a key element of the new economic strategy, and the MOEC implemented several major reforms in 1981. The most important achievements were additional interest rate liberalization, the creation of a more level playing field among existing intermediaries, authorization of several new intermediaries, stronger prudential regulation, the development of several new markets, and the first real steps toward expanding bond and equity markets.

Although the UCD never fully implemented its ambitious original economic program, some accounts of its economic record are too harsh.[93] Financial policy was not the only area where significant economic reforms took place. The MOE made further progress toward adopting a more orthodox monetary policy. The MOF implemented several major fiscal policy reforms, despite severe opposition. The MOC brought exchange rates more into line with market conditions (in the face of strong opposition from importers) and lifted many restrictions on international transactions. It also carried out a fair degree of trade liberalization and eliminated most remaining price controls. Finally, the UCD was able to hold down wage growth by encouraging pacts between unions and employers associations.

In 1982, the PSOE won the third post-Franco elections, ushering in a new era in Spanish politics. As the Socialists took office, speculation raged as to what type of economic policies they might pursue. The financial community wondered specifically whether the PSOE government would increase state intervention in financial markets or continue the process of financial deregulation. The next chapter examines the evolution of financial policy under the Socialists.

CHAPTER 7

Financial Policy under the Socialists

The PSOE won an absolute majority in the Cortes in the 1982 elections. The overwhelming victory of a leftist party, especially significant after the attempted military coup in 1981, unofficially marked the end of Spain's transition to democracy. The PSOE's victory did not reverse Spain's progress toward a more market-based financial system. The Socialists did not, as many anticipated, adopt a policy of heavy state intervention in the economy. Instead, they vigorously and successfully pursued structural reforms, like financial liberalization, aimed at creating more efficient markets. Significantly, their overall economic strategy was in many respects similar to that outlined by the UCD in 1977.

I argue that in seeking structural reforms, the Socialists responded, as the UCD had, to the incentives generated by Spanish electoral institutions to eschew the provision of benefits to particular social groups and instead improve general economic performance to capture broad-based political support. Two factors heightened the interest in structural reforms and affected their character and implementation. First, an intensification of Spain's economic problems in 1982 made reform more urgent and opened a window of opportunity for adopting tough economic measures. Second, Spain officially joined the EC in 1986. Its entry made some economic reforms obligatory and greatly facilitated the implementation of others by creating a consensus that Spain would have to undergo structural adjustment to compete effectively in European markets. In the case of financial policy, however, EC rules did not require the Spanish government to undertake major new initiatives, only to deepen certain ongoing reforms.

The PSOE was much better positioned to implement structural reforms than the UCD had been. First, it held an absolute majority in the Cortes throughout most of the 1980s, providing it with great legislative autonomy. Second, many key political reforms, like the drafting of a constitution, were completed, so government officials could concentrate on economic policy. Third, the PSOE was not as constrained by ties to vested economic interests that opposed structural reforms, like big business. It had strong ties to labor, but this turned out to have advantages (as well as disadvantages) in carrying out economic reforms. Finally, Spain's impending entry into the EC allowed policymakers to argue convincingly that the country needed to create more efficient markets. Still, it would be wrong to argue that the Socialists were able to govern by decree. Although they had the parliamentary majority to pass their agenda, they could not implement it effectively without gaining the cooperation of key social actors, many of whom opposed at least some basic reforms. In the end, the Socialists, like the UCD before them, compromised on some elements of their economic reforms to avoid political and social tensions, particularly after their original electoral mandate began to fade.

The Socialists themselves were not completely unified behind a strategy of structural adjustment. Two factions emerged on economic policy. One faction—which I call the "neoliberals"—advocated deepening the process of structural reforms. In financial policy, the neoliberals wanted to intensify deregulation. The other—which I call the "interventionists"—wished to increase government involvement in the economy. In financial policy, the interventionists hoped to augment control over credit allocation and taxation of the banking sector. As I detail later, the neoliberals prevailed on most major financial policy issues but sometimes had to make important concessions to the interventionists.

The Socialists initially encountered serious constraints in their efforts to liberalize the financial system. The difficulties stemmed from grave problems in the areas of fiscal and monetary policy. Socialist policymakers took office determined to introduce a sounder fiscal policy. In the short term, however, they were unable to implement a more effective system of taxation to pay for greatly expanded government services because of strong social opposition and administrative constraints. This led them to try to extract more revenue from the banking system through dramatic increases in RRs and ARs. RRs and ARs were also used to control money supply growth, an act necessitated by the unavailability of more appropriate monetary instruments like open market operations.

Additional taxation of the banking system exacted a heavy toll. By the mid-1980s, evidence mounted that the efficiency costs of this policy had grown very large and that it was getting difficult to expropriate more seignorage from intermediaries. The Socialists realized that unless they carried out tax reform soon, the state might face a fiscal crisis, as budget deficits were reaching alarming levels. Consequently, the Socialists redoubled their efforts to impose progressive income and value-added taxes and gradually began eliminating taxation of the banking system. Implementing a new tax system was difficult, but the transition had generated social pressure for a more equitable distribution of the tax burden that the Socialists were able to mobilize in their efforts. The fact that the PSOE's natural constituency was labor and not business was a decided advantage.

A surprising element of the Socialists' economic program, often underappreciated by scholars, was their successful attempt to transform the nature of industrial finance. The government wished to diversify corporate financing in order to break the stranglehold of banks over industrial finance, reduce the risk of financial instability, and make a more restrictive monetary stance less punishing for firms. To achieve this goal, the Socialists took several steps to strengthen firm profitability, including efforts to hold down wage growth so that more profits would accrue to capital, and aggressively promoted sources of finance other than bank credit.[1] The financial position of Spanish firms in fact improved dramatically from the mid-1980s onward. Profit margins expanded sharply throughout the 1980s and after-tax profitability was far above the average for the OECD by 1989.[2] The Spanish economy grew robustly in the mid- to late-1980s; annual GDP growth averaged 3.6 percent in Spain, much higher than the OECD average of 2.0 percent.[3]

This period finally saw the success of efforts to improve financial efficiency through measures designed to increase competition within the financial sector. In particular, liberalizing reforms dramatically eroded dominance of the financial sector by large national banks. In the early 1990s, bank margins and profits fell sharply, lowering the cost of financial intermediation. Moreover, banks lost market share in both deposits and loans to the private sector to other financial intermediaries. Disintermediation also rose markedly as firms increasingly turned to bond and equity markets and emerging markets for private fixed income securities to raise investment capital.

This chapter begins by examining the 1982 elections and the reasons behind the PSOE's overwhelming electoral victory. Next, it analyzes the political incentives the Socialists faced upon entering office, their primary economic agenda, and their capacity to implement it. It then describes the divisions within the Socialist party on economic policy. Finally, it examines the evolution of financial policy in the 1980s, concentrating on two analytical issues: (1) the connections between the government's financial and fiscal policies; and (2) the consequences of Spain's entry into the EC for financial policy.

The 1982 General Elections

In August 1982, the UCD dissolved the Cortes and convened general elections (originally scheduled for 1983) for October.[4] As the elections grew near, it became obvious that the PSOE would win; the only question was by how much. Most of its principal opponents were in disarray. The UCD, as discussed in the previous chapter, was in the process of self-destructing.

The PCE also confronted serious problems. Internal dissention, a large pro-Soviet faction, and the desertion of many of its most moderate members projected an excessively radical image to the electorate.[5] In fact, the only true opposition was Coalición Popular (CP, Popular Coalition), a coalition of Alianza Popular, the Christian Democrats of the Partido Demócrata Popular, and the Liberal Party; the CP, however, clearly lacked the support to become Spain's major party.

The PSOE itself had experienced a major crisis after the 1979 elections. Although the party had adopted a catch-all strategy in its 1979 campaign, it had alienated a significant segment of the electorate because of the persistence of a radical image.[6] Felipe González, the party's general secretary, and Alfonso Guerra, its number-two man, calculated that the PSOE needed to disassociate itself from its "Marxist" past if it was to become Spain's dominant party. Their efforts to moderate the party's formal ideology at the PSOE's Twenty-eighth Party Congress in 1979 encountered stiff resistance from party militants and was defeated. However, at an Extraordinary Congress held in September 1979, they were able to push through the desired changes in ideology and organizational structure.[7] Consequently, the PSOE entered the 1982 campaign a unified, moderate party intent upon appealing to a wide spectrum of voters.

Economic concerns had a prominent place in the 1982 election campaign. In general, the major parties paid less attention to financial policy than they had in previous contests. Other economic issues, notably unemployment, had priority in the campaign. In addition, there was simply less opportunity for political entrepreneurs to take advantage of financial policy issues to gain support than there had been in the past.

The results of the 1982 elections are shown in table 7.1. The PSOE won 202 seats, giving it an absolute majority in the Congress of Deputies. Felipe González was named prime minister. The newly created CP emerged as the major opposition party. While its predecessor, the CD, had won only 9 seats in 1979, the CP took 107 in 1982. The biggest loser in the elections was the UCD; whereas it had won 168 seats in 1979, it captured only 11 in 1982. The UCD's defeat was so devastating that the party disbanded within a few months. Finally, the PCE also suffered a huge loss in seats, from 23 to 4.

The PSOE's Economic Strategy

General Economic Policy

Many political observers expected the Socialists to increase government control over markets and adopt more accommodative fiscal and monetary

TABLE 7.1. Results of the 1979, 1982, 1986, and 1989 Elections for the Congress of Deputies

Party	1979		1982		1986		1989	
	% of Votes	Seats	% of Votes	Seats	% of Votes	Seats	% of Votes	Seats
UCD	34.9	168	6.5	11	n/a	n/a	n/a	n/a
PSOE	30.4	121	48.4	202	44.5	184	39.6	175
PCE-PSUC/IU	10.8	23	4.0	4	4.5	7	9.1	17
CD/CP/PP	8.1	10	26.6	107	26.3	105	25.8	107
CDS	n/a	n/a	2.9	2	9.2	19	8.0	14
CiU	2.7	8	3.7	12	5.1	18	5.1	18
PNV	1.7	7	1.9	8	1.6	6	1.3	5
Others	11.6	13	6.2	4	8.8	11	11.1	14
Total	100.0	350	100.0	350	100.0	350	100.0	350

Source: "Anuario El País 1996," 70.

Note:

UCD: Unión de Centro Democrático

PSOE: Partido Socialista Obrero Español and Socialistes de Catalunya

PCE-PSUC/IU: Partido Comunista de España and Partit Socialista Unificat de Catalunya; in 1986, Izquierda Unida

CD/CP/PP: Coalición Democrática in 1979; Coalición Popular in 1982 and 1986; Partido Popular in 1989

CDS: Centro Democrático y Social

CiU: Convergència i Unió

PNV: Partido Nacionalista Vasco

n/a = not applicable

policies. Instead, they implemented tough stabilization measures and an ambitious program of structural adjustment, policies typically associated with more conservative governments.[8] In many respects, the Socialists' overall program resembled the one proposed by the first UCD government in 1977, but not carried out fully, for reasons already identified. Its chief goal was to improve Spain's competitiveness in international markets generally and Europe in particular. A centerpiece of this effort was an industrial restructuring plan, adopted despite vigorous opposition from unions and the management of state-owned enterprises.[9] Its primary objectives were to free up capital and labor for use in more competitive industries and reduce the state expenditures propping up declining sectors. The Socialists also sought to increase state spending on physical and social capital in the belief that government could improve the prospects for long-term economic growth by providing badly needed infrastructure.[10]

The government's initial economic measures in late 1982 illustrated its determination to eliminate internal and external imbalances. Immediately after taking office, policymakers announced a comprehensive stabilization package. First, they cut targeted growth in the money supply (M2) from 15.5 to 13.0 percent annually. Second, they devalued the peseta by 8 percent in December 1982 (and allowed it to depreciate throughout 1983). Third, they stated their determination to achieve fiscal restraint by freezing government spending, especially current expenditures, at 1982 levels.[11] Finally, they stressed wage moderation by attempting to negotiate agreements between the government, labor, and business. Concern over upcoming municipal elections, however, impeded strict adherence to an incomes policy. Still, nominal wage growth fell from 14 to 10 percent between 1982 and 1984.

For many scholars, a key question is why the PSOE followed economic policies that contradicted the "Socialist orthodoxy." One potential explanation is that in the current era of great economic interdependence, governments have little scope to pursue distinctive and independent economic policies, even if they are desirable from the standpoint of domestic political competition or for ideological reasons. In this view, Spain had to become more like other Western countries in order to compete effectively in international markets.

Several authors have challenged the view that governments no longer have autonomy over economic policy. They contend that while convergence has taken place in some areas of economic policy, notably monetary policy, considerable divergence remains in other areas. Garrett and Lange, for example, claim that governments are still able to shape the supply-side policies affecting industry as well as factor markets in accordance with their partisan preferences.[12] Therefore, one cannot assume a priori that the

Socialists could not have pursued a partisan economic agenda; to make this argument, it would be necessary to identify the specific constraining factors that restricted their autonomy.

A related explanation for the Socialists' ambitious economic adjustment strategy focuses on Spain's accession into the EC. Some scholars suggest that the need to meet EC standards and improve the country's competitiveness in European markets once admitted explains the push for basic economic reforms.[13] This argument contains an important element of truth: EC accession helped shape the Spanish reform process. However, it incorrectly treats integration into the EC as exogenously given. The decision to enter the EC was in fact an endogenous policy choice, and in making it, Spanish leaders chose to accept the obligation to undertake certain economic reforms. Therefore, what ultimately needs to be explained is why they accepted this obligation. I contend that the decision to enter the EC was prompted in large part by a fundamental political motive, one that I have already identified as critical in explaining the course of Spanish economic policy: the drive to improve economic performance in order to generate broad-based political support. This does not negate the importance of the other motives behind the Spanish drive for EC membership. The Franco regime, for example, also sought entry into the EC as a means of gaining legitimacy in the eyes of the international community; the UCD and PSOE viewed accession as a means of consolidating democracy and being recognized as a "part of Europe."

It is also important to note that despite the broad agreement among the political elite, most (but not all) business interests, and the general populace that joining the EC was desirable, there was no clear consensus, even among the Socialists themselves, on what structural reforms Spain should undertake or how they should be implemented. Moreover, the constraints imposed on Spain by EC guidelines varied greatly across different economic policy areas. Whereas admission into the EC obliged Spain to undertake basic reforms to meet stringent requirements in commercial and agricultural policy, it did not in the area of financial policy (as I detail later).

My argument is that the Socialists pursued structural reforms in response to the incentives embodied in Spanish electoral rules to capture broad-based support by appealing to encompassing interests. They were willing and able to incur some short-term political costs (e.g., the alienation of labor) to improve long-term economic performance, which they believed would enable them to secure a stable, heterogeneous constituency. The incentive to initiate reform was especially strong when the Socialists entered office in late 1982 because Spain's economy was in serious trouble.[14] The combination of strong electoral results and an economic crisis opened a window of opportunity for adopting tough measures that the Socialists astutely seized.[15]

The evidence indicates that the Spanish electorate put great weight on economic performance in their evaluations of the government. An in-depth study of the determinants of support for the government in the 1980s reveals that voters' views on the efficacy of economic policy were the primary factors influencing the level of support.[16] Perceptions of collective economic conditions were more important in explaining support than economic conditions viewed in personal terms or traditional factors such as religious identification. The study concludes that approval of the PSOE governments was due to "a combination of perceived economic rejuvenation and of the association of government policies with this improvement."[17] Moreover, Spanish voters were very pragmatic when it came to economic issues. Two decades of economic modernization under different political regimes taught Spaniards "that economic well-being need not be associated with clear-cut, dogmatic alternatives between left and right."[18] Indeed, strong support for the PSOE also stemmed from voters' favorable opinions of the pragmatism and technical expertise of its policymakers.

I have no direct evidence that the Socialists were cognizant of the importance that voters' perceptions of economic policy had on electoral backing. One bit of information suggests they were, however. Party leadership believed strongly in the utility of opinion polls and other surveys of the Spanish electorate. They regularly hired the research institute, Centro de Investigaciones Sociológicas, to poll voters on a variety of political, economic, and social issues. Therefore, it is likely that the Socialists were aware of the link between economic policy and electoral support.

The Socialists were able to implement stabilization and structural adjustment programs, despite serious social opposition, without any immediate threat to their political standing for two primary reasons. One, they enjoyed an absolute majority in the Cortes. This meant that if PSOE leadership could maintain party unity (which it usually did), it could pass any legislation it wanted. Two, the PSOE was not beholden to traditionally powerful, narrow interests, like banking and big business. It did have close ties to labor, which influenced its economic policy in important ways (as I discuss later). Nevertheless, the Socialists refrained from simply carrying out their preferred policies without negotiating with other actors. They realized that effective implementation of their initiatives, particularly in the area of industrial restructuring, required winning the cooperation of the social actors affected by them through consultation and bargaining. In other words, their strategy was one of "concertation" and their economic policies reflected some compromise with key social actors.[19] The Socialists also wished to avoid alienating other political parties as they were aware that one day they might need coalition partners.

The Socialists' traditional ties to labor generally bolstered their ability to carry out various structural reforms.[20] Labor was more willing to accept as credible the government's assertions that structural adjustment programs that imposed high costs on the working class (e.g., industrial restructuring) were necessary for Spain's economic recovery. In addition, the PSOE used its links to trade unions to negotiate wage settlements that formed part of an effective incomes policy. The Socialists' connections to labor also had disadvantages. The most serious was that it made labor market reform much more difficult. The government passed several minor reforms in the 1980s but only achieved a more comprehensive (but still inadequate) reform of labor markets in 1994.

Over time, as the Socialists carried out policies that led to layoffs or reduced worker benefits, it confronted accusations from unions that it had "abandoned socialism." This hostility did little to harm the PSOE electorally in the short run, however, because it maintained a broad-based constituency. The Socialists were extremely careful not to rely excessively on labor's support. They prudently avoided giving the appearance that they were favoring labor over general societal interests and made a point of keeping unions at arm's length when making policy. In addition, the importance of unions decreased steadily throughout the 1980s; one indication of this is that only about 10 percent of the workforce was unionized at the end of the decade.[21]

The Struggle over Economic Policy within the PSOE Governments

Although the Socialists generally pursued a coherent economic adjustment strategy, government and party officials were split into two factions on basic policy: the "neoliberals" and the "interventionists."[22] The neoliberals were identified with Miguel Boyer, the first PSOE minister of economics and finance; Carlos Solchaga, the first PSOE minister of industry (and second minister of economics and finance); and Joaquín Almunia, the minister of labor.[23] Boyer was particularly influential during his tenure in office (1982–85); indeed, the press often referred to him as the "super-minister" because he seemed to be dictating the Socialists' economic strategy.[24] The neoliberals advocated stabilization and structural reform programs to correct the fundamental deficiencies of the Spanish economy. They believed that improving economic performance was essential for achieving political stability in Spain as well as the PSOE's long-term acceptance by a wide spectrum of the Spanish electorate.[25]

The interventionists, on the other hand, considered loyalty to labor's interests and the Socialist tradition of extensive state intervention in the economy as central to the party's long-term prospects. They stressed the use of public spending to create employment, the expansion of social and welfare spending, and greater government control over industry and finance. They opposed the government's emphasis on fighting inflation and particularly the use of a tight monetary policy to do so. This faction was closely identified with the vice president of the government, Alfonso Guerra; Enrique Barón, minister of transportation; Nicolás Redondo, the head of the UGT (the union associated with the PSOE); Martín Toval, head of the PSOE's parliamentary group; and Antonio Marugán, Guerra's chief economic advisor.

The two factions took opposing stances on financial policy. The neoliberals proposed gradual but complete financial deregulation to promote economic efficiency. The interventionists advocated using selective credit instruments and the public banking system to direct credit to "priority" activities. They also favored taxing the banking sector to obtain badly needed government revenue and weaken its position of dominance in the Spanish economy.[26]

Felipe González was the final arbiter in the clash between the two factions, and he generally sided with the neoliberals in financial (and other economic) policy matters. González was the PSOE's undisputed leader due to his popularity with Spanish voters—they largely identified the PSOE with his person—and acceptance by all segments of the Socialist camp. He believed that undertaking basic economic reforms was critical to the PSOE's long-term electoral success. In addition, he was determined to see Spain "catch up" with Western Europe and become competitive in international markets. His early contacts with leaders from EC countries strengthened his conviction that structural adjustment was required to place Spain on equal footing with other European countries.[27] Naturally, Spain's entry into the EC also buttressed the position of neoliberal reformers within the government.

Although the interventionists generally lost in the design of the government's overall strategy, they had ways of influencing economic policy. As already noted, a few interventionists held ministerial portfolios and were able to voice their objections to reforms in the Economic Commission and Council of Ministers. More importantly, Guerra, as vice president, chaired the powerful Comisión de los Subsecretarios (Undersecretaries Commission).[28] All legislation had to be approved by this commission before being considered by the Council of Ministers and the Cortes, and the commission could return draft legislation to its sponsor (typically a ministry) for revision. This provided Guerra with a direct means of influencing the legislative process. In addition, he was the organizational mastermind of the PSOE and commanded a large following within the party. Guerra, however, had the least influence over economic

policy of any policy domain, primarily because González staunchly supported his economic ministers and their policy initiatives.[29]

The intragovernment battle over general economic policy occasionally went public, but perhaps the most visible confrontation occurred over
the appointment of a new BOS governor in 1984. González, at the behest
of key economic advisors, nominated Mariano Rubio, who was then subgovernor, for the post. Rubio was a darling of the neoliberals, well known
for his advocacy of stringent adjustment policies and greater central bank
independence. The interventionists immediately launched an acerbic public assault against Rubio's nomination. Their hostility toward Rubio had
several causes. First, they believed that Rubio was the primary architect of
the BOS's tight money policies, which they despised. Second, they felt that
Rubio would seek greater operational independence for the BOS. They
deeply distrusted BOS officials, who they viewed as technocratic allies of
the neoliberals, and wanted a governor who would be amenable to greater
political control over the BOS. Finally, Guerra and Rubio's personal relations were acrimonious. The interventionists' protests were to no avail;
González stuck by his candidate and Rubio became governor.[30] Opposition by the interventionists, however, did help block the move to grant
greater independence to the BOS until the 1990s.

The Links between Fiscal and Financial Policy

The Socialists' early financial policy seemed to indicate that they would
augment state control over financial markets.[31] In 1983, the government
increased RRs for intermediaries sharply, and in 1984 imposed a new type
of ARs on them, called the "public debt" coefficient (PDC). Economic
policymakers, however, claimed that they were firmly committed to the
goal of liberalization.[32] They stated that the aforementioned moves were
only stopgap measures to overcome Spain's urgent fiscal and monetary
crises. Their refusal to augment other types of government intervention in
financial markets despite considerable pressure to do so lent credence to
their claim that they did not seek greater state control. For example, they
mostly resisted the temptation to increase state control over credit allocation.[33] With hindsight, it is in fact easy to see that the Socialists' initial
measures were forced upon it by difficult economic circumstances and
underdeveloped financial institutions. At the time, however, the conflicting evidence meant the financial community could not be sure which direction the PSOE would follow.

This section analyzes how the Socialists' efforts to deal with major
fiscal and monetary crises affected financial policy. It outlines their moves
to increase taxation of the banking system in order to finance deficits and

slow the growth of bank credit to the private sector and describes their borrowing from the BOS to finance government activities. It shows that the growing cost and ineffectiveness of these policies created an ever stronger incentive to abandon financial repression and implement more efficient means of raising government revenue. Finally, it examines the Socialists' adoption of more orthodox fiscal and public finance policies, including the creation of an efficient market for public debt. Overall, economists have given the Socialists high marks for their reform efforts.[34]

The Budget Crisis and Rising Public Debt

Among the most intractable economic problems the Socialists faced upon taking office were large government deficits and a rapidly growing public debt. Budget deficits as a percentage of GNP had increased from 0.3 to 5.6 percent between 1976 and 1982.[35] Consequently, outstanding public debt had risen from 8 billion pesetas in 1975 to 1,063 billion in 1982.[36] The deficits were primarily due to greatly increased spending. Total government revenues had grown from 0.7 to 3.3 trillion pesetas between 1975 and 1983, an increase of 483 percent; meanwhile, total expenditures had climbed from 0.7 to 4.4 trillion in the same time period, an increase of 654 percent.[37] As a percentage of GNP, expenditures jumped from 22.5 to 40.6 percent between 1974 and 1985.[38]

The UCD's difficulties with implementing a more efficient means of taxation to increase government revenues in line with expenditure growth have already been discussed. I focus here on the factors that accounted for the rapid increase in central government expenditure. Two were especially important. First, the UCD governments dramatically increased social expenditures to meet glaring needs and ease political tensions during the transition. Spending on social welfare programs increased by 215 percent between 1978 and 1982; unemployment compensation and pensions rose by 563 and 300 percent, respectively.[39] The inadequate state of Spain's social infrastructure made much of this spending necessary. The Franco regime had simply failed to allocate budgetary resources to social programs. In 1975, government social expenditures totaled only about 10 percent of GDP in Spain, whereas the EC average was 24 percent.[40] Second, transfers to cover the losses of public enterprises jumped from 22.3 to 398 billion pesetas between 1975 and 1984; the 1984 figure represented 7.4 percent of total budget expenditures.[41]

The Socialists did not have a sound basis for dealing with the net public debt they inherited either. The UCD had not created an efficient market for government bonds, choosing instead to rely on Treasury borrowing from the BOS to cover deficits.[42] The Socialists also borrowed from the

BOS, but to a lesser extent. Borrowing from the BOS was politically attractive. First, it did not appear in any form in the General Budget. In contrast, when the government issued public debt, interest payments on it were listed as expenditures in the General Budget. Second, it was seemingly cost-free because no interest was charged on the loans; in fact, since no maturity was specified, the Treasury could defer the return of the principal indefinitely. In reality, borrowing from the BOS reduced state revenue in a direct way. Forced lending to the Treasury involved opportunity costs for the BOS because it had to substitute nonperforming for interest-bearing assets in its portfolio.[43] As the BOS turned over its earnings to the Treasury, the government lost the revenue that would have otherwise been generated by the BOS's interest-bearing assets.

BOS lending to the Treasury had a negative impact on monetary policy since it led to immediate and potentially inflationary increases in the monetary supply. The BOS managed to sterilize money supply increases to limit inflation, but this reduced the flow of credit to the private sector, producing "crowding out." In 1978, for example, although the BOS met its monetary aggregate targets, the composition of domestic credit growth was unsatisfactory; credit to the public sector rose by 40 percent while credit to the private sector increased by only 14 percent.[44]

Aware of growing budgetary and public debt problems, the PSOE's economic team took office determined to establish more conservative and orthodox fiscal policies. That is, it hoped to limit expenditure growth, implement a more effective system of taxation, and create more adequate means of financing deficits (i.e., build efficient public debt markets). Policymakers were also aware that financial deregulation could not proceed much further until the government's fiscal position improved. Without fiscal reform, they would be forced to tax the banking system to obtain badly needed incremental revenue (thereby perpetuating financial repression) and issue huge amounts of government debt (thereby impeding the development of bond markets as a source of private finance). To emphasize the links between financial and fiscal policy, the Socialists combined the Ministry of Economics and the Ministry of Finance into a single ministry, the Ministry of Economics and Finance (MOEF).

The Socialists ultimately succeeded in reducing government deficits but not without a struggle.[45] They confronted the same political constraints that had made it difficult for the UCD to overhaul fiscal policy: vigorous social opposition toward tax reform and rapidly growing demand for state services and entitlement programs. In addition, the administrative capacity required to implement a value-added tax and increase direct taxation was still lacking. The delay in achieving fiscal discipline meant authorities had to finance large government deficits and a rapidly growing stock of public debt, without the benefit of an adequate market for public securities. The following sections explore how they handled these immediate problems as well as how they eventually obtained their goals of achieving fiscal responsibility and a sound framework for public finance.

Taxation of the Banking System

The Socialists, like the UCD before it, initially ran into a wall of social resistance that delayed significant reform of tax policy until the late 1980s. The opposition of business in particular forced the Socialists to proceed warily because they feared firms might withhold investment if they imposed tax reform. Consequently, policymakers continued to rely on indirect taxation, especially of the banking system, to generate needed incremental revenues. Whereas neoliberals disliked this policy and viewed it as a temporary but necessary evil, the interventionists reveled in the chance to shift a larger part of the burden of financing the government onto banks.

Taxation of the banking system took several forms in the 1980s. First, the MOEF imposed very high RRs on intermediaries. In 1983, the government set RRs at 18 percent of intermediaries' liabilities, and they remained at that level until 1989, when they began a slow reduction (completed by the mid-1990s). It also extended RRs to most NBFIs, such as finance companies, and expanded the range of liabilities included in the base for calculating the RRs of all intermediaries. The MOEF justified the increase in RRs as essential for draining liquidity from the banking system. Although raising RRs did serve this function, perhaps a more compelling reason for this measure was to generate government revenue. As discussed in chapter 2, RRs permit the government to use funds deposited at the central bank at zero- or low-interest rate cost. In the mid-1980s, reserves in excess of their optimal level (deemed to be about 2.5 percent) generated approximately 260 billion pesetas of state revenue annually, an amount equivalent to about 1 percent of Spanish GNP.[46]

Intermediaries opposed the increase in RRs because it imposed huge additional opportunity costs on them.[47] They also feared that high RRs could contribute to financial instability by further weakening the numerous banks on the verge of insolvency. Intermediaries, however, recovered part of the opportunity costs imposed by higher RRs by increasing interest rates on loans.[48] They were sharply criticized because of high loan rates but managed to deflect some of the blame onto the government's financial policy, particularly the decision to raise RRs.

A second means of taxing the banking system was set up when the

MOEF established the PDC in 1984, purportedly to help absorb liquidity in the banking system. The PDC required intermediaries to hold a percentage of their assets (initially 3.5 and later 10.0 percent) in the form of short-term public debt. The Treasury negotiated interest rates on public debt with the banking sector and the BOS (see my discussion later in this chapter), but they were always considerably lower than market rates. Therefore, the PDC served as an indirect tax on intermediaries, whatever its utility as a monetary tool. Its use meant a cost savings for the government since the Treasury paid out less interest to finance deficits than if it had sold debt directly to the highest bidder. In 1986, the PDC guaranteed the Treasury purchasers among banks alone for two trillion pesetas of debt at below-market rates. This generated interest cost savings equivalent to 0.4 percent of GDP and 2.4 percent of government revenue.[49] By all accounts, the PDC reduced financial efficiency. It introduced further rigidity into the financial system, increased market segmentation, and distorted short-term interest rates. In addition, it imposed opportunity costs on intermediaries, which they tried to recover by charging higher interest rates on loans.[50]

Finally, the government made use of the inflation tax to reduce the real impact of budget deficits.[51] The financial sector's involuntary holdings of public debt (e.g., 6.5 trillion pesetas in 1986) allowed the state to increase its proceeds from the inflation tax. In 1986, total inflation tax benefits reached 1.3 trillion pesetas or 4.1 percent of Spanish GNP; inflation tax benefits derived from outstanding public debt alone totaled 0.7 trillion pesetas or 2.2 percent of GNP.[52]

Increased taxation angered banks, and bank-government relations were strained in the mid-1980s.[53] They lobbied authorities to eliminate indirect taxation, especially high RRs, and mounted a vigorous public campaign urging the government to reduce its deficits. BOS governor, Mariano Rubio, also criticized the PDC on the grounds that it distorted financial markets and introduced an additional element of rigidity into the financial system.[54]

Creating Effective Public Debt Markets

Until the 1990s, the Spanish public debt market was very small. Intermediaries were the primary purchasers of government securities, often involuntarily. Few others purchased public debt because its yields were well below that of other financial assets. Moreover, until 1981, all debt was medium or long term (i.e., with maturities over three years), and there was practically no secondary market; this made public securities unattractive for investors seeking liquidity.

Under the UCD, the Treasury shortened maturities slightly and raised interest rates to bring them more in line with market rates. However, it did not seriously consider issuing short-term debt to finance government activities until 1981. Barriers to issuing short-term debt were large. Banks strongly opposed the sale of short-term debt at market rates because it represented direct competition for their deposit base, to which they would not able to respond because of interest rate controls. Indeed, the issuance of short-term public debt put banks in a no-win situation: if the government liberalized interest rates to allow them to compete for funds with the Treasury on equal footing, they would face competition for deposits among themselves; if interest rates were not liberalized, they would slowly lose their deposit base to the Treasury.

This issue came to a head in 1983 when the MOEF announced its intention to make a new six-month security, "Pagarés del Estado," its primary debt instrument, and hinted that it would be issued at near market rates. The MOEF introduced Pagarés for several reasons. Although it maintained its goal of keeping the cost of financing government activities low, it realized that the long-term stability and depth of the public debt market required that securities be issued at near market conditions. The MOEF also wished to create a public debt security that the BOS could use for open market operations.[55] Finally, some neoliberals argued that the cost of financing budget deficits should approximate the real opportunity cost of capital in order to force the government to confront the true economic implications of its deficits.

As Pagarés represented a clear disintermediation threat, banks opposed them. Not yet willing to impose additional ARs, the MOEF opted to negotiate with banks on the terms of the debt issue as they had done in the past. It needed the banking sector's cooperation since the Treasury lacked a network for selling government securities directly to the public. Therefore, the MOEF would have to rely on banks to place issues with their customers as it attempted to broaden the public debt market.[56] Moreover, without banks as major purchasers, there might not be a sufficiently large market for public debt issues. The MOEF was uncomfortable with this situation and repeatedly pressured other intermediaries, especially savings banks, to purchase more debt.

Negotiations among the MOEF, BOS, MOC, and private banks on the new short-term debt issues began in early 1983 and continued on into the summer.[57] Banks asked for interest rates on Pagarés that would allow them to continue to compete for deposits (i.e., slightly below market rates). They also requested that the Treasury channel most of the debt issue through the banking system. Government agencies were divided on the conditions of short-term debt issues and had to hold extensive informal negotiations to resolve their differences.[58] The Treasury wanted debt to be channeled through banks at below-market rates to keep the cost of financing low. The BOS wished debt to be sold directly to the public at prevailing market rates so that it could be used in open market operations. The MOC also wanted market rates to attract foreign capital and maintain the parity of the peseta. Finally, some other government officials opposed paying market interest rates when funds could be obtained for less by forcing banks to purchase debt at lower rates. A settlement on short-term debt was finally reached after several months of arduous negotiations.[59] The Treasury was to channel most of the debt issue through banks at near but below-market rates.

In 1984, still faced with a rapidly mounting government deficit, the government changed course and created the PDC (discussed earlier) to guarantee a market for Pagarés among intermediaries. It also passed the 1985 Financial Assets Act to secure a market for Pagarés among other investors. This act decreed that interest earned on Pagarés was tax-free and purchasers could remain anonymous, converting Pagarés into a safe haven for investors seeking to hide their wealth. The favorable treatment given the Pagarés diminished the market for competing short-term assets, especially bank bonds and commercial paper. Intermediaries and corporations protested against this new policy, but to no avail.

The fiscal treatment of Pagarés allowed the Treasury to lower their interest rates to well below those offered on other financial assets. This reduced the cost of financing the deficit (albeit while eliminating the revenue generated by taxes on interest earned by holders of Pagarés) but had several negative consequences. It segmented short-term money markets and distorted interest rates so they did not reflect market conditions. It also made it infeasible for the BOS to use Pagarés in open market operations, which by law could only be carried out with financial intermediaries. Specifically, the BOS could not sell Pagarés to intermediaries to reduce the money supply because they were not willing to purchase more. Consequently, the BOS had to engage in expensive repurchase agreements when it wanted to tighten its monetary stance.

The problems associated with Pagarés, especially their inappropriateness for open market operations, led the MOEF to introduce a new form of public debt, Letras del Tesoro, in 1987. The Letras quickly replaced Pagarés as the principal instrument of public debt and came into use in open market operations. The Letras did not have preferential fiscal treatment nor did they count toward fulfilling intermediaries' PDCs. The government maintained the Pagarés and their fiscal treatment (and corresponding low yields) to take advantage of their captive market among intermediaries and investors attempting to hide their funds. To reduce the transaction costs associated with the sale of public debt and reduce reliance on banks for selling debt, the Treasury started to sell debt through a system of book entries at the BOS.

The economic significance of public debt grew rapidly in this period. The share of current expenditure allocated to interest payments on public debt increased from 1.2 to 3.5 percent of GDP between 1982 and 1985 as the stock of net public debt rose from 18.1 to 27.5 percent of GDP.[60] The effect of these trends on interest rates is not clear, although most scholars believe they might have decreased somewhat in the absence of heavy government borrowing.[61]

Financial Innovation and Limits on Revenue Generation

Increased taxation of the banking system through RRs and ARs led intermediaries to intensify their efforts to circumvent financial controls. In addition, disintermediation due to the expansion of the public debt market encouraged them to develop new financial instruments. Consequently, the 1980s witnessed intense financial innovation, particularly by banks.[62] Innovation reduced the government's ability to extract more revenue from the banking system because growth in intermediaries' assets occurred in areas that public officials could not tap. It also made it difficult for the BOS to set and meet monetary growth targets.

Innovations Stimulated by Financial Controls
The government's increased use of RRs and ARs motivated intermediaries to devise new means of obtaining liabilities that would not be included in the deposit base the government used to calculate their obligations under these (and other) controls. One important innovation was the creation of a secondary market in bank acceptances. As bank acceptances were not considered deposits, they were not subject to interest rate controls or included in the pool of liabilities used to compute their obligations under ICs or RRs. Authorities eventually closed these loopholes. Intermediaries also developed repurchase agreements (discussed later) to circumvent various government controls.

Innovations stimulated by financial controls created tremendous difficulties for monetary authorities. In the early 1980s, the BOS realized that monetary expansion was proceeding at a much faster pace than desired even though it was meeting its M2 and M3 growth targets. This was because M2 and M3—measures of money supply based on traditional deposits—had slowly become outdated. Intermediaries had created so many new liquid assets that these measures no longer provided an adequate picture of financial flows. Consequently, the BOS had to design a

new monetary aggregate—ALP—that included the new forms of quasi
money being held by banks and the public. From 1984 on, monetary
authorities set their primary money growth targets in terms of the ALP but
continued to encounter difficulties due to further financial innovation. As
a result, the BOS slowly shifted the focus of its operations from targeting
the evolution of domestic credit to manipulating short-term interest
rates.[63]

Innovations Stimulated by Disintermediation
Intermediaries faced disintermediation threats from a variety of sources,
but short-term public debt posed by far the greatest challenge. The most
important financial innovations to cope with short-term debt were repurchase agreements and floating-rate bank bonds pegged to Pagarés. In carrying out repurchase agreements, banks sold a portion of their public debt
holdings to clients while agreeing to repurchase it at a designated future
date and price.[64] Through these operations, banks obtained the use of
funds that were not legally considered deposits; therefore, they were free to
offer savers effective yields that exceeded deposit rate ceilings and, hence,
compete with the government for short-term funds. Repurchase agreements were especially troubling for monetary authorities because they created substantial liquid assets on which they had little information. Banks
also issued floating-rate bonds with five-year maturities that typically
offered a 0.5 percent spread over one-year Pagarés in a direct attempt to
capture potential clients of public debt.

The Move toward Fiscal Orthodoxy

Growing budget deficits and the problems created by taxation of the banking system increased pressure on the Socialists to implement more orthodox fiscal policies. Taxation of the banking system was clearly acting as a
drag on the national economy. According to one estimate, the government's financial controls annually generated inefficiency losses of between
0.5 and 1.0 percent of Spain's GDP in the mid-1980s.[65] In addition, the
Socialists realized that unless they reined in spending and implemented
a more effective means of raising revenue the state might soon face a
major fiscal crisis. Consequently, they intensified their efforts to implement needed tax reforms.

   In the mid-1980s, the government successfully reformed private and
corporate income taxes and implemented a value-added tax, thereby establishing a wider and more stable revenue base.[66] Although increasing
direct taxation was difficult, the transition had generated social pressure
for a more equitable distribution of the tax burden that the Socialists were

able to mobilize in their efforts. It helped that the Socialists' natural constituency was labor, which supported a change in tax policy; a conservative party might have found it more difficult to transform the tax system. The reforms helped fiscal receipts as a percentage of GNP to jump from 33.1 to 37.7 percent between 1982 and 1987.[67] As a result, government deficits dropped to about 3.0 percent of GNP in the late 1980s after having reached 6.7 percent in 1985. The reduction in budget deficits was due almost solely to improved revenues since expenditures continued to rise.[68] The Socialists continued to struggle to bring government spending under control into the 1990s.

The success of the government's fiscal policies and the slow emergence of a functional public debt market allowed policymakers to ease taxation of the banking system and curtail the Treasury's borrowing from the central bank. In 1989, the government scheduled a gradual reduction of RRs in excess of their optimal level and began a slow eradication of ARs. In 1987, it imposed a stock limit on the Treasury's borrowing from the BOS, despite stiff opposition from the interventionists and several ministries (which feared that it would lower total government expenditure, thereby leading to reductions in their budgets); BOS lending to the Treasury was completely abolished in 1994.

Financial Policy: 1985–89

An Overview

Starting in 1985, the MOEF undertook a series of reforms that largely completed the transformation of the Spanish financial system into a market-based system. Among the key policies implemented in this period were the following:

1. The complete liberalization of interest rates
2. A dramatic reduction in state control over credit allocation
3. Additional measures to make public banks operate more like private banks
4. Further steps to eliminate differences in the treatment of intermediaries to increase competition among them
5. A complete overhaul of bond and equity markets
6. Measures to reduce business's dependence on bank finance
7. Liberalization of capital inflows and outflows

The MOEF did not issue financial reforms in "packages," as had been past practice, but rather in a piecemeal fashion over several years.[69] The motivating force behind deregulation remained a push for financial efficiency that would improve overall economic performance. Several factors intensified the drive toward financial reform in this period. The most notable were the diminished need to tax the financial sector to obtain revenue (already discussed); the PSOE's landslide victory in the 1986 elections; and Spain's entry into the EC.

The PSOE reaffirmed its position as the leading Spanish party in the 1986 elections. As table 7.1 shows, although the PSOE lost eighteen seats, it easily retained its absolute majority in the Cortes, enabling it to continue to govern alone. The major opposition party, CP, also maintained its status, but did not (as some had expected) gain ground on the PSOE. The other major winners in the elections were Suárez's CDS party and the centrist Catalan nationalist party, the CiU.

The 1986 election results suggested that the PSOE's dominance of Spanish politics was secure for the foreseeable future.[70] The neoliberals believed that the results gave them a mandate to proceed with their program of structural reforms. The interventionists' allegations that the government's economic policies would destroy the PSOE's electoral support had proved to be, at least for the moment, unfounded. Indeed, the elections convinced González and others that the government's economic program was the correct long-term political strategy and an acceptable short-term one. They felt comfortable in intensifying certain structural reforms, including financial deregulation.

Banks and firms moderated their opposition to further deregulation in this period because they now viewed it as inevitable. The interventionists, however, still opposed many financial reforms. They were unable to halt the deregulation process but managed to modify some reforms in ways that reduced their liberalizing impact. Specific examples are discussed later in this chapter.

The Effect of Spain's Entry into the EC on Financial Policy

Spain officially entered the EC on January 1, 1986.[71] The EC's influence on Spanish policy, however, had really begun years before. In the early 1960s, some government officials already believed that Spanish economic policy and institutions would have to become more like those of EC countries if Spain were to compete successfully in the Europe of the future, whether or not that included EC membership. In this sense, the EC served as a focal point for thinking about economic modernization.

As discussed previously, some scholars have argued that Spain's accession into the EC was largely responsible for its ambitious economic adjustment efforts, including financial deregulation. They suggest that the need to meet EC standards in a variety of economic policy areas as well as the need to improve the country's competitiveness in European markets once admitted explains the push for basic economic reforms. This argument, however, treats integration into the EC as exogenously given, whereas the decisions to apply for membership and enter the EC were in fact endogenous policy choices. Moreover, it implies that Spanish policymakers were only willing to undertake reform when highly constrained by external factors, a view that ignores the influence of domestic politics. In the most extreme versions of this argument, the push to enter the EC explains all Spanish economic reforms, even those taken years ago when the prospects of entry were remote; this is highly problematic, for numerous factors have influenced Spanish policy.

In addition, the impact of Spain's accession on its economic policy varied greatly across policy domains. It was not great in the area of financial policy. Spain did have to adopt EC rules on financial matters, and these were more liberal than Spanish regulations in the areas of foreign banking and transborder capital flows.[72] This constraint intensified and deepened liberalization in these areas in the mid-1980s, but it does not account for the bulk of Spain's deregulation efforts, which occurred well before Spain agreed to abide by EC rules. Furthermore, Spanish reforms cannot be attributed to policymakers anticipating EC requirements to facilitate acceptance into the Community.[73] EC financial regulations could only be considered comprehensive and restrictive after the Community issued its "Second Directive" in 1989; until that time, they were ambiguous and limited in scope, granting countries considerable leeway in setting financial policy.[74] Three leading authorities on the Spanish financial system state this clearly:

> In contrast with other policy areas, such as the Customs Union or Common Agricultural Policy, in the financial policy domain there is a great diversity of institutions, financial structures, and legal frameworks, leading to multiple differences across EC countries. It would be wrong, therefore, to think that the EC has a common financial policy with uniform rules; there is not a common banking market, and certainly not a common financial market.[75]

Finally, the most important Spanish financial reforms, at least until the mid-1980s, were concentrated in areas where the EC simply did not have rules (e.g., interest rate policy).

In any case, Spain's financial regulatory regime resembled that of other EC countries throughout much of the postwar period. If anything, according to three Spanish economists writing in 1988, "Spain is much further along than many other EC countries in the process that would be needed to create a common banking system."[76] Certainly, the Spanish government began carrying out major reforms in critical areas of financial policy (e.g., the removal of credit and interest rate controls) before many other EC countries (e.g., France).

In short, Spain's financial reform process was set in motion for reasons not directly related to meeting EC demands; we need to examine domestic political incentives to explain why political leaders deregulated markets. Nevertheless, as already noted, we can attribute some post-1985 reforms directly to Spain's entry into the EC. The most significant impact was further opening of Spanish markets to foreign intermediaries. After a transition period (until 1992), Spain could no longer discriminate against banks from other EC countries. It also had to adopt EC standards on the establishment of intermediaries issued in the "First Directive," although it was given a grace period.[77] The unrestricted entry of foreign banks was a frightening prospect for Spanish banks; moreover, it was not counterbalanced by the promise of profitable expansion into EC countries, as they were less efficient than European banks in almost every respect.[78]

Spanish authorities also had to liberalize capital flows to and from EC countries by 1992. At the time of its entry, Spanish capital controls were fairly typical of those of other EC countries. In fact, removing capital controls was a thorny issue for all EC members because financial assets were not taxed at a uniform rate within the EC.[79] Spain actually liberalized certain types of capital flows before 1992; for example, it removed most restrictions on foreign direct investment in 1987. Finally, authorities abolished limits on the types of international transactions Spanish intermediaries could perform so that they could compete with foreign intermediaries.

Entry into the EC also restricted, in principle, the type of aid that the Spanish government could provide to industry.[80] In the area of financial policy, for example, it was supposed to eliminate the supply of subsidized credit to exporters to EC countries. In practice, governments in most EC countries did not take the aid guidelines very seriously until the early 1990s, and their interpretation remains a highly controversial issue even today. Certainly, no government official ever cited the need to meet EC requirements in the highly contentious debates over reform of selective credit policies, where such a requirement would have been useful in overcoming opposition by affected industries.[81] In any case, Spain had already begun to eliminate most selective credit policies targeted at priority sectors well before its admission. It is also important to note it began dismantling its selective credit instruments prior to several other European countries (e.g., France).

Finally, EC accession provided a greater impetus to the ongoing reform of Spanish bond and equity markets. Although Spain faced no legal requirement to reform its direct markets, Britain's infamous "Big Bang" of 1986 meant that Spain would be unable to compete effectively with the United Kingdom's (and other EC countries') bond and equity markets for funds once capital controls were removed unless it also carried out reforms.

Ultimately, perhaps the most important impact of Spain's entry into the EC on financial policy was that it gave reformers another tool to overcome opposition to further financial deregulation.[82] Policymakers could point to EC standards (where they existed) as external constraints. They also could raise the specter of eventual competition from more efficient European intermediaries to build support among Spanish banks for reforms that would increase their long-run competitiveness.

State Control over Credit Allocation

The New Investment Coefficients
In 1985, the government passed legislation establishing a new legal framework for ICs. Its immediate objectives were to (1) create a single legal framework for ICs to replace the myriad of confusing and often contradictory rules, regulations, and the like that had been issued over the years; (2) establish uniform ICs for all intermediaries to eliminate the competitive advantages stemming from differential treatment; (3) expand the base of liabilities on which ICs were calculated; and (4) raise interest rates on loans granted through ICs to near market rates. The government stated that its long-term goal was to reduce the amount of credit flowing through ICs, thereby decreasing state control over credit allocation and improving financial efficiency. In fact, the MOEF reduced ICs to 23 percent of total liabilities immediately.[83] The law, however, permitted authorities to set ICs as high as 35 percent.

Interventionists tried to derail the legislation, since it reduced state control over credit, but they were unsuccessful. The Undersecretaries Commission held up the draft bill for several weeks, but González exercised his influence to push it through to the Cortes.[84] Regional governments also opposed the bill, claiming that it infringed upon their right to influence the allocation of credit at the regional level.[85] They threatened to challenge (but did not) the legality of the new law in the courts.

The reaction of intermediaries to the new law was mixed. Those previously exempt from ICs (e.g., finance companies) opposed the legislation but lacked the political influence to do anything about it. Savings banks, on the other hand, applauded it because it granted equal treatment to all intermediaries, a goal they had long sought because they had higher ICs.[86] Banks had long pushed for reform of ICs but found fault with this law. They contended that the government was preparing the way to eventually increase state control over credit allocation, because the legislation allowed the MOEF to set ICs as high as 35 percent of total liabilities. In addition, they feared the increased competition that saving banks might represent now that their ICs were identical.

In 1987, the MOEF, to the delight of all intermediaries, decreed it would reduce ICs to only 11 percent.[87] There were several reasons for the dramatic reduction of ICs. First, it was yet another step in the government's ongoing elimination of state control over credit allocation. Second, the government's industrial restructuring plans were nearing completion, so their need for funds was decreasing. Finally, the reduction was intended to compensate banks for the removal of all interest rate controls in 1987.[88]

The beneficiaries of ICs loudly protested this reduction since it effectively cut them off from preferential credit. It should be noted, however, that the central and regional governments continued to provide aid to various sectors through other channels, some new, some preexisting. The most important were preferential fiscal treatment, regional development schemes, and direct subsidies.[89] From an efficiency standpoint, these policies were generally preferable to administrative control of credit flows because they introduced less distortion in factor markets.

The Reform of the Public Banking System
The Socialists moved decisively to reform the public banking system upon taking office, curtailing its role as a conduit of preferential credit. This occurred despite strong opposition from the interventionists, who wished to expand the system to support industrial sectors in crisis. In 1983, the government capped the amount of funds that public banks could obtain from the Treasury to force them to procure more working capital from private markets. In 1987, it announced it would slowly eliminate all government funding of the public banking system. This reform was related to that of ICs. The reduction of ICs had abolished intermediaries' obligation to purchase investment certificates, the instrument the Treasury had used to fund public banks. This meant the Treasury either had to provide funds to public banks directly or force them to obtain more funds on their own.

These measures were aimed at creating a new type of public bank. Public banks were no longer to provide credit at subsidized rates; instead, they were to supply credit at market rates but with longer maturities than private intermediaries. They were to continue to concentrate their lending in "priority" sectors (e.g., housing), but were expected to diversify their lending activity over time. The government began to privatize public banks in the 1990s, setting up the holding company Argentaria to manage the process.

Control over Savings Banks

Spanish savings banks have traditionally been the object of intense political pressures. The conspicuous abuses of savings banks by public officials during the Franquist period motivated the UCD to modify the banks' governance institutions in order to insulate them from political pressures. The UCD's reforms were widely criticized, however, for their failure to grant representation on savings banks' boards to all interested parties. This encouraged the PSOE and other parties to clamor for greater "democratization" of savings banks in the 1979 and 1982 electoral campaigns.

The Socialists announced that they would introduce legislation establishing a new legal framework for savings banks soon after taking office. Savings banks feared that this new framework was intended to permit political parties and unions to use them for political purposes. At its 1983 assembly, CECA's director called upon the PSOE to maintain the current governance structure of savings banks and not permit any one group, especially municipal governments, to gain control over them.[90] The BOS also urged PSOE leadership not to turn savings banks into mere political appendages for municipal governments because this would undermine its attempts to improve financial market efficiency.

To allay their fears, Boyer announced that the MOEF had no intention of politicizing savings banks.[91] The interventionists, however, had other plans, as they had made giving municipal governments, many of which the PSOE dominated, greater control over savings banks a top priority. The interventionists managed to seize control over the legislative process when the savings bank issue made it into the Cortes, due in part to skilful maneuvering by Martín Toval, head of the PSOE's parliamentary group, and they pushed through legislation in 1985 that largely reflected their preferences.

The governing organs of savings banks were modified to have the following representation: local government (40 percent); depositors (45 percent); original founders (11 percent); and employees (5 percent). A savings bank's management was to be chosen by this body. At this time, it is still unclear to what extent savings banks have fallen prey to political forces. Overt politicization has occurred in at most only a few savings banks. On the other hand, several have become highly efficient intermediaries that seem to act solely on the basis of economic criteria. Indeed, a few, such as the Caixa, have become leading and highly respected players in Spanish financial markets.

Measures to Develop Direct Financial Markets

The PSOE passed legislation in 1988 that revolutionized Spanish bond and equity markets in ways similar to the United Kingdom's famous "Big Bang."[92] Although the legislation built upon earlier efforts to reform direct markets, it represented a major qualitative breakthrough. The timing of the reforms was greatly affected by developments in other countries (especially the United Kingdom) and the prospect of the complete liberalization of capital flows in the EC in 1992.

The 1988 legislation unified the four existing stock exchanges and created a single supervisory body, the Comisión Nacional de Valores (much like the United States's Securities and Exchange Commission), to oversee them. It opened up participation in the official exchanges to all financial institutions, breaking up the monopoly that members of the Association of Stock Brokers had traditionally enjoyed. In this regard, the law stipulated that Sociedades del Mercado de Valores (SMV, Stock Market Societies) would be the principal intermediaries on the exchanges. SMV's could be either brokers or dealer-brokers (i.e., market makers). The law prohibited foreign dealer-brokers until 1992 because of widespread concern that their greater expertise and experience would permit them to dominate the market. Finally, it established a continuous market in place of periodic auctions and instructed the exchanges to computerize all operations. In related developments, the government promoted the growth of secondary markets, passed regulations requiring all major firms to submit to yearly audits and disclose in-depth financial information, and took the first steps to eliminate insider trading.

As in the past, banks feared the expansion of direct markets because of the disintermediation threat they posed.[93] Instead of frontally opposing legislation (as they had done earlier), however, they strategically sought to gain a leading role in the new stock exchanges by lobbying for specific changes in the draft law. This change in tactics came about because banks realized that reform of direct markets was inevitable. Policymakers in fact modified their original draft bill to induce banks to drop their opposition to the reforms. They established start-up capital requirements that would make it difficult for anyone but banks to form SMVs and, as noted earlier, prohibited foreign dealer-brokers from entering the market until 1992. Overall, these and other provisions ensured banks a dominant position in the new bond and equity markets (at least temporarily). It should be noted that domestic banks enjoyed a similarly privileged position in many European bourses in the late 1980s.

To help deepen direct markets, the government attempted to increase demand for bonds and equities by encouraging institutional investors, specifically mutual funds and pension plans. The Pension Funds Law of 1987 was one of the most controversial pieces of financial legislation in the late 1980s, again pitting the neoliberals against the interventionists. The original bill would have given firms control over the creation and management of pension funds, as is the practice throughout most of Europe.[94] The interventionists, on the other hand, wished to allow workers to manage the funds through their unions. In this arrangement, a portion of the commissions workers paid for management of their funds would be set aside to finance union activities. A drop in workers' dues caused by declining membership made this especially attractive for union leaders.

The final version of the law reflected the preferences of the interventionists, primarily because of intense lobbying by the UGT. González yielded to the interventionists on the pension funds legislation in exchange for the UGT's acquiescence on the PSOE's general economic policies at a time when tensions between the government and UGT were rising. The law stipulated that workers (i.e., unions) would manage pension funds; however, firms were not obligated to set up pension funds for their employees. To date, the law has had only limited success in promoting the creation of pension funds. As the neoliberals had anticipated, firms had little confidence in pension funds controlled by unions, and they stayed away from them, seeking out alternative arrangements to provide for their employees.

Interest Rate Liberalization and Other Measures to Increase Competition

The government removed all controls on interest rates and commissions in 1987. Policymakers had delayed this reform out of concern over high interest rates in the mid-1980s largely caused by a tight monetary policy (discussed later in this section); they feared that deregulation might push rates even higher unless government deficits and inflation were brought under control first. Moreover, many banks had remained opposed to it.[95] The government also passed the Financial Intermediaries Law in 1987. It established a common set of regulations governing all types of intermediaries and represented the final stage in the promotion of universal banking; this was meant to allow other intermediaries to challenge bank dominance of the financial sector.

These and other measures intended to increase competition had disappointing results in the short run, but yielded their intended outcomes in due course. As table 7.2 shows, bank's financial margins and profits actually increased in the mid- to late 1980s.[96] The best economic explanation for the persistence of high margins is that households dramatically increased their demand for credit in this period, more than offsetting a sharp decline in demand from firms.[97] In addition, banks initially were able to reach and sustain "gentlemen's pacts" to limit deposit rate increases.

The competitive environment changed permanently in late 1989, when the Banco de Santander offered much higher rates on large volume demand deposits ("super accounts") in an effort to augment its share of total deposits. This sparked strong competition for demand deposits among banks, pushing rates on these liabilities over 10 percent. In subsequent years, competition for funds among all intermediaries kept deposit rates high while loan rates dropped (see table 7.3).[98] This competition sharply eroded banks' share of total deposits, as indicated in fig. 7.1, so much so that savings banks actually captured a larger share of deposits by the mid-1990s. The dramatic decline in banks' margins and profits (table 7.2) is compelling evidence that competition-augmenting reforms have led to great improvements in the efficiency of Spanish banking.[99] Banks also encountered stiff competition in their lending to the private sector. Banks lost business to other intermediaries, as seen in a further drop in banks' share of credit to the private sector (fig. 7.2). In addition, disintermediation increased with the development of viable domestic alternatives to bank financing, such as markets for private fixed income securities (e.g.,

TABLE 7.2. Banks' Operating Costs, Financial Margins, Loan-Loss Provisions, and Profits as a Percentage of Total Assets, 1984–95

	[1] Operating Costs[a]	[2] Financial Margin[b]	[3] [2] - [1]	[4] Loan-Loss Provisions	[5] Profits before Taxes[c]
1984	2.75	4.52	1.77	0.94	0.59
1985	2.65	4.32	1.67	0.68	0.73
1986	2.67	4.53	1.86	0.63	0.83
1987	2.67	4.72	2.05	0.66	1.02
1988	2.73	4.98	2.25	0.78	1.38
1989	2.67	4.80	2.13	0.44	1.54
1990	2.74	4.73	1.99	0.62	1.55
1991	2.70	4.43	1.73	0.66	1.41
1992	2.59	4.15	1.56	0.66	1.11
1993	2.30	3.86	1.56	0.89	0.88
1994	2.12	3.10	0.98	0.77	0.65
1995	2.02	3.00	0.98	0.43	0.69

Source: Banco de España, "Boletín Económico," various issues.
[a]Operating Costs = Personnel Costs + General Expenses + Taxes + Amortizations
[b]Financial Margin = Average Yield on Loans – Average Cost of Deposits + Commissions
[c]Profits before Taxes = Column 3 + Other Profits – Column 4

commercial paper) and bond and equity markets, as well as borrowing from abroad.[100]

It should be noted that high interest rates in the 1980s and early 1990s were primarily the product of a tight monetary policy stance aimed at fighting inflation.[101] In addition, authorities used interest rate policy to boost confidence in the peseta after Spain entered the European exchange rate mechanism in 1989. Although this monetary stance reduced inflation, it was not without costs.[102] Perhaps the most serious was that high real rates (by international standards) attracted large capital inflows that made monetary control difficult. Authorities welcomed a huge increase in long-term direct investment, but implemented various capital controls (starting in 1987) to stem short-term capital flows.[103] In addition, they removed controls on outward flows before required to do so by the EC in order to lessen appreciation of the peseta.[104] Monetary control problems led the government to impose temporary quantitative restrictions on bank credit in 1989–90. Capital inflows also further appreciated the peseta, making

TABLE 7.3. The Evolution of Various Interest Rates, 1978–95

	Deposit Rate[a]		Loan Rate[b]		Bank of Spain Rate[c]	
	Nominal	Real	Nominal	Real	Nominal	Real
1978	6.5	−14.1	15.0	−5.6	9.0	−11.6
1979	6.5	−10.4	15.8	−1.1	8.0	−8.9
1980	6.5	−6.9	16.8	3.4	10.9	−2.5
1981	11.4	−1.2	17.4	4.8	10.5	−2.1
1982	12.3	−1.6	17.5	3.6	18.4	4.5
1983	12.3	0.8	17.6	5.8	21.4	9.9
1984	12.3	0.7	18.1	6.5	12.5	0.9
1985	10.5	2.8	16.7	9.0	10.5	2.8
1986	9.0	−2.1	15.4	4.3	11.8	0.7
1987	9.0	3.2	15.9	10.1	13.5	7.7
1988	9.1	3.4	15.2	9.5	12.4	6.7
1989	9.6	2.5	16.4	9.3	14.5	7.4
1990	10.7	3.3	17.5	10.1	14.7	7.3
1991	10.5	3.5	16.5	9.5	12.5	5.5
1992	10.4	3.9	15.9	9.4	13.3	6.8
1993	9.6	5.2	14.6	10.2	9.0	4.6
1994	6.7	2.3	10.9	6.8	7.4	3.0
1995	7.7	2.2	10.1	4.6	9.0	3.5

Source: Banco de España 1988, 1995b, and IMF, *International Financial Statistics.*

[a]Nominal and real rates are for new six-month to one-year deposits; rates were freed from government control after 1981.

[b]Nominal and real rates are for new one- to three-year loans.

[c]Ten-day intervention rate

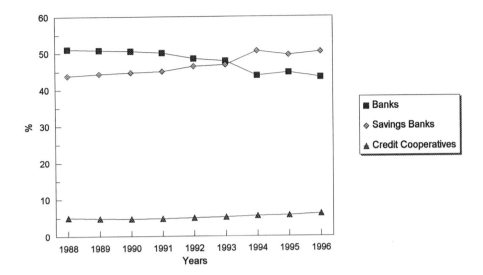

Fig. 7.1.   Share of total deposits by financial intermediary as a percentage of total, 1988–96. (Data from Banco de España, data tape, 1996.)

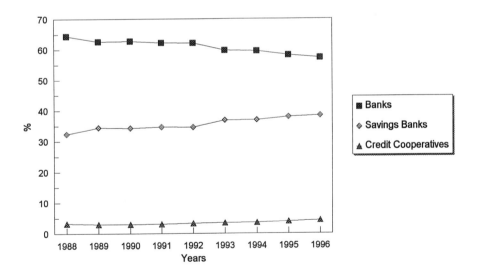

Fig. 7.2.   Share of credit to the private sector by financial intermediary as a percentage of total, 1988–96. (Data from Banco de España, data tape, 1996.)

Spanish exports less competitive and, thus, contributing to a deficit on the current account.

Socialist Policies to Transform Industry's Financial Structure

In the late 1970s, firms sought to lower their dependence on bank financing because of the rising cost of bank credit and tighter monetary policy.[105] The Socialists designed several policies to further reduce industry's reliance on bank financing, particularly after 1985.[106] First, policymakers took several steps to expand and modernize bond and equity markets (as discussed earlier). Second, they promoted NBFIs as alternatives to banks. Third, they followed policies aimed at increasing business profits to enable firms to generate a pool of funds available for self-finance. One principal strategy was to restrain wage growth in order to allow a larger share of earnings to accrue to capital, a remarkable policy for a Socialist party. Finally, policymakers sought to establish macroeconomic stability to encourage a climate propitious for savings and investment.

Three basic motives underlay this strategy. To begin with, policymakers wished to eliminate firms' vulnerability to fluctuations in the banking sector's liquidity. As shown earlier, this vulnerability was a serious constraint on the government's ability to tighten monetary policy. They also believed that a more diversified financial structure would make firm profitability less susceptible to developments in the banking sector, such as increases in the cost of bank credit. Finally, some government officials wanted to reduce banks' perceived control over the real sector based on their ownership of firms and control over financing.

The government's policies apparently were effective and had an immediate impact. As table 7.4 indicates, firm profitability increased significantly during the mid-1980s. Profit margins grew rapidly throughout the 1980s, and after-tax profit became higher than the OECD average.[107] Although this trend cannot be attributed solely (or perhaps even mostly) to the government's policies, many observers believe that they contributed greatly. A study by Alfonso Novales and anecdotal evidence suggest that firms recognized the intent of government policy and funneled profits into investment or reducing debt, instead of distributing greater dividends.[108] Retained earnings increased dramatically while firms held down dividends; retained earnings were negative 56 percent of sales revenue in 1982 but increased to positive 25 percent in 1989.[109] As a result, firms' net financial wealth grew very rapidly from 1980 to 1989.[110] After deteriorating somewhat in the period from 1990 to 1992 (due largely to an economic recession that hit most European countries), the profitability and net wealth of Spanish firms improved again in 1994.[111]

Azofra and Martínez demonstrate that the financial structure of firms also changed dramatically from the 1970s to the mid-1980s.[112] In 1972, the ratio of debt to equity was 1.65; by 1986, it had dropped to only 1.07.[113] In particular, firms reduced their reliance on short-term credit; it fell from 42 percent of their total financing in 1972 to only 13 percent in 1986.[114] Firms increased their self-financing and turned to bond and equity markets for funds as they moved away from bank credit.[115] The impact of these trends on the pattern of bank lending was extraordinary: firms (excluding those in construction) absorbed 62 percent of all bank lending in 1985 but only 17 percent in 1988.[116]

Conclusion

After the 1982 elections, the Spanish financial world waited anxiously to see the course that the PSOE would take in financial policy. Many feared it might attempt to increase state control over financial markets to achieve its political and social goals. Using the financial system to ease the economic crisis (e.g., by funneling funds to "priority activities") seemed to be too great a temptation for a Socialist party to resist. Instead, the PSOE implemented the most far-reaching financial reforms to date. The Socialists promoted financial liberalization, despite considerable opposition from social

TABLE 7.4. **Profitability of Private Firms, 1981–94**

	Income[a] before Taxes	Income[a] after Taxes	Return on Equity Capital[b]
1981	−0.3	−0.3	n/a
1982	−0.7	−1.1	−1.3
1983	−0.1	−0.6	−0.1
1984	0.5	−0.1	0.9
1985	1.7	0.9	3.3
1986	2.9	1.9	5.6
1987	4.8	3.5	9.7
1988	6.3	4.9	12.0
1989	6.4	5.0	12.5
1990	4.6	3.2	10.6
1991	3.1	1.7	5.9
1992	0.4	−0.6	0.8
1993	−1.2	−2.1	−2.2
1994	3.1	1.8	6.2

Source: Banco de España, "Central de Balances," 1991 and 1995.

Note: Private firms are nonfinancial firms providing data to the Bank of Spain. n/a = not available.

[a]Income expressed as a percent of sales revenue.

[b]A different statistical series is used for data from 1991–94.

actors and within the PSOE itself, as one means of improving economic performance and appealing to a wide electoral base.

Spain's fiscal crisis also acted as a powerful force behind financial deregulation. PSOE officials initially augmented taxation of the banking system by imposing high RRs and ARs to generate government revenue. They adopted this policy out of necessity, since other more effective fiscal instruments had not yet been developed. By the mid-1980s, however, it had become apparent that excessive taxation of the banking system was seriously hurting economic performance and could yield little (if any) additional revenues. Consequently, the PSOE stepped up its efforts to implement more efficient means of raising revenue, namely, a progressive income tax and value-added tax. When the government's more orthodox fiscal policies began functioning adequately in the late 1980s, policymakers greatly reduced taxation of the banking system.

Another major force behind financial liberalization was Spain's entry into the EC. Although EC rules did not oblige Spain to undertake many major new reforms, they did require deepening some ongoing reforms. In addition, authorities used EC requirements to soften social and state opposition to further deregulation and prod Spanish intermediaries to modernize. In particular, the large national banks, faced with the imminent entry of more efficient foreign intermediaries, slowly started focusing on improving their competitiveness. Nevertheless, Spanish intermediaries remain relatively uncompetitive vis-à-vis their EC counterparts (albeit with a few notable exceptions) even though authorities have successfully encouraged them to enter into mergers to obtain the economies of scale that they need to compete with large European banks.

CHAPTER 8

Conclusion

This study has explored, both generally and in the case of Spain, why government officials restrict their country's financial system as well as why they may later liberalize it. Using a rational choice perspective, I have argued that public officials provide the dynamic behind the evolution of financial policy. Specifically, I have contended that public officials shape financial markets to advance their own interests—namely, holding power and obtaining government revenue—altering regulatory policy in response to changes in the incentives and constraints generated by their political environment.

This chapter has two purposes. The first is to consider the implications of this study's findings for rational choice approaches that explain economic policy-making by analyzing political institutions and the reward structures they provide political leaders. A brief review of my theoretical and case study results precedes this discussion. The second is to determine whether the finding from the Spanish case that democratization may spur political leaders to undertake structural reforms like financial liberalization is generalizable. To help ascertain this, I analyze the impact of democratization on financial policy in Brazil, South Korea, and Turkey, countries that began their transitions with repressed financial systems. My reasons for choosing these cases are identified later in this chapter. I contend that democratization helped to stimulate financial reform in these three countries, but that several institutional features, notably electoral systems, have influenced the intensity and profile of their reform efforts. This discussion illustrates and elaborates upon the theoretical arguments concerning democratization made in chapter 2.

The Principal Findings and Their Theoretical Implications

A Brief Overview of the Findings

This study contends that public officials design financial policy in order to advance two primary goals, holding power and obtaining government revenue, adapting it to suit the reward structure generated by a country's political environment and institutions. For instance, when institutions encourage political leaders to court narrow special interests instead of the general populace in the pursuit of power, they formulate financial policy that creates the means of distributing credit rents to specific groups. When institutions provide an incentive to appeal to encompassing interests, leaders fashion policy that emphasizes the supply of collective goods, like efficient financial markets.

Seen in this light, restricted and market-based systems have different political merits whose utility for politicians varies across institutional settings. Financial restriction is most useful when a country's institutions motivate political leaders to deliver private benefits to key constituencies in the pursuit of power or to raise revenue indirectly. Interest rate and credit controls enable public officials to retain or win political support by directing available credit at preferential rates to actual or potential supporters. Taxation of the banking system provides an attractive source of government revenue. RRs allow fiscal authorities to tap savings mobilized by the banking system at zero- or low-interest cost; ARs enable them to reduce the cost of financing state activities and also ensures the placement of government bond issues. Leaders often resort to taxation of the financial sector despite its high efficiency costs because a more direct and efficient means of generating revenue is not feasible politically.

Although restriction gives public officials a means of distributing private financial benefits and obtaining revenue, it generally leads to financial inefficiency. Market-based financial systems promise greater efficiency but are more difficult to manipulate for political purposes because they do not allow officials to affect directly the fortunes of particular groups. A more market-based system is politically valuable, however, when a country's institutions encourage politicians to supply collective economic goods instead of private goods in the pursuit of power. For instance, politicians have an interest in creating efficient markets if they must appeal to a broad-based national coalition to win sufficient electoral support, and voters place a premium on economic performance. A system in which market forces determine the allocation and price of credit is also useful when leaders wish to avoid having to favor some constituents over others or need to extricate themselves from costly existing commitments to certain groups. Finally, a more market-based system is politically attractive because it improves the stream of government revenues by promoting long-term growth.

Politicians will deregulate financial markets when changes in institutions or their political environment increase the utility of a more market-based system relative to that of a restricted system. The utility of a market-based financial system for politicians may increase in two ways. First, it may occur when the value of supplying more efficient market arrangements increases relative to that of providing private benefits to select constituents in the pursuit of power. Second, it may happen when more efficient means of taxation become available and politically feasible. I have identified democratization as an institutional change that often has both these effects and, thus, contributes to interest in deregulation. Likewise, leaders may deregulate when the costs of maintaining restriction come to exceed its benefits, turning a restricted system into a political liability. This takes place when restriction so lowers financial efficiency that it impedes growth, giving rivals an issue they can use to challenge current leaders.

This study contends that one must look at the factors that influence the supply of regulation as well as the demand for it to explain financial policy. Public officials do not simply design policy in response to the demands of social groups for regulation, as simple sectoral models contend; they possess distinctive interests and may attempt to use the instruments of the state to shape financial markets to further their goals. Analysis that views regulatory policy as simply reflecting the preferences of dominant social groups or emerging from the struggle among interest groups for influence will be incomplete. The importance of considering the interests of public officials is most clearly seen in the case of deregulation of restricted financial systems. In countries with restricted systems, public officials have provided the impetus behind liberalization, usually in the face of strong opposition from powerful, well-organized private groups benefiting from restriction (e.g., banks) and general indifference on the part of those that might benefit from deregulation (e.g., savers).

Public interest, international, and ideational accounts of financial regulation are also inadequate because political leaders view economic conditions, external pressures, and policy-relevant knowledge through the filter of their own self-interest. The timing and nature of reforms are ultimately determined by domestic political factors, such as the calculations of leaders, the degree of political competition, and the balance of interest group demands. This is evident in the wide variation of response among countries faced with similar international trends or exposed to the same policy-relevant knowledge. Nevertheless, global economic and political trends in particular have become a more important influence on financial policy since they have augmented the political costs of maintaining a closed, restricted financial system.

The Evolution of Financial Policy in Spain
The conceptual framework developed in this study explains the evolution of Spanish financial regulation during the period from 1939 to 1992 very

well. Spain had a restricted system until the 1970s. Early on, Spanish financial policy reflected the strong bargaining power of the banking sector. Government officials permitted banks to earn high, risk-free profits by imposing entry and interest rate controls that limited competition and reduced risk. They also implemented policies designed to limit the growth of bond and equity markets, thereby reducing the threat of disintermediation. Officials in the Franco regime, however, gradually transformed financial regulation so that it could be used to advance their own interests more effectively. In the 1960s, they implemented new regulatory controls that created a means of using financial markets to obtain government revenue and distribute private benefits to secure the support of key social groups. Policymakers established various selective credit programs for controlling the allocation of credit, passing much of the cost of supplying preferential credit onto private banks. They taxed the banking system to fund government activities and deficits at low interest cost. The Franco regime was reluctant to rely on more efficient means of taxation, like direct taxes, because it did not wish to alienate constituents among the middle and upper classes. Government officials did not take full advantage of seigniorage opportunities initially. However, they slowly increased their use of these instruments throughout the 1960s, 1970s, and 1980s.

Spain's experience with financial restriction was typical of that of most countries that have had restricted systems. There is strong prima facie evidence that the political motives that I identify as central in prompting public officials to pursue a strategy of restriction—namely, using the financial system to distribute private benefits to key constituents and raise government revenue—were also important in countries other than Spain. Many governments have used repression to extract large amounts of revenue from the banking system.[1] In addition, studies suggest that public officials have often designed selective credit policies with political purposes in mind, notably to target important constituents.[2] It also warrants repeating that many economists believe that repression has tended to hurt economic performance in most countries (including Spain) where it was followed. Of course, credit and interest rate controls have been more politicized in some countries than in others, and the degree of taxation of the banking system has also varied. Japan, South Korea, and Taiwan stand out as countries that were able to use financial controls to effectively target sectors whose growth was important for economic development and modernization. Explaining why financial restriction in the East Asian cases differed from that of most other countries is beyond the scope of this book, but I address this issue elsewhere.[3]

The Spanish government began liberalizing financial markets tentatively in 1969. Political leaders sought deregulation when they decided that the superior economic performance that a market-based financial system promised to help bring about was essential for staying in power. The Franco regime's concern with growing political unrest in the late 1960s, fueled partly by dissatisfaction with economic policy, was the first event to spark interest in financial liberalization. The regime's inner circle resolved to permit the MOF to pursue limited structural reforms aimed at increasing economic efficiency and growth and lowering inflation. It hoped that rising standards of living and stable prices would reduce hostility toward the regime and eliminate a potential basis of support for opposition groups. MOF officials believed that promoting a more market-based financial system through gradual deregulation was a top priority, so they implemented a series of minor reforms in the early 1970s. They were confident that such a system would help increase economic efficiency as well as improve monetary control. In supporting financial liberalization, regime officials calculated that obtaining the acquiescence of workers and students through better economic performance would be worth losing some support among banks and big business.

As in many countries with restricted systems, the push for liberalization in Spain did not stem at all from a change in the preferences of restriction's private sector beneficiaries or the net balance of interest group demands. Banks, which have led deregulation efforts in countries with well-developed financial systems, aggressively lobbied against most financial reforms. Private groups that stood to benefit from deregulation, namely, savers and firms rationed out of credit markets, were not organized and did not apply pressure on the government to alter financial policy. In short, public officials alone provided the impetus behind financial deregulation.

Financial reform halted after 1974 as the uncertainty surrounding Spain's political future led to virtual paralysis in economic policy-making. It was the country's transition from an authoritarian to a democratic regime that provided a fresh impetus for financial deregulation. The transition ushered in new political institutions that gave politicians a relatively greater incentive to supply collective goods (like efficient markets) rather than private benefits to select groups in the pursuit of power. As shown in chapter 5, Spanish electoral rules encouraged politicians to create large, national parties, not small, sectarian ones. To win office, parties had to build broad-based constituencies by appealing to encompassing interests, since a strategy based on targeting narrow groups was unlikely to obtain sufficient electoral support. The country's general political environment also contributed to heightened interest in supplying collective goods, as I detail later.

The party that won the 1977 elections, the UCD, responded to the political incentives generated by Spain's new democratic institutions. Upon taking office, it took steps to stabilize the economy and introduce badly needed structural reforms designed to promote overall social welfare and abolish special privileges for entrenched economic elites. An important element of its economic adjustment program was a financial reform package. This package represented the first systematic attempt to eliminate inefficient interest rate and credit controls, augment competition in the financial sector, and deepen Spain's links to international capital markets. Significantly, these measures decreased the ability of public officials to use financial policy to distribute private goods to favored groups.

Financial reform slowed starting in 1978 as the government confronted increasingly strident opposition, especially from banks and business associations, and Spain's economic situation deteriorated. UCD leadership decided that more aggressive economic adjustment would have to wait until they completed basic political reforms. In the area of financial policy, additional factors weighing against reform were continuing problems with inflation, a perceived industrial crisis, and a rapidly escalating banking crisis. Consequently, the government resolved to follow a strategy of gradual structural reform concentrating on only a few areas of public policy.

The UCD reopened the process of financial deregulation in 1981 with an important package of reforms. Party leaders realized that the electorate had become disenchanted with the government's inability to formulate coherent solutions to the economic crisis. They decided that further delay in carrying out structural adjustment would destroy the UCD's chances to succeed in the upcoming elections. A realignment of political forces within the party, namely, the ascent of the Social Democrats, helped to encourage a return to a more reform-oriented economic policy. This change in strategy came too late, however: the UCD was crushed in the 1982 general elections, which were won handily by the socialist party, the PSOE.

As the PSOE took office in 1982, many political analysts predicted that the new government would pursue an "orthodox" socialist economic strategy and intervene extensively in the economy, including financial markets. Instead, the Socialists deepened the process of economic adjustment, despite stiff resistance from some party members and traditional constituents, like labor. In the area of financial policy, the Socialists continued the deregulation process. Over the course of the 1980s, they completely liberalized interest rates, dramatically reduced state control over credit allocation, deepened direct markets, successfully augmented competition in the financial sector, and fully integrated Spain's financial system into international markets.

The PSOE, like the UCD before it, responded to the incentives generated by Spain's political institutions to win the support of a heterogeneous national constituency by adopting measures necessary to improve economic performance. In addition, it confronted another reason to liberalize financial markets: a sharp increase in state expenditures engendered by the democratic transition combined with growing evidence that taxing financial intermediaries could yield little (if any) additional revenues. Consequently, the PSOE stepped up its efforts to implement a progressive income tax and began to eliminate taxation of the banking system. Reform of fiscal policy, which was not permitted by the Franco regime, was also made possible by the transition. Democratization generated social pressure for a more equitable distribution of the tax burden that the Socialists were able to mobilize in their efforts.

Other factors have also affected the evolution of Spanish financial regulation. The most important were changes in economic conditions, alterations in the composition of the economic policy-making team, and Spain's entry into the EC. Spanish accession into the EC made some financial reforms obligatory and facilitated the implementation of others by generating a consensus that the country had to undergo structural adjustment to compete effectively in European markets. But it cannot account for most of Spain's deregulation efforts. Significant liberalization occurred well before Spain agreed to abide by EC rules, and those reforms cannot be attributed to policymakers anticipating EC requirements to facilitate acceptance into the Community. Finally, the decision to enter the EC was itself endogenous. It was partly explained by the same variable that I highlight as important in motivating structural reforms: the need to provide strong economic performance to sustain broad-based political support.

Implications of the Findings for Rational Choice Theorizing about Economic Policy-Making

What do the case study results tell us about the explanatory power of the conceptual framework developed here? I suggest that this study's rational choice hypotheses are able to capture differences in the reward structures provided political leaders by authoritarian and democratic regimes and demonstrate how these differences affect economic policy-making. But they are unable to explain inter- and intragovernmental variances in the behavior of politicians facing similar institutional constraints after democratization; this variance must be explained by an entirely different set of factors. The broader implication is that rational choice approaches that seek to explain political behavior solely by specifying the institutional reward structure confronting politicians are bound to be incomplete; they must be supplemented by attention to variables at other levels of the political system and the interactions among them. I examine some of these other variables after first identifying which political outcomes in the Spanish case can be attributed to changes in institutional constraints and incentives.

Democratization in Spain fundamentally changed the reward structures facing political leaders, making the supply of public goods more attractive and a narrow defense of special interests much less feasible as a means of staying in power. The impact of the new incentive structures on political behavior is seen in the remarkably similar electoral strategies adopted by newly formed parties. With only one exception, the major parties devised catch-all strategies designed to attract heterogeneous, national constituencies. In addition, they emphasized their intent to provide for the public good rather than deliver benefits to particular groups. Significantly, the only major party that failed to heed electoral incentives to seek broad-based support, the AP, was punished severely. The AP's 1977 electoral campaign, which seemed to suggest the party was catering to particular interests, led to a humiliating defeat that literally destroyed the party; its successors, the CD and CP, subsequently developed catch-all strategies. The fate of the AP suggests that Spanish parties must respond "rationally" to electoral incentives if they wish to be major participants in the country's political life and shape its economic policies.

Moreover, the two parties that formed governments, the UCD and PSOE, attempted to follow a similar economic strategy—featuring stabilization and structural adjustment programs intended to promote aggregate social welfare—once in office, despite huge differences in their core constituencies, historical policy preferences, ideologies, and party structures. In addition, they resisted temptations to implement policies that would unduly favor their natural constituencies over others. What most distinguished the two parties was their ability to carry out their policies effectively. The Socialist governments had several advantages in pursuing economic reforms such as financial deregulation. Two stand out. First, they enjoyed an absolute majority in the Cortes throughout the 1980s, which permitted them great autonomy in passing legislation. Second, the PSOE was not as constrained by ties to vested economic interests opposed to many structural reforms as the UCD had been. The PSOE's long-standing links to labor may have actually helped it to implement some economic reforms because it had greater credibility in the eyes of the working class (who were asked to bear part of the burden of adjustment). It is testimony to the powerful influence of institutional reward structures that the UCD attempted to provide for the collective interest despite being an internally mobilized party with every incentive to retain office by taking advantage of its connections to well-established social groups.

An analysis of formal institutions, like electoral rules, however, cannot entirely explain why Spanish parties appealed to the public interest in pursuit of office or supplied collective goods once there; we also need to consider variables associated with Spain's general political environment. One key factor is that Spanish politicians placed a premium on economic and political stability and energetic state action because they feared a return to the divisiveness and policy incoherence characteristic of the 1930s. These concerns, of course, had contributed to the choice of Spain's particular electoral institutions in the first place. In addition, Spanish voters had a pragmatic orientation toward public policy that stressed good outcomes, not particular content. They viewed parties that favored public policies that seemed to benefit only select groups as illegitimate, because such an orientation reminded them of the arbitrariness and favoritism of much government policy during the Franco years. I illustrate the importance of factors related to a country's political climate further when I compare the impact of democratization on financial policy in Spain and Turkey later in this chapter. Democratic transitions resulted in similar institutional structures in both countries, but variations in their overall political environment have contributed to different economic policy outcomes.

The limits of the rational choice approach are also seen in the existence of divergent perspectives on overall political and economic strategy within individual parties, notably the UCD and PSOE. Stated simply, all Spanish politicians faced similar reward structures, but their calculations of how to maximize electoral representation differed markedly.[4] Specifically, not every Spanish politician viewed policies aimed at supplying collective goods as the optimal way to maximize electoral support.

In the UCD, the divisions on economic and political strategy stemmed largely from diverse calculations regarding how the UCD could best secure votes.[5] Suárez and his closest political associates believed that the biggest bloc of voters was located somewhat to the left of center. Thus, they asserted that the UCD had to reach out beyond its natural conservative constituency and appeal to a broad electorate, including labor, by designing progressive, reform-minded economic policies that would promote aggregate welfare. The Christian Democrats (and some others), on the other hand, wanted to create a party based on close, institutionalized links to key constituent groups, especially banks and established business, to which they already had special ties. They feared that appeals to a wider array of voters through more reformist policies might alienate the party's core supporters. The UCD's organizational structure, especially the freedom it granted the barons to pursue their own political agendas, permitted conflicting viewpoints to flourish within the party; this ultimately proved to be an insurmountable obstacle to creating a coherent political and economic strategy.

In the PSOE, the battle over general economic and political strategy was waged by two internal factions, the "neoliberals" and the "interventionists." The neoliberals, generally supported by Prime Minister Felipe González, argued that the PSOE had to put together a broad-based constituency that extended beyond labor if it were to enjoy long-term political success; in particular, they considered gaining the confidence of business as essential for governing effectively. They contended that improving economic performance was imperative for building a heterogeneous national coalition and felt that the party should adopt a pragmatic, reformist approach to policy and not allow itself be bound by the dictates of the socialist tradition. Although the leader of the interventionists, Alfonso Guerra, recognized the importance of a catch-all electoral strategy, he believed that the PSOE had to remain faithful to core Socialist values and its natural constituency, labor, if it was to succeed long term. Thus, he insisted that macroeconomic policy should be expansive and the state should play an active role in guiding the economy. In addition, the ideology of the interventionists made it difficult for them to embrace policies that favored business interests. Unlike the UCD, however, the PSOE maintained cohesiveness despite the existence of conflicting viewpoints, due to the strong, unchallenged leadership of González and an organizational structure that emphasized party discipline.

It is significant that although the UCD and PSOE experienced internal divisions over strategy, they ultimately followed policies consistent with the reward structure of Spain's political institutions. The PSOE ignored the temptation to design its economic policy to favor labor or intervene excessively in the economy. Instead, it vigorously pursued many structural reforms, such as financial deregulation, aimed at advancing aggregate social welfare. In other words, the split within the PSOE was almost always resolved in favor of the "correct" strategy. The UCD started out by aggressively pursuing more efficient markets but slowed basic reforms when confronted by economic and political adversity. Nevertheless, it did not bow to pressure from well-established elites, like big business and banking, to reshape its economic policy to advance their interests at the expense of the public good. By 1981, it had recognized its mistake and renewed its adjustment efforts. Significantly, the UCD's failure to persist with its original strategy eventually created public disillusionment that contributed to the party's dramatic decline and dissolution.

The preceding discussion suggests that an analysis of electoral rules and other formal institutions can identify an important set of incentives and constraints facing politicians and the likely costs they incur if they fail to heed them. This can prove very useful in explaining long-term patterns of policy-making, including those that involve very different sorts of parties or politicians. They cannot, however, provide determinate accounts of political behavior, since this is influenced by factors found at various levels within the political system. Specifically, intra- and intergovernmental differences of the sort discussed earlier must be explained by an entirely different set of variables. As the Spanish case study shows, intragovernmental differences in political and economic strategies emerge from different views of how to best attract voters, beliefs about where voters are located on the left-right spectrum, values and ideological preferences, ties to specific constituencies, and personal ambition, to name but a few variables.[6] Intergovernmental differences stem in part from variations in a government's ability to carry out its agenda. The Spanish experience suggests that a government's capacity to act depends on its parliamentary strength, the nature of its ties to powerful special interest groups, and prevailing domestic and international economic conditions. A ruling party's ideology probably also has an impact on the nature of a government's economic strategy. Garret, Lange, and Hibbs, among others, have shown that partisan differences remain important in shaping the course of a government's economic policy.

The Impact of Democratization on Financial Policy: Three Case Studies

Perhaps the most significant theoretical finding from the Spanish case study is that democratization stimulated political leaders to liberalize financial markets. Democratization will not necessarily lead to deregulation, however. As argued in chapter 2, the form of democracy that emerges from the transition matters. Political institutions may be adopted that do not give leaders an incentive to supply collective goods, like efficient financial markets. Moreover, the "right" political institutions may not be sufficient to spur public officials to undertake appropriate reforms. A variety of other factors, for example, the ideology of national leaders or their cohesiveness, also has an impact on policy decisions. Finally, public officials who wish to liberalize markets may lack sufficient autonomy from powerful interest groups that resist changes to the economic status quo.

This section examines the impact that democratization has had on financial policy in three countries: Brazil, South Korea, and Turkey. Although not a random sample, these three countries are representative of democratizing states facing the necessity of undertaking structural reforms.[7] Brazil, South Korea, and Turkey share one important common feature: their transitions to democracy have promoted financial liberalization to a lesser degree than in Spain. Their new democratic institutions gave leaders weaker incentives to supply collective goods, like efficient markets, in their pursuit of elected office than was the case in Spain. Indeed, the motivation to retain financial controls as a means of distributing private goods to key constituents remained important in all three cases.

One aim of this section is to determine how democratization contributed to financial deregulation in these countries. I do not claim that democratization was the only or even principal force behind liberalization in any of the three, but I do contend that it was an important factor in all; certainly, the most intense financial reform occurred after political liberalization began in each case. Another objective is to ascertain how differences in economic and political institutions, especially electoral and party systems, across the cases led to varying financial policy outcomes. The purpose of this inquiry is to gain an understanding of when democratization is most and least likely to spark structural reform.

The choice of political institutions, like electoral systems, in the transition period has a large endogenous element. The question of why politicians adopt different institutional arrangements in different contexts is a complex one beyond the scope of this book. As I have argued in the Spanish case, various fundamental political variables (e.g., the character of the previous authoritarian regime) as well as the strategic interaction of political groups seeking to win power influence their design. Nevertheless, electoral and other institutions, once established, have important independent effects, since they push political actors to follow the logic of existing rules or suffer the consequences.

Turkey

Turkey is an interesting case for my purposes because democratization affected its financial policy somewhat differently than in Spain, despite several similarities between the two countries' political institutions, especially their electoral systems. The differences between Spain and Turkey illustrate a theoretical point made earlier: formal institutions are an important but not determinate influence on political behavior. In one sense, Turkey may seem like an odd choice for examining the impact of democratization on financial policy, since it had a democratic regime for much of the post–World War II period. However, Turkey's return to democracy in the early 1980s after intense political instability and a period of military rule places it in the class of countries that have recently undergone a "transition to democracy" in the eyes of many scholars.[8] In any case, Turkey returned to democracy with a very different set of electoral rules, so its redemocratization represents a basic institutional change.

An authoritarian, monoparty regime created the modern Turkish state in 1923. It surrendered office in 1950, giving way to a democracy that was characterized by a lack of political competition. A strong central bureaucracy dominated the political system, which featured weak parties and a disorganized public. In particular, interest associations were few and uninfluential, and they lacked institutional links to the state. State intervention in the economy was extensive, and traditional clientilistic relations dominated economic policy-making. In the realm of finance, government policy fostered a highly repressed financial system.[9] Policymakers imposed strict credit, entry, and interest rate controls and taxed the banking system heavily to obtain revenue. The state relied upon taxation of the banking system because it found it difficult to generate revenue through direct taxes or finance outstanding debt through orthodox means. Public officials ostensibly used financial controls to channel preferential credit to sectors, typically dominated by state-owned enterprises, whose growth was deemed important for economic development, but political factors clearly played a major if not dominant role in credit allocation.[10]

A military interregnum led to a new democratic constitution in 1961. In the 1960s and 1970s, political competition increased sharply but in a way that eventually resulted in instability and further military intervention. Electoral laws encouraged the emergence of many small parties, contributing to great fragmentation of the party system.[11] Moreover, polarization and ideological confrontation escalated throughout this period, deepening traditional cleavages based on ethnicity, class, attitude toward religion, and socioeconomic status. The result was an unstable political system permeated by tenacious clientilistic networks, in which politicians attempted to win support through the dispersion of patronage, including cheap credit delivered through the financial system.[12] On the economic policy front, Turkey pursued a strategy of import substitution industrialization that led government officials to deepen state control over financial markets.

The military ruled Turkey again between 1980 and 1983, after intervening in response to a breakdown in economic and social order in the late 1970s. Turkey's return to democracy occurred under terms wholly dictated by the military. Elections were held in 1983 under a completely new set of electoral rules, with the participation of parties and former politicians severely circumscribed. Military leaders designed electoral institutions to eliminate the problems that they believed had made political authority ineffectual in the pre-1980 period: excessive fragmentation of the party system and the growing importance of small parties in forming coalition governments.[13] Their ideal was a two-party system consisting of a moderate center-right party and a moderate center-left party. To accomplish this objective, the military chose a PR system, but, as in the Spanish case, included correctives (e.g., threshold requirements) meant to exclude minor parties and overrepresent the party that obtained the most votes.[14] The party that won the 1983 elections, the Motherland Party or ANAP, headed by Turgut Özal, instituted reforms before the next general elections in 1987 to further strengthen the tendency of the electoral system to produce majorities. ANAP remained in power until 1991, when another major center-right party, the True Path, won sufficient votes to form a coalition government. The True Path stayed in office until 1996.

The Reforms

The ANAP government implemented stabilization and structural adjustment programs after winning the 1983 elections. Some reforms were initiated during the period of military rule, but the military was not the primary force behind structural adjustment; it lacked a coherent economic agenda and did not sustain a number of reforms already underway.[15] As in Spain, progress in the structural reform process has varied across issue areas. Financial and trade reform have moved ahead quickly, but fiscal reform and privatization have lagged badly behind. Still, Turkey's overall achievements have been considerable.[16]

Policymakers implemented most financial reforms in the mid- and late 1980s.[17] However, the first major step toward liberalization, partial interest rate deregulation, took place in 1980. Interest rate controls were reimposed in 1982 after widespread financial instability (including numerous bank failures) ensued, mainly caused by excessive risk taking by banks. In the mid-1980s, the government authorized foreign banks and NBFIs and promoted direct markets to increase competition in the financial sector. At first, smaller banks and NBFIs captured market share at the expense of larger, established banks. The latter, however, subsequently recaptured the ground they had lost.[18] Overall, the banking system remains uncompetitive and inefficient by international standards.[19] In addition, direct financial markets are still only a secondary source of financing despite the rapid growth of the Istanbul Stock Exchange.

With redemocratization, the government initially expanded selective credit programs slightly but, soon after, began dismantling them.[20] Financial policymakers also gradually reduced intermediaries' RRs and transaction taxes. But the central bank stopped paying interest on reserves, and intermediaries' "liquidity" requirements were increased; thus, the net reduction of indirect taxation of intermediaries was greatly mitigated.[21] Continued taxation of intermediaries contributed to financial margins that were high by international standards.[22] Finally, the government removed virtually all capital controls, permitting direct and portfolio investment to flow into and out of the country unhindered.

What factors account for the movement toward deregulation and the pattern of the reforms? The onset of a severe economic crisis, featuring huge balance-of-payments problems, was central.[23] The crisis encouraged policymakers to try to increase domestic savings, attract additional flows of foreign capital, and improve resource allocation by liberalizing financial markets. In addition, Turkey turned to the IMF and World Bank to obtain financing for its adjustment program. Financial deregulation was a key element in the Structural Adjustment Loans negotiated with the World Bank, and a number of Turkey's reforms matched the Bank's prescriptions. It would be incorrect, however, to assert that the World Bank's influence was the critical factor in the reform process. Özal and his policy-making team took office determined to liberalize the financial system. Moreover, scholars point out that Turkey's geostrategic importance gave it greater bargaining power vis-à-vis international agencies than other countries obtaining loans from them.[24] Turkey was able to resist some World Bank and IMF demands it did not like and attain agreements that more closely fit its preferences.

Redemocratization also generated interest in financial liberalization. Özal, ANAP's undisputed leader, believed that strong economic performance was critical for the party's long-term prospects, as well as for the stability of the democratic regime, and was determined to pursue a strategy of structural adjustment once in office. Özal and his economic team deemed financial deregulation an essential step in the adjustment process because they thought repression was a primary cause of Turkey's economic woes. In the electoral arena, the ANAP sought to build support based on the notion that its economic policy, in contrast to that of its predecessors or the opposition, was effective.[25] Opposition parties have used criticism of the incumbent party's economic record as a primary means of capturing votes in subsequent elections, often focusing on issues of collective interest, like bringing inflation under control.[26] In general, economic issues have tended to dominate major electoral campaigns since 1983.[27]

The ANAP was simultaneously pulled in another direction, however. Turkish parties traditionally consolidated political support by dispensing patronage to key groups, and groups supporting the ANAP expected it to follow this practice. In addition, the ANAP felt a great deal of pressure to compensate the losers of economic adjustment through discretionary flows as structural reforms deepened. In Waterbury's words, "[the ANAP] has promoted deregulation and liberalization in the name of efficiency *and* increased the scope of discretionary allocations in the economy."[28] In financial policy, the incentive to wield discretionary authority was manifested in an initial increase in preferential credit and the wild expansion of "extrabudgetary funds."[29] Extrabudgetary funds, pools of money raised by levies on particular goods or activities to finance "priority activities," were an attractive means of distributing private benefits because they were off budget and outside of democratic control.

Over time, clientilism revealed its limitations as a political strategy. As Öniş and Webb note, "control of state resources became a disadvantage as the dispensing of favors led to growing resentment and reaction on the part of the wider populace."[30] With regards to financial policy, some private groups came to believe that it was better to have a predictable, nonarbitrary regulatory regime to one in which they might get favors today but lose them tomorrow.[31] Political leaders dismantled several directed credit programs in the mid-1980s. But they discovered that they had lost control over the extrabudgetary funds. These funds had become numerous and extraordinarily complex, and the various ministries administering them had slowly shifted control over their operations away from the prime minister's office into their own hands.[32]

The Spanish and Turkish Experiences Compared

The impact of democratization on Turkish financial policy resembled the Spanish experience in some respects. In both countries, democratization raised the political costs for national leaders of poor economic performance. ANAP's leaders, like those of the UCD and PSOE, perceived that rival parties would replace them if voters believed that they were not handling the economy in a way that would increase prosperity and stability. In addition, they believed, as did UCD leaders, that the future of democracy depended on the new regime's ability to provide satisfactory economic performance.[33] Consequently, the ANAP governments took major steps toward implementing sound economic policies, although they failed to act decisively to resolve certain pressing problems, notably ballooning government deficits caused by runaway spending and ineffective taxation policies.[34] The difficulty of establishing a sound fiscal policy has been an obstacle in reducing taxation of the banking system, as it initially was in Spain.

The most significant divergence in the two countries' experiences was that the motivation to maintain the means of delivering private goods was stronger in Turkey, notwithstanding similarities in their formal institutional structures, especially electoral laws. This was most clearly seen in their respective treatment of credit controls. Spanish leaders moved to dismantle selective credit policies, despite substantial social opposition, immediately after democratization; Turkish leaders retained preferential credit longer and expanded another form of delivering financial benefits, extrabudgetary funds. Turkish leaders eventually moved to dismantle selective credit policies as the limits of clientilism became evident, but the ability to wield discretionary authority has remained very important.

Several factors accounted for the varying incentive to supply private benefits. First, politics in Turkey were more divisive and fragmented.[35] Turkish society continued to be beset by deeper cultural, ideological, and social cleavages than in Spain, although these have slowly dissipated. This meant that constructing electoral coalitions based on encompassing interests was more difficult in Turkey, thereby increasing the temptation to pursue a strategy of creating a minimum winning coalition by fashioning deals with a number of narrow groups. Further complicating matters, most Turkish parties did not have closed and blocked electoral lists, giving party leaders less control over individual parliamentary representatives than leaders in Spanish parties. Antagonism among top Turkish politicians also ran deep, making it difficult for political parties to enter into necessary strategic alliances. In particular, traditional animosities between the leaders of ANAP and the other major center-right party, the True Path, prevented them from joining forces into a grand center-right coalition that could have easily won an absolute majority; this occurred even though the two parties had similar policy preferences, especially concerning the economy. This rivalry affected the character of their economic policies when they held office. Each party feared that its hold on office was very shaky and felt compelled to compete with its arch opponent for specific blocs of voters by providing material benefits (e.g., wage increases to government employees).

Second, the state's presence in the economy was considerably greater in Turkey, and reformers could not build upon previous liberalization efforts as they did in Spain. Therefore, it was more difficult for Turkish elected officials to extricate the state and its powerful bureaucracy from the financial system and dismantle firmly entrenched patronage networks.[36] The ANAP, for instance, had to devote a great deal of effort to wresting control over economic policy away from the old "etatist bureaucrats" who resisted many economic reforms.[37]

Finally, effective peak interest associations were rare in Turkey. This encouraged influential private actors to strike individual deals with bureaucrats and politicians and discouraged the negotiation of broad social agreements to develop collective solutions to national problems. In contrast, Spanish business and labor generally attempted to organize and channel their demands to the government collectively, not individually. Consequently, Spain's political leaders were able to forge agreements with key social actors at critical junctures (e.g., the Moncloa Pacts) that aided in the design of effective economic policies and their legitimation.

South Korea

South Korea has sometimes been held up as an example of a country that has managed financial deregulation successfully. It has been lauded mainly because the government has liberalized financial markets gradually after first having achieved macroeconomic stability.[38] Korean financial reform efforts began in 1979 but mostly languished until the late 1980s and early 1990s, when, I contend, they received a new impetus from democratization. The incentive to deregulate in South Korea was also not as strong as in Spain, but for reasons that differ somewhat from the Turkish case. The Korean case demonstrates that when the government has acquired a huge stake in the success of sectors favored by past financial policy, liberalization may be an economically and politically risky strategy.

South Korea's road to democratization was marred by periods of violence. Political opposition to authoritarianism rose sharply in the late 1970s and early 1980s, only to be brutally suppressed. Massive political protests finally led to a new constitution and free presidential elections in 1987, followed by parliamentary elections in 1988. Since that time, democracy has slowly consolidated.

South Korea has a presidential system.[39] Seats in the National Assembly are mostly chosen through a single-member district system, but some at-large seats are allocated through a PR scheme. A multiparty but non-fragmented party system has emerged, with parties tending to drift toward the center of the political spectrum; since 1990, the major center-right parties have joined forces in an effort to establish a grand conservative ruling coalition in the tradition of Japan's LDP. Party support is mostly region-based, stemming from the appeal of individual leaders (who draw their political strength from popularity in their home regions).[40] According to Lee, "this personalistic party regionalism [has] hindered a transition to consensual democratic governance."[41] In general, parties do not exercise strong control over their members and lack extensive institutional ties to society.[42] Individual politicians tend to emphasize their local or regional ties, a rational strategy in a mostly single-member district system where party control is weak. As a result, the political agenda has tended to concentrate on parochial concerns and traditional interregional rivalries, not on national public policy issues.

In South Korea, most authority over economic policy has traditionally resided in the executive branch. The new democratic National Assembly has not proved to be an effective balancer of the executive's power in economic policy, although it has blocked some of its initiatives at several junctures. Consequently, economic policy is still largely run by ministers that are appointed and dismissed by the president.[43]

The Reforms

South Korea had a highly repressed financial system prior to 1979 (when the reform process tentatively began), which was insulated from international markets by strict capital controls. The state implemented extensive interest rate and credit controls as the key means of attaining its development goals.[44] Authority over credit allocation was centralized in the hands of well-insulated industrial policy activists, who could control directly the allocation of credit to industrial sectors (as well as specific firms) through the state-owned banking system in line with development objectives. Over time, the relationship between business and the state became one of strategic interdependence, with industrial conglomerates, known as *chaebol,* gaining considerable influence over the allocation of preferential credit as their economic power grew. By the 1970s selective credit policy was highly politicized, and it was difficult to specify whether the *chaebol* or the government actually controlled Korea's credit allocation policy.[45] This turn of events demonstrates that even strong states with well-insulated policy-making teams may find it difficult to intervene in credit markets without eventually falling prey to clientilism. Finally, although the Korean government sometimes ran budget deficits, overall it exercised "relatively tight fiscal discipline."[46] Therefore, taxation of the banking system was not heavy in South Korea (though not insignificant) and, hence, its elimination has not been a major item in the financial deregulation agenda.

Financial deregulation in South Korea began with policymakers opening markets to new entrants. The government authorized the creation of NBFIs in the 1970s, although it limited the range of their activities.[47] Over the 1980s, it relaxed most restrictions on NBFI activities, permitted additional intermediaries (including a handful of foreign banks) to enter the market, and promoted bond and equity markets. The government privatized state-owned commercial banks as well but retained informal authority over them. Government officials were slow to reduce control over credit allocation and international financial transactions. In the 1980s, government credit programs actually expanded slightly (by some accounts) and have only begun to shrink significantly in recent years.[48] Policymakers, however, raised interest rates on preferential credit after 1982, bringing them into line with market rates. Controls on capital inflows and outflows were gradually lifted starting in the mid-1980s, with the most intense liberalization occurring between 1991 and 1994. Finally, officials began deregulating interest rates after the 1988 elections.[49] Several interest rates were officially freed in 1988, but the government encouraged banks to informally regulate rates amongst themselves. More aggressive and complete interest rate reform took place in 1991. In 1993, the government announced a blueprint for comprehensive financial reform that is supposed to result in virtually total deregulation by 1997.

Some scholars have asserted that worsening economic problems motivated financial reform. South Korea, like many other countries, experienced high inflation, balance-of-payments difficulties, and slowing aggregate growth starting in the late 1970s due to a global recession and various external shocks. The most significant impact of these macroeconomic problems on financial policy was that they led numerous firms, many of them targeted by government policy during the 1970s, to default on their loans.[50] The consequent deterioration of bank loan portfolios raised the specter of widespread financial instability, so the government poured in large sums of money to shore up both industry and the banking sector in the short term; it also began restructuring industry to rationalize production in the longer term. These events made government leaders painfully aware of the moral hazard problems that financial policy had created among firms, and they concluded that the state could no longer continue to socialize so much economic risk through interest rate and credit controls.[51] In addition, monetary authorities discovered that it was difficult to implement a tighter money policy because increases in interest rates would endanger South Korea's highly leveraged firms.

Financial distress in the 1980s was very serious indeed, but it cannot entirely explain the timing of financial reform. Financial instability had arisen at various times since the 1960s, with an especially bad episode occurring in the early 1970s.[52] In the early 1970s, the government's response had been to increase control over financial markets, by imposing stricter interest rate and credit controls, not to deregulate. The existence of financial distress, therefore, does not tell us how the government will choose to respond and, by itself, cannot account for the decision to liberalize financial markets.

I suggest that government leaders gained interest in liberalization at the time they did because the political costs of sustaining an increasingly inefficient policy of restriction were rising. These costs grew especially after the transition to democracy. South Korea's new democratic leaders felt considerable pressure to maintain the strong economic performance that the country had enjoyed under its authoritarian predecessors because failure to do so would have damaged the democratic regime's legitimacy.[53] Technocrats who believed in a more laissez-faire economic policy, many of them U.S.-trained economists, used political leaders' anxiety over economic performance to convince them of the desirability of trying a new financial strategy.[54] Voters, in fact, have paid a great deal of attention to economic issues. Slowing growth and other economic problems were among the major issues in the 1992 national elections, for example.[55]

But perhaps the most direct impact of democratization was that it permitted budding resentment among the populace toward a financial policy designed to privilege a few at the expense of many to blossom fully. Opposition parties were able to win political support by sharply criticizing government leaders for directed credit policies that fostered close financial ties between themselves and the *chaebol*.[56] This lowered the political appeal of restriction considerably and prompted government officials to begin reducing administrative control over credit in the late 1980s. Significantly, even some beneficiaries of prevailing financial policy, notably several of the *chaebol,* started to favor some deregulation as a way of escaping from what they considered excessive state control and the high cost of currying favor with state officials to obtain preferential finance.[57] The *chaebol* also began to search for ways to diversify their funding sources in order to rely less on condition-laden policy loans, turning mostly to domestic and foreign bond and equity markets.[58]

Finally, one cannot ignore the role that U.S. pressure played in the opening of Korean markets to foreign institutions and the removal of capital controls, and possibly in sparking other reforms as well.[59] It is unlikely that Korean officials would have opened the country's markets without external pressure, though many economic policymakers viewed this step as a means of improving efficiency.[60] Furthermore, the entry of foreign banks had tremendous ramifications. Along with new NBFIs, they were not subject to interest rate ceilings and, therefore, had a competitive edge over domestic banks. As the "economic theory" of regulatory policy would suggest, this led domestic banks to push for greater deregulation to level the playing field.

The Korean and Spanish Cases Compared
Democratization in South Korea did not push government officials to liberalize financial markets as aggressively as in Spain. Increased political competition after the Korean transition raised the political costs for government leaders of poor economic performance. This and the continued North Korean threat prompted them to find ways to maintain the country's traditionally high growth rates. In addition, the 1980s made clear that restriction had many economic and political disadvantages as a financial strategy. Financial controls created moral hazard problems among their beneficiaries, and resentment among the populace grew dramatically over perceptions that financial policy favored a select few over general interests. Although movement toward a more market-based system has been substantial, the reform process has proceeded very gradually and with numerous setbacks. In particular, the government has been very slow to dismantle selective credit policies.

What accounts for the differences between Korea and Spain? One key factor is that Korean political institutions did not provide as strong an incentive for politicians to concentrate on broad national issues, like financial policy. As already discussed, the Korean electoral and party systems gave politicians a parochial focus, and politics tended to center on local and interregional concerns, not national policy issues. Politicians hesitated to dismantle interest rate and credit controls because the ability to target specific groups, notably the *chaebol* (which are still a huge source of political contributions), continued to be important in the pursuit of power. In contrast, Spanish institutions encouraged the emergence of national, all-encompassing parties that vied for the support of broad-based constituencies. Parties had to appeal to the collective interest because they could not obtain sufficient electoral support by targeting narrow groups.

The huge stake the government obtained in certain industrial sectors due to past policy also hampered financial liberalization in South Korea.[61] Officials found it difficult to eliminate preferential credit to targeted sectors because of the potential for a major industrial crisis due to massive defaults. In addition, as banks had been forced to extend credit to these sectors, a series of defaults would have jeopardized the solvency of the banking system. As Choi asserts, "insofar as the government was ultimately responsible for the accumulation of nonperforming debts in the banking system, it could not avoid rescuing the banks."[62] The Spanish government faced the same set of issues. Its bailout of industry and banking was also costly, but the problems were less severe and had fewer long-term repercussions (see chap. 6). This was because Spanish industry was not as concentrated in huge and powerful conglomerates like South Korea's *chaebol,* and bank lending had always been more diversified (though still too concentrated).

Finally, the *chaebol*'s enormous economic and political weight was another impediment to liberalization. Although they complained of excessive state intervention, many *chaebol* still depended on preferential finance and worried about the impact of interest rate deregulation on the cost of credit. In addition, the health of the *chaebol* remained the key to the country's economic stability, making it difficult for policymakers to implement financial reforms that might jeopardize their solvency. The government has recently taken several measures to undermine the dominance of the *chaebol,* but progress has been slow.[63] Significantly, the *chaebol* have found a way to maintain their disproportionate share of available domestic funds despite the financial deregulation that has occurred, thereby spoiling the government's plans to allocate credit more efficiently across all users. They aggressively purchased NBFIs in the 1980s, enabling them to secure the ample funds mobilized by these new entities at low cost.[64] In contrast, Spanish authorities regulated who could establish or control new intermediaries and put limits on their lending activity to avoid excessive economic and political concentration.

Brazil

The impact of democratization on financial policy in Brazil presents major contrasts with the experiences of the other countries that I have examined in this study. Brazil's new democratic institutions have supplied politicians with far fewer collective action incentives to undertake basic structural reforms than in South Korea, Spain, or Turkey. This difference can be traced in large part to Brazil's electoral and party systems. According to Scott Mainwaring, "the Brazilian case is an extreme example of electoral rules that encourage individualism among politicians and loose linkages between parties and politicians."[65] In addition, traditional economic and social structures remain firmly in place in Brazil, permitting powerful established economic elites to resist reforms. Consequently, financial reform has been slow in coming.

Brazil had a limited democracy from 1945 until a military coup in 1964. Democracy only fully returned to the country in 1985, though there was some political opening from 1975 on. Brazil has a presidential system with several unique features.[66] Especially noteworthy about this system is that members of the congressional Chamber of Deputies are chosen in an open list PR system. Parties present a list of candidates for each state, with party candidates competing against each other for election. Seats from a state are first divided proportionately among parties according to the total number of votes cast for each party's candidates and then within parties according to the number of personal votes. In this system, party leaders have little control over individual legislators, and party loyalty and discipline are very low. Deputies have a parochial focus, loyal not to party policy but to the local or regional interest groups that got them elected. The tendency toward regionalism in the political system is augmented because a great deal of authority over public policy is vested in the state governments. Among other things, this has meant that issues related to interregional rivalries have often dominated the political agenda.[67] Finally, electoral rules have tended to produce a highly fragmented party system: since 1985, at least seventeen parties have been represented at any one time in the legislature, and Brazil's effective number of parties is much higher than in the other cases examined in this study.[68]

Brazil's financial policy has been characterized by restriction, though there was one experiment with limited deregulation in the mid-1960s.[69]

The government has maintained an extensive network of interest rate and credit controls in the post–World War II period. In 1987, government credit programs accounted for 70 percent of the credit outstanding to the private and public sectors.[70] An elaborate system of public banks, featuring the National Economic Development Bank, has been especially important in implementing directed credit policies. Taxation of the banking system has sometimes been significant; policymakers have imposed very high RRs on banks at times (as much as 40 percent) and relied upon the related mechanism of the inflation tax to generate state revenue.[71] Finally, the government has permitted capital inflows but channeled foreign funds into favored sectors (at least until the late 1980s).[72] Foreign banks have been permitted, but their activities have been strictly controlled.

Some scholars claim that the state's original decision to pursue a developmentalist industrial policy has mostly determined the shape of financial strategy.[73] Nevertheless, financial policy has also served political purposes. Public officials have used public banks to distribute preferential credit to secure political support, especially after 1975.[74] In addition, financial regulation has clearly been shaped by the demands of private groups, notably intermediaries and firms, which have been active in lobbying for policies associated with financial repression (e.g., entry and deposit rate ceilings).[75]

The Reforms

Financial liberalization in Brazil has moved at a snail's pace, although there has been some progress in recent years. The government retains considerable control over the cost and allocation of credit, but it is slowly declining. The private banking sector is still quite oligopolistic—if anything, concentration has increased—and inefficient, highly politicized public banks continue to dominate many areas of financial activity.[76] Some state-owned corporations have been privatized, which has released some credit for alternative uses (thereby improving financial efficiency), but progress has been uncertain.[77] A severe fiscal crisis, caused in part by the difficulty of implementing tax reform, has discouraged the government from reducing indirect taxation of the banking system.[78] On the other hand, the government has deepened financial opening, especially with respect to foreign portfolio investment, and permitted the entry of additional foreign intermediaries (although they remain subject to many restrictions).[79] Bond and equity markets have also been modernized and deepened.

Restriction has persisted in spite of a growing consensus among many political leaders and technocrats that financial reform is necessary to improve economic performance. Throughout the 1980s and early 1990s, economic conditions deteriorated, sharply augmenting the costs of maintaining existing financial controls. Slower growth called attention to the deficiencies of the financial system and greatly increased the political incentive to do something about it.[80] Moreover, Brazil faced a huge debt crisis, which made it imperative to mobilize domestic resources more fully and use them more efficiently. In particular, public officials realized that the state could no longer afford to supply large sums of preferential credit to inefficient state-owned enterprises, since Brazil's fiscal situation continues to deteriorate.[81] Finally, public resentment arose over the oligopolistic nature of the banking sector and the high profits earned by banks relative to other sectors.[82]

On a related point, Leslie Armijo argues that a perceived erosion of state decision-making capacity also generated interest in financial deregulation. Many private and public actors were willing to accept state intervention in financial markets when they believed that policymakers were competent and government guidance was required for economic development. But they lost their willingness to allow technocrats to dictate the course of financial and industrial development as the failures of the developmentalist model became evident.

Finally, democratization has augmented the attractiveness of financial reform. Leaders with a national constituency, most notably, the president, have begun to feel tremendous pressure to improve economic performance because they must compete for a broad-based electorate that increasingly demands greater prosperity.[83] The Brazilian electorate is weary of high inflation, sluggish growth, and other problems and now seeks out candidates who seem capable of improving economic performance. In the last presidential elections, Fernando Henrique Cardoso went from being a virtual political unknown to a successful presidential candidate on the strength of his victory over inflation as minister of finance.[84] Consequently, the executive has proposed various liberalizing reforms, most notably several aimed at curtailing and depoliticizing the activities of state banks and increasing the attractiveness of Brazil for foreign investors.[85]

Why has more extensive economic reform not occurred? The answer lies largely with Brazil's democratic institutions, which do not give most politicians collective action incentives to carry out structural reforms. National leaders recognize the need for economic adjustment, and both Cardoso and his predecessor, Fernando Collor, have actively sought it. But the nature of the party system, featuring weak, undisciplined parties with members beholden to local interests, and the procedure for ratifying most reforms, have made structural change an uphill battle. Although economic policy-making is centered in the executive branch, many fundamental reforms require a constitutional amendment, which demands a 60 percent vote in the highly fragmented and parochial legislature; even members of the president's own party have been known to vote against the government regularly. In addition, since authority over much public policy is shared with the states, passage of legislation requires complex logrolling, and governors of large states can effectively veto legislation. Consequently, the executive has relied upon presidential decrees to move reforms along. Significantly, most decrees have not been overturned by the legislature because members recognize that the country's economic collapse would jeopardize their own political careers; in effect, their inaction permits reform to occur but allows them to tell constituents who oppose changes in policy that they had no part in them.

An additional problem for reformers is that interest groups that oppose financial reform are still firmly entrenched and powerful. Large private banks have prospered under restriction and have fought against regulatory changes that threaten their dominance of the financial sector. Public banks have a vast constituency, ranging from targeted agricultural and industrial sectors to state governments, and they have vigorously resisted efforts to curtail their activities. Finally, some public officials still cling to the belief that the state should lead development; they view financial controls as useful tools in carrying out this enterprise.[86]

In Brazil and South Korea, then, electoral and party systems supply fewer incentives to politicians to carry out long-term structural reforms than in Spain. Moreover, powerful private interests in both countries pose difficult obstacles to would-be reformers. The result has been a slow and halting financial reform process. Long term, it will probably be more difficult to attain reform in Brazil. In South Korea, the president can push his economic initiatives through at the governmental level fairly easily, since the legislature has not been an effective balancer of executive power.[87] In Brazil, most major reforms must go through a recalcitrant, fragmented legislature whose members think mainly in terms of their local interests. Parties are extraordinarily weak and undisciplined, making it difficult for leaders to energize the political class for coordinated action. The executive can use presidential decrees to initiate certain reforms, but this tactic is probably inadequate for effecting long-term change. These problems have led many Brazilian politicians, most recently, Cardoso and Collor, to recommend a drastic overhaul of electoral institutions, with Germany's electoral system often mentioned as an ideal.[88]

Conclusions

What conclusions can be drawn from the comparative material about the hypothesis that democratization encourages politicians to deregulate financial markets? Overall, the evidence suggests that democratization generated interest in deregulation among political leaders in all the countries studied but that its specific impact varied greatly across countries.

In all the cases, transitions to democracy raised the political costs of maintaining financial restriction for government leaders. With democratization, their management of economic affairs became subject to approval in periodic elections. Leaders were pushed to design better financial policy in order to prevent competitors from taking advantage of declining economic performance to capture electoral support. In all the countries examined here, the nature of economic problems made financial deregulation an essential element of any structural adjustment program. The strength of the motivation to implement fundamental reforms varied significantly, however, depending on the nature of the country's political institutions. The political incentive to take the steps necessary to create efficient markets was the strongest in Spain and the weakest in Brazil. In Spain, institutions encouraged leaders to seek broad-based electoral support by supplying collective economic goods; further, the general political environment after the transition led the political class to emphasize economic stability. In Brazil, institutions prompted politicians, with the exception of officials with a national constituency, like the president, to build political support by appealing to narrow regional groups, not encompassing interests. But even in the Brazilian case, members of the highly parochial legislature have recognized that the country's economic collapse would jeopardize their own political careers, and they have often permitted executive decrees instituting reforms to take effect.

The incentive to supply collective goods in the pursuit of electoral support was balanced to a certain degree by the countervailing incentive to use financial controls to benefit important sets of constituents in all the cases. This helps to explain why Turkish officials retained or even increased certain forms of discretionary authority while they proceeded to liberalize the economy and why Korean politicians have taken so long to dismantle directed credit programs. Nonetheless, the Korean and Turkish cases, along with that of Spain, support the contention that political leaders have an incentive to dismantle selective credit policies after democratization to eliminate the need to respond to increased demands by social groups for preferential credit or in reaction to charges that financial policy unfairly benefits some groups at the expense of others.

Finally, the comparative material supports my contention that we need to examine the political calculus of public officials to understand how factors like changes in economic conditions, international constraints and opportunities, or new policy-relevant knowledge affect the course of financial regulation. Scholars are correct in asserting that international economic and political trends have increasingly limited the range of options open to governments by increasing the costs of maintaining a tightly regulated, closed financial system. But the case material bears out the view that these trends cannot explain variations in the pace or depth of financial deregulation, nor shed light on the long-term prospects for its success.

Of the cases examined here, Turkey best supports the view that economic and international factors shape the course of financial policy. A deterioration of Turkey's economic situation, especially its external financial position, played a central role in its reform efforts. But it does not tell the whole story. Turkey had long suffered serious economic problems, so the state of the economy cannot explain the timing of reform; arguing that previous crises were not "severe enough" to cause reform merely begs the question: how severe must a crisis be before reform ensues?[89] Turkey also needed to tap the IMF and World Bank for short-term financing, and the funds it received came with conditions that prompted some financial reform. Its geostrategic importance, however, gave it greater freedom of maneuver vis-à-vis international agencies than most countries enjoy. Furthermore, Turkish policymakers had an interest in deregulating financial markets that was independent of international pressure.

In Spain, economic and international variables were important but not determining factors. A deteriorating economy sometimes acted as a catalyst for reforms, but at other times it did not; leaders' political calculations ultimately determined whether economic problems resulted in financial reform. Pressure by foreign banks and governments helped open Spanish financial markets but mainly because it strengthened the position of domestic actors who were already seeking such reforms. Entry into the EC deepened the liberalization process, but deregulation had already progressed very far for reasons unconnected to EC regulations. In short, the Spanish case shows that external pressures are not a necessary condition for financial deregulation.

Brazil best illustrates the point that international or economic trends that generate pressure to liberalize financial markets are not a sufficient condition for reform. Brazil experienced a severe economic crisis in the 1980s, which, in purely economic terms, provided tremendous incentives to deregulate the financial system. It also confronted external pressure to liberalize, particularly from international agencies like the IMF and World Bank that provided condition-laden balance-of-payments and structural adjustment loans.[90] Moreover, Brazilian policymakers were exposed to the diffusion of new policy-relevant knowledge about financial policy (e.g., through their contacts with the World Bank), and many changed their beliefs about what sort of financial policy was best for their country. Nevertheless, none of these factors has been sufficient to generate sustained financial reform because of the character of domestic politics.

All told, this book's analytical focus on the calculus of self-interested political leaders is a useful way of organizing our thinking about financial regulation as well as examining the influence of diverse forces that affect its evolution. Yet it is also obvious that more research needs to be completed on the factors that give leaders a political motive to deregulate financial markets. A focus on domestic political institutions—which generate many of the constraints and incentives public officials confront when designing regulatory policy—as well as on their interaction with economic and international variables, promises to be an especially fruitful area for these efforts.

Notes

Chapter 1

1. Two classic accounts of the role of financial markets in the economy are McKinnon 1973 and Shaw 1973.

2. Zysman 1983, chap. 2, is an excellent discussion of this topic.

3. Many developing countries have or have recently had restricted financial systems. Among them are Algeria, Argentina, Brazil, Chile, Costa Rica, Ghana, India, Nigeria, Peru, the Philippines, Sierra Leone, South Korea, Taiwan, Tunisia, Turkey, Zaire, and Zambia. Several developed countries, for example, Spain and Japan, have also had restricted systems at one time.

4. See Fry 1988 and McKinnon 1973 and 1991 on the characteristics of restricted systems. I discuss restricted systems in greater detail later. Of course, the features of restriction vary across countries.

5. Several recent studies of financial liberalization have focused primarily on opening vis-à-vis international markets. For example, see Haggard and Maxfield 1996. This book considers *all* elements of financial deregulation. Economists generally view the removal of credit, entry, and interest rate controls as the first and most important steps in the process of liberalization. For example, see Fry 1988, McKinnon 1991, and World Bank 1989. I adopt this perspective in this study. Among the countries that have liberalized in recent years are Chile, Indonesia, Morocco, Portugal, South Korea, Spain, Sri Lanka, and Turkey. Faruqi (1994) and World Bank (1989), chap. 9, discuss the experiences of several of these and other countries.

6. For example, see Andrews 1994 and Goodman and Pauly 1993.

7. An example of a sectoral political economy model is Frieden 1991a. Sectoral models of financial policy include Hammond and Knott 1988 and Rosenbluth 1989.

8. See Institute of Latin American Studies 1986, Smith 1989, and Stallings and Kaufman 1989 for examples of this argument. The empirical evidence on this point is mixed. See Lindenberg and Devarajan 1993 and Remmer 1990. The first post-Franco elections were held in 1977.

9. The term *public officials* refers to both political leaders as well as bureaucratic policymakers. In constructing my analytical framework, I initially argue at a high level of abstraction, concentrating on political leaders and their goals. Moreover, I assume that these officials have homogeneous preferences and that principal-agent problems are limited; that is, bureaucrats carry out the directives of their

political superiors and design policy in accordance with their superiors' preferences. In the case study of Spain, presented in chapters 3 through 7, and at certain points in the theoretical discussion, I distinguish between the preferences of various types of public officials. To minimize repetition, I sometimes use the term *politicians* in place of *political leaders.*

10. I use Hall's definition of institutions as "formal rules, compliance procedures, and standard operating procedures that structure the relationship between individuals in various units of the polity and economy" (Hall 1986, 19). I assume that institutional structure is greatly influenced by historical forces, as Spruyt (1994) contends, but that private and public actors can sometimes reshape institutions, as Levi (1988) argues.

11. For example, Wiarda 1992.

12. For example, see Bermeo and García Durán 1994.

13. This does not imply that the other objectives behind the drive for EC membership, for example, the goal to consolidate democratic institutions, were unimportant. I discuss these other motives in chapter 7.

14. Following Munck (1994), I define democratization as a process consisting of three basic phases: (1) the transition from authoritarian rule; (2) the installation of democratic institutions; and (3) the consolidation of the newly installed democracy.

15. For example, see Lindblom 1977.

16. Bates 1983, Geddes 1994, Haggard and Kaufman 1995, Hall 1986, Noll 1983, and Rosenbluth, 1989, are representative works.

17. For example, see Cole and Wellons 1989.

18. See Amsden 1989, Johnson 1987, Wade 1990, and Zysman 1983. Late industrializers are countries that initiate industrialization when technologically more advanced firms exist in other countries. The concept derives from Gerschenkron 1962.

19. For example, see Calder 1993 and Woo 1991. The use of selective credit as a policy instrument is the primary focus of an excellent volume on financial policy in developing countries edited by Haggard, Lee, and Maxfield 1993. Rosenbluth (1989) adopts a more comprehensive approach in examining financial restriction in Japan.

20. Fry (1988) reviews the economic literature on financial deregulation. Notable recent works on the political economy of financial deregulation in developing countries are Haggard, Lee, and Maxfield 1993; Maxfield 1990; and Woo 1991.

21. For example, see Hamada and Horiuchi 1987, Hammond and Knott 1988, and Rosenbluth 1989. The economic theory was developed by Becker 1983; Peltzman 1976 and 1989; and Stigler 1971.

22. As I discuss in chapter 2, later versions of the economic theory raise the possibility that public officials may also initiate deregulation. These versions of the theory have not found their way into the financial policy literature.

23. Disintermediation occurs when savers lend funds directly to the final users of credit, thereby eliminating the intermediary services performed by banks.

24. A financial system is said to lack depth when it has underdeveloped bond

and equity markets (e.g., as operationalized by market capitalization), intermediaries other than banks are scarce, and the range of financial products available is small. See Fry 1988, chap. 10.

25. The issue of when state- or society-centered analysis is most appropriate in understanding economic policy-making has long preoccupied social scientists. For examples of state-centered approaches, see Krasner 1978, Skocpol 1985, and Zysman 1983. For examples of society-centered approaches, see Frieden 1991a, Gourevitch 1986, and Milner 1988.

26. Gowa 1988 is one study that has reached this conclusion.

27. For example, see Harper 1986 and Loriaux 1991.

28. For example, Fry 1988, 245.

29. See Faruqi 1994 and World Bank 1989, chap. 9.

30. Goodman and Pauly 1993.

31. Andrews 1994, Cerney 1993, and Kurzer 1993 make this argument.

32. For example, Webb and Shariff 1992.

33. The debate over whether the variables that most influence economic policy-making are found at the international or domestic level is long-standing. One important contribution to it is the edited volume, Ikenberry, Lake, and Mastanduno 1988. Haggard 1990, Kahler 1992, and Stallings 1992 are among the recent works that also address this issue.

34. See Frieden 1991b and Kurzer 1993 on this point.

35. RRs oblige financial intermediaries to keep a percentage of their liabilities in the form of cash or deposits at the central bank. ARs require intermediaries to purchase public debt securities with yields below market rates.

36. In countries where banks played a major entrepreneurial function or were set up by and for industrialists, the government's role in establishing a bank-based financial system was not necessarily central. As Gerschenkron has pointed out, "late industrializers" tend to have bank-based financial systems. See Gerschenkron 1962, chap. 1.

37. For example, see Cole and Wellons 1989. Stiglitz (1989) and Wade (1990) are skeptical about the ability of developing countries to implement an effective market-based system even today.

38. World Bank 1989, chap. 4.

39. Prudential regulation seeks to prevent excessively risky behavior by lenders (e.g., through regular inspection of intermediaries' loan portfolios) and to force lenders to address problems promptly if they occur (e.g., by instituting loan-loss provisions). The ultimate objective of prudential regulation is to ensure the solvency of the banking system.

40. World Bank 1989, 108. An example of such policies was that firms had to issue equities at a substantial discount to market value.

41. In a securities market-based system, a significant portion of available financial resources are allocated by decentralized markets (as opposed to bank executives or government officials). The United States is the clearest example of such a system. The features of bank-based financial systems are discussed later. Zysman (1983, chap. 2) contrasts securities market-based and bank-based financial systems.

42. Tobin 1965. See Fry 1988, chap. 1, and Meier 1984, chap. 6, for reviews of earlier work advocating restriction.

43. An additional rationale for deposit and loan rate controls is that they help to safeguard the solvency of the banking system by eliminating price competition for deposits and prohibiting banks from pursuing risky, high-return loans. Most economists believe that interest rate controls constitute a second-best solution for limiting the level of default risk in the banking system. They argue that prudential regulation is a superior form of preserving the system's solvency. Instituting effective prudential regulation, however, has proved to be a costly and difficult endeavor, as recent experience in various countries, including advanced industrial countries like Japan and the United States, has shown. For elaboration, see Lukauskas 1992.

44. For example, Buffie 1984 and Taylor 1983.

45. See McKinnon 1973 and 1991.

46. For example, Cole and Wellons 1989 and Dalla and Khatkhate 1995.

47. See Amsden 1989, Wade 1990, and Zysman 1983.

48. Fry 1988, chap. 16, and Kane 1977.

49. See Amsden 1989, Gerschenkron 1962, Patrick 1994, Stiglitz 1989, Wade 1990, and Zysman 1983. One proposal for creating a strong banking system is to implement interest rate and entry controls to enable banks to earn large profits and build up internal reserves. See Patrick 1994, 375–76.

50. Bank-based systems may take several forms. Banks may own shares in firms and play a direct managerial role in their operations, or they may provide the bulk of project finance and exercise only indirect influence over firm activities. Alternatively, industrial groups may set up and own banks in order to create a secure supply of cheap finance. Scholars who favor bank-based systems generally advocate some variation of bank influence over the activities of firms, not situations where banks are subordinate to industrial groups.

51. See Porter 1992.

52. See Lee 1992 and Wade 1990, chap. 11.

53. Patrick 1994, 385, and Stiglitz 1989. Monitoring includes assessment of new projects and evaluation of the firm's ongoing activities.

54. In Japan, for instance, a distressed firm's "main bank" takes special responsibility for its rescue, shouldering costs greater than its formal exposure because of built up trust between the two parties and concern over reputational effects. See Patrick 1994, 359.

55. Moral hazard occurs when actors have contracts or other assurances that will reimburse them against loss. Protected against losses, such actors may have an incentive to not exercise proper caution against loss or even to pursue risky courses of action.

56. The extent of moral hazard problems seems to vary across countries. Loriaux (1991) suggests that they were great in France, whereas Patrick (1994) asserts they were not significant in Japan, mainly because the economic and reputational costs of abuse were high.

57. The Spanish case is discussed in chapter 6. See World Bank 1989, 71–72, for

a listing of countries that have experienced financial crises recently; close bank-firm ties played a role in several of these crises.

58. Fry 1988, 288–89. East Asian countries with restricted systems are partial exceptions. They have exhibited high savings rates but also high intermediation costs.

59. See Cho 1986.

60. See Loriaux 1991 and Zysman 1983 on France; Patrick 1994 on Japan; Amsden 1989 on South Korea; and Wade 1990 on Taiwan.

61. Lanyi and Saracoğlu 1983.

62. Ibid., 28.

63. World Bank 1989, 32. See also McKinnon 1991, 19–22.

64. World Bank 1989, 64. The Bank also notes that two countries that recently adopted positive interest rates—Malaysia and Thailand—experienced tremendous financial deepening. M2/GDP jumped from 31% in 1970 to 75% in 1987 in Malaysia and from 34% in 1980 to 60% in 1987 in Thailand. In contrast, M2/GDP in Argentina, which had a severely negative interest rate policy, dropped from 50% in the late 1920s to 30% in 1970 and only 18% in 1987.

65. It found that countries with positive, moderately negative, and severely negative real interest rates had ratios of change in GDP to investment of 36.7%, 31.1%, and 21.7% in 1965–73, respectively, and 22.7%, 17.3%, and 6.2% in 1974–85, respectively. See ibid., 31–32. Higher ratios indicate higher investment productivity.

66. The drop in savings occurs as a shift from deposits in the local currency into foreign or tangible assets, or by creating a bias in favor of current consumption. See Shaw 1973, 61. See Olson and Bailey 1981 on the theory underpinning the view that savings are interest rate elastic. Other theorists argue that deposit interest rates do not affect national savings because the demand for savings is inelastic with respect to interest rates. For example, see Modigliani 1986.

67. World Bank 1989, 27.

68. A summary of Fry's empirical analysis is found in Fry 1988, chap. 6. Fry claimed that national savings increased by 0.1% on average when real interest rates rose by 1.0%.

69. Giovannini 1985.

70. Gupta 1987.

71. Wade 1990, 31.

72. See Cole and Wellons 1989; Fry 1988, chap. 16; Galbis 1986; Haggard, Lee, and Maxfield 1993; Kane 1977; and McKinnon 1991 for general discussions of this issue and case studies of individual countries.

73. Interest rate controls make it feasible for policymakers to supply credit to favored sectors at preferential rates. Chapter 2 examines why this is the case.

74. Fry 1988, chap. 16.

75. Ibid., 414.

76. Ibid., 162–64.

77. World Bank 1989, 60.

78. See Fry 1988, chaps. 14 and 16, and McKinnon 1994, chap. 4.

79. See Amsden 1989.

80. Krugman 1983 and Riedel 1988 are representative works.

81. See Calder 1993 and Horiuchi 1984.

82. Cole and Wellons 1989, 85.

83. This analysis is beyond the scope of this book, but I consider it in Lukauskas 1996.

84. Scholars do not concur on the sources of East Asia's superior economic performance. See Amsden 1989, Bedeski 1994, Cummings 1987, Johnson 1982 and 1987, and Wade 1990 for important views.

85. See Corbo and Melo 1985 and Edwards 1985.

86. See Akyüz 1990 and Gokce 1993.

87. See Dalla and Khatkhate 1995.

88. World Bank 1989, 126.

89. See McKinnon 1973 and World Bank 1989.

90. Within the remaining portfolio of bank deposits, it causes a shift away from long-term assets (e.g., certificates of deposit) toward short-term assets (e.g., currency and sight deposits). This shift means that intermediaries must increase their reserves (since RRs are higher for short-term liabilities), which also restricts liquidity. In addition, intermediaries usually curtail long-term lending to the private sector as they seek to match the maturities of their assets to that of their liabilities.

91. See Fry 1988, chap. 13, and McKinnon 1991, chap. 3.

92. Government borrowing in developing countries, many of which have restricted systems, consists of 46.7% from the central bank; 38.3% from foreign sources; 6.7% from deposit banks; and 8.3% from other domestic sources. In developed countries, government borrowing consists of 11.6% from the central bank; 9.7% from foreign sources; 22.7% from deposit banks; and 56.0% from other domestic sources. See World Bank 1989, 62.

93. See Fry 1988, 344, and Goldstein 1995. I discuss the Spanish case in chapter 6.

94. See Fry 1988, chaps. 10 and 11; Galbis 1986; and McKinnon 1991, chap. 7.

95. Stiglitz and Weiss 1981.

96. McKinnon 1991, chap. 7.

97. Recent experience in Japan and the United States indicates that government officials in developed countries also have trouble safeguarding the solvency of financial institutions.

98. Cole and Wellons 1989, 85.

99. The optimal policy is to set each bank's premiums according to the riskiness of its loan portfolio. In practice, authorities often lack the information to implement this policy effectively, and so establish the same premiums for all intermediaries.

100. Cho 1986.

101. See Galbis 1986.

102. Fry 1988, 271–72, and Galbis 1986. Pacts to maintain deposit rate ceilings have a prisoners' dilemma incentive structure; therefore, it remains to be explained how banks in these countries were able to enforce collusive arrangements. The Spanish case is discussed in later chapters.

103. Universal banks carry out the functions of both commercial banking (col-

lecting deposits and making loans) and investment banking (issuing, underwriting, placing, and trading company securities). See World Bank 1989, 50. This strategy is not risk-free, as universal banks may have conflicts of interest that hurt their clientele and provoke financial instability.

104. Ibid., 127.

Chapter 2

1. Patrick 1994, 369.
2. See Bates 1988 on this approach.
3. Rational choice approaches posit that individuals seek to maximize expected utility subject to budget constraints. In this book, I assume that actors exhibit "bounded rationality"; that is, they have only imperfect information about their environment and the consequences of their actions, do not necessarily examine all alternative courses of action, and may only attempt to "satsifice." On the problems of collective action, see Olson 1965.
4. Stigler 1971, 3.
5. Peltzman 1976.
6. Becker 1983. See also Keeler 1984.
7. For example, see Moran 1984 and Pérez 1997.
8. The view that bureaucrats can dominate regulatory policy free of political control has been sharply criticized in recent years. For two important works in this vein, see Derthick and Quirk 1985 and Wilson 1980. As Rosenbluth (1989) and others have pointed out, the degree of principal-agent problems depends on several institutional factors and varies considerably across countries.
9. Rosenbluth 1989, 132. See also Calder 1993, 66.
10. Becker (1983), Buchanan and Tullock (1962), Peltzman (1976), and Stigler (1971) are among the many scholars who make the analytical assumption that obtaining and retaining political office is the primary goal of politicians.
11. Bates 1994, 30.
12. See Levi 1988 on the argument that generating government revenue is a central goal of public officials. Unlike Levi, I do not contend that public officials necessarily seek to maximize revenue; rather, I suggest that, at a minimum, they attempt to generate enough revenue to provide essential services, leaving open the possibility that they may wish to raise much more. A variety of factors, including a country's political institutional structure, influence whether public officials will appropriate revenues for themselves or spend them responsibly. While holding power and raising revenue are usually complementary goals, politicians sometimes must make trade-offs between them. For instance, politicians may hurt their prospects for political survival if they tax constituents excessively; but they may lose out to rivals if they cannot obtain sufficient revenue to provide essential services. I assume here that politicians strive to achieve both these goals, devising trade-offs between them as circumstances require. In the case study, I examine how Spanish political leaders handled this set of issues.
13. Levi 1988, 3.

14. For example, see Garrett and Lange 1991, Hibbs 1987, and Hicks and Swank 1992.

15. In modern usage, seigniorage is any benefit that is derived from the creation of money. Banks obtain seigniorage when they accept deposits and subsequently supply credit, since this creates money. The government can expropriate a portion of this seigniorage by immobilizing the banking sector's deposits (e.g., by imposing RRs) and using these funds itself. See Dornbusch and Fischer 1981, chap. 8, for a discussion of how banks create money by providing credit. See Fry 1988, chaps. 1 and 12, and Giovannini and Melo 1993 for a discussion of predatory public finance.

16. A brief review of the development economics literature in this period is Meier 1984, chap. 6. U.S. officials, the Bank of England, and various international agencies promoted the view that financial systems designed along Anglo-Saxon lines were best. They were most active in East Asia but also attempted to influence policy in Latin America. See Armijo 1993, 288, Calder 1993, 41–44, and Choi 1993, 25.

17. Unfortunately, even hindsight does not allow us to ascertain definitely which view is correct. For instance, one cannot conclude that officials were not motivated by the public interest because financial policy led to poor results; they might have believed they were following the right model or well-designed policy might have been implemented poorly by subordinates. Even the continued choice of policy that is dysfunctional from a social welfare perspective may not be evidence of self-interested behavior, since public-minded officials may misinterpret information they receive from the feedback loop.

18. In recent years, several other authors have also addressed the topic of which institutional variables help determine whether politicians strive to provide for the public good. For examples, see Bates 1983, Geddes 1994, and Widner 1994.

19. Credit rents arise from the difference between ceiling or preferential interest rates and market interest rates. Selective credit policies help to determine which groups obtain credit rents.

20. In addition, the Stiglitz and Weiss model (discussed in chap. 1) suggests that intermediaries voluntarily cap their loan rates in order to prevent the problems caused by adverse risk selection and incentive effects (Stiglitz and Weiss 1981). Intermediaries may still be vulnerable to "interest rate" risk even when there is a fixed spread between deposit and loan rates. If they borrow short but lend long, a sharp increase in interest rates (e.g., due to rapid inflation) may mean that the cost of funds exceeds the return on some loans. Intermediaries can guard against this risk by matching the term structure of their loan portfolio to that of their liabilities. The significance of entry controls is discussed later in this chapter.

21. "It is generally believed that large banks gave up their opposition to deposit insurance in exchange for prohibition of interest payments on demand deposits and ceilings on other rates" (West 1983, 367 n. 4).

22. When loan rate ceilings are binding, demand for credit exceeds supply since the prevailing loan interest rate is below the equilibrium rate (that is, the rate that would clear the market). Thus, rationing must occur, and the total supply of loans offered by intermediaries will be lower than in the absence of loan rate ceilings.

23. Firms may find it difficult to predict precisely who will have access to credit in a rationed market. Thus, they may not be certain which position they should take on interest rate controls.

24. When authorities implement deposit rate ceilings, the supply of savings will probably decrease because savings are generally believed to be positively related to real interest rates. As noted in chapter 1, the empirical record on the effect of ceilings on the level of savings is not conclusive.

25. Deposit rate ceilings reduce the cost of deposits for intermediaries and, thus, make it viable for the government to impose loan rate ceilings. For the same reason, they make it possible for public officials to create the selective credit programs that provide credit at preferential rates.

26. Zysman (1983, 10) first recognized the political significance of credit rationing.

27. Peltzman 1976.

28. Scholars frequently cite the political uses of credit controls. For example, see Galbis 1986 and Kane 1977, and the in-depth case studies of credit programs in Haggard, Lee, and Maxfield 1993. Fry identifies five major categories of selective credit instruments. (1) Differential rediscount rates: intermediaries are compensated for lending at subsidized rates of interest to priority borrowers when they rediscount preferential loans at the central bank on concessionary terms. (2) Direct budget subsidy: the negative differential between preferential and market loan rates is financed by budget appropriations. (3) Credit floors: policymakers set minimum percentages of total credit or deposits that must be lent by intermediaries to priority borrowers. (4) Credit ceilings: authorities set ceilings on the aggregate volume of credit to the private sector, but grant exemptions for loans made to priority sectors. (5) Specialized financial institutions: funds are extracted from private intermediaries (e.g., by ARs) and are channeled to priority sectors on concessionary terms by specialized public financial institutions. See Fry 1988, chap. 16, for a more complete description of these instruments.

29. Bureaucrats may follow a different political logic if their political superiors delegate authority over credit controls to them. They may, for example, attempt to allocate funds to groups that make lucrative employment offers or provide valuable information. These may or may not be the same groups that politicians would like to favor. I examine the implementation of selective credit policies and the principal-agent issue in Spain in chapter 3.

30. Becker (1983) develops this analytical argument about the design of regulatory policies in general.

31. On the factors that influence private demand for preferential credit, see Haggard and Maxfield 1993. Mexico and Thailand are two countries where demand for preferential finance was relatively low. See Maxfield 1993 and Doner and Unger 1993.

32. See Haggard and Maxfield 1993, 305–12, and Maxfield 1994.

33. A bank's opportunity cost roughly equals the difference between market and subsidized interest rates multiplied by the volume of subsidized credit it must supply.

34. In addition, there may be positive covariance among the expected returns of

projects undertaken by priority borrowers to general macroeconomic conditions. As a result, macroeconomic conditions leading one priority borrower to default may cause several others to default as well. See McKinnon 1991 on this point.

35. Goodhart 1989, chap. 7.

36. A numerical example illustrates this point. A bank lends $100 for a year at 10% (the loan rate ceiling), but requires the borrower to deposit 20% of the loan in a non-interest-bearing account. In this operation, the borrower receives $80 but pays interest on $100. The effective interest rate on this transaction is 12.5%, 2.5% over the loan rate ceiling.

37. The Spanish government inadvertently provided banks with the means to circumvent deposit rate ceilings in this way. Repurchase agreements are feasible only when the asset traded is risk-free and perfectly liquid. Before short-term public debt was issued, few assets in Spain met these criteria.

38. See Fry 1988, chap. 16, and World Bank 1989, 59, on this point.

39. World Bank 1989, 60.

40. See Fry 1988, chap. 16.

41. RRs in excess of this optimum level do not add to the stability of the banking system and, in fact, may detract from it. See Andreu 1987a. In a new practice, some governments now pay interest on a percentage of the reserves intermediaries must deposit at the central bank.

42. This is called the Courakis effect in the economics literature (Fry 1988, 109–18). If there are perfect substitutes for bank deposits and loans in financial markets, the entire tax will fall on banks; conversely, in the absence of substitutes, banks will transfer the tax in full to their clients.

43. Giovannini and Melo 1993.

44. See Fry 1988, especially chap. 5; Giovannini and Melo 1993; and McKinnon 1973.

45. The most basic measure of financial margins is the difference between the gross cost of borrowing and the net return on lending. Higher financial margins reduce the flow of resources to the final users of credit and, thereby, lower levels of investment. For this reason, gross earnings margin is often considered one of the best measures of the efficiency of intermediation. See Fry 1988, 234–37, on this topic.

46. See Goode 1984, chap. 8.

47. See Fry 1988, part 1.

48. It is not impossible, however. The government can attempt to influence the flow of credit within direct markets by qualifying bond and equity issues. Nevertheless, as this policy curtails the growth of direct markets sharply, policymakers can hope to influence the allocation of at most a small percentage of total financial resources in this way. Spain adopted this strategy, and I discuss its features and results in chapter 3.

49. These controls take a variety of forms, including: general foreign exchange controls on banks, individuals, and firms; strict conditions on foreign direct or portfolio investment; and limits on the sorts of international transactions domestic banks can undertake.

50. This was certainly the case in Spain, as I discuss in chapter 3. Until the

1970s, Japanese economic officials also maintained a relatively closed financial system, in part to be able to retain strict control over investment flows. See Hills 1983.

51. See Goldstein 1995.

52. Economic Commission for Latin America and the Caribbean 1992 provides a brief review of the benefits of foreign direct investment.

53. Frieden 1981.

54. See Fry 1988, chap. 11.

55. Some authors believe that these policies may be justified if they help to build a bank-based system. See chapter 1.

56. Rosenbluth makes a similar argument. See Rosenbluth 1989, chap. 4.

57. Policymakers use moral suasion when they attempt to gain compliance with a specific policy without issuing legally binding regulations. A central bank's "request" that intermediaries voluntarily comply with a proposed policy is often successful since it can greatly influence the conditions under which they obtain funds.

58. Applications of the economic theory to financial policy include Hamada and Horiuchi 1987, Hammond and Knott 1988, and Rosenbluth 1989.

59. As already noted, the economic theory also raises the possibility that public officials will initiate deregulation if the existing regulatory regime begins to generate large deadweight economic losses, since consumer and producer surpluses are also sources of political support. See Becker 1983 and Keeler 1984.

60. See Hammond and Knott 1988. U.S. authorities have already begun to remove restrictions on geographic and product competition.

61. Hamada and Horiuchi (1987) and Harper (1986) examine these factors.

62. See Fry 1988, 245, for a more complete discussion of the differences between restricted and nonrestricted systems. A financial system's depth is a product of both a country's economic history and government policies.

63. Ibid., 245. Curb markets are informal financial markets.

64. This is true unless inflation is high and deposit ceilings are set so low that savers engage in massive capital flight, or heavily substitute from deposits to tangible assets or curb markets (if they are available). If policymakers authorize the entry of foreign banks or nonregulated NBFIs, domestic banks may begin to lose market share, eventually giving them an interest in financial reform. This occurred in Mexico and South Korea, for instance.

65. Woo offers one exception. She claims that beneficiaries of selective credit programs in South Korea came to oppose them late in the day because they felt overly controlled by government officials. See Woo 1991, 199–201.

66. For example, there was some divergence in stances among Spanish banks toward deregulation. I discuss this in later chapters, particularly chapter 6. Rosenbluth notes similar divisions among Japanese banks. See Rosenbluth 1989, 133.

67. See Fry 1988, chap. 11. In contrast, banks in several Southern Cone countries competed avidly for deposits after interest rates controls were removed.

68. "Conglomeration in developing countries is often motivated strongly by the desire to avoid interest rate ceilings and other regulations on lending, such as credit ceilings" (Fry 1988, 284–85). This means that banks and firms in conglomerates may care less about certain aspects of financial policy (e.g., credit controls) than

banks and firms that are not. Galbis finds that conglomerates have typically opposed efforts to liberalize financial systems (1986, 127–28). See also Haggard and Maxfield 1993 on this issue.

69. Banks from restricted systems may wish to follow their clients as they expand into foreign markets in order to supply services best provided locally. They may also want to gain access to lower cost funds in Eurocurrency markets. Frieden (1991a) and Silva (1993) contend that internationally oriented conglomerates sought the removal of capital controls in Chile. Among other things, liberalization allowed these conglomerates to obtain dollar-denominated funds from abroad and reloan them at highly profitable rates to domestic borrowers.

70. For example, Indonesia. See Cole and Wellons 1989, 69–84.

71. See Meier 1985 on the U.S. financial regulatory environment.

72. For example, see Cole and Wellons 1989, Harper 1986, and Loriaux 1991.

73. For instance, see Fry 1988, 245.

74. See Loriaux 1991, 295–99.

75. See Rodrik 1994, 22–23.

76. See Levi 1988 and North 1981.

77. See Bates and Krueger 1993 and Krueger 1993.

78. Governments have sometimes undertaken major reforms when economic conditions were not critical. See Rodrik 1994, 20. This suggests that an economic crisis is not even a necessary condition for reform and prompts us to consider other variables (e.g., the political calculations of leaders) as important factors in determining whether and when reform takes place.

79. See Haggard and Kaufman 1995 and Nelson 1993, 442–47.

80. The literature on the role of external pressures in economic policy-making is large. Recent work includes Kahler 1992 and Stallings 1992.

81. Webb and Shariff 1992.

82. For example, see Calder 1988a on Japan.

83. See Pauly 1988.

84. An excellent review of the literature on this topic is Cohen 1996.

85. Goodman and Pauly 1993.

86. Frieden 1991b, Gill and Law 1989, and Kurzer 1993.

87. Andrews (1994), Cerney (1993), and Kurzer (1993) make this argument.

88. A similar conclusion about the impact of international factors on financial policy in diverse settings is reached by Kapstein (1994), Sobel (1994), and Wilson (1994). Garret and Lange (1991) conclude that greater international financial integration has not eliminated the ability of leaders to shape national economic policies in accordance with their partisan preferences.

89. A discussion of this point is found in Bryant 1987. A recent report by the U.S. Treasury confirms that barriers to international financial intermediation (i.e., capital controls and discriminatory treatment of foreign intermediaries) remain large in most countries outside the Organization for Economic Cooperation and Development (OECD). See *Financial Times,* December 5, 1994, 4. Nevertheless, substantial capital flight from developing countries in the 1980s suggests that their capital controls are also becoming more porous. See *Economist* 1993. In addition, some developing countries have recently promised to give foreign intermediaries

greater access to their markets in talks on liberalizing financial services under the auspices of the World Trade Organization. It is unclear what policy changes will actually be carried out, especially as the talks have stalled.

90. See Kahler 1992 and Nelson 1990.

91. Pauly 1988, 154. More generally, Pauly contends, "politics within distinct state structures remains the axis around which international finance revolves" (1988, 2). See also Sobel 1994.

92. For example, see Fry 1988, 245.

93. For example, see Pastor 1989.

94. Weir (1989) is another scholar who contends that the impact of ideas is mediated by domestic political institutions.

95. See Dalla and Khatkhate 1995. Amsden and Euh (1993) believe restriction is still the best policy for South Korea (and other countries) and criticize its recent liberalization efforts.

96. For example, see Bates and Krueger 1993, Callaghy 1993, Haggard and Webb 1994, and Nelson 1993.

97. Haggard and Kaufman (1995) agree that the initiation of reforms requires centralization of authority in the hands of an insulated economic team but contend that their consolidation requires the development of what Evans calls "embedded autonomy."

98. Bates (1983) reaches a similar conclusion in his study of the circumstances under which politicians have the greatest incentive to design agricultural policy in order to be able to supply private benefits.

99. Downs (1957) argued that when political power is highly dispersed, as in a democracy with universal suffrage and accountable administrative functions, diffuse interests have a stronger voice in public policy. Drawing on the work of Downs, Aronson and Ordeshook (1985) contended that a two-party democracy produces an optimal level of public goods. In a similar vein, Becker (1983), Stigler (1982), and Wittman (1989) also claimed that the greater political competition of democracy brings about more efficient policy choices. The primary difference between authoritarian and democratic regimes is that the latter grant opposition groups the right to contest incumbent rulers and replace them through competitive elections.

100. Lake (1992), Maravall (1994), and Verdier (1994) are among the scholars who make this argument.

101. Kiewiet 1983. See also Lewis-Beck 1988.

102. Kiewiet 1983, 21.

103. Empirical work on the relative economic performance of different regime types is inconclusive: some studies indicate that democratic regimes exhibit higher growth rates than autocratic regimes, whereas others find the opposite result or little difference between regime types. Barro (1989), Grier and Tullock (1989), and Kormendi and Meguire (1985) suggest that democracies enjoy superior economic performance. Helliwell (1994) finds that differences in economic performance between authoritarian and democratic regimes are not statistically significant. Most empirical studies of the impact of regime type on economic growth are cross-

sectional and, thus, do not directly test the contention that, for a given country, democratization should lead to superior performance.

104. Olson posited that the voting majority needed to win office in a democracy has an encompassing interest in maximizing a country's productivity. As a result, democratic systems tend to supply more public goods than authoritarian regimes (Olson 1993).

105. Haggard and Kaufman 1995, 7.

106. See Calder 1993.

107. See Calder 1988b.

108. Among the important attempts to get at these issues are Bates 1983, Geddes 1994, Haggard and Kaufman 1995, and Haggard and Webb 1994.

109. Lijphart 1994, 1. A full discussion of these variables is found in ibid., chap. 2. See also Taagepera and Shugart 1989.

110. Geddes 1994 and Mainwaring 1991 discuss the importance of closed and open party lists.

111. See Linz and Valenzuela 1994 and Mainwaring 1993. Shugart and Carey (1992) dispute this view.

112. Stepan and Skach 1993, especially 16–22.

113. See Mainwaring 1993.

114. Haggard and Kaufman caution, however, that parties in such systems sometimes turn into elite-dominated patronage machines (1992a, 344). This points out that electoral institutions alone cannot provide the determinants of behavior. I examine this issue in chapters 5 and 8.

115. See Arnold 1979, chap. 1.

116. See Olson 1993.

117. Przeworski 1991, chap. 4.

118. Nelson 1993, 447.

119. Przeworski, "The Games of Transitions," unpublished manuscript, 1990. Cited in Maravall 1993.

120. See Levi 1988, chap. 6.

Chapter 3

1. Torrero Mañas 1982, cuadro 1. Direct markets' share of credit to the private sector as a percentage of total credit was 5.8% in 1962, 7.1% in 1970, and 2.4% in 1980.

2. In 1964–65, the percentage of self-finance in total industrial financing in Spain was only 27%. In contrast, it was 54% in the United States, 49% in West Germany, and 42% in England (in 1968–70). See Lieberman 1982, 241.

3. Preferential credit as a percentage of total private sector financing was 30.4% in 1962, 32.5% in 1966, 39.8% in 1970, 34.8% in 1974, and 33.0% in 1978. (Poveda Anadón 1986, cuadro 2). Preferential credit includes financing granted by banks, savings banks, credit cooperatives, public banks, and the central bank to the private sector because of selective credit policies.

4. Interviews with former Ministry of Finance and Planning Commission officials, July 1989 and February 1990.

5. Pérez (1997) makes this argument.

6. The Opus Dei is a Catholic lay organization that was founded in 1928. The "technocrats" were a group of economists trained at the Opus Dei-run University of Navarra. The most important early technocrats were Mariano Navarro Rubio, the minister of finance; Alberto Ullastres, the minister of commerce; and Gual Villalbi, minister without portfolio and president of the Council of the National Economy. Their champion within the regime was Carrero Blanco, the secretary of the presidency, later vice president. For more on the technocrats, see Lancaster 1989 and Miguel 1975.

7. See González Temprano 1981, Muñoz 1969, and Pérez 1977 for capture theory views of Spanish financial policy in the Franco period.

8. See Payne 1987, chap. 7, on Franco's rise to power.

9. Gunther 1980, 30–32. The notion of limited pluralistic competition was developed by Linz (1964).

10. See Carr and Fusi 1981, chap. 8, and Miguel 1975 on the various political groups that made up the regime.

11. See Preston 1986, chaps. 2 and 3.

12. These issues were (1) matters of public order, (2) church/state relations, (3) the army, and (4) the succession to power in the event of his retirement or death. See Gunther 1980, 163.

13. See ibid., chap. 9.

14. Esteban 1976.

15. Ibid., 91, and Lieberman 1982, 188. Real wages fell precipitously after the Civil War because the war had destroyed much of Spain's capital stock, thereby sharply reducing labor productivity.

16. The government erected high tariff barriers, imposed strict capital controls, and established a confusing system of multiple exchange rates. Overvalued official rates slowed Spanish exports and stimulated imports. See Lieberman 1982, 176–78. See Clavera et al. 1978, Esteban 1976, Harrison 1985, and Lieberman 1982 for more on Spain's autarkic economic policies.

17. Esteban 1976, 90.

18. See, especially, Donges 1976, chap. 3, and Lieberman 1982, chap. 3.

19. See Schwartz and González 1978 on the foundation and evolution of INI. In practice, INI played a limited role in guiding industrial development, in part because of disagreements within the regime over the proper scope of its activities.

20. Esteban 1976, 93. The drop in the level of output below pre–Civil War levels was largely due to the war's devastation.

21. See Velarde 1968 on the Primo de Rivera regime and its policies.

22. See Preston 1976, 137–39.

23. Esteban 1976, 93–94.

24. Clavera et al. 1978, 246.

25. The dissent took the form of increased labor strikes and student protests. Lieberman 1982, 187–92, details the protest activities in this period. See also Preston 1976, 139–40.

26. See Anderson 1970, González 1979, Lieberman 1982, and Wright 1977 for in-depth studies of the Stabilization Plan.

27. See Muns 1984.

28. Carrero Blanco became Franco's closest subordinate after entering the government as undersecretary of the presidency in 1941. Carrero was vice president of the government and secretary of the presidency during much of the Franco era. By all accounts, he was the second most powerful figure within the regime during its last two decades. In 1973, he took over the post of president, making him the clear successor to Franco. He was killed by terrorists in December 1973.

29. Preston 1986, 7.

30. Ibid., chap. 1.

31. For example, Wiarda 1992. Anderson (1970) believes that Spanish policymakers sought to improve public welfare but did not always succeed in achieving their stated objectives.

32. See González 1979, Lieberman 1982, and Sampedro 1975.

33. López Rodó, quoted in Wright 1977, 59.

34. See Alcaide Inchausti 1989 and Martín Rodríguez 1989 for detailed analyses of this issue.

35. See Donges 1976, Fuentes Quintana 1989, González 1979, Lieberman 1982, Sampedro 1975, and Wright 1977.

36. Tourist receipts were $2.8 billion in 1973 when 34 million tourists visited Spain (Wright 1977, 145). Workers' remittances rose steadily throughout the 1960s, reaching a high of $913 million in 1973. See ibid., 148. Foreign direct and portfolio investment increased from $156 million to $1,013 million between 1960 and 1970; this foreign investment financed 10% of gross fixed capital formation and 20% of gross industrial investment (González 1979, 316). Gross capital formation increased by an annual average of 11.4%, considerably higher than the EC average of 6.4%. See ibid., 301–2. The value of capital per worker in Spain (in 1972 constant pesetas) increased from 353,050 in 1963 to 565,650 in 1973. See Lieberman 1982, 236.

37. Universal banks' share of total credit to the private sector declined after the policy changes implemented by the 1962 Banking Law, but they recaptured some of their lost share in the 1970s. Figure 4.1 shows the shares of total credit to the private sector for various intermediaries in the 1970s. Caution is required in interpreting long-term trends since the data set used for the 1970 decade differs somewhat from this data set.

38. The regulations consisted of a series of ministerial orders and laws promulgated between December 1939 and May 1942. See Alvarez Llano and Andreu 1982, 108, and Muñoz 1969, 60–62.

39. For this reason, I make no further reference to commercial banks in this study. I distinguish between industrial and universal banks only when it is important to do so. In all other instances, the term *bank* refers to an universal bank.

40. See especially González Temprano, Sánchez Robayna, and Torres Villanueva 1981 and Muñoz 1969.

41. See González Temprano, Sánchez Robayna, and Torres Villanueva 1981, chaps. 4 and 5.

42. Chapter 4 through 7 examine these reforms. Ironically, the most favorable legislation for banks was passed when they had few government representatives.

43. The Spanish press and memoirs of financiers reveal numerous anecdotes detailing the feuding among the major banks. See Graham 1984, chap. 5, and Rivases 1988.

44. They are Banesto, Central, Bilbao, Hispano Americano, Santander, Vizcaya, and Popular. Mergers have reduced their current number to four.

45. Graham 1984, 98–99.

46. See Hernández Armenteros 1986 and Sáez Fernández 1975. The government has recently begun to privatize public banks.

47. Banco de España, *Boletín Estadístico,* various issues. Rural savings banks have provided up to one-third of total private credit to agriculture.

48. There is virtually no literature on the Spanish curb market. It probably played its most significant role in the 1940s, when general black market activity was high and in the 1970s when monetary policy drained liquidity from the banking system.

49. Before 1962, the Dirección General de la Banca, Bolsa e Inversiones (Directorate of Banks and Capital Markets) carried out this function.

50. See Gunther 1980 for an exceptional study of the budgetary process in the Franco era and the MOF's role in it. In the 1960s, the Planning Commission became powerful, challenging the dominance of the MOF. I discuss this later.

51. See Martinez Cortiña 1971, chap. 2.

52. See chapter 6 on this point.

53. Interview with a former BOS official, February 1990.

54. Some Spanish economists pointed out the dangers of this policy to policymakers. For example, see Gala 1969. See Cho 1986 for the mainstream economic view.

55. The Junta de Inversiones determined whether a company's security would be included on a list of assets that intermediaries could purchase to fulfill credit controls. If a firm's securities were not included, it had no chance of placing it among investors.

56. In the 1950s and 1960s, "the Junta required firms to offer a yield of 6.25% on their bonds (after taxes); this yield on bonds, with maturities of 15 to 20 years and no option of resale on a secondary market, was not attractive for savers." See Poveda Anadón 1982, 63 n. 4.

57. Similar institutional arrangements had equally dampening effects on bond markets in Japan, forcing firms into greater reliance on bank credit. See Hamada and Horiuchi 1987, 236, and Rosenbluth 1989, 141–47

58. González Temprano, Sánchez Robayna, and Torres Villanueva 1981, 27.

59. See Banco de España 1968, 473.

60. About 75% of all bank credit had maturities of ninety days or less (Lieberman 1982, 243). In practice, banks rolled over short-term credits indefinitely, thereby increasing the effective term of loans.

61. Payne 1987, 470.

62. See Trías Fargas 1970. Chapter 4 provides data on financial margins in the 1960s.

63. The Banking Law of 1946 allowed new banks to enter the market with prior approval by the CSB. The ample representation that existing private banks enjoyed

in the CSB allowed them to block all but a few applications. The Banking Law of 1962 relaxed entry requirements and granted the MOF the power to authorize new banks. The MOF authorized twenty-two new banks in the remainder of the decade (Alvarez Llano and Andreu 1982, 119). There is evidence that competition within the banking sector increased in the 1960s. See Fanjul and Maravall 1985.

64. See Muñoz 1969, 60, and González Temprano, Sánchez Robayna, and Torres Villanueva 1981, 33.

65. Payne 1961, 201.

66. Ridruejo 1954, 71, and Muñoz 1969, 65. Banks could not distribute all of these profits as dividends, however, because of restrictions imposed in 1940 (discussed later).

67. Muñoz 1969, 61–62.

68. The largest five banks increased their number of offices by 50% from 1941 to 1954, while other banks increased theirs only slightly. See Ridruejo 1954, 74–75.

69. From 1941 to 1966, the six largest banks absorbed seventy-eight banks, compared to only twelve for the period 1918–40 (Muñoz 1969, 65).

70. Ibid., 158–59. The total number of banks in Spain was 126.

71. See Fanjul and Maravall 1985.

72. The Japanese government placed similar restrictions on banks in the postwar period. The purpose, in contrast to Spain, was to build up capital in the banking sector. See Patrick 1994, 394.

73. The largest five banks increased their capital by 700% between 1940 and 1960. Muñoz 1969, 65.

74. See Payne 1961 on the Falangists and their views on political economy.

75. The MOF prohibited savings banks from acquiring equity in firms, encouraging them instead to deposit extra funds with banks at low interest rates.

76. Muñoz 1969, 290.

77. The largest six banks alone had representatives on the boards of directors of 696 firms in 1957 and 955 firms in 1967 (ibid., 291). Rivases (1988) suggested that banks retained significant representation on the boards of industrial firms in the 1980s.

78. See Lancaster 1989 and Tamames 1977.

79. See Miguel and Linz 1963.

80. The view that banks may lead industrial development in late industrializers is developed by Gerschenkron 1962, chap. 1.

81. Lieberman, Navarro Rubio, and Torrero Mañas contend that banks did not play a primary role in guiding industrial development in the Franco era. See Lieberman 1982, chaps. 3 and 4; Navarro Rubio 1972; and Torrero Mañas 1989a. Torrero Mañas explicitly states, "Spanish banks have a tradition of participating in industrial firms, but it has not centered on supervision and control of operations, nor have banks developed departments for creating their own industrial groups. The difference with German banking is considerable in this regard" (1989a, 135). For dissenting opinions, see Graham 1984, chap. 5, and Muñoz 1969.

82. See Donges 1976, Lieberman 1982, Schwartz and González 1978, and Wright 1977 for in-depth studies of government efforts to shape industrial development.

83. In 1965, for example, Franco expressed grave concern over the economic power wielded by banks when he vetoed the proposed merger between the Banco Central and Hispano, two of the Big Seven. See López Rodó 1990, 592.

84. Fanjul and Maravall 1985, 238. It also deserves recalling that the 1962 Banking Law sought the creation of industrial banks whose mission was to provide long-term finance to new firms, which policymakers believed was sorely lacking. In practice, the promotion of industrial banks was a half-hearted, short-lived, and unsuccessful endeavor. See Muñoz 1969, 81–85.

85. Martinez Cortiña 1971, 183–84. The large national banks actually increased their holdings of private stock and bonds by 80.6% from 1962 to 1967. See Muñoz 1969, 220.

86. See Muñoz 1969, chap. 8.

87. In 1938, the Nationalists, who had already gained control over much of the state bureaucracy, dismantled the CSB and gave the MOF sole authority to set interest rates. The Banking Law of 1946 reestablished the CSB and required the MOF to consult with it and the National Economic Council, another advisory board, before modifying interest rates.

88. It might be argued that authorities implemented interest rate and entry controls to ensure bank solvency, especially in light of the dramatic bank failures that hit Europe in the 1930s. While it is impossible to discount this notion entirely, I do not believe it was a principal concern of Spanish policymakers since Spanish banks weathered the 1930s with no difficulty and were healthy after the Civil War.

89. Gil 1973. Occasionally, banks also used these agreements to fix deposit rates at levels below the ceilings set by authorities.

90. Banks did engage in non–price competition for deposits by offering free services or gifts. They also invented various means of paying large depositors higher returns on an ad hoc basis.

91. Gala 1969, 39. In 1969, the MOF began to mandate loan rate ceilings through official regulations.

92. See International Bank for Reconstruction and Development 1963 and OECD 1966, 1969.

93. See Donges 1976, 132.

94. A good summary of these controls is López Roa 1981, chap. 5.

95. Public officials, including dignitaries at the regional and local levels, exercised particularly great pressure on savings banks. See Graham 1984, 98–99.

96. In 1969, for example, interest rates on long-term preferential credit ranged from 5.1 to 6.5%. Rates on ordinary short- and medium-term loans ranged from 6.5 to 8.0%. See Gil 1973.

97. Interview with a former banker, July 1989.

98. A complete list of beneficiaries is found in Poveda Anadón 1986.

99. See Anderson 1970, chap. 8.

100. Several in-depth studies conclude that the allocation of privileged credit was greatly influenced by noneconomic criteria. For example, see González 1979, chap. 6, and Tortella and Jiménez 1986, chaps. 5 and 6. Directed credit programs aimed at exports were probably justified on economic grounds but were implemented arbitrarily. See chapter 4 in this book on this point.

101. On South Korea and Taiwan, see Amsden 1989 and Wade 1990, respectively. On the failure of Spanish selective credit policies to improve export performance or productivity, see González 1979 and Jiménez and Tortella 1986. Donges (1976) offers a somewhat less critical assessment.

102. The Matesa Affair is discussed in chapter 4.

103. See Fuentes Quintana 1989 and OECD 1966, 1969, 1971.

104. Martí (1975) argued that the regime imposed the planning apparatus in response to pressure from social groups that eventually benefited from it. His argument faces a traditional problem with interest group approaches: policy outcomes that favor a group's interests are viewed as proof that the group's pressure was behind the policy. Martí offers no evidence in this regard, nor is such evidence apparent in other accounts of the period. In fact, most studies, such as Gunther 1980, stress the absence of aggregated social demands on economic policy during the period of Franquist rule. Moreover, many of the actors that benefited from the development planning were simply not organized into interest groups before the plans were put in place.

105. Lieberman 1982, 216. See also Fuentes 1991 and González 1979, chap. 6.

106. Interviews with former PC and MOF officials, January and February 1990. This is consistent with Gunther's description of the process by which public sector investments were allocated across ministries. See Gunther 1980, chap. 7.

107. See Donges 1976, chap. 3, sec. 3.

108. Interviews with several economic policymakers, June 1989 and February 1990. This finding is also consistent with Gunther's description of how many lower-order budget decisions were made in the Franco period. See Gunther 1980, chaps. 8 and 9.

109. See Poveda Anadón 1972. Pérez argues that selective credit policies were designed to harness credit expansion to enable Spanish authorities to keep inflation under control while pursuing a policy of cheap credit, not to serve as instruments of political discretion. See Pérez 1997, especially 177–78. Instead of harnessing credit growth, however, selective credit instruments actually fueled inflation. As noted in chapter 1, this is a common problem with directed credit programs.

110. See Gala 1969 and Wright 1977 on credit rationing in Spain.

111. Wright 1977, 116. See also Muñoz 1969, 206–10.

112. See Gunther 1980, especially chap. 8.

113. See Poveda Anadón 1982.

114. Several recipients of subsidized credit without sound reasons for expansion built up excess productive capacity in response to the availability of cheap capital. They later faltered when demand for their products did not increase rapidly. See García Delgado 1980.

115. Chapter 6 discusses Spain's banking crisis and how defaults by privileged borrowers contributed to it.

116. Alvarez Llano and Andreu 1982, 15.

117. Ibid., 24.

118. Tortella 1973, 314–17. Ortega Fernández notes that the government later

renewed the Bank's privileged position only in exchange for further concessions on credit (1987a, 201).

119. Martín Aceña 1987, 110–11.

120. Cuervo García, Parejo Gámir, and Rodríguez Sáiz 1988, 348.

121. Tortella 1973. See also Kindleberger 1984, chap. 8.

122. On taxation under the Franco regime, see Gunther 1980, especially chaps. 2 and 3.

123. In 1971, Spanish fiscal receipts, including social security, totaled about 20% of GNP, whereas in OECD countries receipts averaged about 32% of GNP. See OECD 1974, 36.

124. Comín 1990, 891.

125. Esteban 1976, 92.

126. Gunther 1980, 58–60.

127. Clavera et al. 1978, 292.

128. Until the 1970s, their sole monetary instruments were quantitative credit restrictions and manipulation of the discount rate.

129. Navarro Rubio 1972, 5.

130. Policymakers also abolished rediscounting to alleviate the monetary control problems noted earlier. This became more pressing after the Stabilization Plan, as monetary growth had to be made consistent with the new requirements of peseta convertibility.

131. See Sáez Fernandez 1975, 85–87, and Tortella and Jiménez 1986, chap. 5.

132. A lack of data made it impossible for me to replicate exactly the methodology used in the Giovannini and Melo study (discussed in chap. 2); thus, my results are not strictly comparable to theirs.

133. Calculated from data found in Banco de España, *Boletín Estadístico,* various issues. The choice of years for the estimates was determined by data availability, although an attempt was made to pick years that did not over- or understate the amount of revenue typically generated by restriction.

134. Calculated from data in Hernández Armenteros 1986 and Banco de España, *Boletín Estadístico,* various issues.

135. See Gunther 1980, especially chap. 2.

136. Ortega Fernández 1987a, 190. This statistic is somewhat deceptive, however, as the government undertook large expenditures after 1962 that did not appear as budgetary items. Some expenditures were covered by BOS lending to government agencies or state-run enterprises at zero-interest cost. This lending was a form of inflation financing since the BOS simply printed money to make the loans. As already noted, banks also provided low-cost funds that permitted the MOF to fund state-run enterprises and public bank activities without budgetary expenditure.

Chapter 4

1. See especially Pérez 1997.

2. See Fry 1988, part 3, and Galbis 1986. On the appropriateness of Spanish reforms in this regard, see OECD 1988, chap. 2.

3. Fry 1988, part 3, and Galbis 1986.

4. This conclusion is at odds with the work of Pérez (1997), who contends that policymakers did not take steps to emend the narrow and oligopolistic structure of the Spanish financial system because they were constrained by what she calls a compact of reciprocal consent with the banking sector. As evidence, she points to the fact that banks continued to enjoy high margins and profits while nonfinancial sectors faced high real financing costs. I suggest that Pérez underestimates the difficulty of liberalizing oligopolistic markets and confuses policy outcomes with the intent of policymakers. Her account also does not identify many of the reforms undertaken by authorities nor take full account of the dramatic changes that have swept the Spanish financial system, particularly since the late 1980s. I develop these points later, especially in chapter 7.

5. On these points, see chapter 3. Firms targeted by credit controls were less active in this period because serious efforts to eliminate government credit programs did not begin until 1977. Their lobbying in this period consisted mostly of efforts to increase the amount of preferential credit they received and keep its cost low.

6. Torrero Mañas 1982, cuadro 7.

7. Savings banks favored some financial reforms, particularly those that would have allowed them to compete on more equal terms with banks. However, they did not begin to lobby for deregulation actively and effectively until the mid-1970s. For this reason, their role in financial policy will be discussed primarily in the chapters that follow.

8. It might also be argued that private actors did not seek liberalization because they were not aware of its potential benefits for them. This was probably not the case, however, as several studies in this period demonstrated that prevailing financial policy favored some groups at the expense of others. See Hornillos García 1970 for a representative work.

9. Anderson 1970, 73.

10. A policy of targeting growth in monetary aggregates is incompatible with interest rate controls because it is impossible to simultaneously determine quantity and price in any market. For a thorough discussion of the links between financial deregulation and monetary control in the Spanish context, see Martinez Méndez 1980.

11. A representative critique by a Spanish economist is Trías Fargas 1970. For reports by international agencies, see International Bank for Reconstruction and Development 1963 and OECD 1963, 1969, 1971. The BOS's widely read *Annual Reports* also challenged the logic of prevailing financial policy, especially after 1967. The Matesa Affair is discussed in detail later.

12. See Donges 1976.

13. On these issues, see the works cited in note 11. See also the analysis of selective credit policies in chapter 3.

14. Financial economists, such as Revell, view "gross earnings margin" (column 2) as the best measure of the costs of intermediation. As table 4.1 indicates, financial margins in Spain were the third highest among OECD countries. Fry

notes that in uncompetitive markets, the cost of intermediation is one of the best measures of overall financial efficiency (1988, 264).

15. See OECD 1963, 1969. See also Fuentes Quintana 1990 on this point.

16. Preston 1986, 11.

17. Until the mid-1960s, strike activity had been sporadic. There had been several episodes of labor unrest, notably in 1951, 1956–57, and 1962, and they had contributed to changes in economic policy (see chap. 3). Strike activity, however, clearly accelerated after 1967. In 1967, 402 strikes affected 272,964 workers and led to 2,456,100 hours of labor lost; in 1974, 1,193 strikes affected 625,971 workers and led to 18,188,895 hours lost (Payne 1987, 555, and Preston 1986, 13–15). See also Maravall 1978.

18. Carr and Fusi 1981, 145–46.

19. Lieberman 1982, 250–56.

20. See Cooper 1976, and Preston 1986, chaps. 1 and 2.

21. Payne 1987, 557–60, and Preston 1986, chap. 2.

22. Wright 1977, 88. Alcaide Inchausti presents statistical evidence that supports this assertion, albeit for a slightly different time period. Spain's Gini coefficient, a measure of income inequality, increased from .421 in 1964 to .457 in 1970. The percentage of GDP held by the bottom 20% of Spanish society dropped from 4.74% to 4.57%, while that of the top 20% increased from 49.26% to 53.02% (Alcaide Inchausti 1989, 663).

23. Alcaide Inchausti 1989, 651. The average for other OECD countries in 1970 was about 70% (ibid., 653).

24. Lieberman 1982, 253.

25. Preston 1986, chaps. 1 and 2 (especially pp. 23–25). See also Payne 1987, chaps. 20 and 21.

26. Preston 1986, 13, and Payne 1987, chaps. 20 and 21.

27. See Payne 1987, 543–48, and Tortella and Jiménez 1986, chap. 6, on the Matesa Affair and its political consequences.

28. The complexity of Matesa's organizational structure made it difficult for BCI's undermanned inspection staff to discover the discrepancies at first. Nonetheless, by 1968, the BCI had become aware of many irregularities and brought them to the attention of MOF officials. The MOF's failure to take timely action against Matesa fed speculation that top regime officials were implicated in the affair.

29. In addition to the claim that Opus Dei officials had chosen to ignore the irregularities, "it was loudly whispered that some of the funds unaccounted for had been sent abroad to finance the activities of Opus Dei in other countries" (Payne 1987, 544).

30. Ibid., 546. The Asociación Católica Nacional de Propaganda was also a Catholic lay organization.

31. Carrero had been pushing Franco for the formation of a new cabinet for eighteen months (Preston 1986, 23–24).

32. The regime declared frequent states of exception to deal with increasingly strident student protests and strikes. It imprisoned leaders of the clandestine opposition and labor unions and executed several suspected terrorists. Finally, it even used ultraright terrorism to intimidate and kill its opponents. See Carr and Fusi

1981, chap. 9. Nonetheless, the regime also implemented a few cautious political reforms in this period. See Payne 1987, 554–55.

33. Interview with a former MOF official, February 1990.

34. The proposed merger of two of the Big Seven banks in 1965 was vetoed by Franco himself because of his concern that the resulting bank would be too powerful. See López Rodó 1990, 592.

35. The most influential book was Muñoz 1969.

36. The most famous example involved Alberto Monreal Luque, minister of finance from 1969–73, who was forced to resign immediately after presenting a major tax reform proposal to the Council of Ministers. See Gunther 1980, 93–98.

37. Interview, February 1990. One of these economists, José Toribio Dávila, a student of Milton Friedman at the University of Chicago, became the general director of financial policy in the first Unión de Centro Democrático government. Several others, notably Mariano Rubio, Luis Rojo Duque, Raimundo Poveda Anadón, and Angel Madroñero, later held high-ranking posts in the BOS. Mariano Rubio and Luis Rojo Duque, for instance, went on to become the governor of the BOS.

38. Interview with a former PC official, July 1989.

39. The most important of these were the *técnicos comerciales y economistas del estado.* These high-level economic civil servants were recruited and trained by the MOC, but many of them later found their way into other ministries. See Dehesa 1994, 139.

40. Interview with a participant in this committee, February 1990.

41. Liberalization would have increased the cost of credit, but there is little reason to believe that it would have significantly altered the growth rate of the Spanish economy. Real interest rates were extremely low or negative in this period, and demand for credit exceeded supply. Evidence from a later period (the mid-1970s) indicates that demand for credit in Spain was very inelastic. See Argandoña 1981. Thus, a reasonable conclusion is that firms would have continued to demand funds at higher rates and carry out productive investment.

42. See chapter 3 on the features of SRLs.

43. Quantitative controls had been responsible for a "stop-and-go" pattern of economic activity throughout the 1960s. In most instances, the implementation of controls had led to protracted periods of recession since the MOF had usually erred by making them overly restrictive.

44. The MOF originally intended to liberalize loan interest rates for maturities of eighteen months or more. It changed this to three years or more after firms protested.

45. RRs differed greatly from one type of intermediary to another, creating both economic policy problems (e.g., the difficulty of controlling monetary aggregates as funds shifted from one type of intermediary to another) and political controversy (notably, charges that there was an uneven playing field). These issues were only resolved in 1978 when the MOF applied uniform RRs to all intermediaries.

46. ICs affected only banks, as savings banks continued to be regulated by a different and more stringent set of coefficients. (The MOF later imposed ICs on

savings banks as well.) Authorities initially established the total ICs for universal banks at 22% of total liabilities (15% to "public funds," 7% to favored industrial sectors). Industrial banks were free of the "public funds" component of the ICs initially (although later they also had to invest in public funds). The MOF set interest rates on loans provided through ICs at well below prevailing market rates. See Poveda Anadón 1986 for a thorough discussion of ICs.

47. Interview with a banker, February 1990.

48. Foreign reserves jumped from $1.79 billion at the end of 1970 to $6.78 billion by the end of 1973. As a result, the stock of high-powered money grew by 28% in 1973 alone, causing inflation to reach 14% that year. See Rojo and Pérez 1977, 10.

49. Martínez Méndez 1980, n. 14.

50. Ibid., 6.

51. See Hernández Armenteros 1986, chap. 1.

52. Poveda Anadón notes that in 1979 "commissions charged for discounting operations were set at about 64% of the interest rate charged on these operations (9%); this fixed the cost of discounting at 14.5%, a full 5.5% over the legally established rate of 9%" (1982, 64).

53. Interview with a former MOF official, February 1990.

54. One respondent in the BOS claimed that in the early 1970s most firms' sophistication in financial matters was low because rigid financial controls had not given them much incentive to gain technical expertise. Interview, June 1989.

55. See Preston 1986, chaps. 2 and 3, and Payne 1987, chaps. 21 and 22.

56. Payne 1987, 593.

57. Strike activity, for example, continued to rise. There were 811 strikes affecting 441,042 workers and leading to 11,120,251 hours of labor lost in 1973; in 1976, there were 1,568 strikes affecting 3,638,952 workers and leading to 110,016,240 hours lost. See Payne 1987, 555.

58. Ibid.

59. Preston 1986, 55.

60. Interview with a former MOF official, February 1990. On the "Barrera reforms," see Pérez de Ayala 1974.

61. The real sector reforms consisted of measures to dismantle the still-extensive system of state price controls, subsidies, and protectionist barriers and overhaul Spain's antiquated fiscal policies. They were never implemented.

62. Banks denounced this tactic. For example, see "Editorial," *Banca Española,* November 1974.

63. On the 1974 reforms, see López Roa 1981, chap. 7, sec. 2.

64. In the period 1978–85, Spain experienced a massive banking crisis. The crisis was partly attributable to the failure to implement prudential regulation in conjunction with the 1974 reforms. This topic is discussed in chapter 6.

65. See López Roa 1981, chap. 7.

66. "Operating costs" in Spanish banking statistics have four components: personnel expenses, general expenses, taxes, and amortization. Amortization and taxes as a percentage of total assets remained relatively stable throughout the 1970s and 1980s; therefore, changes in operating costs were due to higher person-

nel costs and general expenses. See Torrero Mañas 1982, chap. 2, on this issue. Not all banks were equally successful in handling the increase in costs produced by expansion. Most scholars believe that cost increases in this period helped push some banks into insolvency after 1977. For example, see Cuervo 1988, sec. 3.1.2.

67. Spanish banks continued to have the highest ratio of profits before tax to volume of business of banks in any country studied by Revell (1980). In 1976, Spanish banks had a ratio of 1.66%, whereas banks in all other countries had ratios of less than 1% except for Switzerland 1.44%, West Germany 1.11%, and Canada 1.00%.

68. No data are available on how the reforms affected the intermediation efficiency of financial entities other than banks in this period.

69. For an example of the banking sector's reaction, see *Banca Española*, November 11, 1974.

70. Banks were able to make gentleman's pacts work in the 1980s, as discussed in chapter 6.

71. See Preston 1986, chap. 3, for an overview of this period.

72. Carr and Fusi speculate that Arias was the best choice of the three candidates forwarded to the king by the Council of the Realm. By law, the king could only choose one of these three candidates. See Carr and Fusi 1981, 212.

73. Discussions of economic policy in the transition period are Lieberman 1982, chap. 5; López Roa 1978; Martínez Méndez 1982; and Ros Hombravella 1987.

74. Public bank lending increased about 23% annually from 1973 to 1977. See Banco de España, *Boletín Estadístico,* January 1979.

75. Martínez Méndez noted that authorities met all their M3 growth targets for the period 1974 to 1977. He argued that, given the sharp increases in salaries and the price of petroleum products in these years, "a less accommodating monetary policy would have had little effect on the evolution of prices, but a very strong impact on economic activity and employment." Consequently, he concluded that the BOS carried out the strictest feasible policy, preventing even more dramatic increases in inflation in the period. See Martínez Méndez 1982, 51.

Chapter 5

1. See McDonough, Barnes, and López de Piña 1986.

2. The UCD's and PSOE's overall economic programs varied in some important respects. These contrasts, however, stemmed mainly from their differing ability to implement certain elements of essentially similar economic programs. Chapters 6 and 7 develop this point more fully.

3. *Wall Street Journal,* November 9, 1995.

4. See the discussion in Lancaster 1989. Chapter 3 of this book examines the composition and influence of the financial oligarchy.

5. See Pérez Díaz 1990, 1993.

6. New democracies seem to have greater success implementing structural adjustment programs when they are able to build upon the reform efforts of a pre-

ceding authoritarian regime. See Callaghy 1993 and Haggard and Kaufman 1995 on this point.

7. Gunther 1996, 28 n. 20. Spain was actually a net creditor in international capital markets.

8. For example, Maravall 1993 and Pérez Diaz 1987.

9. Lancaster 1989.

10. In 1982, the OECD noted that the UCD made considerable progress in economic adjustment, especially considering the tough conditions of the period. See "Informe de la OCED sobre la Economía Española, 14 de mayo de 1982," cited in Linde 1990, 53. Critics of the UCD may be unduly harsh because they have focused on the party's failures in the areas of energy, industrial, and labor policy. These areas remain problematic today.

11. Gunther 1989. Gunther describes three cases of seemingly irrational behavior by party elites in the early 1980s.

12. See Gunther, Sani, and Shabad 1988; Maravall 1982; and Preston 1986, chap. 4, on this period.

13. Suárez used several tactics to achieve this result. Some recalcitrant deputies were sent on an official junket to Panama via the Caribbean. Suárez promised others seats in the future Senate. See Preston 1986, 101.

14. Gunther 1989, 838.

15. Ibid., 837.

16. As Donaghy and Newton note, the term *Cortes* has come to refer to the national Parliament, whether expressed through one or two chambers (1987, 37). The two chambers are the Congress of Deputies and the Senate.

17. The D'Hondt method allocates seats to parties on the basis of highest average. The highest average is obtained by dividing the number of votes received by a party by the number of seats already obtained plus one. The party with the highest average is awarded the seat, and the process is repeated until all seats are assigned. See Lijphart 1994, app. A, for more on the mechanics of the D'Hondt method.

18. As Gunther indicates, the D'Hondt method penalizes small parties in the extreme unless the district size is very large or the party system is highly fractionalized. These conditions generally do not hold for Spain. See Gunther 1989, 838–41. The impact of the D'Hondt formula and district size on vote distribution for three different types of Spanish provinces is shown in Gunther, Sani, and Shabad 1988, 48–50.

19. Disproportionality measures the deviation of seat shares from vote shares. Gallagher (1991) computed disproportionality values for eighty-two elections in twenty-three countries based on three different indices. Spain scored highest on all three indices for countries with PR systems; it had the fifth highest scores when countries with majoritarian systems were included.

20. Tagepera and Shugart 1989, 147 n. 4. The effective number of parties is a measure that indicates "the number of hypothetical equal-sized parties that would have the same effect on fractionalization of the party system as have the actual parties of varying sizes" (ibid., 79). Table 5.2 is an updated version of a table appearing in Gunther 1994.

21. See Lijphart 1994, chap. 3, on these concepts.

22. Gunther 1989. Strategic behavior by voters and contributors involves voting for or donating money to a party with good electoral prospects instead of a preferred party that is perceived to have little hope of winning. Strategic behavior by politicians is discussed later in this chapter.

23. Ibid., 836.

24. See Gunther 1989.

25. See McDonough, Barnes, and López de Piña 1986. For instance, the electorate generally lacked economic policy preferences derived from firm partisan identification; however, it did hold the government responsible for economic prosperity. For more on the political predispositions of the Spanish populace, see Gunther, Sani, and Shabad, chaps. 5–8.

26. Gunther, Sani, and Shabad (1988) examine the general political and electoral strategies of the major Spanish parties in the period 1977–86. Stepan and Linz also point out that Spain's first elections were unionwide, not regional; they suggest that if regional elections had come first, "the incentives for creation of all-union parties and an all-union agenda would have been greatly reduced" (1992, 127).

27. The Partido Popular was the primary force behind the creation of the UCD. The UCD did not present an elaborate electoral program; it only published a short statement of principles a week before the election that did not discuss its economic program in great detail.

28. See *Banca Española,* January 1977.

29. See *Banca Española,* May 1977.

30. Rivases 1988, 28.

31. Preston 1986, 124.

32. Ibid., 123.

33. Shefter 1978.

34. Ibid., 415.

35. Ibid.

36. See Caciagli 1986; Gunther, Sani, and Shabad 1988, particularly 127–45; and Huneeus 1985.

37. I refer to Suárez and his cohorts as "party leadership" because until 1980, Suárez exercised considerable control over the party and its strategies. After 1980, Suárez's authority eroded as his popularity declined and the influence of the barons grew. This is examined in chapter 6.

38. Suárez required all deputies to submit an undated letter of resignation before taking office. Suárez delegated the composition of electoral lists to Calvo Sotelo, the UCD's secretary, and until 1981, a close collaborator.

39. See Gunther, Sani, and Shabad 1988.

40. See *Actualidad Económica,* April 12, 1977, 18–31. The economic program he sought to implement once in office closely matched the recommendations outlined in the interview.

41. Several published reports recounted this demand. For example, see *Actualidad Económica,* December 31, 1977.

42. The IMF provided $300 million to ease Spain's balance-of-payments prob-

lems but did not influence the decision to implement a stabilization package and structural reforms. See Muns 1984.

43. Inflation was running at an annual rate of 25% in July 1977, and economists predicted 30% inflation by year's end. The 1976 balance-of-payments deficit was $4.3 billion (4.0% of GNP), and the deficit for 1977 had already reached $3.2 billion by July. Growth in the period 1975–78 had slowed to an annual average of 2.3%, down from around 6.0% in the early 1970s. See Martínez Méndez 1982 for further details.

44. Indeed, as recently as 1975, the Spanish economy had suffered a significant slowdown in growth (to 1.1%), negative growth in industrial production and capital investment, and serious balance-of-payments deficits (3.3% of GNP).

45. Gunther, Sani, and Shabad 1988, 143–44.

46. The creation of the MOE was part of a larger administrative reform. The UCD implemented the reorganization by decree, not through legislation, thereby avoiding a debate in the Cortes on the matter. See *El País,* July 5, 1977.

47. Several studies have identified the cohesiveness of the economic policy-making team as a variable that greatly affects a government's ability to formulate and implement appropriate economic policies. For example, see Nelson 1990.

48. Interview, February 1990.

49. Pérez Díaz 1987, 229.

50. On the Pacts, see Bermeo and García Durán 1994 and Pérez Díaz 1987.

51. The UCD told the leaders of the recently formed Confederación Española de Organizaciones Empresariales (CEOE) that the government would keep them abreast of the negotiations but would not involve them formally. (The next section examines the CEOE.) Díaz and Guindal suggest that the UCD adopted this policy to avoid granting the CEOE status as the legitimate representative of the business community. The UCD hoped that this would keep business weak and divided, facilitating the passage of controversial reforms (like the overhaul of the fiscal system). See Díaz and Guindal 1990, 143.

52. See *El País,* October 13, 1977, and November 25, 1977, for representative declarations.

53. See Díaz and Guindal 1990, especially chap. 8.

54. Maravall 1993 and Przeworski 1991, chap. 4.

55. Inflation dropped to 16.5% by mid-1978. See Banco de España, *Boletín Estadístico,* April 1979.

56. The Inter-Confederation Framework Agreement 1980, the National Agreement on Employment 1981, the Inter-Confederation Agreement 1983, and the Economic and Social Agreement 1984 all represented efforts to restrain wage growth, usually in exchange for government or employer concessions on other labor issues (e.g., unemployment compensation). This has led some observers to argue that a form of "neocorporatism" has emerged in Spain. See Pérez Díaz 1987, especially 227–39, and Roca 1987.

57. Pérez Díaz 1987, 224. See also Díaz and Guindal 1990, chap. 3.

58. See Linz 1981, 401.

59. Rivases 1988 and Graham 1984, chap. 5.

60. Roca 1987, 250.

61. Martínez and Pardo 1985.

62. The CEPYME remained an independent organization and was granted a permanent seat on the CEOE's executive committee.

63. The AEB remained an independent organization and was given a permanent seat on the CEOE's executive committee.

64. A particularly divisive set of issues concerned the causes of high interest rates and what should be done to lower the cost of credit. Chapter 6 examines these issues and the views of banks and firms.

65. The government also raised wage taxes slightly to give the appearance that the cost of tax reform would be shared fairly.

66. As the next two chapters show, the UCD's inability to establish an efficient means of raising revenue and control government spending led policymakers to increase taxation of the banking system and the inflation tax to fund government activities well into the 1980s. This had dire consequences for the health of financial markets and the economy generally.

67. Blasco Sànchez 1984, 175.

68. See Díaz and Guindal 1990 and Gunther, Sani, and Shabad 1988, 125.

69. García Díez 1991, 38.

70. See Banco de España, *Boletín Estadístico*, September 1978.

71. See *El País*, July 13, 1977, for an example of statements by union leaders.

72. For details on the reforms, see Cuervo García, Parejo Gámir, and Rodríguez Sáiz 1988; López Roa 1981; and Toribio 1983.

73. See Armijo 1993 and World Bank 1989, chaps. 4 and 9. The Brazilian case is examined in chapter 8.

74. Approximately 80% of all preferential credit originated in the ICs imposed on intermediaries; either directly, through bank lending to favored companies, or indirectly, through banks' obligatory purchases of investment certificates from the Treasury (which used the proceeds to finance the public banking system).

75. See Lukauskas 1992, chap. 6, for details on the timetable.

76. The MOE raised interest rates on most preferential credit by 33% to 50%. See ibid. for details.

77. See *Actualidad Económica*, April 12, 1977, and July 1, 1977.

78. The gross opportunity cost imposed on intermediaries roughly equaled the difference in interest rates between voluntary loans and those provided through ICs, multiplied by the volume of credit supplied through the ICs. Poveda Anadón estimated that in 1979 the gross opportunity costs imposed by ICs on all intermediaries totaled 200 billion pesetas (roughly $3 billion). Net opportunity costs, however, were probably considerably lower. Intermediaries (particularly banks) cross-subsidized these loans by increasing interest rates on lending not controlled by the state. See Poveda Anadón 1982, especially p. 114, and Torrero Mañas 1982.

79. Interviews with former MOE officials, February 1990. Some firms called for the elimination of ICs in November 1977. However, this demand was only one of a number of proposals dealing with economic policy and was not repeated subsequently. See *Actualidad Económica*, December 6, 1977.

80. Funds channeled through ICs to the sector had totaled 118 billion pesetas

in 1977 but would only amount to 80 billion pesetas in 1978 if the reductions were implemented as planned. See *Actualidad Económica,* November 15, 1977.

81. In addition to requesting a halt in reductions of ICs, capital goods producers asked for increased export credits for their sector, a domestic content requirement (requiring forward-linked industries to buy Spanish-produced capital goods), and greater import restrictions. See *Actualidad Económica,* October 18, 1977.

82. *Actualidad Económica,* December 6, 1977.

83. The MOE also wished to establish uniform RRs across intermediaries to alleviate monetary control problems stemming from the movement of funds among different types of deposits or intermediaries. See Martínez Méndez 1980, sec. 3.

84. A clear statement of savings banks' demands may be found in the record of the Forty-fifth Assembly of Spanish Savings Banks, held in June 1977. See *El País,* July 1, 1977, for a summary of the assembly's proceedings.

85. A particularly acrimonious statement of the banking sector's position is "Editorial," *Banca Española,* March 1976. Banks were correct in asserting that savings banks enjoyed considerable fiscal advantages. Nevertheless, most neutral observers agreed that savings banks were at a serious disadvantage vis-à-vis banks overall because of the government's extensive control over their allocation of credit.

86. Leasing companies purchase goods (e.g., machinery) and lease them to firms. For firms, leasing is often an excellent alternative to taking out a loan from financial intermediaries to purchase goods.

87. Banks had been advised of possible financial reforms, including interest rate deregulation, in informal consultations with government officials in early 1977. See *El País,* March 9 and 11, 1977.

88. Barallat López 1988, 215. Several bankers interviewed for this study corroborated this analysis (interviews, July 1989). They stressed, however, that even institutions that viewed interest rate reform more favorably remained very cautious.

89. A study commissioned by the savings banks concluded, "for savings banks, [the removal of interest rate controls] is incompatible with the maintenance of the current system of investment coefficients; we cannot offer higher deposit rates to maintain market share since we cannot cover their higher cost by increasing our loan rates" (Confederación Española de Cajas de Ahorros 1978, 112).

90. *Actualidad Económica,* January 15, 1977.

91. Spanish banks in fact initiated an expansion abroad, opening branches in Europe, the United States, and Latin America. See Graham 1984, 100.

92. One former MOE official stated that the opening Spanish markets to foreign banks generated the greatest banking sector opposition of any of the financial reforms implemented in this period (interview, February 1990).

93. The UCD issued its new foreign banking rules by executive decree because it believed that it would be difficult to get a bill through the Cortes.

94. See Díaz and Guindal 1990 and Rivases 1988, chap. 1.

95. A third possible form of foreign bank was the "representative office," but it

had little practical importance. See Cuervo García, Parejo Gámir, and Rodríguez Sáiz 1988, 180.

96. See Alvarez Canal 1982, 73.

97. Cuervo García, Parejo Gámir, and Rodríguez Sáiz 1989, 183.

98. Alvarez Canal 1982, 74–75.

99. Foreign banks were also responsible for the development of an efficient secondary market for discounted paper, the introduction of floating rate loans, and several new forms of deposits. See Cuervo García, Parejo Gámir, and Rodríguez Sáiz 1989, 183–84; and OECD 1987, 61.

100. See Martínez Méndez 1980.

101. The volume of completed transactions in the interbank market grew from 38 million pesetas in 1979 to 412 million in 1985. See Banco de España, *Boletín Estadístico,* April 1986.

102. Before 1979, only a few Spanish firms were allowed to raise capital abroad, and their borrowing was subject to restrictions.

Chapter 6

1. Interviews with several economic policymakers, February 1990.

2. See *El País,* February 24, 1978.

3. See *Actualidad Económica,* December 12, 1977. Oliart and Fuentes also clashed publicly over the formulation of a national energy plan. See *El País,* February 15, 1978.

4. *El País,* February 24, 1978, and *Actualidad Económica,* March 4, 1978.

5. Rumors also circulated that the CEOE, angered by Fuentes's fiscal reforms, had pressured UCD leadership to dismiss him. See Caciagli 1986, 249.

6. Suárez first offered the post to Fernández Ordoñez, who favored policies similar to those of Fuentes. Fernández Ordoñez declined the offer for personal reasons. See *El País,* February 25, 1978.

7. Ibid.

8. Most business leaders, however, were not happy with the choice of Rodríguez because his views were not representative of those of the business community. They also noted ironically that Rodríguez was Suárez's brother-in-law.

9. ETA is a Basque separatist organization that emerged in the 1960s. The most radical faction, ETA-Militar, has pursued terrorism against the institutions of the central government, especially the Guardia Civil.

10. Díaz and Guindal 1990 present a detailed journalistic account of the relations between the UCD and CEOE.

11. Opposition parties called a special parliamentary session to demand an explanation for Fuentes's resignation and debate the direction of future economic policy. The Cortes subsequently passed a motion condemning the UCD's handling of economic policy. See *Actualidad Económica,* April 25, 1978.

12. Preston 1986, 141.

13. The improvement in the balance of payments was mainly due to the devaluation of the peseta in 1977. Spanish imports as a percentage of GNP dropped from 16.5% in 1977 to 14.4% in 1978; exports rose from 14.4% to 15.1%.

14. See *Actualidad Económica,* February 11, 1978.

15. Argandoña Ramiz (1981) estimated that real credit to the private sector fell by 2.3% in 1978.

16. Cuervo 1988, 54. Cuervo notes, however, that it was a drop in product margins rather than the higher cost of credit per se that was responsible for the problems facing Spanish firms in this period (1988, 54–60).

17. Argandoña Ramiz 1981.

18. *Actualidad Económica,* June 10, 1978.

19. Some prominent economists, notably Antonio Torrero Mañas, supported business's position. Torrero contended that the lack of competition in the financial sector allowed banks to transfer any increases in the price paid for liabilities or operating costs to the real sector in the form of higher interest rates and commissions. He also agreed that interest rate reform was hurting the real sector by driving up rates to socially excessive levels. See Torrero Mañas 1982.

20. See Asociación Española de la Banca Privada (AEB) 1979 and Termes's frequent declarations in *El País* (e.g., June 27, 1980).

21. Provisions for bad loans jumped from an average of 0.1% of total assets between 1970 and 1975 to 0.7% between 1978 and 1980.

22. Argandoña Ramiz 1981 is an important study on this issue.

23. The AEB's proposal, "La financiación crediticia a medio y largo plazo," is summarized in *Actualidad Económica,* July 7, 1979.

24. Aware of the UCD's interest in reducing the cost of credit, the AEB continued to propose reforms that it contended would contribute to lower interest rates. In 1979, for instance, banks asked the MOE to decrease the required ratio of paid-in capital to total deposits from 8% to 4%. They suggested that this would permit them to reduce interest rates since they could achieve an acceptable return on equity while charging less for credit.

25. The number of firms in suspension of payments and declaring bankruptcy increased by 70% and 45%, respectively, from the period 1975–77 to 1978–80. The liabilities involved in these actions increased by 170%. See Cuervo 1988, cuadro 3.6.

26. The number of workers affected by the elimination of jobs, layoffs, and workday reductions increased by 150% from the period 1975–77 to 1978–80. See Cuervo 1988, cuadro 3.5.

27. In 1981–82, the thirty nationalized firms had losses totaling 71.7 billion pesetas and employed 66,000 workers (García Fernández 1984, 197). In this period, the government was already supplying state-owned companies held by INI with an average of ninety-five billion pesetas of working capital annually. See Martín Aceña and Comín 1989, 154.

28. By 1984, these institutions were required to lend 20% of their deposits to priority sectors. Authorities also imposed reserve and capital adequacy requirements on these intermediaries. See Poveda Anadón 1986, 57–61, for details.

29. The UCD announced its "Plan de Ordenación Industrial" in 1978. It issued several decrees in 1981 and passed a law covering industrial restructuring in 1982. See Albentosa 1985.

30. See González Grimaldo 1982 and Cuervo García, Parejo Gámir, and Rodríguez Sáiz 1988 on SGRs.

31. SGRs proved to be ineffective in increasing the flow of credit to SMCs. Intermediaries were suspicious of the guarantee offered by the SGRs and often refused to lend to SMCs unless they provided additional collateral. The creation of the Sociedad Mixta de Segundo Aval (Second Guarantee Society), whose purpose was to provide the secondary collateral that intermediaries requested, a few years later improved the flow of credit to SMCs only slightly.

32. For example, see Patrick 1994, 402.

33. Interviews with two former MOE officials, February 1990. See also *El País,* January 26, 1978. Entrepreneurial activity by some major political parties, especially the PCE and PSOE, also had an impact. These parties sought the support of SMCs by attacking the government's financial policies as prejudicial to these firms. See *El País,* January 15, 1978, and *Actualidad Económica,* February 17, 1979. This tactic proved partially successful: the Catalan Association of SMCs encouraged its members to vote for either the PCE or PSOE in the 1979 elections, and CEPYME withheld its anticipated endorsement from either the UCD or Coalición Democrática (CD, Democratic Coalition), the former AP party. See Gunther, Sani, and Shabad 1988, 186.

34. Interviews with two former MOE officials, February 1990.

35. Cuervo (1988) notes that official figures are conservative because they exclude banks that failed but were not included on the official list of insolvent banks for various reasons.

36. The most complete account of the Spanish banking crisis is Cuervo 1988.

37. In fact, it was common practice for banks to list the new loan as a performing asset and register liquidation of the old loan as a profit on their balance sheet (even though no profit had occurred). See Juan 1988.

38. Of course, not all bank-based systems have experienced major banking crises, and securities market-based systems have not been free of similar problems (e.g., the United States).

39. Cuervo 1988, 66–70.

40. See table 6.5. The 1974 reforms are discussed in chapter 4.

41. Interviews with several former bankers and BOS officials, February 1990.

42. See Lukauskas 1992, chap. 7, for a summary of the evolution of the crisis and government actions to remedy it.

43. The expropriation was later extended to all 647 companies belonging to the Rumasa group. At the time of expropriation, seventeen of the eighteen banks were in danger of immediate failure. The government took over management of the banks and floated public debt to cover the cost of making these banks solvent. Most banks fully supported the expropriation of the Rumasa banks, as they had been deeply disturbed by their irregular operations. Moreover, they accepted the government's assurances that the expropriations would not lead to permanent nationalization of Rumasa or the expropriation of other banks. The government in fact later privatized these banks.

44. Cuervo 1988, chap. 5.

45. *Actualidad Económica,* October 9, 1980.

46. On this point, see Argandoña Ramiz 1981, 61–64.

47. Ibid., 67.

48. Huneeus 1985, 207.

49. The measures came as somewhat of a surprise. It had been widely believed that the MOE was preparing major financial reforms, including further interest rate deregulation, a greater reduction of credit floors, and measures to modernize the stock exchanges. See *Actualidad Económica,* December 9, 1978.

50. External borrowing rose by 108% between 1976 and 1979. See Banco de España, *Boletín Estadístico,* September 1980.

51. *Actualidad Económica,* September 8, 1979.

52. The AEB argued that the government should not promote greater competition in the banking system because it would jeopardize its solvency. See AEB 1979. However, banks' lobbying efforts were concentrated on other issues, namely, reducing the opportunity cost of selective credit policies.

53. Interview with an official involved in drafting the legislation, February 1990.

54. Interview with two BOS officials, May 1989 and February 1990.

55. See Preston 1986, 170–72. One poll indicated that more than half of those who had voted for the UCD in the 1979 general elections would not vote for it again. There was deep dissatisfaction with the UCD's economic record, especially the sharp increase in unemployment.

56. See Linde 1990, 46–47.

57. In 1980, for instance, a debate raged over the best way to manage unemployment and the energy shortage. García Díez and Bustelo favored immediate structural reforms of labor and energy markets, whereas Abril and Leal advocated delaying them. See Huneeus 1985, 276; Preston 1986, 173; and *El País,* May 2, 1980.

58. Preston 1986, 174.

59. The ministries of Economics and Commerce were combined in 1980.

60. The leader of the Social Democrats, Fernández Ordoñez, eventually joined the PSOE.

61. Huneeus 1985, 276–77. Several individuals identified with a more interventionist approach also became or remained ministers, notably Ignacio Bayon Mariné (Ministry of Industry), Jaime Lamo de Espinosa (Ministry of Agriculture) and José Luis Alvarez (Ministry of Transportation). Bayon, for example, favored a policy of supplying preferential credit to industrial firms targeted for restructuring (although he was committed to intensifying the process of restructuring, not simply using state funds to support declining sectors as the UCD had tended to do in the past). The presence of these officials in the cabinet continued to make it difficult for the UCD government to develop a coherent, forceful economic plan.

62. See Linde 1990, 46–47.

63. See *Banca Española,* June 1980.

64. Interview with a former MOEC official, February 1990. See also *El País,* January 6, 1981.

65. AEB 1980. The AEB continued its deceptive tactic of equating the process of financial liberalization with the elimination of credit controls. Therefore, it

could state that it favored deregulation despite its opposition to most of the reforms being considered.

66. In early 1980, two of the Big Seven banks had stated publicly that they favored interest rate deregulation, raising hope among MOEC officials that the others might as well. See *Actualidad Económica,* February 23, 1980, and April 5, 1980. It soon became apparent, however, that most Big Seven banks actually opposed it. Small- and medium-sized banks, some of them deregulation proponents, also took a stand against the removal of controls because they feared that increased competition could lead to additional bank failures and takeover attempts. See *Actualidad Económica,* January 15, 1981.

67. *El País,* June 19, 1980, and January 6, 1981.

68. See Confederación Española de Organizaciones Empresariales 1980 and "Reflexiones sobre el sistema financiero," summarized in *El País,* January 2, 1981. A later restatement of the CEOE's views is Confederación Española de Organizaciones Empresariales 1981.

69. The ICs of banks were to be lowered by 0.10% every month instead of every two months; the ICs of savings banks were to be reduced by 0.25% every month instead of 0.10% every month.

70. The MOEC promised to subsidize loans to the housing sector in exchange for bank commitments to provide an agreed-upon quantity of credit at a fixed interest rate. Banks showed little interest in participating in the pacts because they were asked to supply loans at below-market rates. Consequently, the pacts generally failed to meet their goals.

71. *El País,* January 21, 1981.

72. See *El País,* January 18, 1981, and *Actualidad Económica,* January 15, 1981.

73. On Suárez's resignation, see Gunther, Sani, and Shabad 1988, 420–23, and Huneeus 1985, chap. 7.

74. See Linde 1990, 49–50, and Ros Hombravela 1987, 219–21.

75. See Linde 1990, 47–54.

76. See *Actualidad Económica,* October 14, 1982, on the stance of various market participants on the expansion of direct financial markets.

77. On the Japanese case, see Rosenbluth 1989, chap. 5.

78. Interviews, July 1989 and February 1990.

79. See Toribio 1983 on the reforms.

80. See Torrero Mañas 1989a, chap. 4.

81. In an effort to deepen money markets, policymakers also promoted the existing secondary market in discounted paper and created a market for commercial paper.

82. See Santillana del Barrio 1982 on the law and its consequences.

83. In "cross lending," bank A lends to firms controlled by bank B while bank B lends to firms controlled by bank A. Crossed lending emerged as a way to circumvent controls on concentration of risk.

84. OECD 1988, 58.

85. Public banks also gained market share, but this was due to government policy that funneled more lending through the public banking system.

86. See OECD 1991, 58.

87. See Öniş and Riedel 1993, chap. 11.

88. See Galbis 1986.

89. See Rivases 1988 on the points that follow.

90. Nevertheless, the cohesiveness of the Big Seven banks was coming under increasing strain. Graham notes that a generational change in management had occurred in the Bilbao, Popular, Vizcaya, and Hispano banks, whereas the "old guard" remained in place in the Central, Banesto, and Santander banks. The generation gap between the two groups of banks exacerbated their rivalries and differences. See Graham 1984, 99.

91. The incremental output/capital ratio equals real GDP growth divided by the national capital investment rate. Higher ratios indicate greater allocative efficiency. Various factors, for example, external supply shocks, may distort the validity of the ratio as an indicator of efficiency.

92. Interviews, July 1989 and February 1990.

93. See Lancaster 1989, Maravall 1993, and Pérez Diaz 1987. Their focus on industrial and energy policy, I believe, leads them to an overly critical view of the UCD record.

Chapter 7

1. Pérez (1997) suggests that financial policy neglected the needs of domestic producer groups, imposing high real financial costs on Spanish firms. As I detail in a later section, this view is not supported by the evidence.

2. After-tax profitability was 4.7% (as a percentage of total sales) in Spain versus an average of roughly 3.5% in the majority of OECD countries (OECD 1992, 59–60).

3. Figures are for the period 1986–92. Spain's average annual GDP growth was 1.2% between 1980 and 1985 (World Bank 1994).

4. The UCD's parliamentary group had shrunk from 168 to 123, due to the desertion of groups like the Social Democrats and key individuals like Suárez. The UCD concluded that it could not survive a vote of confidence. In addition, it hoped that early elections would give new rivals, such as Suárez's recently formed CDS party, less time to organize.

5. Gunther, Sani, and Shabad 1988, 402.

6. Ibid., 407. The radical rhetoric of the party's declarations and its occasional threats to unleash "mass mobilizations" frightened many voters.

7. The most salient change was the demotion of Marxism from the status of official doctrine to one of several intellectual traditions within the party. Also, the PSOE dropped references to mass mobilizations and eliminated its "assembly style" of internal deliberations, thereby enabling party leaders to increase discipline over party membership. See ibid., 409.

8. See Bermeo and García Durán 1994, Dehesa 1994, Gunther 1996, López Claros 1988, and Maravall 1993 for reviews of Socialist economic policy.

9. Most accounts of the period highlight the PSOE's ability to carry out its restructuring plan despite high political costs. Díaz and Guindal contend that the

program actually implemented was less ambitious and harsh than the original formulation. See Díaz and Guindal 1990, 230–31.

10. Maravall 1993, 94–96, and Gunther 1996, 31–34.

11. They did not meet this objective, however, as there were sharp increases in transfers to firms and pension and unemployment compensation payments.

12. Garrett and Lange 1991.

13. See especially Bermeo and García Durán 1984.

14. See López Claros 1988 and Maravall 1993 on Spain's economic situation in the early 1980s.

15. Maravall 1993, 114. Keeler (1993) develops this argument more generally.

16. McDonough, Barnes, and López de Piña 1986. See also Maravall 1993, 121–22.

17. McDonough, Barnes, and López de Piña, 466.

18. Ibid., 449.

19. See Maravall 1993.

20. See Garrett and Lange 1986 on how the links between leftist governments and labor affect economic performance and policy-making.

21. Fishman 1990, 187.

22. See Díaz and Guindal 1990 for a journalistic treatment of the divisions within the Socialist governments on economic policy.

23. Other key officials also supported economic adjustment. In the area of financial policy, the most important were Guillermo de la Dehesa and José Borrell, both secretaries of the economy, and Raimundo Ortega Fernández and Pedro Méndez, both directors of the treasury and financial policy.

24. Boyer resigned his post in 1985 after becoming involved in a fierce power struggle within the upper levels of the Socialist party and government. Boyer had asked for the dismissal of several ministers who he believed were resisting the government's overall strategy. He also requested to be made vice president of economic affairs in order to establish greater personal control over other economic ministries. González declined these requests when other PSOE leaders protested. Boyer refused to retract his demands and had no choice but to resign.

25. The failure of the orthodox Socialist strategy in France also greatly influenced these officials. The French Socialists' efforts to expand the public sector, nationalize key industrial sectors and banking, and increase employment led to sluggish growth, inflation, balance-of-payments problems, and dramatic capital flight. Spanish Socialists did not want to commit the same mistakes.

26. See *El País,* November 11, 1983, for a clear statement of interventionists' views on financial policy.

27. Interview with a former MOEF official, February 1990. See also Maravall 1993, 94.

28. Undersecretaries are directly responsible for the administration of a ministry's programs and play a critical role in communications between the different bureaus within a ministry and across ministries.

29. *El País Internacional,* Sección Revista, March 18, 1991. González took to heart the advice of several of his European Socialist colleagues that a prime minister should firmly support his minister of finance. See Maravall 1993, 123.

30. See *Actualidad Económica,* February 9, 1984, for an example of the public attacks on Rubio's appointment. The controversy over Rubio and the BOS's policies resumed in 1988 when Rubio faced reappointment as governor. He was reappointed.

31. Given some of the PSOE's previous statements on financial policy, this start lent credence to the interpretation that the Socialists favored greater state intervention in financial markets. In previous years, the PSOE had asserted that if elected, it would (1) seek to "democratize" savings banks and rural savings banks by modifying their governing organs to give local government greater control over them; (2) halt the reduction of ICs at current levels; (3) expand the public banking system; (4) call for pacts between banks, industry, and the government to fund its industrial policy; and (5) promote the expansion of direct financial markets. See *Actualidad Económica,* November 5, 1981, and *Banca Española,* September 1982.

32. In 1983, the government announced a three-year financial plan that stated that further liberalization was necessary to improve the efficiency of the financial system. See *El País,* November 11, 1983.

33. The Socialists instituted only one additional credit control. In 1984, the high cost of industrial restructuring led the government to create a credit floor (dubbed *capital riesgo*) that required banks to provide credit for restructuring efforts. As discussed in a later section, policymakers began dismantling many selective credit programs in 1985.

34. OECD 1992, 48.

35. Banco de España, *Boletín Estadístico,* various issues. It was 1.8% in 1978 and 2.7% in 1980.

36. Ortega Fernández 1987a, 190.

37. Blasco Sánchez 1984, 175.

38. Ortega Fernández 1987b, 130.

39. Rodríguez Saiz and Parejo Gámir 1984, 69.

40. Maravall 1993, 84. See also pp. 100–1 on this point.

41. Durán Herrera 1984, 211. Direct subsidies to private firms also increased sharply. See Gimeno 1984, 93.

42. See Ortega Fernández 1987a. In the early 1980s, the market for public debt was very small; consequently, it would have been unable to absorb the large volume of bond issues required to cover deficits even if authorities had wished to pursue this course. UCD policymakers actually did take some initial steps (discussed later) in creating a functional public debt market in 1977. Until 1989, the Treasury had the legal right to borrow up to 12% of all state expenditures from the BOS at zero interest cost with no specified maturity.

43. Nonperforming assets, most of them loans to the Treasury, went from 31.6 to 43.4% of the BOS's portfolio between 1975 and 1987. See ibid., 193.

44. Banco de España, *Boletín Estadístico,* March 1980. On crowding out in this period, see Arasa Medina 1985 and López Roa 1984.

45. As already noted, when the PSOE entered office in 1982, the deficit as a percentage of GNP was 5.6%; after reaching a high of 6.7% in 1985, it dropped to around 3% in the late 1980s (which was about the OECD average). Government

budget deficits rose again in the 1990s, creeping back over 6%, as Spain suffered through a period of slow growth. See World Bank 1994.

46. See Andreu 1987a, 2,427.

47. See *El País,* December 10, 1982. The CEOE also criticized this policy on the grounds that it would increase the cost of bank credit.

48. López Claros notes that taxation of the banking system "contributed to the substantial spread between lending and deposit rates, as financial institutions attempted to preserve profitability through relatively high lending rates on that portion of their assets not subject to RRs and through relatively low rates on deposits." He adds, "not surprisingly, over time the spreads between borrowing and lending rates tended to be as large as the tax on the financial system implied by the reserve and investment coefficients" (López Claros 1988, 13, 21).

49. Calculated from data found in Banco de España, *Boletín Estadístico,* various issues.

50. The opportunity costs were low in 1984 but increased sharply afterward as the yield on public debt fell sharply. At most times, however, the yield on public debt still exceeded deposit interest rates, meaning that bank holdings at least generated a positive cash flow. See López Claros 1988, 21.

51. The inflation tax equals $I_t x (M_{t-1} + B_{t-1})$, where I_t is inflation in year t, M_{t-1} is the monetary base in year $t - 1$, and B_{t-1} is outstanding public debt in year $t - 1$. See Andreu 1987b on this point.

52. Ibid., 3,970.

53. PSOE-banking relations had not begun as poorly as some press reports originally indicated (see e.g., *El País,* December 10, 1982). González had assured bankers before the elections that the Socialists would not attempt nationalizations or implement several other unpopular changes in financial policy (e.g., an expansion in public banking). See Rivases 1988.

54. See *Actualidad Económica,* May 6, 1986.

55. Confronted with rapid money supply growth, the BOS had issued its own securities, called CRMs, to drain liquidity from the banking system. Operations with CRMs had been extremely costly for the BOS since private banks refused to purchase them unless their yields matched those prevailing in the interbank market. Interest paid on CRMs reached 275 billion pesetas in 1983 alone. This figure represented 98% of the Bank of Spain's financial costs that year. As this reduced revenue to the Treasury, the MOEF ordered the BOS to stop issuing them. See Ortega Fernández 1987b, 131 and n. 3.

56. At one point, the Treasury proposed using Postal Savings Banks to sell its securities directly to the public. Fierce banking sector opposition led the government to shelve the plan. Interview, BOS official, February 1990.

57. See *El País,* January 9, 1983, March 28, 1983, and May 23, 1983.

58. Interview with a participant in these negotiations, July 1989.

59. See *El País,* June 18, 1983.

60. López Claros 1988, 13.

61. Torrero Mañas 1989b reaches this conclusion.

62. See Barallat López 1988 on financial innovation in Spain.

63. See Sanz and Val 1993.

64. For the client, the yield on this operation equals the remainder of the repurchase price minus the sale price, divided by the sale price (adjusted for the maturity period).

65. OECD 1988, 63.

66. The contribution of income taxes to total revenues rose to 27% in 1987, up from only 22% in 1982. See López Claros 1988, 13.

67. Ibid.

68. Government expenditures as a percentage of GNP jumped from 36.7% in 1982 to 41.2% in 1987 (ibid). The biggest increases occurred in spending on physical and social infrastructure.

69. The principle architects of most reforms were Raimundo Ortega Fernández and Pedro Martínez Méndez, both directors of the treasury and financial policy; Guillermo de la Dehesa, secretary of the economy under Solchaga; and Raimundo Poveda Anadón, a top economist at the BOS.

70. The PSOE also won elections in 1989 and 1993 but lost its outright majority in the Cortes. The PSOE suffered a narrow loss to Partido Popular in the 1996 elections.

71. Spain applied for EC membership numerous times beginning in the early 1960s but was rebuffed due to EC displeasure over the Spanish political situation. The country's transition to democracy finally opened the door to accession, and its application for membership was formally accepted in 1977.

72. See Cuervo García, Parejo Gámir, and Rodríguez Sáiz 1988 and Gil 1985 for discussions of EC regulations and their impact on Spanish financial policy.

73. All the economic policymakers I interviewed (1989, 1990, 1992) asserted that Spain's wish to enter the EC was of less importance in shaping financial policy than the more basic motives of improving efficiency and monetary control. They affirmed that EC rules did influence policy in other areas (e.g., commercial policy) before Spain's entry into the EC.

74. The EC's "White Book" on financial service liberalization, a set of proposals that served as the basis for the Second Directive, was published in 1985.

75. Cuervo García, Parejo Gámir, and Rodríguez Sáiz 1988, 254.

76. Ibid., 285.

77. The EC issued the First Directive in 1977. The Directive "was not an important step in the process of harmonizing legislation across EC countries because its scope was limited and its principles vague" (Cuervo García, Parejo Gámir, and Rodríguez Sáiz 1988, 257). Spanish policymakers passed several regulations to comply with the First Directive in 1985.

78. Operating costs represented 3.3%, 2.1%, and 2.0% of total assets for Spanish, Italian, and French banks, respectively, in 1983 (*Actualidad Económica,* December 20, 1984). Spanish banks were much smaller than most European banks. To the extent that economies of scale are important in banking, this left Spanish banks at a competitive disadvantage. See *Noticias CEE,* November 1985. For a realistic analysis of the prospects of Spanish banks by a Spanish banker, see Boada Vilallonga 1985.

79. Without a uniform tax rate on financial assets, capital was likely to flow to

countries with the lowest tax rates once controls were removed, creating all sorts of economic and political problems.

80. Countries wishing to provide aid to industry had to request previous authorization from the EC Commission. The Commission would base its ruling on whether (1) the aid would transfer economic problems (e.g., unemployment) to other member states; (2) it would enable the firms in question to become economically viable; and (3) the aid was "transparent."

81. Government officials instead focused on why dismantling selective credit policies was critical for improving financial efficiency. For example, see the parliamentary debates on the reform of ICs, reproduced in *Papeles de Economía Española: Suplementos sobre el Sistema Financiero,* vol. 11, 1986. The failure to bring up EC rules is significant because authorities always invoked the need to meet EC regulations as a rationale for financial reform whenever possible in their efforts to implement other reforms.

82. See Ikenberry 1986 and Putnam 1988 on how leaders may use international constraints to achieve domestic policy goals.

83. The reduction in ICs was between 2% and 8.75% depending on the intermediary. The law established two categories within the ICs: the existing PDC and a new "special investments" coefficient (SIC). The MOEF fixed the PDC at 10% and SIC at 13% (with a minimum of 8% in the Treasury's investment certificates). This meant that all other "special investments" lending (e.g., to export industries) would account for only 5% of total lending. Among the private sector beneficiaries of the SIC were housing, sectors undergoing industrial restructuring, shipbuilding, and exporters.

84. Interview with a MOEF official, February 1990.

85. See *Actualidad Económica,* June 1, 1985.

86. In fact, the reduction of savings banks' ICs quickly improved their bottom line, as they were able to switch funds to lending yielding higher returns. See Sastre 1992, 52.

87. Intermediaries retained the obligation of investing 10% of their funds in public debt; thus, the reduction in ICs fell entirely on the "special investments" segment, virtually eliminating forced lending to the private sector.

88. Interview with a former high-ranking MOEF policymaker, February 1990.

89. See Lasheras and Alvarez 1988 and Prieto Pérez 1987.

90. *Actualidad Económica,* June 30, 1983.

91. Ibid.

92. See Bengoechea 1988, Bultó Millet 1988, and Dehesa 1988 on the reforms.

93. See Termes 1987 for an example of the banking sector's views on direct markets.

94. This is the usual practice because firms normally must make up the difference between the pensions they promise employees and the funds actually generated by their own and employees contributions to pension plans.

95. *Actualidad Económica,* November 3, 1986.

96. Spanish bank profits were almost 1% higher than those of banks in other EC countries. See Andreu 1992, 89. The trends described for banks also held true for savings banks, although they were less pronounced.

97. See Torrero Mañas 1989b and Banco de España 1993, 102.

98. Banco de España 1992, 99, 101–2.

99. Banco de España 1995a, supplement, 14–15.

100. See Banco de España 1991, 106–7, and Banco de España 1992, 99.

101. See OECD 1993, 33. Until the mid-1980s, monetary authorities did not attempt to influence interest rates directly, as they targeted monetary aggregates; high interest rates in this period reflected meager growth in domestic credit levels. After 1987, monetary authorities did try to influence interest rates directly. Table 7.3 shows the evolution of the BOS's ten-day intervention rate.

102. Inflation dropped from 11.5% in 1981–85 to 7.4% in 1986–90. Banco de España, *Boletín Estadístico,* August 1992. Economists believe that it was largely the result of annual growth in the money supply dropping 50% from 1981–85 to 1986–90. See OECD 1992, 55.

103. Direct investment constituted the bulk of capital inflows until 1991, when the Spanish government removed restrictions on portfolio investment. Capital controls in the 1987–89 period are discussed in Banco de España 1991, 82–83.

104. OECD 1992, 33.

105. See Cuervo 1988, 52–60.

106. It should be noted that, upon taking office, the Socialists had proposed a plan to encourage banks to purchase equity in industrial firms undergoing restructuring in exchange for an increase in interest rates on credit provided by banks through ICs. The government's motivation was to reduce the cost to the state of restructuring by pulling in private capital. See *Actualidad Económica,* January 10, 1983. This plan failed, as banks were not interested in investing in firms in declining sectors. Later on, the Socialists also encouraged certain banks (such as the BBV) to finance new enterprises or activities and to become core shareholders in the state-owned enterprises being privatized.

107. Profit margins in Spain grew at 4.4% and 3.5% in the periods 1981–85 and 1986–90, respectively; the OECD average for these periods were 2.3% and 0.6%. As already noted, after-tax profit in Spain was 4.7% in 1989, higher than the OECD average of 3.5%. OECD 1992, 59–60.

108. Novales (1988) indicated that private firms lowered their debt, whereas public enterprises increased their capitalization. Anecdotal evidence comes from several interviews (July 1989 and February 1990) and articles published in the financial press from 1988 onward.

109. Banco de España, *Central de balances,* November 1991, 37.

110. Banco de España 1993, 103, and Banco de España 1995a, 124.

111. Banco de España 1993, 100–106, and Banco de España 1994, 119–26.

112. Azofra and Martínez 1988. See also Saá 1991, which examines trends in the critical period 1984–88.

113. Azofra and Martínez 1988. The ratio was 1.33 in 1978 and 1.26 in 1982. The debt-to-equity ratio dropped further in the early 1990s. It was 0.80 in 1990 and 0.98 in 1994. See Banco de España, *Central de balances,* November 1995, 74.

114. Ibid. It was 41% in 1978 and 40% in 1982. Short-term financing as a percentage of total financing remained low in the early 1990s: it was 16.3% in 1990 and 16.0% in 1994 (ibid., 73).

115. See Banco de España, *Central de balances,* November 1991, 26–37, and Saá 1991, 148–54.

116. Torrero Mañas 1989a, 78.

Chapter 8

1. See Fry 1988, part 1, and Giovannini and Melo 1993.

2. For a general survey of interest rate and selective credit policies, see Fry 1988, chaps. 15 and 16. An excellent set of in-depth case studies of selective credit policies is found in Haggard, Lee, and Maxfield 1993. See especially the studies by Hutchcroft and MacIntyre. Chapter 2 has additional cites on this topic.

3. See Lukauskas 1996.

4. Moreover, as Gunther points out, not all Spanish politicians viewed maximizing electoral representation as their predominant goal. They sometimes gave greater priority to ideological or programmatic objectives. See Gunther 1989.

5. More comprehensive treatments of the issues discussed here are Caciagli 1986; Gunther, Sani, and Shabad 1988, 127–45; and Huneeus 1985.

6. Gunther provides a more comprehensive discussion of this issue. See Gunther 1989.

7. Specific reasons for choosing each of these countries are detailed later.

8. See Sunar and Sayari 1986.

9. Akyüz 1990 and Barchard 1990, chaps. 4 and 5, discuss the characteristics of financial repression in Turkey.

10. See Öniş and Riedel 1993, chaps. 3–6, on state efforts to direct the economy. State-owned banks were the primary conduits of preferential finance, and they were notoriously vulnerable to political pressures. See Barchard 1990, 96–97.

11. Sunar and Sayari 1986, 178–79.

12. See Öniş and Webb 1994 and Sunar and Sayari 1986.

13. Turan 1994, 49.

14. See Turan 1994 on electoral engineering in Turkey. As in Spain, the rules succeeded in overrepresenting the winners of elections. In 1983, for example, the party that won the largest number of votes, the Motherland Party, received 46% of the votes but 53% of the seats in parliament. See ibid., 55, on the distribution of votes and seats in the post-1980 general elections.

15. Öniş and Webb 1994, 132–33. It is significant that Özal was minister of finance during much of the period of military rule between 1980 and 1983. He stepped down after an initial attempt to deregulate interest rates went awry.

16. See Öniş and Riedel 1993.

17. Summaries of the reforms are found in Akyüz 1990; Bachard 1990, chaps. 4 and 5; and OECD 1993.

18. See Barchard 1990, chap. 4, and Öniş and Riedel 1993, chap. 11.

19. See *Financial Times* 1995b, 4, and OECD 1990, 91–95.

20. The percentage of total credit flows affected by government credit programs dropped from 49% in 1980 to 18% in 1987. The proportion of selective credit provided on preferential terms declined from 53% in 1983 to 35% in 1987. See World Bank 1989, 56.

21. OECD 1996, 49.

22. Barchard 1990, chap. 4, and OECD 1990, 91–95.

23. See Öniş and Riedel 1993.

24. See Taylor 1990.

25. Öniş and Webb 1994, 133–34, 140. See also Finkel and Hale 1990.

26. Finkel and Hale 1990.

27. See ibid. on electoral campaigns in the 1980s.

28. Waterbury 1992, 128.

29. Öniş and Webb 1994, 151–53.

30. Ibid., 176.

31. Ibid., 149.

32. Ibid., 153, 176. A movement is currently underway to put these funds back into the budget. See Canevi 1994, 192.

33. Kuruç 1994, 142–45.

34. True Path governments in the 1990s have also failed to resolve these problems, despite frequent announcements of major reform programs designed to do so.

35. On Turkey, see Sunar and Sayari 1986, 178–83. See chapter 5 of this book on the Spanish political environment.

36. Öniş and Webb 1994, 136.

37. Ibid., 148–49.

38. See particularly Dalla and Khatkhate 1995. Its reforms, in fact, have avoided several of the problems that other countries have faced in their liberalization efforts (see chap. 1).

39. Cheng and Kim 1994 describes the electoral system and its politics.

40. It is also a legacy of previous authoritarian governments, which were seen as favoring the interests of some regions at the expense of others. See Bedeski 1994, 48, and *Economist* 1995b, 8–10.

41. Lee 1994, 153.

42. Bedeski 1994, chaps. 2 and 3, and Lee 1994, 152–53.

43. *Economist* 1995b, 9.

44. See Amsden 1989, Choi 1993, and Dalla and Khatkhate 1995.

45. See Choi 1993, especially 38–40, and Woo 1991. Significantly, returns on investment in sectors targeted by credit controls dropped below those in nonfavored sectors in the 1970s.

46. See Cooper 1994. Korea's fiscal discipline was atypical for an industrializing country but not as impressive as that of other East Asian countries.

47. In addition to increasing competition, introducing NBFIs was a way of pulling in money from "the uncontrolled, unofficial financial market to a more deregulated, but official financial market." See Woo 1991, 197.

48. Choi reported that over 60% of total bank credit was in the form of "policy loans" (i.e., preferential credit mandated by the government) in the 1970s. This percentage fell from the mid-1980s on as the government began to rely more on specialized banks like the Korean Development Bank to provide preferential credit. Nevertheless, policy loans still make up about 50% of private bank lending. See Choi 1993, 52, and *Economist* 1995b, 10 and 16. A different source indicates that

policy loans as a percentage of credit supplied by *banks* remained fairly steady from 1975 until 1992 at about 45%. However, policy loans as a percentage of *total* domestic credit dropped markedly after 1980 and again after 1990 (to roughly half the percentage of the late 1970s), as NBFIs and direct markets became more important in providing credit. See Cargill 1995, 61. Policy loans are to be eliminated entirely by 1997.

49. See Dalla and Khatkhate 1995 and Kim 1992 on Korea's program of interest rate reform.

50. Choi 1993 and Woo 1991, chap. 7.

51. Ibid. See also Dalla and Khatkhate 1995, 3–7.

52. See Choi 1993, 29–30, and Woo 1991, chap. 4.

53. Lee 1994, 152.

54. Choi 1993, 42. See also Woo 1991, chap. 7. Chung notes that there has been a widespread consensus among Korean economists for a comprehensive liberalization program during the last two decades. See Chung 1994, 261.

55. Bedeski claims they were the primary issue. See Bedeski 1994, 53–54.

56. See Bedeski 1994, 85; Haggard and Collins 1994, 93 and 102; Ro 1994, 179; and Woo 1991, 169–75, 195.

57. See Woo 1991, 199–201. The *chaebol* remained dependent on preferential credit, however, and did not favor an immediate end to selective credit programs. They were also concerned that interest rate deregulation would increase the cost of credit substantially. See Choi 1993, 42.

58. Bond and equity issues accounted for 55% of total financing in 1991, up from 27% in 1987. See Dalla and Khatkhate 1995, 19.

59. See Frankel 1992 for a review of U.S.-Korean financial policy talks.

60. Woo 1991, 193–94.

61. On this point, see especially Cargill 1995, 65–67.

62. Choi 1993, 53.

63. *Economist* 1995b, 15.

64. Choi 1993, 46.

65. Mainwaring 1991, 26.

66. An excellent analysis of the Brazilian electoral system and its political consequences is Mainwaring 1991. In Brazil, the president is elected by an absolute majority. The legislature is bicameral, with a senate and chamber of deputies. Senate seats are chosen in plurality (first-past- the-post) elections, while chamber seats are filled through a PR system.

67. *Financial Times* 1996, 3.

68. The effective number of parties was 5.54, 3.85, 3.45, and 2.72 in Brazil, Turkey, South Korea, and Spain, respectively. The Spanish figure is from Lijphart 1994, 162. Figures for the other countries are from Haggard and Kaufman 1995, table 4.3.

69. See Armijo 1993, 269–71. A comprehensive overview of the Brazilian financial system is Lees, Botts, and Cysne 1990.

70. World Bank 1989, 55.

71. Ibid., 62.

72. See Frieden 1991a, chap. 4.

73. For example, see Armijo 1993, 260.

74. Ibid., 280; *Economist* 1995a; and Frieden 1991a, chap. 4.

75. See Armijo 1993; Frieden 1991a, chap. 4; and Minella 1994.

76. *Economist* 1995a and Minella 1994.

77. *Economist* 1995a, 16–21.

78. Economist Intelligence Unit 1993b, 10–11.

79. Economist Intelligence Unit 1993a, 48.

80. Average annual growth of GNP per capita between 1985 and 1994 was –0.4%. World Bank 1996, 189.

81. Armijo 1993, 278–84.

82. Minella 1994.

83. The president's incentive to carry out reforms once in office is weakened somewhat by a prohibition against reelection. However, recent presidents (Cardoso in particular) have held hopes of reforming the constitution so that they could return for a second term. In addition, presidents must still concern themselves with the effect of their policies on their party's electoral prospects in future elections.

84. See *Financial Times* 1995a, 5.

85. On financial reforms, see *Economist* 1995a, 9, 13–14, and Economist Intelligence Unit 1993a, 48. Economist Intelligence Unit (1995, 4–5), discusses several general structural reforms that affect financial policy.

86. Armijo 1993, 289.

87. Haggard and Collins (1994) caution that the independence of economic agencies has begun to erode as a consequence of democratization.

88. *Financial Times* 1995a, 5.

89. See Rodrik 1994, 22–23.

90. In particular, Brazil and the World Bank entered into negotiations in the late 1980s centered on reforming the financial system. In exchange for a commitment to deregulate the financial system, the World Bank was to provide over $500 million in assistance. See Armijo 1993, 283–84.

Bibliography

Articles, Books, and Documents

Akyüz, Ylimaz. 1990. "Financial System and Policies in Turkey in the 1980s." In T. Aricanli and D. Rodrik, eds., *The Political Economy of Turkey: Debt, Adjustment, and Sustainability.* Houndmills, Basingstoke, Hampshire, UK: MacMillan.

Albentosa, Luis. 1985. "La política de ajuste aplazada: Reconversión industrial." *Información Comercial Española* 617/618: 175–92.

Alcaide Inchausti, Julio. 1989. "La distribución de la renta." In J. L. García Delgado, ed., *España, economía.* Madrid: Espasa Calpe.

Alvarez Canal, Pilar. 1982. "La banca extranjera en España." *Papeles de Economía Española* 9: 68–77.

Alvarez Llano, R., and J. M. Andreu. 1982. "Una historia de la banca privada en España." *Situación* 3: 9–140.

Amsden, Alice. 1989. *Asia's Next Giant: South Korea and Late Industrialization.* New York: Oxford University Press.

Amsden, A., and Y. Euh. 1993. "South Korea's 1980s Financial Reforms: Goodbye Financial Repression (Maybe), Hello New Institutional Restraints." *World Development* 21: 379–90.

Anderson, Charles. 1970. *The Political Economy of Modern Spain.* Madison: University of Wisconsin Press.

Andreu, José Miguel. 1987a. "El coeficiente de caja óptimo y su posible vinculación con el déficit público." *Boletín Económico de Información Comercial Española* 2,091: 2,425–27.

———. 1987b. "Una nota sobre la medición económica del déficit público." *Boletín Económico de Información Comercial Española* 2,108: 3,967–71.

———. 1992. *Un informe sobre los determinantes de los tipos de interés bancarios en España.* Madrid: Ministerio de Economía y Hacienda, Dirección General de Política Económica.

Andrews, David. 1994. "Capital Mobility and State Autonomy: Toward a Structural Theory of International Monetary Relations." *International Studies Quarterly* 38: 193–218.

Arasa Medina, Carmen. 1985. *La política monetaria en España 1973–1984.* Tesis doctoral, Universidad Complutense, Madrid.

Argandoña Ramiz, Antonio. 1981. "El coste del crédito y la liberalización del sistema financiero." *Papeles de Economía Española* 7: 52–67.

Armijo, Leslie. 1993. "Brazilian Politics and Patterns of Financial Regulation." In S. Haggard, C. Lee, and S. Maxfield, eds., *The Politics of Finance in Developing Countries.* Ithaca: Cornell University Press.

Arnold, R. Douglas. 1979. *Congress and the Bureaucracy: A Theory of Influence.* New Haven: Yale University Press.

Aronson, P., and P. Ordeshook. 1985. "Public Interest, Private Interest, and the Democratic Polity." In R. Benjamin and S. Elkin, eds., *The Democratic State.* Lawrence: Kansas University Press.

Asociación Española de la Banca Privada. 1978. "Texto íntegro del informe de Don Rafael Termes, Presidente de la AEB, a la Asamblea General Ordinaria." Madrid.

———. 1979. "Comentarios al programa económico del gobierno." Madrid.

———. 1980. "Informe de la AEB sobre la liberalización del sistema financiero." Madrid.

Azofra Palenzuela, V., and A. Martínez Bobillo. 1988. "Cambios recientes en el modelo de financiación de la empresa privada española." *Actualidad Financiera* 43: 2,271–97.

Banco de España. 1968, 1971, 1985, 1987, 1988. *Informe Anual.* Madrid.

———. 1991, 1992, 1993, 1994, 1995a. *Annual Report.* Madrid.

———. Various years. *Boletín Económico.* Madrid.

———. Various years. *Boletín Estadístico.* Madrid.

———. Various years. *Central de balances.* Madrid.

———. 1995b. *Cuentas financieras de la economía española, 1985–1994.* Madrid.

Barallat López, Luis. 1988. *Proceso de innovación en el sistema financiero español: Experiencia reciente y tendencias futuras.* Madrid: Instituto de Empresa.

Barchard, David. 1990. *Turkey: Investing in the Future.* London: Euromoney Publications.

Barro, Robert. 1989. "A Cross-country Study of Growth, Savings, and Government." Working Paper 2855, National Bureau of Economic Research, Cambridge.

Bates, Robert. 1983. *Essays on the Political Economy of Rural Africa.* Berkeley and Los Angeles: University of California Press.

———. 1988. "Macro-Political Economy in the Field of Development." Working Paper 40, Duke University Program in International Political Economy, Durham, North Carolina.

———. 1994. "Comment on 'In Search of a Manual for Technopols' by J. Williamson." In J. Williamson, ed., *The Political Economy of Policy Reform.* Washington, DC: Institute for International Economics.

Bates, R., and A. Krueger, eds., 1993. *Political and Economic Interactions in Economic Policy Reform.* Cambridge: Blackwell.

Becker, Gary. 1983. "A Theory of Competition among Pressure Groups for Political Influence." *Quarterly Journal of Economics* 98: 371–400.

Bedeski, Robert. 1994. *The Transformation of South Korea: Reform and Reconstruction in the Sixth Republic under Roh Tae Woo, 1987–1992.* New York: Routledge.

Bengoechea, Mariano. 1988. "Nuevas instituciones del mercado de valores español." *Economistas* 32: 8–11.

Bermeo, N., and J. García Durán. 1994. "Spain: Dual Transition Implemented by Two Parties." In S. Haggard and S. Webb, eds., *Voting for Reform: Democracy, Political Liberalization, and Economic Adjustment.* New York: Oxford University Press.

Blasco Sánchez, Tomás. 1984. "Hacia una transparencia en el control de la liquidez monetaria del estado." *Hacienda Pública Española* 88: 157–80.

Boada Villalonga, Claudio. 1985. "El reto de la CEE para la banca española." *Noticias CEE* 10: 27–30.

Bryant, Ralph C. 1987. *International Financial Intermediation.* Washington, DC: Brookings.

Buchanan, J., and G. Tullock. 1962. *The Calculus of Consent.* Ann Arbor: University of Michigan Press.

Buffie, Edward. 1984. "Financial Repression, the New Structuralists, and Stabilization Policy in Semi-Industrialized Economies." *Journal of Development Economics* 14: 305–22.

Bultó Millet, Víctor. 1988. "La reforma del mercado de valores español en el contexto de otras reformas europeas." *Economistas* 32: 12–15.

Caciagli, Mario. 1986. *Elecciones y partidos en la transición española.* Madrid: Centro de Investigaciones Sociológicas.

Calder, Kent. 1988a. "Japanese Foreign Economic Policy Formation: Explaining the Reactive State." *World Politics* 40: 517–41.

———. 1988b. *Crisis and Compensation: Public Policy and Political Stability in Japan, 1949–1986.* Princeton: Princeton University Press.

———. 1993. *Strategic Capitalism: Private Business and Public Purpose in Japanese Industrial Finance.* Princeton: Princeton University Press.

Callaghy, Thomas. 1993. "Political Passions and Economic Interests: Economic Reform and Political Structure in Africa." In T. Callaghy and J. Ravenhill, eds., *Hemmed In: Responses to Africa's Economic Decline.* New York: Columbia University Press.

Cameron, Rondo. 1967. *Banking in the Early Stages of Industrialization: A Study in Comparative Economic History.* New York: Oxford University Press.

Canevi, Yavuz. 1994. "Turkey." In J. Williamson, ed., *The Political Economy of Policy Reform.* Washington, DC: Institute for International Economics.

Cargill, Thomas. 1995. "Will Korea's Liberalization Serve as a Model for the Other Emerging Pacific Basin Economies?" In Korean Economic Institute, *Economic Cooperation and Challenges in the Pacific.* Washington, DC: Korean Economic Institute.

Carr, R., and J. P. Fusi. 1981. *Spain: Dictatorship to Democracy.* London: Harper Collins Academic.

Cerney, Phillip. 1993. "The Deregulation and Re-regulation of Financial Markets in a More Open World." In Cerney, ed., *Finance and World Politics: Markets, Regimes, and States in the Post-Hegemonic Era.* Aldershot, England: Edward Elgar.

Cheng, T., and E. M. Kim 1994. "Making Democracy: Generalizing the South

Korean Case." In E. Friedman, ed., *The Politics of Democratization*. Boulder, CO: Westview Press.

Cho, Yoon Je. 1986. "Inefficiencies from Financial Market Liberalization in the Absence of Well Functioning Equity Markets." *Journal of Money, Credit, and Banking* 18: 191–99.

Choi, Byung-Sun. 1993. "Financial Policy and Big Business in Korea: The Perils of Financial Regulation." In S. Haggard, C. Lee, and S. Maxfield, eds., *The Politics of Finance in Developing Countries*. Ithaca: Cornell University Press.

Chung, Choon Taik. 1994. "Financial Sector Reforms and Liberalization in the Republic of Korea: Current Status and Prospects." In S. Faruqi, ed., *Financial Sector Reforms, Economic Growth, and Stability: Experiences in Selected Asian and Latin American Countries*. Washington, DC: World Bank.

Clavera, J., J. Esteban, A. M. Mones, A. Montserrat, and J. Ros Hombravella. 1978. *Capitalismo español: De la autarquía a la estabilización 1939–1959*. Madrid: Editorial Cuadernos para el Diálogo.

Cohen, Benjamin. 1996. "Phoenix Risen: The Resurrection of Global Finance." *World Politics* 48: 268–96.

Cole, D., and P. Wellons. 1989. "The Financial System, Financial Reform, and Economic Development." Working Paper 312, Harvard Institute for International Development, Cambridge.

Comín, Francisco. 1990. "Reforma tributaria y política fiscal." In J. L. García Delgado, ed., *España, economía*. Madrid: Espasa Calpe.

Confederación Española de Cajas de Ahorros. 1978. *Las Cajas de Ahorros y la reforma del sistema financiero*. Madrid: C.E.C.A.

Confederación Española de Organizaciones Empresariales. 1980. *Medidas urgentes para luchar contra el paro: Actuaciones básicas*. Madrid.

———. 1981. *Una nueva política de empleo*. Madrid.

Consejo Superior Bancario. 1986. *Anuario estadístico de la banca privada 1986*. Madrid.

Cooper, Norman. 1976. "The Church: From Crusade to Christianity." In P. Preston, ed., *Spain in Crisis*. London: Harvester Press.

Cooper, Richard. 1994. "Fiscal Policy in Korea." In S. Haggard, R. Cooper, S. Collins, C. Kim, S. Ro, eds., *Macroeconomic Policy and Adjustment in Korea, 1970–1990*. Cambridge: Harvard University Press.

Corbo, V., and J. Melo. 1985. "Overview and Summary." *World Development* 13: 863–66.

Cuervo García, Alvaro. 1988. *La crisis bancaria en España 1977–1985*. Barcelona: Editorial Ariel.

Cuervo García, A., J. A. Parejo Gámir, and L. Rodríguez Sáiz. 1988. *Manual de sistema financiero: Instituciones, mercados y medios en España*. 2d ed. Barcelona: Ariel Economía.

Cummings, Bruce. 1987. "The Origins and Development of the Northeast Asian Political Economy: Industrial Sectors, Product Cycles, and Political Consequences." In F. Deyo, ed., *The Political Economy of the New Asian Industrialism*. Ithaca: Cornell University Press.

Dalla, I., and D. Khatkhate. 1995. "Regulated Deregulation of the Financial System in Korea." World Bank Discussion Paper 292, World Bank, Washington, DC.

Dehesa, Guillermo de la. 1988. "La reforma del mercado de valores." *Economistas* 32: 4–7.

———. 1994. "Spain." In J. Williamson, ed., *The Political Economy of Policy Reform.* Washington, DC: Institute for International Economics.

Derthick, M., and P. Quirk. 1985. *The Politics of Deregulation.* Washington, DC: Brookings.

Díaz Varela, M., and M. Guindal. 1990. *A la sombra del poder.* Barcelona: Tibidabo Actualidad.

Donaghy, P., and M. Newton. 1987. *Spain: A Guide to Political and Economic Institutions.* Cambridge: Cambridge University Press.

Doner, R., and D. Unger. 1993. "The Politics of Finance in Thai Economic Development." In S. Haggard, C. Lee, and S. Maxfield, eds., *The Politics of Finance in Developing Countries.* Ithaca: Cornell University Press.

Donges, Jürgen B. 1976. *La industrialización en España.* Barcelona: Oikos-tau.

Dornbusch, R., and S. Fischer. 1981. *Macroeconomics.* 2d ed.. New York: McGraw-Hill.

Downs, Anthony. 1957. *An Economic Theory of Democracy.* New York: Harper and Row.

Durán Herrrera, Juan José. 1984. "Comportamiento de la empresa pública y el déficit público." *Hacienda Pública Española* 88: 207–16.

Economic Commission for Latin America and the Caribbean. 1992. *World Investment Report: Transnational Corporations as Engines of Growth.* New York: United Nations.

Economist. 1993. "New Ways to Grow: A Survey of Third-World Finance." September 25.

———. 1995a. "A Survey of Brazil: Half Empty or Half Full?" April 29.

———. 1995b. "A Survey of South Korea: The House That Park Built." June 3.

Economist Intelligence Unit. 1993a. *Brazil: Country Profile, 1993/1994.* London: Economist Intelligence Unit.

———. 1993b. *Brazil: Country Report, First Quarter, 1993.* London: Economist Intelligence Unit.

———. 1995. *Brazil: Country Report, First Quarter, 1995.* London: Economist Intelligence Unit.

———. 1996. *Turkey: Country Profile, 1995/1996.* London: Economic Intelligence Unit.

Edwards, Sebastian. 1985. "Stabilization with Liberalization: An Evaluation of Ten Years of Chile's Experiment with Free-Market Policies, 1973–1983." *Economic Development and Cultural Change* 33: 223–54.

Esteban, Joan. 1976. "The Economic Policy of Francoism: An Interpretation." In P. Preston, ed., *Spain in Crisis.* London: Harvester Press.

Fanjul, O., and F. Maravall. 1985. "Competencia y rentabilidad del sistema bancario." *Papeles de Economía Española* 18: 237–49.

Faruqi, Shakil, ed. 1994. *Financial Sector Reforms, Economic Growth, and Stabil-*

ity: Experiences in Selected Asian and Latin American Countries. Washington, DC: World Bank.

Financial Times. 1995a. "Brazil: Special Survey." May 17.

———. 1995b. "Turkey: Special Survey." June 12.

———. 1996. "Brazil and the State of Bahia: Survey." June 6.

Finkel, A., and W. Hale. 1990. "Politics and Procedure in the 1987 Turkish General Election." In A. Finkel and N. Sirman, eds., *Turkish State, Turkish Society.* New York: Routledge.

Fishman, Robert. 1990. *Working Class Organization and the Return to Democracy in Spain.* Ithaca: Cornell University Press.

Frankel, Jeffrey. 1992. "Foreign Exchange Policy, Monetary Policy, and Capital Market Liberalization in Korea." In Korean Economic Institute, *Korean-U.S. Financial Issues.* Washington, DC: Korean Economic Institute.

Frieden, Jeffrey. 1981. "Third World Indebted Industrialization: International Finance and State Capitalism in Mexico, Brazil, Algeria, and South Korea." *International Organization* 35: 407–31.

———. 1991a. *Debt, Development, and Democracy: Modern Political Economy and Latin America, 1965–1985.* Princeton: Princeton University Press.

———. 1991b. "Invested Interests: The Politics of National Economic Policies in a World of Global Finance." *International Organization* 45: 425–51.

Fry, Maxwell. 1988. *Money, Interest, and Banking in Economic Development.* Baltimore: John Hopkins University Press.

Fuentes Quintana, Enrique. 1989. "Tres decenios de la economía española en perspectiva." In J. L. García Delgado, ed., *España, economía.* Madrid: Espasa Calpe.

———. 1990. *Las reformas tributarias en España.* Barcelona: Editorial Crítica.

———. 1991. "Prólogo." In R. Termes, ed., *Desde la banca,* vol. 1. Madrid: Ediciones Rialp.

Gala, Manuel. 1969. "El sistema financiero español." *Moneda y Crédito* 111: 31–64.

Galbis, Vicente. 1986. "Financial Sector Liberalization under Oligopolistic Conditions and a Bank Holding Company Structure." *Savings and Development* 10: 117–40.

Gallagher, Michael. 1991. "Proportionality, Disproportionality, and Electoral Systems." *Electoral Studies* 10: 33–51.

García Delgado, José L. 1980. "Crecimiento y cambio industrial en España 1960–1980: Viejos y nuevos problemas." *Economía Industrial* 197: 13–27.

García Díez, Juan Antonio. 1991. "La economía de la transición española." *Claves,* 32–39.

García Fernández, Julio. 1984. "Política empresarial pública: Tiempos de capitulación 1974–1984." *Información Comercial Española* 617/618: 193–211.

Garrett, G., and P. Lange. 1986. "Performance in a Hostile World: Economic Growth in Capitalist Democracies, 1974–1982." *World Politics* 38: 517–45.

———. 1991. "Political Responses to Interdependence: What's Left for the Left?" *International Organization* 45: 539–64.

Geddes, Barbara. 1994. *The Politician's Dilemma: Reforming the State in Latin America.* Berkeley and Los Angeles: University of California Press.

Gerschenkron, Alexander. 1962. *Economic Backwardness in Historical Perspective.* Cambridge: Oxford University Press.

Gil, Gonzalo. 1973. "La evolución de los controles sobre los tipos de interés en España." Madrid: Banco de España.

———. 1985. *Aspectos financieros y monetarios de la integración española en la Comunidad Económica Europea.* Estudios Económicos 37, Banco de España, Madrid.

Gill, S., and D. Law. 1989. "Global Hegemony and the Structural Power of Capital." *International Studies Quarterly* 33: 475–500.

Gimeno, Juan. 1984. "Las causas del déficit público." *Hacienda Pública Española* 88: 85–105.

Giovannini, Alberto. 1985. "Savings and the Real Interest Rate in LDCs." *Journal of Development Economics* 18: 197–217.

Giovannini, A., and M. de Melo. 1993. "Government Revenue from Financial Repression." *American Economic Review* 83: 953–63.

Gokce, Deniz. 1993. "The Political Economy of Financial Liberalization in Turkey." Ankara, Turkey: Central Bank of the Republic of Turkey.

Goldstein, Morris. 1995. "Coping with Too Much of a Good Thing: Policy Responses for Large Capital Inflows in Developing Countries." Policy Research Working Paper 1507, World Bank, Washington, DC.

González, Manuel Jesús. 1979. *La economía política del franquismo 1940–1970.* Madrid: Editorial Tecnos.

González Grimaldo, Mariano Carmelo. 1982. "Las sociedades de garantía recíproca y el segundo aval." *Papeles de Economía Española* 9: 181–88.

González Temprano, A., D. Sánchez Robayna, and E. Torres Villanueva. 1981. *La banca y el estado en la España contemporánea 1939–1979.* Madrid: Editorial Gráficas Espejo.

Goode, Richard. 1984. *Government Finance in Developing Countries.* Washington, DC: Brookings.

Goodhart, Charles. 1989. *Money, Information, and Uncertainty.* 2d ed. Cambridge: MIT Press.

Goodman, J., and L. Pauly. 1993. "The Obsolescence of Capital Controls? Economic Management in an Age of Global Markets." *World Politics* 46: 50–82.

Gourevitch, Peter. 1986. *Politics in Hard Times: Comparative Responses to International Economic Crises.* Ithaca: Cornell University Press.

Gowa, Joanne. 1988. "Public Goods and Political Institutions: Trade and Monetary Policy Processes in the United States." *International Organization* 42: 15–32.

Graham, Robert. 1984. *Spain: Change of a Nation.* London: Michael Joseph.

Grier, K., and G. Tullock. 1989. "An Empirical Analysis of Cross-national Economic Growth, 1951–1980." *Journal of Monetary Economics* 24: 259–76.

Gunther, Richard. 1980. *Public Policy in a No-Party State: Spanish Planning and Budgeting in the Twilight of the Franquist Era.* Berkeley and Los Angeles: University of California Press.

――――. 1989. "Electoral Laws, Party Systems, and Elites: The Case of Spain." *American Political Science Review* 83: 835–58.

――――. 1994. "Electoral Laws, Party Systems, and Elites: The Case of Spain." Paper presented at the conference on Electoral Reform and Democratization, Columbia University, April 30, 1994.

――――. 1996. "Spanish Public Policy: From Dictatorship to Democracy." Working Paper 1996/84, Instituto Juan March de Estudios e Investigaciones, Madrid.

Gunther, R., G. Sani, and G. Shabad. 1988. *Spain after Franco: The Making of a Competitive Party System.* Berkeley and Los Angeles: University of California Press.

Gupta, Kanhaya. 1987. "Aggregate Savings, Financial Intermediation, and Interest Rates." *Review of Economics and Statistics* 69: 303–11.

Haggard, Stephan. 1990. *Pathways from the Periphery: The Politics of Growth in the Newly Industrializing Countries.* Ithaca: Cornell University Press.

Haggard, S., and S. Collins. 1994. "The Political Economy of Adjustment in the 1980s." In S. Haggard, R. Cooper, S. Collins, C. Kim, S. Ro, eds., *Macroeconomic Policy and Adjustment in Korea, 1970–1990.* Cambridge: Harvard University Press.

Haggard, S., and R. Kaufman. 1992a. "Introduction: Institutions and Economic Adjustment." In S. Haggard and R. Kaufman, eds., *The Politics of Economic Adjustment.* Princeton: Princeton University Press.

――――. 1992b. "Economic Adjustment and the Prospects for Democracy." In S. Haggard and R. Kaufman, eds., *The Politics of Economic Adjustment.* Princeton: Princeton University Press.

――――. 1995. *The Political Economy of Democratic Transitions.* Princeton: Princeton University Press.

Haggard, S., C. Lee, and S. Maxfield, eds. 1993. *The Politics of Finance in Developing Countries.* Ithaca: Cornell University Press.

Haggard, S., and S. Maxfield. 1993. "Political Explanations of Financial Policy in Developing Countries." In S. Haggard, C. Lee, and S. Maxfield, eds., *The Politics of Finance in Developing Countries.* Ithaca: Cornell University Press.

――――. 1996. "Financial Internationalization and the Developing World." *International Organization* 50: 35–68.

Haggard, S., and S. Webb. 1994. "Introduction." In S. Haggard and S. Webb, eds., *Voting for Reform: Democracy, Political Liberalization, and Economic Adjustment.* New York: Oxford University Press.

Hall, Peter. 1986. *Governing the Economy: The Politics of State Intervention in Britain and France.* New York: Oxford University Press.

Hamada, K., and A. Horiuchi. 1987. "The Political Economy of the Financial Market." In K. Yamamura and Y. Yasuba, eds., *The Political Economy of Japan.* Stanford, CA: Stanford University Press.

Hammond, T., and J. Knott. 1988. "The Deregulatory Snowball: Explaining Deregulation in the Financial Industry." *Journal of Politics* 50: 3–30.

Harper, Ian R. 1986. "Why Financial Deregulation?" *Australian Economic Review:* 37–49.

Harrison, Joseph. 1985. *The Spanish Economy in the Twentieth Century.* New York: St. Martin's Press.

Helliwell, John. 1994. "Empirical Linkages between Democracy and Economic Growth." *British Journal of Political Science* 24: 225–48.

Hernández Armenteros, Juan. 1986. *La banca pública española.* Madrid: Instituto de Estudios Fiscales.

Hibbs, Douglas. 1987. *The Political Economy of Industrial Democracies.* Cambridge: Harvard University Press.

Hicks, A., and D. Swank. 1992. "Politics, Institutions, and Welfare Spending in Industrialized Democracies, 1960–1982." *American Political Science Review* 86: 658–74.

Hills, Jill. 1983. "The Industrial Policy of Japan." *Journal of Public Policy* 3: 63–80.

Horiuchi, Akiyoshi. 1984. "The 'Low Interest Rate Policy' and Economic Growth in Postwar Japan." *Developing Economies* 22: 349–71.

Hornillos García, Carlos. 1970. *Problemas de la pequeña y mediana industria en España.* Madrid: Confederación Española de Cajas de Ahorros.

Huneeus, Carlos. 1985. *La Unión de Centro Democrático y la transición a la democracia en España.* Madrid: Centro de Investigaciones Sociológicas.

Hutchcroft, Paul. 1993. "Selective Squander: The Politics of Preferential Credit Allocation in the Philippines." In S. Haggard, C. Lee, and S. Maxfield, eds., *The Politics of Finance in Developing Countries.* Ithaca: Cornell University Press.

Ikenberry, John. 1986. "The State and Strategies of International Adjustment." *World Politics* 39: 53–77.

Ikenberry, J., D. Lake, and M. Mastanduno. 1988. "Introduction: Approaches to Explaining American Foreign Economic Policy." *International Organization* 42: 1–14.

Institute of Latin American Studies. 1986. *The Debt Crisis in Latin America.* Monograph 13, Institute of Latin American Studies, Stockholm.

International Bank for Reconstruction and Development. 1963. *The Economic Development of Spain.* Baltimore: John Hopkins University Press.

International Monetary Fund. (Various). *International Financial Statistics.* Washington, DC.

Johnson, Chalmers. 1982. *MITI and the Japanese Miracle.* Palo Alto, CA: Stanford University Press.

———. 1987. "Political Institutions and Economic Performance: The Government-Business Relationship in Japan, South Korea, and Taiwan." In F. Deyo, ed., *The Political Economy of the New Asian Industrialism.* Ithaca: Cornell University Press.

Juan, Aristóbulo de. 1988. "Does Bank Insolvency Matter?" Mimeo, World Bank, Washington, DC.

Kahler, Miles. 1992. "External Influence, Conditionality, and the Politics of Adjustment." In S. Haggard and R. Kaufman, eds., *The Politics of Economic Adjustment.* Princeton: Princeton University Press.

Kane, Edward. 1977. "Good Intentions and Unintended Evil: The Case against Selective Credit Allocation." *Journal of Money, Credit, and Banking* 9: 55–69.

Kapstein, Ethan. 1994. *Governing the Global Economy: International Finance and the State.* Cambridge: Harvard University Press.

Keeler, John. 1993. "Opening the Window for Reform." *Comparative Political Studies* 25: 433–86.

Keeler, Theodore. 1984. "Theories of Regulation and the Deregulation Movement." *Public Choice* 44: 103–45.

Kiewiet, D. Roderick. 1983. *Macroeconomics and Micropolitics.* Chicago: University of Chicago Press.

Kim, Tae-Joon. 1992. "Perspective on Korea's Financial Liberalization." In Korean Economic Institute, *Korean-U.S. Financial Issues.* Washington, DC: Korean Economic Institute.

Kindleberger, Charles. 1984. *A Financial History of Western Europe.* London: George Allen & Unwin.

Kormendi, R., and P. Meguire. 1985. "Macroeconomic Determinants of Growth." *Journal of Monetary Economics* 16: 141–63.

Krasner, Stephen. 1978. *Defending the National Interest: Raw Materials Investments and U.S. Foreign Policy.* Princeton: Princeton University Press.

Krueger, Anne. 1993. *Political Economy of Policy Reform in Developing Countries.* Cambridge: MIT Press.

Krugman, Paul. 1983. "Targeted Industrial Policies: Theory and Evidence." In Federal Reserve Bank of Kansas City, *Industrial Change and Public Policy.* Kansas City: Federal Reserve Bank of Kansas City.

Kuruç, Bilsay. 1994. "Economic Growth and Political Stability." In M. Heper and A. Evin, eds., *Politics in the Third Turkish Republic.* Boulder, CO: Westview Press.

Kurzer, Paulette. 1993. *Business and Banking: Political Change and Economic Integration in Western Europe.* Ithaca: Cornell University Press.

Lake, David. 1992. "Powerful Pacifists: Democratic States and War." *American Political Science Review* 86: 24–37.

Lancaster, Thomas D. 1989. *Policy Stability and Democratic Change: Energy in Spain's Transition.* University Park: Pennsylvania State University Press.

Lanyi, A., and R. Saracoğlu. 1983. "Interest Rate Policies in Developing Countries." Occasional Paper 22, International Monetary Fund, Washington, DC.

Lasheras, J., and J. Alvarez. 1988. "Las ayudas financieras a las empresas." *Economía Industrial* 21: 59–67.

Leal, José Luis. 1982. *Una política económica para España: Lo necesario y lo posible durante la transición.* Barcelona: Planeta.

Lee, Chung H. 1992. "The Government, Financial System, and Large Private Enterprises in the Economic Development of South Korea." *World Development* 20: 187–97.

Lee, Heng. 1994. "Uncertain Promise: Democratic Consolidation in South Korea." In E. Friedman, ed., *The Politics of Democratization.* Boulder, CO: Westview Press.

Lees, F., J. Botts, and R. Cysne. 1990. *Banking and Financial Deepening in Brazil.* London: Macmillan Press.

Levi, Margaret. 1988. *Of Rule and Revenue.* Berkeley and Los Angeles: University of California Press.

Lewis-Beck, Michael. 1988. *Economies and Elections: The Major Western Democracies.* Ann Arbor: University of Michigan Press.

Lieberman, Sima. 1982. *The Contemporary Spanish Economy: A Historical Perspective.* London: George Allen & Unwin.

Lijphart, Arend. 1994. *Electoral Systems and Party Systems: A Study of Twenty-seven Democracies, 1945–1990.* New York: Oxford University Press.

Lindblom, Charles. 1977. *Politics and Markets.* New York: Basic Books.

Linde, Luis. 1990. "La profundización de la crisis económica: 1979–1982." In J. L. García Delgado, ed., *Economía española de la transición y la democracia.* Madrid: Centro de Investigaciones Sociológicas.

Lindenberg, M., and S. Devarajan. 1993. "Prescribing Strong Medicine: Revisiting the Myths about Structural Adjustment, Democracy, and Economic Performance in Developing Countries." *Comparative Politics* 25: 169–82.

Linz, Juan. 1964. "An Authoritarian System: Spain." In E. Allardt and Y. Littunen, eds., *Cleavages, Ideologies, and Party Systems: Contributions to Comparative Political Sociology.* Helsinki: Translations of the Westermarch Society, vol. 10.

———. 1981. "A Century of Politics and Interests in Spain." In S. Berger, ed., *Organizing Interests in Western Europe: Pluralism, Corporatism, and the Transformation of Politics.* Cambridge: Cambridge University Press.

Linz, J., and A. Valenzuela, eds. 1994. *The Failure of Presidential Democracy.* Baltimore: Johns Hopkins University Press.

López Claros, Augusto. 1988. "The Search for Efficiency in the Adjustment Process: Spain in the 1980s." Occasional Paper 57, International Monetary Fund, Washington, DC.

López Roa, Angel Luis. 1978. "La política económica de la crisis 1973–1977." In Fundación Foessa, *Síntesis actualizada del III informe Foessa.* Madrid: Fundación Foessa.

———. 1981. *Sistema financiero español.* Alicante: Nueva Generación Editores.

———. 1984. "El déficit público y el sector financiero privado." *Hacienda Pública Española* 86: 195–206.

López Rodó, Laureano. 1990. *Memorias.* Barcelona: Plaza & Janes.

Loriaux, Michael. 1991. *France after Hegemony: International Change and Financial Reform.* Ithaca: Cornell University Press.

Lukauskas, Arvid. 1992. *The Political Economy of Financial Deregulation: The Case of Spain.* Ph.D. diss., University of Pennsylvania, Philadelphia.

———. 1994. "The Political Economy of Financial Restriction: The Case of Spain." *Comparative Politics* 27: 67–89.

———. 1996. "Financial Repression in Comparative Perspective." Unpublished manuscript, Columbia University, New York.

McDonough, P., S. Barnes, and A. López de Piña. 1986. "Economic Policy and Public Opinion in Spain." *American Journal of Political Science* 30: 446–79.

MacIntyre, Andrew. 1993. "The Politics of Finance in Indonesia: Command, Confusion, and Competition." In S. Haggard, C. Lee, and S. Maxfield, eds., *The Politics of Finance in Developing Countries.* Ithaca: Cornell University Press.

McKinnon, Ronald. 1973. *Money and Capital in Economic Development.* Washington, DC: Brookings.

———. 1991. *The Order of Economic Liberalization: Financial Control in the Transition to a Market Economy.* Baltimore: Johns Hopkins University Press.

Mainwaring, Scott. 1991. "Politicians, Parties, and Electoral Systems: Brazil in Comparative Perspective." *Comparative Politics* 24: 21–43.

———. 1993. "Presidentialism, Multipartism, and Democracy." *Comparative Political Studies* 26: 198–228.

Maravall, José M. 1978. *Dictatorship and Political Dissent: Workers and Students in Franco's Spain.* London: Tavistock.

———. 1982. *La política de la transición 1975–1980.* Madrid: Taurus.

———. 1993. "Politics and Policy: Economic Reforms in Southern Europe." In L. Bresser Pereira, J. Maravall, and A. Przeworski, eds., *Economic Reforms in New Democracies: A Social-Democratic Approach.* New York: Cambridge University Press.

———. 1994. "The Myth of the Authoritarian Advantage." *Journal of Democracy* 5: 17–31.

Martí, Luis. 1975. "Estabilización y desarrollo." *Información Comercial Española* 500: 42–55.

Martín Aceña, Pablo. 1987. "Development and Modernization of the Financial System, 1844–1935." In N. Sánchez-Albornoz, ed., *The Economic Modernization of Spain, 1830–1930.* New York: New York University Press.

Martín Aceña, P., and F. Comín. 1989. "La financiación del INI 1941–1986." *Papeles de Economía Española* 38: 135–58.

Martín Rodríguez, Manuel. 1989. "Evolución de las disparidades regionales: Una perspectiva histórica." In J. L. García Delgado, ed., *España, economía.* Madrid: Espasa Calpe.

Martínez Cortiña, Rafael. 1971. *Crédito y banca en España: Análisis y estructura.* Madrid: Editorial Moneda y Crédito.

Martínez Méndez, Pedro. 1980. "Monetary Control by Control of the Monetary Base: The Spanish Experience." Documento de trabajo 8005, Banco de España, Madrid.

———. 1982. *El proceso de ajuste a la crisis.* Madrid: Banco de España.

Martínez, R., and R. Pardo Avellaneda. 1985. "El asociacionismo empresarial español en la transición." *Papeles de Economía Española* 22: 84–114.

Maxfield, Sylvia. 1990. *Governing Capital: International Finance and Mexican Politics.* Ithaca: Cornell University Press.

———. 1993. "The Politics of Mexican Financial Policy." In S. Haggard, C. Lee, and S. Maxfield, eds., *The Politics of Finance in Developing Countries.* Ithaca: Cornell University Press.

———. 1994. "Financial Incentives and Central Bank Authority in Industrializing Nations." *World Politics* 46: 556–88.

Meier, Gerald. 1984. *Emerging from Poverty: The Economics That Really Matter.* New York: Oxford University Press.

Meier, Kenneth. 1985. *Regulation: Politics, Bureaucracy, and Economics.* New York: St. Martin's Press.

Miguel, Amando de. 1975. *Sociología del Franquismo.* Barcelona: Editorial Euros.

Miguel, A., and J. Linz. 1963. "Los empresarios españoles y la Banca." *Moneda y Crédito* 84: 3–112.

Milner, Helen. 1988. *Resisting Protectionism: Global Industries and the Politics of International Trade.* Princeton: Princeton University Press.

Minella, Ary Cesar. 1994. "The Discourse of Brazilian Business Leaders: The Voice of the Bankers." Translated by Jeffrey Hoff. First published in *Ensaios FEE* 15, no. 2.

Ministerio de Comercio. Various years. *Balanza de pagos.* Madrid.

Ministerio de la Gobernación, Dirección General de la Política Interior. 1977. *Elecciones Generales 1977: Resultados Congreso por Provincias.* Madrid.

Ministerio del Interior, Dirección General de la Política Interior. 1979. *Elecciones Generales 1979: Resultados Congreso por Provincias.* Madrid.

Ministerio de Justicia e Interior. 1996. *Elecciones Generales 1996: Software Package.* Madrid.

Modigliani, Franco. 1986. "Life Cycle, Individual Thrift, and the Wealth of Nations." *American Economic Review* 76: 297–313.

Molinas, C., J. Baiges, and M. Sebastian. 1987. *La economía española: Datos, fuentes, análisis.* Madrid: Instituto de Estudios Fiscales.

Moran, Michael. 1984. *The Politics of Banking: The Strange Case of Competition and Credit Control.* New York: St. Martin's Press.

Munck, Gerardo. 1994. "Democratic Transitions in Comparative Perspective." *Comparative Politics* 26: 355–75.

Muns, Joaquín. 1984. "España y el F.M.I." *Información Comercial Española* 612: 57–66.

Muñoz, Juan. 1969. *El poder de la banca en España.* Madrid: Edita Zero.

Navarro Rubio, Mariano. 1972. *Los condicionantes políticos en la marcha de la economía.* Madrid: Raycar.

Nelson, Joan. 1990. "Conclusions." In Nelson, ed., *Economic Crisis and Policy Choice: The Politics of Adjustment in the Third World.* Princeton: Princeton University Press.

———. 1993. "The Politics of Economic Transformation: Is Third World Experience Relevant in Eastern Europe?" *World Politics* 45: 433–63.

Noll, Roger. 1983. "The Political Foundations of Regulatory Policy." *Journal of Institutional and Theoretical Economics* 139: 377–404.

North, Douglass C. 1981. *Structure and Change in Economic History.* New York: W. W. Norton.

Novales, Alfonso. 1988. "Evolución del saneamiento financiero de las empresas industriales en España: 1984–1986." Documento 88-11, Banco de España, Madrid.

Olson, Mancur. 1965. *The Logic of Collective Action.* Cambridge: Harvard University Press.

————. 1982. *The Rise and Decline of Nations.* New Haven: Yale University Press.

————. 1993. "Dictatorship, Democracy, and Development." *American Political Science Review* 87: 567–76.

Olson, M., and M. Bailey. 1981. "Positive Time Preference." *Journal of Political Economy* 89: 1–25.

Öniş, Z., and J. Riedel. 1993. *Economic Crisis and Long-Term Growth in Turkey.* Washington, DC: World Bank.

Öniş, Z., and S. Webb. 1994. "Turkey: Democratization and Adjustment from Above." In S. Haggard and S. Webb, eds., *Voting for Reform: Democracy, Political Liberalization, and Economic Adjustment.* New York: Oxford University Press.

Organization for Economic Cooperation and Development (OECD). 1963, 1966, 1969, 1974, 1988, 1991. *Economic Surveys: Spain.* Paris.

————. 1971. *Le marché financier. Les mouvements internationaux de capitaux: Les restrictions sur les operations de capital en Espagne.* Paris.

————. 1990, 1993. *Economic Surveys: Turkey.* Paris.

Ortega Fernández, Raimundo. 1984. "El déficit público y su financiación." *Hacienda Pública Española* 88: 23–37.

————. 1987a. "Un repaso histórico al recurso del Tesoro al crédito del Banco de España." *Hacienda Pública Española* 107: 181–206.

————. 1987b. "Tendencias recientes y problemas inmediatos de la política de deuda pública." *Papeles de Economía Española* 32: 130–147.

Pastor, Manuel. 1989. "Latin America, the Debt Crisis, and the International Monetary Fund." *Latin American Perspectives* 16: 790–810.

Patrick, Hugh. 1994. "The Relevance of Japanese Finance and its Main Bank System." In M. Aoki and H. Patrick, eds., *The Japanese Main Bank System: Its Relevance for Developing and Transforming Economies.* New York: Oxford University Press.

Pauly, Louis W. 1988. *Opening Financial Markets: Banking Politics on the Pacific Rim.* Ithaca: Cornell University Press.

Payne, Stanley. 1961. *Falange.* Stanford, CA: Stanford University Press.

————. 1987. *The Franco Regime.* Madison: University of Wisconsin Press.

Peltzman, Sam. 1976. "Toward a More General Theory of Regulation." *Journal of Law and Economics* 19: 211–40.

————. 1989. "The Economic Theory of Regulation after a Decade of Deregulation." *Brookings Papers on Economic Activity* (special issue): 1–41.

Pérez, Sofia. 1997. "From Cheap Credit to the EC: The Politics of Financial Reform in Spain." In M. Loriaux, M. Woo-Cumings, K. Calder, S. Maxfield, and S. Pérez, eds., *Capital Ungoverned: Liberalizing Finance in Interventionist States.* Ithaca: Cornell University Press.

Pérez de Ayala, José L. 1974. "La Reforma Barrera en materia fiscal y económica." In *España perspectiva 1974.* Madrid.

Pérez Diaz, Víctor. 1987. "Economic Policies and Social Pacts in Spain during the Transition." In I. Scholten, ed., *Political Stability and Neo-Corporatism: Corporatist Integration and Societal Cleavages in Western Europe.* Beverly Hills, CA: Sage Publications.

————. 1990. "The Emergence of Democratic Spain and the Invention of a Democratic Tradition." Working Paper 1, Instituto Juan March de Estudios e Investigaciones, Madrid.

————. 1993. *La primacía de la sociedad civil.* Madrid: Alianza Editorial.

Porter, Michael. 1992. *Capital Choices: Changing the Way America Invests in Industry.* Washington, DC: Council on Competitiveness.

Poveda Anadón, Raimundo. 1972. *La creación de dinero en España, 1956–1970: Análisis y politica.* Madrid: Instituto de Estudios Fiscales.

————. 1982. "Funcionamiento del mercado financiero español." *Papeles de Economía Española* 9: 42–67.

————. 1986. "Las financiaciones privilegiadas de las entidades de depósito." *Papeles de Economía Española, Suplementos sobre el Sistema Financiero* 11: 5–121.

Preston, Paul. 1976. "The Anti-Francoist Opposition: The Long March to Unity." In Preston, ed., *Spain in Crisis.* London: Harvester Press.

————. 1986. *The Triumph of Democracy in Spain.* New York: Methuen.

Prieto Pérez, Francisco. 1987. "Ayudas financieras y otros incentivos a las empresas inversoras y generadoras de empleo." *Actualidad Financiera* 18: 916–31.

Przeworski, Adam. 1991. *Democracy and the Market: Political and Economic Reforms in Eastern Europe and Latin America.* New York: Cambridge University Press.

Putnam, Robert. 1988. "Diplomacy and Domestic Politics: The Logic of Two-Level Games." *International Organization* 42: 427–60.

Remmer, Karen. 1990. "Democracy and Economic Crisis: The Latin American Experience." *World Politics* 42: 315–35.

Revell, Jack R. S. 1980. *Costs and Margins in Banking: An International Survey.* Paris: Organization for Economic Cooperation and Development.

Ridruejo, Epifanio. 1954. "El sistema bancario español." *Moneda y Crédito* 51: 35–83.

Riedel, James. 1988. "Economic Development in East Asia: Doing What Comes Naturally?" In H. Hughes, ed., *Achieving Industrialization in East Asia.* Cambridge: Cambridge University Press.

Rivases, Jesús. 1988. *Los banqueros del PSOE.* Barcelona: Ediciones B.

Ro, Sung-Tae. 1994. "Korean Monetary Policy." In S. Haggard, R. Cooper, S. Collins, C. Kim, S. Ro, eds., *Macroeconomic Policy and Adjustment in Korea, 1970–1990.* Cambridge: Harvard University Press.

Roca, Jordi. 1987. "Neo-corporatism in Post-Franco Spain." In I. Scholten, ed., *Political Stability and Neo-Corporatism: Corporatist Integration and Societal Cleavages in Western Europe.* Beverly Hills, CA: Sage Publications.

Rodríguez Saiz, L., and J. Parejo Gámir. 1984. "Déficit público, crisis económica, y política monetaria." *Hacienda Pública Española* 86: 67–83.

Rodrik, Dani. 1994. "Understanding Economic Policy Reform." Unpublished manuscript, Columbia University, New York.

Rojo Duque, L., and J. Pérez. 1977. "La política monetaria en España: objetivos e instrumentos." Estudios Económicos 10, Banco de España, Madrid.

Rosenbluth, Frances McCall. 1989. *Financial Politics in Contemporary Japan.* Ithaca: Cornell University Press.

Ros Hombravella, Jacint. 1987. *Materia de política económica.* Barcelona: Oikostau Ediciones.

Saá, Jesús. 1991. "Los determinantes de las decisiones sobre fuentes de financiación de las empresas españolas." *Moneda y Crédito* 193: 147–75.

Sáez Fernández, Felipe. 1975. *El crédito oficial en el sistema financiero español.* Madrid: Instituto de Estudios Económicos.

Sampedro, José Luis. 1975. "El Plan de Desarrollo español en su marco social." In J. Ros Hombravella, ed., *Trece economistas.* Barcelona: Oikos-tau Ediciones.

Santillana del Barrio, Antonio. 1982. "La nueva ley del mercado hipotecario." *Papeles de Economía Española* 9: 161–70.

Sanz, B., and M. Val. 1993. "Monetary Implementation Techniques in Spain." *Economic Bulletin/Banco de España* April: 37–45.

Sastre, María Teresa. 1992. "Determination of the Lending and Borrowing Rates of Banks and Savings Banks." *Economic Bulletin/Banco de España* July: 45–53.

Schwartz, P., and M. J. González. 1978. *Una historia del INI.* Madrid: Tecnos.

Shaw, Edward S. 1973. *Financial Deepening in Economic Development.* New York: Oxford University Press.

Shefter, Martin. 1978. "Party and Patronage: Germany, England, and Italy." *Politics and Society* 7: 403–51.

Shugart, M., and J. Carey. 1992. *Presidents and Assemblies: Constitutional Design and Electoral Dynamics.* New York: Cambridge University Press.

Silva, Eduardo. 1993. "Capitalist Coalitions, the State, and Neoliberal Restructuring: Chile, 1973–88." *World Politics* 45: 526–59.

Skocpol, Theda. 1985. "Bringing the State Back In: Strategies of Analysis in Current Research." In P. Evans, D. Rueschemeyer, and T. Skocpol, eds., *Bringing the State Back In.* Cambridge: Cambridge University Press.

Smith, William C. 1989. "Heterodox Shocks and the Political Economy of Democratic Transition in Argentina and Brazil." In W. Canak, ed., *Lost Promises: Debt, Austerity, and Development in Latin America.* Boulder, CO: Westview Press.

Sobel, Andrew. 1994. *Domestic Choices, International Markets: Dismantling National Barriers and Liberalizing Securities Markets.* Ann Arbor: University of Michigan Press.

Spruyt, Hendrik. 1994. *The Sovereign State and its Competitors: An Analysis of Systems Change.* Princeton: Princeton University Press.

Stallings, Barbara. 1992. "International Influence on Economic Policy: Debt, Stabilization, and Structural Reform." In S. Haggard and R. Kaufman, eds., *The Politics of Economic Adjustment.* Princeton: Princeton University Press.

Stallings, B., and R. Kaufman. 1989. "Debt and Democracy in the 1980s: The Latin American Experience." In Stallings and Kaufman, eds., *Debt and Democracy in Latin America.* Boulder, CO: Westview Press.

Stepan, A., and J. Linz. 1992. "The Exit from Communism." *Daedalus* 121: 123–39.

Stepan, A., and C. Skach. 1993. "Constitutional Frameworks and Democratic Consolidation: Parliamentarianism versus Presidentialism." *World Politics* 46: 1–22.

Stigler, George. 1971. "The Theory of Economic Regulation." *Bell Journal of Economics and Management Science* 2: 3–21.

———. 1982. "Economists and Public Policy." *Regulation* 6: 7–13.

Stiglitz, Joseph. 1989. "Financial Markets and Development." *Oxford Review of Economic Policy* 5: 55–68.

Stiglitz, J., and A. Weiss. 1981. "Credit Rationing in Markets with Imperfect Information." *American Economic Review* 71: 393–410.

Sunar, I., and S. Sayari. 1986. "Democracy in Turkey: Problems and Prospects." In G. O'Donnell, P. Schmitter, and L. Whitehead, eds., *Transitions from Authoritarian Rule: Southern Europe.* Baltimore: John Hopkins University Press.

Taagepera, R., and M. Shugart. 1989. *Seats and Votes: The Effects and Determinants of Electoral Systems.* New Haven: Yale University Press.

Tamames, Ramón. 1977. *La oligarquía financiera en España.* Barcelona: Planeta.

Taylor, Lance. 1990. "Turkish Experience: Summary and Comparative Notes." In T. Aricanli and D. Rodrik, eds., *The Political Economy of Turkey: Debt, Adjustment, and Sustainability.* Houndmills, Basingstoke, Hampshire, UK: MacMillan.

Taylor, Lawrence. 1983. *Structuralist Macroeconomics: Applicable Models for the Third World.* New York: Basic Books.

Termes, Rafael. 1987. "La reforma de la Bolsa desde el punto de vista bancario." *Análisis Financiero* 43: 29–36.

Tobin, James. 1965. "Money and Economic Growth." *Econometrica* 33: 671–84.

Toribio Dávila, Juan J. 1983. "La reforma del sistema financiero español." *Papeles de Economía Española* 15: 175–92.

Torrero Mañas, Antonio. 1982. *Tendencias del sistema financiero español.* Madrid: H. Blume Ediciones.

———. 1989a. *Estudios sobre el sistema financiero.* Madrid: Espasa Calpe.

———. 1989b. "La formación de los tipos de interés y los problemas actuales de la economía española." *Economistas* 39: 35–47.

Tortella, Gabriel. 1973. *Los orígenes del capitalismo en España.* Madrid: Editorial Tecnos.

Tortella, G., and J. Jiménez. 1986. *Historia del Banco de Crédito Industrial.* Madrid: Alianza Editorial.

Trías Fargas, R. 1970. *El sistema financiero español.* Barcelona: Editorial Ariel.

Turan, Ilter. 1994. "Evolution of the Electoral Process." In M. Heper and A. Evin, eds., *Politics in the Third Turkish Republic.* Boulder, CO: Westview Press.

Velarde Fuertes, Juan. 1968. *Política económica de la Dictadura.* Madrid: Guadiana de Publicaciones.

Verdier, Daniel. 1994. *Democracy and International Trade: Britain, France, and the United States, 1860–1990.* Princeton: Princeton University Press.

Wade, Robert. 1990. *Governing the Market: Economic Theory and the Role of Government in East Asian Industrialization.* Princeton: Princeton University Press.

Waterbury, John. 1992. "Export-Led Growth and the Center-Right Coalition in Turkey." *Comparative Politics* 24: 127–46.

Webb, S., and K. Shariff. 1992. "Designing and Implementing Adjustment Programs." In V. Corbo, S. Fischer, and S. Webb, eds., *Adjustment Lending Revisited: Policies to Restore Growth.* Washington, DC: World Bank.

Weir, Margaret. 1989. "Ideas and Politics: The Acceptance of Keynesianism in Britain and the United States." In P. Hall, ed., *The Political Power of Economic Ideas: Keynesianism across Nations.* Princeton: Princeton University Press.

West, Robert C. 1983. "The Evolution and Devolution of Bank Regulation in the United States." *Journal of Economic Issues* 17: 361–67.

Wiarda, Howard. 1992. *Politics in Iberia.* New York: Harper Collins College.

Widner, Jennifer. 1994. "Single Party States and Agricultural Policies: The Cases of Ivory Coast and Kenya." *Comparative Politics* 26: 127–48.

Wilson, Bruce. 1994. "When Social Democrats Choose Neoliberal Economic Policies: The Case of Costa Rica." *Comparative Politics* 26: 149–68.

Wilson, James Q. 1980. "The Politics of Regulation." In Wilson, ed., *The Politics of Regulation.* New York: Basic Books.

Wittman, Donald. 1989. "Why Democracies Produce Efficient Results." *Journal of Political Economy* 97: 1395–1424.

Woo, Jung-en. 1991. *Race to the Swift: State and Finance in Korean Industrialization.* New York: Columbia University Press.

World Bank. 1989, 1996. *World Development Report.* New York: Oxford University Press, for the World Bank.

———. 1994. *World Data, 1994: World Bank Indicators on CD-ROM.* Washington, DC: World Bank.

Wright, Alison. 1977. *The Spanish Economy: 1959–1976.* London: Macmillan Press.

Zysman, John. 1983. *Governments, Markets, and Growth: Financial Systems and the Politics of Industrial Change.* Ithaca: Cornell University Press.

Newspapers and Periodicals

Actualidad Económica. Various issues. Madrid.

Banca Española. Various issues. Madrid

El País. Various issues. Madrid.

Financial Times. Various issues. New York edition.

Noticias CEE. November 1985. Madrid.

Wall Street Journal. Various issues. New York.

Index

Abril Martorell, Fernando, 99, 157, 158, 159, 164, 170, 174, 185
Alianza Popular (AP), 128, 131, 132, 190
allocative efficiency of intermediation: in Spain, 87, 103–4, 184
Almunia, Joaquín, 195
Amsden, Alice, 6, 13, 17, 255n, 256n, 263n, 270n, 295n
Andreu, José Miguel, 260n, 268n, 270n, 290n, 292n
Andrews, David, 251n, 253n, 262n
Argandoña Ramiz, Antonio, 161, 283n, 285n
Arias Navarro, Carlos, 114–15, 119–20, 127
Asociación Española de la Banca Privada (AEB), 140–41, 142, 171; proposals by to lower cost of credit, 164; stance on 1981 reforms, 175–76, 178
asset restrictions (ARs), 253n; financial innovation and, 38, 204; ill effects of, 37, 205; in Spain, 91, 92–93, 94, 201, 203, 204, 206, 292n; revenue generation and, 10, 29, 37, 38

balance of payments: financial policy and, 21, 47, 49, 235; in Spain, 68, 69, 70, 136, 159, 173, 192
Banco de Crédito Industrial (BCI), 106, 113
bank-based financial systems, 10, 13–15, 167; monetary policy and, 14, 113, 218

banking crisis of 1979–85, 73, 80, 90, 167–69
banking industry: entry controls and, 40; interest rate controls and, 31–33, 35–36, 44–45; selective credit policies and, 17, 34; stance on deregulation, in countries with restricted vs. non-restricted financial systems, 44–45
Banking Law of 1962, 72, 73, 76, 83, 268n
Bank of Spain (BOS), 76–77, 88, 91, 197; government and, 108–9, 137, 172–73, 197; government borrowing from, 198–99, 206, 289n; monetary policy and, 97, 103, 107, 110–14, 143–44, 153, 160, 162, 180, 203, 204–5; prudential regulation and, 180–81; reform of, 139, 140, 172–73; selective credit policies and, 86, 87, 92, 271n; stance on financial liberalization, 97, 103, 104, 107–8, 114–15, 169, 175, 203; stance on issue of short-term debt, 202–3
banks in Spain: classification of institutions, 72; collusive behavior by, 73, 84, 117, 184, 215; degree of concentration, 81–82, 83, 268n, 269n; divisions among, 74, 81, 140–41, 149–50, 184, 267n; dominance of financial markets by, 63, 72, 79, 81, 82, 83, 100, 148, 189, 215–16; Franco regime and, 73–74, 77, 85, 100; industry and, 79–80, 82–84, 89, 142, 189, 218–19, 293n; margins of,

317